MANAGING DEVELOPMENT FOR FUTURE
A Study in Transition and Change Management

MANAGING DEVELOPMENT FOR FUTURE
A Study in Transition and Change Management

SATISH C. SETH

GYAN PUBLISHING HOUSE
New Delhi-110002

MANAGING DEVELOPMENT FOR FUTURE
A Study in Transition and Change Management
[*Management*]

ISBN: 81-212-0678-2 (Set)
ISBN: 81-212-0736-3 (Vol. II)

14th March, 1932
Painting on Front Cover: Satish C. Seth

Published in 2001 in India by
Gyan Publishing House
5, Ansari Road
New Delhi 110 002
Phones: 3261060, 3282060, Fax: 3285914
e-mail: gyanbook@del2.vsnl.net.in
visit our website at: http://www.gyanbooks.com

Laser Typeset at: Alphabet, Delhi
Printed at: Mehra Offset Printers, New Delhi

To

My Wife, Padma Seth

for her continued support
and guidance

Contents

APPENDICES

PREFACE

Clearly, as we enter the new millennium, the 21st century, demands a different approach to meet the challenges of the socio-economic and technological developments. Above everything else it needs a great deal of foresight knowledge and wisdom. We need to know now how "future" shall unfold itself.

Indian developments are in a state of rapid transition and looking back today, there is enough realization that the key instruments of development, whatever they might have been in the past, have to remain hereafter, more responsive to future oriented innovations in education, technology and management. Development thus is the cumulative result of a vision and change for the betterment of the quality of life of people. Development is indeed preparation for change. By generating scenarios, a nation chooses its right policy for future? Every system such as education, health, defence, communication, rural and urban life, agriculture and industry has to figure out new images of change. Above all, development, emphatically means making decisions for choosing a new future. Administration and management systems have to seize future opportunities. Development thus involves an understanding of the emerging world, besides being a grand exercise in long range planning and preparation. We need to make strategic decisions to help our people, our children so that they can live a better life, become self-confident, problem solvers and innovative and creative citizens. Also, let not development be seen as a display of economic statistics. Good development also specifies how many and who all in India is being benefited by it. Also our systems have to become alert and ready in time to prevent disasters and overcome likely crisis, with the help of new technology and new management and through a futuristic development stance.

Secondly, 21st century demands that our teachers and students community be future oriented. Let's not turn their tomorrows into yesterdays. Going back to past is important as it provides us useful guidelines of why we failed or succeeded. But we have to live the rest of our lives in future.

Let's therefore, stop grovelling in the past; instead we should look ahead. Be it the bureaucracy or the captains of industry and its management, they all need to identify and go for tomorrow's technologies. Indians have sufficient ability to be innovative and make quantum leaps forward. Therefore, let us not feel hesitant to take risks. Let us not smother the dreams and creative endeavours of our people for development and meaningful change.

The paramount change that come during the period of transition of the last two and half decades, before the advent of twenty-first century of India had been the future orientation in diverse sectors, in terms of much needed changes in education management and technology consciousness.

A major question that also arose was: How to maintain the continuity, in thinking and learning about the future development? Another question was should or should not future studies (futurology) be introduced in Indian system? It was also felt that the managerial training programme and human resource development activities be futurised, if so how?

The Indian Council of Management and future along with its All India Futuristic Network responded to these questions. In response to the University Grant Commission (UGC) demand, future studies curricula was developed for M.Phil / M.Tech, course for the University system.

In response to the Central Board of Secondary Education (CBSE), New Delhi, a curricula was developed for the IX and XIIth classes of the school system. Likewise the need for bibliographical references was also developed. In the Seventh Five-Year Plan period the UGC India approved the syllabus prepared and awarded Rs. 20 lakh each for a five-year period to ten Indian University to start M.Phil/ M. Tech course in future studies. In the year 1990 at the World Federation of Futures Studies (WFSF) Conference held on Budapest, Hungary. This Indian syllabus was rated as the most comprehensive and the best out of amongst 70 odd 'Syllabuses on Futurology' used World over.

This volume contains some illustrative scenarios and the text of the original documentation of the M.Phil/M.Tech, syllabus and the syllabus developed for the CBSE, for the school system. In addition, this volume also documents the select editorials drawn from the Council's journals. A select bibliography has also been included here.

The author hopes that the valuable documentation given in this volume of the book will help the University Professors, training managers in industries and the school teachers to promote future consciousness. Let it be mentioned, that reading, writing and arithmetic was the *first literacy*; the computer education is *the secondary literacy*. However, the world is moving towards futurisation of all systems. Sector by sector nations and premier institutions of the world are busy rewriting their growth patterns and onward course, and sub course in future oriented strategic terms. It is clear, that futures studies, Futurology/Technology forecasting/Perspective and long range planning; Trend and Systems analysis, the chaos theory and scientific understanding of the 'complexity' - are indeed the key integrated components of futures studies. Thus, constituted as I have called it at every national and international flora I deemed as the '*third literacy*'. I do hope our country too will pursue it vigorously with a new vision to give a quality of life to a billion fellow Indians.

Satish C. Seth

PART FIVE

Selective Sectoral Scenarios

URBANISATION POLICY: TECHNOLOGICAL CONSIDERATIONS

Satish C. Seth

There have been several attempts in the past to evolve a National Urbanisation Policy for India. A firm view on the matter seems to be necessary to enable us to opt for such schemes and programmes which can make the 7th Five Year Plan period a foundational period on which the successive Five Year Plans can be built to serve the future of this society well. In this process a balanced view is equally vital to opt for such technologies which can serve the urban development in a meaningful way. For this, we need to do future scanning and prepare threat and opportunity inventories (See Appendix 'A'). And on that alone can we identify the technological options for: (i) urban growth, and (ii) urban preservation.

However, since India is an unhomogeneously developed country and since India simultaneously lives as agraria, industria and post-industria, we have a situation where there is scope for both the less sophisticated technology options as well as sophisticated technology options.

When we examine available urban scenarios for and towards future for India, we find that whatever scenario one may opt for finally, the future urbanisation pattern for India shall reflect some of the following features:

(a) Metropolitan cities where improvement, renewal and new provision of spatial development exists, will continue to enhance the functioning of large economies which act as catalysts of regional development. The demographic growth and urban sprawl will, however, be limited. It is debatable if by an absolute increase in population, the percentage share of respective State's urban population will gradually be reduced. There need not be a population of 16 to 20 million or an expanded second metropolis around the mother metropolis. This shall enhance, if not well taken care of, the numbers of the informal sector, slums and urban poor, even when the agro-villages or towns will increase at the periphery.

(b) District and sub-divisional towns where growth and development will receive greater emphasis shall become nodal centres in the sub-region and polarisation process will occur in a way.

(c) New industrial towns and growth centres will be in the backward region.

(d) There will be proliferation of the agro-cities and market towns—one market town within 150 or 250 sq. km. of area. The Agro-cities and market towns will have service centre for agriculture and small industries.

(e) One can also witness the distribution of urban functions in rural area through new growth centres as (i) cellular pattern or hierarchial distribution so that the minimum needs of physical, economic and social infrastructure are spread throughout the State, (ii) development of isolated areas due to the peculiar human settlement pattern for geo-technical and climatic reasons, (iii) skeletal linear corridor with goods and services to be linked with transportation and utility.[1]

Technological choices by themselves cannot usher in a certain preferred future. They may facilitate the process. The question before us would therefore be, to decide in what direction we wish the contribution of fiscal outlays for the 7th Five Year Plan to emerge. Is it for expansion? Is it for consolidation? Or, is it for intermediate urbanisation and reduction of urban sickness as it is visible in the urban sector partly because of the accelerated growth of slums and partly due to the migratory trends.

The roles for the appropriate technology as well as for capital intensive advanced technology relevant to the urban scene can be stated as follows:

Case for Less-sophisticated Appropriate Technology and Intermediate Urbanisation

The intermediate urbanisation problems are to be solved through an appropriate technology which may be a combination of different technologies. Intermediate urbanisation should not be confused with development of intermediate technology or establishment of intermediate towns between large and small cities. As the urbanisation is viewed as a process, not as a product, the desired process will be the universal system of facilities hitherto known as urban facilities (piped water supply, metalled roads, etc.) to be provided to both the urban and the rural areas.

This can be connected with the minimum needs programme in urban as well as in rural areas. The major emphasis in this will be on the economic functioning of such places and not merely on overcoming physical deficiencies which is generally the traditional town planner's view about the improvement of the physical infrastructure.

The low level of technology, high population resource, percentage share of population living in rural areas and dependence on agriculture, will influence the planners to view the process of urbanisation as one based *inter alia* on universal modernisation of agriculture, maintaining the forest wealth and the eco-balance of the region. Between the industrial development and modernisation of agriculture, there will be a service sector, the growth of which will lead to urbanisation also. If to this, we also add the considerations of energy growth and lifestyle—a pattern for technological option for such growth becomes obvious.

The specific areas where the intermediate process will be applicable are:

(a) Within the cities where slums and squatters have developed with shelters built of shack materials and in areas deficient in environmental facilities. These areas may be rebuilt under urban renewal programmes with multiple land use or people from some areas will be diverted to fringe areas.

(b) In the fringe areas of the cities either on the fringe of urban agglomeration or outside the standard urban areas or in between the urban corridors which are likely to be urban within the next few years. This may be termed as "agrovillage", agro-towns where the production in such villages in dairy, poultry, handicrafts, etc., will be oriented to the urban need.

On the other hand, they will utilise the resources out of waste and garbage produced in cities. One can also foresee emergence of bio-industrial centres for recycling of such waste products. This will be a resource conserving plan and the technological process may include water recovery from the waste water, recovery of materials and heavy solid, land reclamation and sludging and composting for agriculture and development of poultry, dairy, slaughter house products, etc. The recycling of waste is, however, a sophisticated process. The new urbanisation nodes in rural areas and agricultural based urbanisation, may be turned into 'agro-towns'.

It can be said that the new technology as Santosh Ghosh has pleaded in the study (see ibid) can be adopted in three urban spheres:

(a) Hierarchial distribution or cellular pattern so that the minimum needs of physical, economic and social infrastructure are spread out throughout the country and specially in backward areas.
(b) Development of isolated areas due to the peculiar human settlement pattern with geo-technical and climatic conditions.
(c) Skeletal Linear corridor where intermediate urbanisation can serve large amount of areas with goods and services. This can be linked with transportation linkages and utility system. A cumulative system may be adopted.

Case for Highly Sophisticated Capital Intensive Technology

Whereas in the rural India labour intensive approach combined with appropriate technological options would be a valid level of progressive urbanism, however, in the case of larger urban agglomeration, the traditional methods of design and construction and the importance of quality of life will have to yield to sophisticated technology and modernisation. Intermediate technology alone will not solve the problems of large metropolitan towns whose population by the turn of the century, according to one forecast, will be of the following order:

Megalopolitan areas	*Population in the Year 2000 (in million)*
1. Mumbai-Ahmedabad-Pune	38.60
2. Calcutta	23.60
3. Chennai-Bangalore	19.70
4. Delhi	19.00
5. Lucknow-Kanpur	10.00

Source: Short Studies in Futures Research, NCST (1976-1978)—*Decentralized Metropolitan Developments in India in the year 2000 AD* by Dr Rashmi Mayur.

It will be difficult to indicate here what sophisticated technologies one should opt for except, in principle, to state that for the 9th Five Year Plan, as far as possible, one should opt for tomorrow's technology today, to work for a preferred future to be attained by the turn of this century (2000 AD) characterised by the following basic achievements:

(1) We should opt for consolidation of the quality of life of the existing urban centres.

(2) We should eradicate, and in an accelerated manner, decelerate the process of urban sickness as visible in slums growth or traffic congestion.

(3) Greater attention be paid to sewage treatment and water supply. (This should be done both for the large metropolitan towns as well as for Class I medium, small towns, including the growth centre and the rural service centres).

(4) For the housing sector, technological inputs should come for manufacturing under the public sector umbrella basic construction material and other inputs to serve the urban and rural poor.

Conclusion

Like many cities of the world, the cities of India, particularly, the metropolitan towns, which already indicate, sector by sector, systems break-down are moving towards an almost predictable chaos. On the other hand, given the will, the potentials of achieving medium quality of life for all whether they live in the cities or in the rural areas are unlimited.

We have thus to opt for an orderly urban future where considerations of economy in energy utilisation and maintenance of a clean and healthy environment should be ensured.

When we link it with the question of life style, the Indian social order is being nurtured on the basis of duality, We have two kinds of dispensation. One for the rich and the well-to-do and the other for the poor and economically weaker person. This will need rationalisation. We must not forget technology is also a great equalizer. Urban Managers can help a lot if they keep this fact in mind.

To sum up: In the succeeding Five Year Plan at least, we can ensure that:

(i) 70 per cent of all fiscal outlay for technology, is given for ameliorating the conditions of less well-to-do people living in the urban settlements and

(ii) 30 per cent investment for technologies should go to the elimination of the urban sickness of such big towns which have a population of more than a million: "Firstly, we need to eliminate the unholy nexus between the politicians and rich land grabbers, all over the country."

NOTES AND REFERENCES

1. Santosh Ghosh's Short Study in Futures Research (1976-78) Reglopolis 2000-A Study in Intermediate Urbanisation with New Growth Centres, pp.1-61.

RURAL FUTURES: CYBERNETIC MANAGEMENT

Author

It is often and rightly remarked that rural and urban divide is part of a single continuum. But in our developmental approach, we invariably treat them as two distinct sectors. At the moment what links them are roads, migration and other allied modes of communications. Perhaps, it may not be wrong that the rural people also see, even if it be a belated process, the same movies, and, of late TV transmissions, wherever they are available.

Any developmental framework, thus cannot escape identifying a set of social indicators which *inter alia*, also have a strong spatial facet to it.

It is clear that today and in the coming days, any study of the rural scene, be it to connect people, or, for augmenting their income level or stepping up of work-opportunities (not traditional job related employment) should take the following facts into account.

	Local	*National*	*Global*
Education	Literacy 5 to 15 per cent; Skills-traditional-based on knowledge of past experience; the familiar and the known.	Literacy-40 per cent; skills-both traditional and modern; knowledge-a little more based on science (rational and analytical mode).	Rational-scientific, mode dominates the world of Edn: with proliferation of Interdisciplinarity (Advancing knowledge explosion).
Technology	Traditional crafts, predominant poverty coexists with excellence of skills.	Technological plurality, bullock-cart-to-space, several technologies abound.	What Next: Culture High-tech based on Tech. Forecasting, systems and analytical enquiring mode.
Management	Native wisdom and feudalistic mobilisation of manpower for agricultural pursuits crafts (exploitative mode).	Colonial mould through acquiring new gloss here and there. Bureaucratic culture delayed dawn of computer culture.	Management modes dominated by industrial and post-industrial society specialisation and electronic computer dominated information cybernetic culture.

	Local	*National*	*Global*
Life-style	Nature-dominated run by customs Faith-folk tradition. Future opportunity growth. Skills sought more from the past. Flow of information is opening aspiration spectrum.	Urbanisation, westernised living; faith still dominates so does the hold of tradition Opportunities and growth cells lie in and recent 20 years pheno-menon.	Institutionalism High-Tech rationalised systems; here and there articulated with fundamentalism and social fragmentation war psychosis. Nucleus family alternative lifestyles.

The aspirations of the rural people today and tomorrow are near identical to those cherished by the rest of their countrymen.

By the same token they will now or in future not be satisfied by a 'dual-dispensation'. Their future is linked to identical opportunities for one and all, whether they are living in a village, in a big medium town or a metropolitan city. The new principle criteria being what is good for "goose should be good for gander as well'.

The rural India will be as autonomous and functional as it shall command the educational, the management and the technological means. A mere cry of decentralisation is not enough, it needs to be matched with the availability and command over resources.

A glimpse into 'rural-features', in the context of the previous Five-Year Plans shows no definite direction of development and growth in 'quantum-jump terms'. It is seen more as an 'Incremental-augmentation' and 'enhancement'. In a sense, even in the Seventh Five Year Plan, at least in 60 per cent of its plan programmes for development, appear only as the seventh variation of the first Five-Year Plan of India.

Finally, the time has come when, we should set-up our vision beyond the piggery and poultry and glimpse the growth and development of the rural sector as a "cybernetic-phenomenon" par-excellence, a growth network which is information and knowledge based and where, extension hierarchies of agriculture, health, education, etc., are not operating in a counter-productive mode causing undue `information load'.

This approach, to my mind, is our best option to bridge the developmental gap between the rural-urban divide of India.

How to Choose a Future?

We now run to examine the limits and possibilities of how to choose a future for the rural India? Here we need to grapple with three dilemmas.

Firstly, whose perception of rural development for and towards future are we looking at? Is it the rural people's perception who live at the grass-roots or the planner's perception some of whom have yet to see a village? It is another point whether the rural people can quite articulate their perception. Perhaps, this is our policy maker's failure and that of the Indian intellectual elite/ who work with inadequate social science measurement tools. Perhaps, we need to improve upon these tools. Surely, there could be a way out to understand the nature and intensity of rural people's hopes, fears and expectations.

We need to ask: when we are being 'prescriptive', in our inventory of 'solutions', has our design-exercise on rural futures, taken a system's view of the matter? A political scientist's opinion, which covers some of these points to a large extent, is worth noting.

Dr Rajni Kothari, as the convenor of the GOI Futurology Panel's interim report of the technical sub-group on rural development observed.

> It is necessary to consider here a widespread belief that rapid development cannot be carried out in a participatory framework, that only a determined and authoritarian elite can bring it about, that this indeed is the lesson of contemporary history. Or answer to such a position is that it mistakes appearance for reality, that the issue is not one's choice between liberal democracy dominated by machine politics and state socialism in which a small bureaucratic elite seeks to perpetuate itself, that both these systems are authoritarian as far as the large numbers of the people are concerned there is far greater similarity between the two than appears at first sight, and that the real issue relates to the classic predicament of political life, namely, the relationship between those in power and those out of power, between the government and the people. Seen in this light it is not surprising that the demand of authoritarianism has

> normally come from members of the privileged classes; the businessmen, the bureaucrats, and the technocrats, often reinforced by the analysis and prescriptions of foreigners.
>
> Our model of a participatory system is not conceived in terms of simple political reforms. Rather, it is expressed in a number of sectors-concerning economic organisation and its governance, the nature of education, location of work and enterprise, choice of technology, size of units economics, political, demographic, communications, and the nature of work. Participation is not some process of involving every one and reducing all to a common denominator. Rather, it consists in evolving institutional structures from which diverse individuals get a sense of dignity and self-respect, as beings that are to determine their own destinies. Poverty and inequality are themselves reflections not just of prevailing relations of production but rather of structures and values that deny dignity to the human beings.
>
> Nor is our thinking on participation conceived in terms of establishing idyllic and isolated small communities. Our conception of a social and spatial continuum goes against such a utopia. We are also convinced that given the numbers of human beings we have to deal with; such a utopia is no longer feasible. Our concern, rather is to imbibe into structures at various levels and of various sizes the value of participation as integral to our model of just society and our conception of autonomy and dignity of all human beings. It is only through such an integral view of the various components of our model that an alternative political perspective can emerge and policy issues can be discussed in a meaningful manner.

This 'participatory perspective', *inter alia* in its operational-design will imply that most plan options, for the urban section as well as the rural section be complimentary, supportive and reinforcing in character. And the net outcome of rural growth strategies and the urban-industrial-transportation and habitat mode be such that at some point the output of State-welfare measures melts into a "synergistic" growth profile.

Much of this, of course, shall happen if firstly, we have chosen our option on a sound "systems analysis". Secondly, basic needs fulfilment, quality of life and ecological considerations, *inter alia* be our prime concerns, before plan-options get catalogued and thirdly we adopt and work out a cybernetic growth-mode to bring about, a qualitative and substantial policy change in the educational, managerial and technological support structures and practice.

Role of New Technologies

The advancements in the field of Science and Technology have both a direct and indirect impact on the rural sector. It is a mistaken notion that whatever is happening in space, ocean, remote sensing, micro-electronics, computers, lasers, fibre optics, atomic sector, etc., has nothing to do with the rural development.

The truth of the matter is that it is only through the new Science and Technology and its conquests and their multiple application that one can generate qualitatively superior natural resource database on many aspects relating to land-use and the concomitant Scientific and Technological (S & T) developments in agriculture, forest and mineral resources. It is the new science that can sustain the developmental tempo over a long range time-frame on the one hand, and further create the conditions whereby communications and human resource development and removal of illiteracy can indeed be quickly augmented for the larger good.

The cybernetic *inter alia* approach would demand two basic developments: The setting up of an information network and the setting up of an Early Warning System (EWS) as can, for example, be glimpsed in terms of the Agro-Met Network. We need to develop these for many other areas.

If the development personnel for the different rural sectors can be provided linkages to such networks, to receive in time locally available and usable information and data base, then, we can easily place the age-old impoverished millions on a working pedestal of contemporary techno-managerial work ethos. Here the barrier, if any, would not be the lack of education of the rural masses or the local language handicap. The Indian peasant has amply demonstrated its resilience to absorb and use new S&T inputs for better agricultural achievements. They can indeed do it in any other field as well.

Extension of Cybernetics Applied Research to Rural Socio-economic Futures

We have since independence looked at the rural India merely as an isolated, independent phenomenon of poverty and neglect. Our extension services and plan schemes too have been implemented in a linear and non-integrated manner. In fact, conventional, incremental developments seem to have reached a saturation point. At the top of all this we continue to maintain that the urban-rural divide is a reality and that these two segments need not be treated as a single mega-system.

In fact, we need to treat the rural system as a large, complex cybernetic system enmeshed with an equally large, complex urban system which ought to be subjected to the methods and techniques of cybernetics to attain accelerated visible development.

Firstly, it will mean that the rural system and the production and economic systems available there be deemed as integral to the management of the national economy. We thus need to use Systems Analysis for:

* Mathematical economic analysis of the rural sector.
* Develop an optimum model for rural development.
* Carry out social and psychological studies.
* Formulate precise goals and tasks.
* Improve the grass-root planning systems.
* Improve the grass-root management systems.
* Examine a futuristic man-machine system to optimise inter-sectoral Rural Resource Development.
* Develop appropriate criteria based on the hierarchy free of 'goals' tasks and well-defined 'realisation' time.
* Work out the economic correlations on the branch sectoral basis.
* Replace isolated local, parochial tendency of village development by a regional perspective enmeshing it further to the national planning criteria, as formulated in the Five-Year Plans for a multiple of specialised projects, like an accelerated expansion of roads and road transportation, or the control of water and air pollution.

Indeed we need to redefine the inter-sectoral coordination or 'overall common goal' through 'cybernetic feedback loops' from one sector to the other establishing numerous hidden, invisible interrelationships, like the nexus between primary health care to clean drinking water or that of 'roads' to Human Resource Development or that of energy to the forests, etc.

One can enumerate many more such cybernetic steps characteristic of new management approach where (i) information requisition and transmission, (ii) interaction of constituent sub-systems with one another locally and with other systems nationally, and (iii) introduction of numerous rural specific 'Control Systems'—automatic or otherwise be soon established.

In fact, it would be a challenging task, if both the social scientists and cybernetic experts in togetherness, discover, identify, develop and install 'Servo-Mechanisms' in the Rural Sectors — be they set-up through 'Community Participation' or emerge through the Computer applications to step-up the local, agriculture and industrial outputs, through new 'Evolutionary Growth Models' and 'Net Working'.

Rural Futures, it is being submitted here, cannot now be regulated by the 19th or 20th century conventional wisdom. Instead, we need to go to the forecasting and quantum jumps course in order to supplement our numerous approaches by the cybernetic wisdom and Anticipatory Management-Interactive-approach relevant to the expectations related to the 21st century.

We can broadly sum up the 20-25 years likely rural future development with the help of two obvious scenarios: The Scenario-I can be described as a marginal change Scenario. The Scenario-II can be described as the Optimum Change (Cybernetic-Quantum Jump) Scenario.

The Marginal Change Scenario

In this scenario we find that notwithstanding the several Five Year Plan Inputs, the next would record only an incremental, marginal change in the rural India. Even after twenty year the poverty shall persist: electricity, potable drinking water, adequate tele-com facilities and road would still not be available in all the 600,00 villages. At the same time, the next seven thousand days, would also witness a record Indian population of a billion Indian or more. Out of these 6[illegible] per cent would be the denizens of the rural India, looking for employment, zero-private-cost sources of energy, adequate nutrition and other things which go to provide a certain quality of life. Undoubtedly, many families and households who were earlier below poverty line, would have moved out of it while more will be entering this zone.

The conventional incremental development, if it continues, shall not bring any big change in the social, developmental thinking and concepts. Consequently, the operative structures attached to and flowing out of those earlier growth concepts, be they for housing, communications, for developing Rural Managers, human resource development or health care, notwithstanding, a quantitative network and welfare services expansion in these sectors, would continue still to prove highly inadequate, if for no other reason but for ever expanding 'need element' due to persistent "population explosion".

In the marginal change scenario, the technology plurality would still be sharply visible even after 2005 AD in the future as it is today. In this scenario, the rural future of India does not display any facets of a 'sea-change' nature, in any walk of life. Turbulence, dissatisfaction, social agitation, agrarian discontent, shortages, either man made or through 'climatic traumas', such as drought and floods shall abound as hitherto. Notwithstanding a greater informational awareness, as is already witnessed, thanks to the present developments in the field of mass-media and telecommunication, initially they would only enhance and not diminish people's struggle for survival. Regretably, it is not a very comfortable scenario. It does not seem at all to enable the disadvantaged to redeem or even partially fulfil what Galbraith, in the Indian context, described as the 'Revolution of aspirations of the millions'.

The Optimum Change Scenario

The Cybernetic Approach

This scenario is based on the assumption that India is well poised, as of today, to cope with its problems, if it takes to a policy shift, sector-by-sector with a futuristic vision and a political will, which consciously seeks people's active participation to make selective 'Quantum leaps' towards the future. This can, however, become possible only if India, simultaneously mercilessly discards the vestiges of the past and overhauls its managerial framework and work ethics. And additionally, as said earlier, India in its management approach also takes to a cybernetic approach.

All this calls for a New Systems Design. As already noted, such a systems design, more so, if it is based on a consideration that Indian rural system is Indeed a complex entity made up of several sub-systems interacting within and with other sub-sets as well as with all other systems, in which the urban sector stands immersed. In this connection, it can be clearly seen that the cybernetic method does not mean a simple shift of an agrarian data computational work on to a digital computer. What is being advocated here is a new and futuristic developmental approach wherein, the use of cybernetic methods shall imply a fundamental change in the methodology of technical and economic studies. A novel approach to these studies, so as to bring out and assess the ramified internal relationships and identify the feedback and feed forward loops which remain hidden or unnoticed in the conventional approach. Thus, the analysis of the existing system and the design of the new cybernetics approach helps seek novel technical and economic decisions supported by more accurate and realistic data, not merely to augment piggery and poultry approach, but to go for these developments which are based on forecasting and trend-analysis so that the inputs in one sector do not cause a mismatch in another sector.

The quantum jump scenario is based on the non-linear thinking. We need to think of things which hitherto we have considered as 'impossible'. We need to stretch the limits of the possible. This requires a new attitude towards the people. For instance, in this approach, the people of the rural India would be considered as a resource and not as a drag on the national socio-economic development. The cybernetic approach can open-up a hoard of opportunities. To attain this, the incremental historical path of step-by-step growth can be skipped. Instead we should make selective 'jumps' in all sectors to usher a scenario which can offer a better quality of life to all people (both rural and urban and not for a few as in the case now.)

It is only through a non-linear thinking system analysis,

feedback studies and technological blending that a new design for better rural futures can emerge. In the design of this scenario, policy makers and planners key task is to identify the levels of quantum jumps and leap-frog into future not with the help of sub-critical technology as we have been doing hitherto. The rural sector too deserves the best of technology. Will this get rooted? The answer is yes. Through Green Revolution and the White Revolution our people have demonstrated enough that a cybernetic treatment can give us several directions of accelerated growth.

And our search should continue to find best of means to provide for the quality of life in villages while remembering Gandhi's words that 80 per cent of India lives in villages. It is worth noticing that the current policies have not yet provided even clean drinking water to 680,000 villages of India, what to say about literacy standards or health care or good roads or a telephone connection.

RECOMMENDATIONS OF THE SECOND FUTUROLOGY CONVENTION-CUM-SEMINAR ON RURAL DEVELOPMENT BY 2000 AD*

Noting that India has made significant achievements in different sectors such as industry, agriculture, science and technology and social welfare.

Accepting the millions of Indian citizens are still living below the poverty line and that 76 per cent of India is rural based and more innovative and radical steps need to be taken to improve the quality of life for all its citizen by 2000 AD.

Expecting that the administrators, managers, planners, educationists, policy-makers and futurists/futurologists will present different and various alternatives to achieve the socio-economic development for a better future for millions of fellow citizens; and

Reaffirming our faith in the greatness of India and determination of its people; the convention in which more than 60 experts and Futurologists took part, hereby views and recommends as follows:

The Convention recognises that time-bound future studies for each department should be completed quickly, say, before the end of 1983 and accordingly recommends to governments of the States and at the Centre to initiate task forces, where it has not already been done, to fulfil the above objectives and to prepare a 20 year long perspective plan.

The Commission for the Future, as has been set-up in countries like New Zealand and Poland, may be set-up in the States and at the Centre. For this purpose the passage of an Act by the Central Government could be an important starting point. One of the primary objectives of the task forces mentioned above would be the framing of a draft legislation for the State

---

* Recommendations of the Second National Futurology Convention-cum-Seminar on Rural Ddevelopment by 2000 AD, (May, 1982) by ICMF, Hyderabad and J.N.T. University, Hyderabad.

and Central Governments, apart from active participation by one and all.

Further, each department/ministry itself or two related departments (for example, education and health) could set-up individual or combined task forces for preparing futuristic plans and complete this work preferably before the end of 1983, as time is already running out.

The convention strongly recommends to the Central Government and the Planning Commission to set-up a National Centre for Futures Studies. This will have to be located under the overall charge of the Prime Minister on the lines of the 'Secretariat for Futures' which had been set-up in Sweden under the control of the Swedish Prime Minister.

The convention has noted that under the auspicies of the Department of Science and Technology's Futurology Panels, a technical sub-group on "Teaching and Research in Futurology" was set-up which has made several recommendations for the introduction of futures studies at appropriate levels in the Indian education system. The convention urges upon the University Grants Commission and the Central Government to follow this up and have it implemented by 1983.

It is understood that the UGC will consider concrete proposals from a few Universities and Colleges to set-up "Futurology Cells" during the Sixth Five Year Plan. The convention would like to bring this to the notice of all the Vice-Chancellors in the country.

Education

1. There is need to bring the student back to his environment, to make him participate in the teaching-learning process and to explore the possibility of students becoming nearer to decision-making of the educational programmes. There is also need to permit departures from the written syllabus in text-books to introduce field work for the student so that he is not cut-off from the environment from which he comes.

   It is necessary to build into the syllabus is schools, colleges and universities, Courses on futurology. Expert groups should be formed to identify the syllabus. Efforts must be made to have a second look at examination systems as it exists at present. Setting up of separate institutions to conduct examinations for applicants seeking jobs by different private and public sector agencies and governments may be extended.

Research

2. A minimum 1 per cent of the plan of energy sectors (of both States and Centre) should be devoted every year to Research and Development in the area of alternative sources of energy. There is great need to make Industries take part in and finance associated and relevant research areas in the Universities or establish their own R&D organisations if they have a big enough universe of operations.
As there is a need for a vast network of good teachers, the training programmes of teachers, is to be redrawn to fulfil the needs of 2000 A.D.
There is need to accord a comprehensive role to the modern media in educational systems. Objectives of education should not be merely to enable a person to get a job in government or private employment.
Health Education, Population Education and Moral Education should become part of general school and college syllabus.
Government must reorient technological education towards achieving developmental objectives of rural areas positively in the next ten years.
The convention recommends the setting up of an Open University, if possible in each State, or at least in each region in order to increase the facilities for Continuing Education. The use of modern technology including radio and television, as a major component of the methodology of teaching in the University is advocated.

Medical Education

3. In order to reach health to all citizens particularly in rural areas, measures should be taken to increase institutional facilities to bring out many more hundreds of doctors in the next two decades. The present population control and family

welfare programmes are to be intensified as otherwise by 2000 AD a serious disequilibrium will set in.

Medicine

4. It should be advisable to consider in an experimental way the use of a computerized system for feeding symptoms of diseases of rural folk in a given area and given written instructions for relief, by the same medium to the Rural Health Assistants for further action.

Technology

5. India should no doubt take pages out of foreign technological books. But its own book of technology should not be full of such pages. The Central Government must set-up a national agency to control, absorb and indiginize the imported techniques and technologies.
6. Rural technology needs a professional hand for its management. Hence governments at Central and State levels should do well to develop special cadres of rural managers who could be recruited both in private and public sectors of development. This is all the more necessary because introduction of different forms of energy sources in rural environment is likely not only to confuse the consumers but may even lead to conflicting claims and counter claims as to the cost, optimal efficiency, etc., of these sources. Further, the maintenance of such systems needs a broad-bases infrastructure to put in which, both government and private sectors have to be given separate roles and responsibilities.
7. Government should give in its plans the highest priority to popularising certain established forms of technology—like indigenous manufacturing plants, rural protected water supply equipment (pipes, taps, repairing facilities), dairy products technology, rice milling technology, soil analysis and concrete technology, fertilizer technology, etc.

   Systems should be set-up to collect and organise the research and study experience on effects/acceptance of technology transfers in different rural environments. Realising that certain technologies (Assembles of electronics parts, watch parts, etc.) can be introduced into rural environments as parts of cheap supply to big factory assembly lines. Governments must compel big industries to introduce the industries into rural areas.

Housing

8. There is need to recognise that a vast shortage in housing will lead finally to individual and group dissatisfactions and frustrations and hit the very fabric of society. But it is difficult to ensure a house for every family. The costs are stupendous and not manageable by Central, State Government and local bodies alone.

9. Recognising the need for a selective approach to the problems in the provision of rural and urban housing, the convention recommends that clear policy directions are to be given by the Centre and State Governments so as
   (i) to discourage transfer of population from rural and semirural to urban conglomerations by providing dispersed and regional facilities such as markets for rural products and also educational and medical facilities which after all attract people to urban towns.
   (ii) to encourage private efforts in housing for rural people through a system of beneficiary-contribution as a pre-condition for credit facility from lending agencies (Banks, LIC, etc.) and for construction facilities by housing boards and corporations.
   (iii) There is need to develop inexpensive yet artistic models of houses and an adequate technology, in the use of wood, stone, brick and mud and other building materials plentifully available locally and adoption of traditional methods of construction. This is all the more necessary because not only is a house to become a home but a conglomeration of these houses must become a harmonius human habitat.
   (iv) To maintain a constant dialogue between technological institutions and universities for updating knowledge, improving quality of thatched houses so as to resist pests and withstand cyclonic winds and fire hazards.

HOUSING PERSPECTIVES: IDENTIFYING PLANNING OPTIONS

Satish C. Seth

The delineating of the housing perspective for the next 17 years to coincide with the turn of the century is as obvious and complex a task as for any other sector in which the socio-economic planning of India is trying to seek meaningful and speedy development. It is obvious to this extent that, even though we are a population of 700 million (±) now, we shall be a billion people by the turn of the century, we shall continue to have problems connected with the urban-rural divide. Above all, much depends on the rate of economic growth.

Against this obvious perspective, the scenario for a marginal change in the housing sector would be somewhat as shown in Table 1 as follows:

TABLE - 1
MARGINAL CHANGE SCENARIO IN THE HOUSING SECTOR

Indian Societal Features (Co-existence and Continuation into Future of Agraria, Industria Post-industria)	*Early Warning Signals: Likely Future Threats (It is not an Exhaustive List)*
1	2
1. Large Human System (1983 AD: 785 m±; 2000 AD: 1-Billion)	1. Resources Depletion: Demand-Supply imbalance. 2. Resources Overload and Sectoral Breakdown in commodity supply in services, etc. 3. Erosion and malfunctioning in the system(s) for both justice and distributive justice. 4. Others: Not identified here.
2. Acute Poverty Conditions	1. Disability of 60 to 70 per cent of population to acquire any consumer personality to benefit from the new technological dispensation. (There may be more houses built yet

(Continued on next page)

(Table 1 continued)

1	2
	majority will be unable to buy even a low cost hut). 2. Urban overload (1981 AD: 130M±; 2000AD:330M±) due to mass migration from rural to urban areas. (Water, housing, traffic breakdowns and sharp decline in the quality of life in urban areas). 3. Others.
3. Uneven state of development	1. Accentuation of rurai urban divide leading to social rift and tensions. 2. Environmental degradation (Forest depletion: Likelihood of the occurrence of fuel famine and fuel riots in some parts in India: Acute paper crisis); Rise in costs of building materials. 3. Others.
4. Value Plurality	1. Crisis arising from awkward unhomogeneous social change and lifestyle disparities. 2. Increased labour and youth unrest (Partly due to politicisation of labour and student community). 3. Emergence of anti-social forces mainly due to traditional social malaise arising from caste, language, religion, sects and inadequate management know-how in administering a highly socially fragmented society. 4. Others.
5. Technological Plurality	1. India enters the 21st century with sophisticated technology in several areas, but without a technological culture (Also continued coexistence of bullock-cart age with space age). The same holds good for the housing sector). 2. Inadequate horizontal diffusion to technology. 3. Increased failure of maintenance system both in the private and the public sector. 4. Others.

• The key-elements outlined in the above-mentioned Marginal Change Scenario, makes it imperative to seek such a National Housing Policy which can overcome the visible threats of today and tomorrow.

• Any future-oriented analysis clearly indicates that the housing policy must not be viewed as an instrument to provide shelters but rather as an instrument of social policy to achieve growth with social justice.

• In administrative terms, to identify the policy options for planning, a clear view needs to be taken on the following aspects which are fairly well-known points:—

— the "Settlement Pattern" for the overall development of townships;
— a proper land-use policy;
— ways and means for dispersal of population and to curb the influx of migrants into metropolitan cities;
— means for slum squatter settlements clearance;
— evolve uniform need-based standards by rationalising the scales of accommodation;
— provide for the use of new substitute building materials; and
— make adequate financial provisions as investment in housing which so far has been meagre.

Optimal Change Scenario

Before we identify the various schemes for the 7th Five Year Plan in the housing sector, it is imperative that we pay all attention that we possibly can to identify both "conceptually" and in terms of "methodology of implementation" and seek such approaches whereby we can achieve by the turn of the century optimal change in the national housing scene. For this, we shall have to ask ourselves several questions:

(1) Are we treating housing as an independent activity of the total environment?
(2) So far, housing has had a low priority. What is the nature of priority which we should now boldly seek?
(3) Have we been taking decision for investment in housing so far on extra social consideration paying little attention to what people need and "what is the paying capacity"

of the family and the "minimum housing standard" they can afford? What is the attitude of our housing agencies which sometimes act as a good marketing organisation? Do the urban and rural poor figure anywhere in the scheme? (Enough statistics exist in terms of the backlog and dwelling and the housing shortage and in terms of the average income of the rural and urban poor).

(4) Can we make our housing agencies accept the fact that their market is or should be this large percentage of household (below 90 per cent) of low income group level? Or, their job is only to cater to 10 per cent of India's population?

(5) Is construction of houses a more prudent form of investment *vis-a-vis* indirect investment and development of infra-structure facilities like making available plots, providing social health and cultural amenities, buildings and employment centres, etc.

(6) In what way can private houses investment be geared to achieve the social objective and with what incentives, if any?

(7) If slums cannot be totally eliminated, can the hut settlements be given all the public amenities? Can we take the attitude of "best or nothing"?

Until and unless we adopt a radical attitude on the above illustrative aspects of housing, (These are only illustrative and not exhaustive points) all we will achieve, is the extrapolation of present levels of achievements and failures into the future.

The Forecasts/Housing Scenarios

A clear idea of the National Land Use Policy, Urbanisation Policy and Economic Growth is a basic prerequisite to draw up a national perspective. In the forecast picture developed by P.M. Apte: In the next 17 years (i) the number of households by 2001 AD are estimated to be about 201 million under the assumption of 35.6 per cent growth between 1971 to 2001; (ii) the percentage annual growth rate of households between the base year (1970-71) and the terminal year (2000-01 AD) works out to 2.8; (iii) contrary to the trend noticed in the past, the household size by the turn of the century is expected to decrease from 5.7 persons in 1971 to 4.7 persons in 2000 AD; (iv) there are varying figures for the current housing shortage in India. One estimate placed it at 61 million dwelling units comprising of 55 million in rural areas and 6 million in urban areas as of 1971. It is likely to increase by 2 million units per annum. As against this, the construction rate is 300,000 units (or 15 per cent of the total demand) per annum. During 1976 to 2001, it is estimated that some 61.15 million households consisting of 33.77 million in rural areas and 27.38 million in urban areas will be added to the already existing backlog. To provide housing accommodation to such a large population will not be an easy task unless some radical measures are taken.

Land Requirements

The total land requirement for non-agricultural uses is estimated at 22.0 million hectares consisting of 42 per cent for residential purposes and the remaining for non-residential purposes. This necessitates a clearly defined national housing policy in harmony with a normal land use policy. Separate policies for rural and urban housing need to be formulated and their financial implications taken into account.

Housing Needs

The housing shortage in India has been variously estimated between 14 million and 61 million dwelling units, of which 3 to 6 million are in urban areas. The estimates of shortage, however, greatly vary with a change in the definition of 'kuchcha' and 'pacca' houses. However, it is important to have the basic facts and data before approaching the solution to any problem.*

According to the Futurology Panel's Housing Technical Sub-Group's Interim Report the following emerges:

India has reached the billion population mark just before the beginning of the this century. The available housing stock at that time is estimated to touch between 126 million and 170 million housing units. Today 105 households manage with 100

* (See P.M. Apte's Study on "Planning for Human Settlements - Housing". In *Short Studies in Futures Research*, NCST Panel on Futurology's Publication).

houses. In the year 2000, 153 households may live in the same number of houses under unfavourable growth rates of related factors. The housing situation under favourable growth rates also deteriorates, i.e. there will be 120 households per 100 houses. Thus, in either case, no farreaching improvements are likely by the turn of the century. Further 65 to 71 per cent of the housing stock is expected to consist of houses built with semi-*pucca* and *kuchcha* building materials. It is observed that a minimum of 75 per cent of the rural households, as compared to 35 per cent of the urban households. are likely to have tiled and thatched-roof houses in 2000 AD.

The urban households with amenities increase from 50 per cent in 1971 to 63 per cent under unfavourable growth and 73 per cent under favourable growth. On the contrary, 76 per cent and 66 per cent of the rural households in 2000 AD, under unfavourable and favourable growth, will be without exclusive amenities. Moreover, the rural scene may not change significantly — 66 to 76 per cent of the rural households will have no basic amenities for their exclusive use. That is to say, two-thirds of the total households in the country will be without exclusive basic amenities.

Desired Rate of Net Additions to Housing Stock

In order to meet the housing needs of the country, under favourable and unfavourable conditions of determining factors, the housing activity has to be greatly accelerated. The expected rate of completions (new houses) per 1000 population should be stepped up by 3.6 times during 1971-81, 2.6 times during 1981-91, and 2.4 times during 1991-2000 under unfavourable conditions. Under favourable conditions, the desired rate of completions should be 3.1 and 1.7 times higher than the expected rates of completions during 1971-81 and 1981-91 respectively.

The decennial rate of completions in the developed countries of the world is observed to be between 80 and 120 per 1000 population. The United Nations has also recommended a decennial addition of 100 dwellings per 1000 population for Asian and Far Eastern countries. In so far as India is concerned, even half as many completions as recommended by the UN will considerably ease the pressure on housing in the country.

This analysis brings into focus rather depressing housing conditions in the country. Since the growth rate of households, or demand for housing, outweighs completions, people will be forced to inhabit houses otherwise only fit for demolition. Improvements on the housing front that one would generally associate with rising per capita income in the country are not likely to be realised. The emerging scenario is pretty grim characterised by housing shortages both qualitative and quantitative.

Building Materials and Other Resources' Requirements

Compared to the scale of housing demand the national resources are tragically low. For instance, the income of 25 per cent of the families in India will buy them about 2 square metres of built up construction, the next 50 per cent can buy upto 5 square metres. Nor is it merely a matter of finance; steel, cement, and other material resources are equally crippling constraints.

The following resources deserve attention :

1. Finance;
2. Building Materials;
3. Land; and
4. Skilled and unskilled labour.

Finance

Investments in housing have been too meagre to have any impact on the situation. It is estimated that the housing needs of the country could be fully met if expenditure on the residential sector is raised from the less than one-sixth to about one-third of the projected expenditure on the construction industry.

Households that do not afford to own houses and, therefore, need subsidy may range between 50 million to 92 million in the year 2000 (12-13 million in urban areas and 37-70 million in rural areas).

Subsidies ranging between Rs 335 billion and Rs 610 billion are required if all the low and middle-income groups were to be provided with a standard R.C.C. house at rates prevailing in 1971. The enormity of required subsidies calls for changes in the prevailing housing concepts. Priority should be accorded to shelter masses, specifically those in the low-income groups, in other than permanent, but fairly habitable houses. In a tropical country like ours, environment built by open space around a shelter is no way less important than a shelter provided with roof, particularly for the low income households.

Ways and means should be explored to bring down the unit costs. For example, the cost of a 385 square feet of thatched house, or 200 square feet of tiled house, or 125 square feet of asbestos house or 70 square feet of R.C.C. houses, are approximately the same. This may give an idea how a variable can be put to use for an optimum utilisation of financial resources as well as human needs. By enforcing revised standards (as to type and area of a standard house), households that cannot afford a standard house are reduced to between 17 million and 45 million. Required subsidies will accordingly come down to anywhere between Rs 7 billion and Rs 200 billion during 1971 and 2000. In any eventuality, the cost of a house remains beyond the paying capacity of a household in the lowest income group.*

It was categorically pointed out at a Futurology Workshop "that housing has to be judged in terms of 'lifestyle patterns' and should be based amongst other things, on (1) community living, (2) lesser hazards to life from traffic, etc., (3) moving the new habitats of peripheral regions, (4) construction of new buildings in metropolitan areas by government and other recognised bodies, (5) improved communication and transport facilities. Other than this, emphasis was laid on mass house-building based on establishment of pre-fabrication modules. There will be, it is expected, a massive public participation which will be initiated, guided and controlled by popular governments."**

A decentralisation of housing activity on the basis of development modules and rationalisation of the various existing statutory constraints involving housing was also suggested in the preferred scenario. Based on these two approaches, an action plan was suggested on the following lines:

1. Need-based standards of housing both in regard to lifestyle and house style should be worked out and this should be

* (See Interim Reports on 'Housing'- NCST panel on Futurology's publication).

** Futurology Workshop on 'Housing' organised by the Department of Science & Technology, held at the Institute for Techno-Economic Studies, Madras, during February 20 to 26, 1978.

propagated to all sections of people through a suitable and imaginative communication programme and media.

2. Training of both skilled and unskilled labour in new housing technologies, particularly prefabrication.
3. Rationalisation of methods of contracts, tax laws, etc., concerning housing.
4. Centres such as Functional Industrial Estates for producing house building materials and components are to be established.
5. Existing substandard units have to be upgraded.
6. Government should take initiative to mobilise the available financial, organisational, material and administrative resources, if at all a sizeable dent is to be made in the housing problem in the next 22 years, (Chairman : B. Natrajan, (Economist).

Conclusion: Key Contextual "Values" for determining Housing Perspectives

All the three scenarios given above do provide somewhat familiar yet "pointed" guidelines to draw up a "Housing Perspective" for India. Thus, the first and foremost important consideration is that in India we are also dealing with a large human system and as we move towards the future, we need to cater to the needs of many, as against, that of a few. We have to gear up our resources and systems to serve a billion people. Are we ready for it?

Secondly, we should abandon, as far as possible, the approaches that only helped the nation in moving towards a "Marginal Change Scenario in the Housing Sector", as is evidenced by our inadequate progress made during the 5th and the 6th Five Year Plans. (See Mid-Term Plan Appraisal for details). Instead, we should work for an "Optimum Change-Scenario".

Finally, such a commitment calls for several bold "Value-Shifts" and pursuing of such "housing schemes" which may enable us to make a "quantum leap" into future in order to work towards the normative goal of "Housing for all by 2000 AD". It is in this context that we should identify the first phase of our perspective plan encompassing the schemes of the VII Plan period from 1985-1990.

In brief, one would personally like to emphasise that, sector by sector, it is extremely difficult to deliver on an equitable and rational basis dispensation to one and all on a per capita basis. Even though housing influences an environment yet environmental consideration should predetermine the housing pattern. And the societal context must be our key reference point. Planning must take into account the social reality.

If house is something which provides privacy, comfort and above all shelter, then let this be determined by a hard look at the sociology of housing in the Indian context.

Our schemes should generate cohesion and participation, imparting a certain quality of life to our settlements. To sum up: One of the things, for and towards future that we need to critically examine is how we can in our Housing Policy, instead of a household being treated as a unit, lay greater emphasis on "community togetherness" and "community living" as an overall criteria. And which could decide our options/choices/schemes for housing.

If looking at a long range perspective has any single message to offer in the housing sector, then it surely is that in choosing the 7th Plan targets and schemes we should opt for those schemes/ incentives which can accommodate, at least a part, if not the entire future demand that shall devolve on us, in our current day investments in the housing sector.

Above all, we need to respond and accept candidly the new values and new future related context. A deep insight will certainly help us to synthesise the claims as between the traditional housing pattern, our current decade's response and the imperatives of future.

LAKSHADWEEP FUTURES SCIENCE AND TECHNOLOGY OPTIONS*

A.D. Damodaran, A.G. Mathere and S.C. Seth

Lakshadweep Islands have been in existence for one thousand years with human inhabitants. However, the people's demand for change towards improved quality of life has been gaining momentum in recent years. Dr S.C. Seth, Department of Science and Technology has proposed that this workshop can help in drawing normative scenarios for the future development of Lakshadweep Islands. According to him, futurology is a study that provides early warning systems with possible alternate technological options. Future technological options are provided by integrating technological forecasting and technology assessment with social forecasting. The function of technological forecasting is to match the demands of society with the demands of technological development.

All decisions aimed at development of Lakshadweep islands are taken by its administration. Decisions taken by the Administration of Lakshadweep Islands is guided by the Five Year Plan proposals of Government of India. Hence there is a demand on the workshop to keep in view the 7th Five Year Plan proposals for Lakshadweep islands while drawing normative scenarios for its future development.

Mr. V. Ramachandran, (Chief Secretary, Government of Kerala) emphasised that while drawing future scenarios, lessons from both the failure and the success cases should be kept in view. Therefore, lessons from the success or failure of Karim Nagar case in its efforts to develop through Scientific and Technological inputs should be kept in view while launching development programmes for Lakshadweep islands. He particularly reminded that in some instances in the past, the prediction of futurologists have been proved wrong, for example, in the matter of raw materials availability. Delay in implementation of programmes is one of the

* Summary report on indicators of Change Management (1986).

causes of failure which is due to poor coordination among different implementation agencies, departments and ministries. Therefore, it is a prerequisite to ensure that the programmes of development initiated by local bodies or island administration or state government are approved by the Central Government and adequate financial and human resources are mobilized in a responsible and accountable way, so that the programmes are sucessfully implemented.

Dr A.D. Damodaran, (Director, Regional Research Laboratory, Trivandrum) expressed his desire that the workshop evolves data base policy options for implementation.

Mr P.M. Sayeed, (Member of Parliament representing Lakshadweep Islands), opined that though the people in the Islands have been living for centuries without much scientific and technological (S & T) inputs but their aspirations for improved quality of life are increasing in recent times. Their aspirations for improved quality of life can be realised through S & T inputs including improved job oriented education. Further he observed that though the Islands are rich with marine (fisheries) and mineral (calcium) resources, no public sector industry is established to exploit these resources. In line with Prime Minister's wishes, it is necessary to go for a massive investment to introduce modern S & T inputs to ensure development without disturbing the eco-system of the Islands. Mr Sayeed appealed to the workshop to give thought over the following aspects:

(1) Means and methods to increase fish production to, say, one hundred thousand tonnes by 2000 AD.

(2) Means and methods to establish industries to produce, say, white cement utilising about 300 million tonnes of calcium resources of the Islands. It is necessary to identify suitable techniques to mine the resources within 1-3 metres deep without disturbing the eco-balance.

Mr Jagdish Sagar gave a description of the Islands and its peoples. Based on the aspirations of the people, he outlined some desirable and likely changes that may come about in the future. Lakshadweep consists of 36 islands made of corals of which 10 are inhabited. The area of the largest island is 4.8 sq. km. and the smallest one is 10 hectare. Total area of islands is 32 sq. km.

Territory appears to be larger if the lagoon area is taken into account which amounts to 4200 sq. km. of territorial water and 400,000 sq.km. of exclusive economic zone.

As per 1981 census, there were about 40,249 people living in an area of 28.5 sq. km. Population density is said to be high which is 1256 per sq. km. The projected population in 2005 AD is 60,000.

Majority of population in the islands are Muslims. The people speak Malayalam except in Minicoy where they speak Mahi. Since 1956, the people in the Island have been classified as Schedule Tribes. There are 9 high schools and 2 junior colleges. Literacy has gone up from 23 per cent in 1961 to 55 per cent in 1981 which according to a neutral forecast should exceed 80 per cent by 2005 AD. The people in the Islands live in houses made of limestones, shingle and coral stones. Roofs used to be thatches in early days but are now replaced by Mangalore tiles. Residential houses increased from 3795 in 1961 to 6320 in 1981. There are about 1700 government buildings of which one third are residential. These buildings have been mostly built from materials mainly brought from the mainland.

Coconut cultivation in the islands has surpassed natural vegetation. Average density of coconut trees cultivated is 220 per hectare which is considered to be above optimum size. There are about 18000 small holdings of coconut gardens. There are about 5000 cattle and 14000 goats in the island. There is about 150 km. of foot path and cycle track. About 36 km. length of road is surfaced one. All the roads are likely to be surfaced by 2005 AD. Vehicular traffic is of recent origin. There are about 360 two-wheelers, 27 tractors, 114 power tillers with pulling trailors a few thousands of bicycles.

Goods and passengers are moved by the sea. Two ships regularly operate, one cargo-cum-passengership (800 tonnes and 242 passengers) and another passengership with capacity to carry 380 people.

Traditional occupation of the people of Islands is fishing, *copra* and coir making. Island people get rice from the mainland in exchange of fish, copra and coir.

The introduction of engine driven boats by the local administration has increased fish catch from 500 tonnes to 5000 tonnes. There are about 300 mechanised fishing boats, each requiring 9-10 people to operate. The catch goes to the mainland as mas or smoked tuna with a shelf life of 1-2 years. In addition about 75 tonnes of tuna are handled by the government canning factory at Minicoy. According to the estimates of the Fishery Department, the value of fish catch in 1984 was Rs. ·24 crore giving Rs. 570 per capita.

Two-third of copra produced in the Islands goes for direct consumption. The surplus, about 2000 tonnes, is marketed by the Lakshadweep Co-operative Marketing Federation. The per capita income earned by sale of copra in 1983-84 (which was the best year) was about Rs. 930. There appears to be little scope for extending coconut cultivation beyond the present level.

In the seventies, the local administration employed about 1400 people of whom 50 per cent were from the Islands. In the eighties, government employment increased to 2500 persons of which 68 per cent were from the Islands. According to a pessimistic scenario in 2005 AD, the Islands are seen covered with houses and buildings both government and private for the much increased population which includes about 6000 government employees and another 6000 people working for the government on daily wages.

The Administrator has visualized the future development of Lakshadweep islands in the following areas:

(1) Planned use of land and regulated construction of buildings.

(2) Development of transport and communication systems through sea, air and land.

(3) Employment generation through increased activities in the areas of fisheries, coconut processing, tourism and vocationalization of education.

(4) Identification of appropriate technologies that work efficiently within the constraints of scarcity in the areas of energy, fisheries, agriculture, animal husbandry, port development, transport, communication, building, industries and protection of sea shore.

Mr Omesh Saigal, (Joint Secretary, Admn., CSIR and former Administrator of Lakshadweep) observed that it is not true that any small work done in the islands disturbs the eco-balance. He held that people are backward and that it needs massive investment to overcome their backwardness. According to Mr Saigal, the growth of Lakshadweep is dependent on the growth of living corals. Therefore, developmental plans should ensure uninterrupted growth of corals. Lakshadweep Islands have been in existence for several centuries and have withstood natural calamities like cyclones that occurred in 1940. People of Lakshadweep Islands are backward only in terms of poverty, as 60 per cent of them live below the poverty line but not in terms of culture and social values. The people are most resourceful in the sense that they carefully utilize their local resources to meet their requirements. Development of Islands is never held up for lack of funds, but if held up, it is only due to lack of proper perspective and absence of appreciation of the importance of S & T inputs to improve the living conditions of the people. It is necessary to improve the living standards of people through improved health, education, communication, transport and employment. Exploitation of ocean resources within the radius of economic zone provides employment to the majority of the people of the islands.

Table 1 indicates optimum scenario drawn for certain sectors of Lakshadweep Islands that could be the basis for deriving normative scenarios for the future development of Islands.

Table 2 presents the institutional linkages as seen from the participants in the workshop for sectoral development of Lakshadweep Islands. This modular matrix can be enhanced to cover other institutions as and when the need arises.

TABLE - 1
OPTIMUM SCENARIO FOR CERTAIN SECTORS OF LAKSHADWEEP ISLANDS

Sector	*1981 (Base)*	*1986*	*1991*	*1996*	*2001*	*2031*
Population	40,249	43,848	47,070	50,064	52,872	65,562
Houses	6,320	6,775	7,273	7,780	8,281	10,837
Fisheries output (tonnes/annum)	3,300	4,335	5,668	7,407	9,682	47,516
Educated employed	1,200	1,743	2,570	3,622	4,847	11,052
Educated unemployed	970	3,292	5,110	6,538	7,655	12,838

TABLE - 2
INSTITUTIONAL LINKAGES FOR SECTORAL DEVELOPMENT - LAKSHADWEEP

	Ocean & Marine Resources Developt.	*Mineral Resources Dev.*	*Fisheries*	*Agriculture (coconut)*	*Post-harvest Tech.*	*Road & Building*	*Transport*	*Water*	*Energy*	*Health*	*Tourism*	*Education Training Futuristic*	*Industries*
CMFRI			x										x
CIFT			x										x
NIO	x												
CSMCRI	x							x	x				x
IIT,M									x			x	x
CPCRI				x									
RRL, T					x	x							
Coir Board						x							
CBRI						x							
HUDCO						x							
KWWWA								x					
NEERI								x		x			x
NATPAC							x						
Dept. of Tourism											x		
CSI	x	x											
DST												x	
LDA	x	x	x	x	x	x	x	x	x	x	x	x	x

MARINE RESOURCES AND OCEANOGRAPHY

Fisheries Development

In view of the small population of the islands, but an extensive EEZ area surrounding them, fisheries development of Lakshadweep should be considered an integral part of the marine fisheries development of India as a whole. Research studies have shown that the potential for tuna fish catch is 50,000 tonnes per annum. However, the actual catch is only 3,500 tonnes. There is a good potential for other fishes like sharks, perches, carangids and seer fishes in the region. Current exploitation of tuna is mainly in the near-shore waters through pole and line fishing using motorised boats with provision to keep bait tanks. Bait fish is an important input in the pole and line fishery. But the limitations on the availability of live-baits is hindering the growth of tuna fishery. It is known from the studies that undue exploitation of live and dead corals and dredging of lagoons for navigational purposes contribute to the destruction of live corals which ultimately lead to the decline of bait-fish and consequently tuna fish. According to National Institute of Oceanography, Goa (NIO) studies, it is understood that the presence of coral enhances the growth of baits and removal of corals reduces baits and increase erosion of the shore.

Suggested areas for further evaluation

(1) Systematic estimation of total fish resources including assessment of stocks of tunas and baits.
(2) Assessment of the role of environmental parameters including coral system on the productivity of marine resources with special reference to artificial propagation.
(3) Assessment of systems for conservation of coral eco-system and extraction of biochemicals from corals.
(4) Conservation of Turtles by intensive farming.
(5) Cultivation and harvesting of marine algae.
(6) Development of new methods for fish catching, processing, storage and product diversification.
(7) Survey of the potential for and development of mariculture in the islands.
(8) Development of live-bait resources for tuna fishing.

(9) Consideration of joint venture for rapid development of tuna fishing.

(10) Survey and estimation of the resources of ornamental fishes.

Participant Institutions in the Programme

(1) Lakshadweep Administration.

(2) Central Marine Fisheries Research Institute, Cochin.

(3) National Institute of Oceanography, Goa.

(4) Central Institute of Fisheries Technology, Cochin.

(5) Central Salt and Marine Chemicals Research Institute, Bhavnagar.

Ocean Thermal Energy

Development of Lakshadweep Islands is conditioned by the adequate supply of energy. Though the island covers a small land area of about 30 sq. km. it has potential to utilize ocean resources covering an area of 700,000 sq. km. it is necessary to identify a reliable source of energy to sustain the developmental programmes like mining and processing of mineral and ocean resources. At present there is only 2,000 kw capacity installed in the islands to generate power. The entire power requirement is met by diesel power generation. Diesel requirement is met from the mainland sources which leads to high cost of power generation being 10 times that of the mainland. Ocean Thermal Energy Conversion (OTEC) as one of the reliable sources of energy is helpful in this direction. Besides OTEC, utilisation of tidal energy, salinity gradient energy, wave energy and wind energy could also be thought of. It is estimated that an OTEC plant of one MW capacity requires Rs 95.35 million towards fixed capital investment.

Participant Institutions in the programme

(1) Lakshadweep Administration.

(2) Indian Institute of Technology, Madras.

(3) Department of Non-Conventional Energy Sources, New Delhi.

(4) National Institute of Oceanography, Goa.

Agricultural Resources

Coconut is the most important crop covering an area of about 2,780 hectare. All other crops are grown in only 47 hectare.

Rice and fish form the main staple food of the islanders. Rice is obtained from the mainland. Principal source of agricultural economy of Lakshadweep Islands is based on sale of copra and coir products to the mainland. The ecology, soil fertility and ground water potential of the Islands in general does not permit an intensive agricultural development programme. Since the density of population (1957 persons per sq. km.) is very high, efforts should be made towards effective and efficient utilization of land for different developmental programmes.

Assuming 2.65 per cent per annum growth rate, the island population reaches 68,000 by 2000 AD. Accordingly the estimated demand for the essential food items is two times more than the present consumption as projected in Table 3.

TABLE - 3
ESTIMATED DEMAND FOR FOOD ITEMS FOR THE POPULATION OF LAKSHADWEEP ISLANDS IN 2000 AD

Food Item	*Per Capita Requirement*	*Total Requirement*
Rice	125 kg	8,500 tonnes
Pulses	185 kg	1,250 tonnes
Meat	20 kg	1,360 tonnes
Eggs	100 nos	6.8 million nos
Milk	18.25 kg	1,240 tonnes
Vegetables	90 kg	6,000 tonnes
Fruits	75 kg	5,000 tonnes

Suggested Areas for Further Evaluation

(1) Intensive cultivation of tuber crops like tapioca is done as intercrop in coconut gardens to supplement the requirement of major food items like rice. Attempts should be made to develop certain high yielding varieties of coconut which require less water. Attempts should be made to try certain water holding agents to conserve the surface water.

(2) S&T inputs are given to enhance the productivity of land and crop.

(3) Land utilization according to the following proposal is explored:

Out of 2,600 hectares cultivable and available land, 120 hectares is allocated for cultivation of fruit crops like banana, papaya and bread fruit. About 104 hectares of land is allocated for cultivation of vegetables like tomato, potato, egg plant, beans and chillies and 25 hectares is allocated for the cultivation of castor which grows very well within the island conditions.

(4) Establishment of coconut processing units to produce quality fibres, coir ropes, coconut oil, desicated coconut powder, partially defatted coconut gratings, coconut cream and bottling of coconut water for soft drink purposes.

(5) Attempts be made to try certain water harvesting technologies to conserve the surface sweet water.

Participant Institutions in the Programme

(1) Coconut Development Board, Cochin.
(2) Central Plantation Crop Research Institute, Kasaragod.
(3) Regional Research Laboratory, Trivandrum.
(4) Coir Board, Cochin.
(5) Lakshadweep Administration.

Land and Buildings

There has been a steep rise in recent years in building activity of Lakshadweep Islands. Many government offices have been recently established causing demand for more housing facilities. Lakshadweep Administration alone built residential houses covering plinth area of 50,000 sq.m and non-residential buildings covering plinth area of 105,000 sq.m. It has completed construction of 1085 quarters during VI Five Year Plan period, though the requirement is for 3102 quarters. It is envisaged to construct 2700 additional quarters of different categories during VII Five Year Plan period. Demand for growth of buildings exerts pressure on land and building materials which are considered as scarce in the Islands.

According to the 1981 census, Lakshadweep Island is a land of 32 sq. kms. with a population of 40,237 and high population density of 1257 persons per sq. km. against the national average of 221 persons per sq. km. Thus the land is a scarce resource which people are not willing to part with for any purpose. Except a few houses, all other houses in the Islands are quite good and two-storeyed buildings are easily constructed. Such double-storey building pattern is not expected to disturb the eco-balance of the Lakshadweep Islands. Private construction so far has been using coral shingles, coral sand and lime as building materials. Timber brought from the mainlands is used as rafters and roof structures. Coconut leaf thatch is used as roofing material. Government buildings till recently have used pre-cast cement concrete blocks made of coral concrete blocks made of coral shingles and sand. A.C. sheets or Mangalore tiles are used as roofing materials. Large-scale mining of coral shingles is likely to affect the ecology of the Islands. It is estimated that about 5.5 lakh cu.m. of shingles 3 lakh cu.m. of sand have been already quarried for construction purposes. Conventional building materials such as bricks, river sand, steel, cement become costly due to high cost of transportation. Hence there is a need for development of newer materials and newer designs.

Suggested Areas for Further Evaluation

(1) Detailed studies should be done to determine the soil stability of the Islands for the purpose of introducing double-storeyed buildings.

(2) Development and use of prefabricated panels made of local resources like coconut leaves, roofing structures made of trunks of coconut and palm trees, cement bonded coconut fibre boards, hallow clay blocks, similar light weight building blocks based on clay, ferrocement products, asphaltic corrugated roofing sheets and precast stone masonry blocks.

(3) Design of double-storeyed buildings with high strength and light structure materials.

(4) Educating people to create an awareness towards the need for adopting newer design/systems of houses.

(5) Training and demonstration to the people by the government about the methods of houses using newer designs and materials.

Participant Institutions in the Programme

(1) Lakshadweep Administration.

(2) Central Building Research Institute, Roorkee.

(3) Housing and Urban Development Corporation, Bangalore.
(4) Regional Research Laboratory, Trivandrum.
(5) Regional Engineering College, Calicut.
(6) Technical Education Directorate, Trivandrum/ Engineering College, Trivandrum.

Water

Main source of limited sweet water in the Lakshadweep Islands is the rain water that percolates through porous sandy soil to form sweet water lens above the saline water. In Bitra the requirements are met by a solar desalination plant. Since all the islands relatively consists of coral sand or shingles, the water is always in contact with ground water. The close proximity of sea water introduces saline water into fresh ground water even without over drafts. The sewage disposal by means of septic tanks and numerous burial grounds scattered all over the Islands cause pollution to the sweet water. High concentration of pollution (1250 persons per sq. km.) causes contamination of open air.

The volume of ground water estimated at Kavaratti is 0.33×10^6 cu.m. The estimated annual rainfall is 5.4×10^6 cu.m. The estimated recharge of fresh water lens per annum is 0.51×10^6 cu.m. The estimated annual requirement of drinking water in Kavaratti during the years 1998 and 2013 AD are 0.232×10^6 cu.m. and 0.346×10^6 cu.m. respectively. There are above 165 government wells and many private wells. Community wells are unhygienically maintained. Ground water is available at a depth of 1.5 m. Indiscriminate use of small hand pumps for domestic purpose is likely to deplete water resources. Information so far available indicate that ground water resources alone are inadequate to meet all the demands of water supply. A plan for tapping ground water in Kavaratti by underground tank supplemented by feeder tanks as presented by KWWA has a promise to meet the need for adequate supply of water in the Islands.

Suggested Areas for Further Evaluation

(1) Development of organised water supply and sewerage system for the Lakshadweep Islands.
(2) Adoption of a suitable plan for tapping ground water in other islands

(3) Installation of plants for desalination of sea water by reverse osmosis technique and/or electrodialysis technique to the Island people.

Participant Institutions in the Programme

(1) Lakshadweep Administration.
(2) National Environmental Engineering Research Institute, Nagpur/Cochin.
(3) Kerala Water and Waste Water Authority, Alwaye.
(4) National Institute of Oceanography, Goa/Cochin.
(5) Central Salt and Marine Chemicals Research Institute, Bhavnagar.

Industry, Energy and Environment

According to the Government of India's declaration, Lakshadweep is a no Industry Island. Causes attributed for such a situation are: lack of infrastructure like land, transport, power and market; lack of technical knowledge and skilled manpower; high cost of power generation and lack of entrepreneurship of the people. According to 1981 census, out of 19,743 male population, 7,949 were workers. The marginal workers in the Islands are 1157 males and 713 females. About 19.74 per cent of population constitutes main workforce. Out of total workforce, 22.18 per cent are engaged in fishing and allied activities, and 13.68 per cent are engaged in household industry.

Coconut is the main source of economy in the Lakshadweep Islands. About 85 per cent of land is utilized for coconut cultivation. There are about 6 lakh coconut trees with annual yield 23.6 million nuts. Coir production in the Islands is declining over the years. This is inferred from the declining of coir procurement from 1,210 quintals in 1971-72 to 160 quintals in 1984-85 under coir monopoly scheme of Lakshadweep. This is attributed to the non-remunerative prices earned by the coir producers.

Fishing is the second economic activity of the people in the Islands. Lakshadweep has a potential of fishing wealth extending to an area of half a million sq. kms. of sea water. The estimated potential of marine wealth is about one lakh tonnes of which only 6 per cent have been exploited.

It is observed by experts that out of 2000 million tonnes of calcarious sand reserve in the lagoons of Islands, 712 million tonnes can be safely exploited. It is estimated that there are 92,460 tonnes of phosphate reserves also.

The Island's only source of power generation is the diesel generators. All the ten inhabited islands have been electrified using diesel electric generators whose capacity ranges from 5 kw to 128 kws. Present installed capacity is 2,790 kw. Power consumption in the Islands is increasing steadily from 1,785 kw in 1982-83 to 3193 kw in 1984-85. It is envisaged to add another 300 kw generating capacity during VII Five year Plan. 60 per cent of power is consumed by household sectors mainly for lighting purposes. Consumption of HSD oil is increasing from 1009 kl in 1982-83 to 1652 kl in 1984-85. The estimated demand for HSD oil during VII Five Year Plan is about 3,380 kl.

There are no medium and large-scale industries in the Lakshadweep Islands. About 35 tiny industries are engaged in saw milling, bakeries, soda making, fibre retting and extraction, flour mills, book binding, etc.

Suggested Areas for Further Evaluation

(1) Development of communication, transport and power generation systems to widen the market scope for industrial products of Lakshadweep Islands.
(2) Establishment of mechanised units for fibre extraction and manufacture of coir yarn, ropes, mats and maltings.
(3) Establishment of a Marine National Park, prevention of soil erosion and protection of the eco-balance of the coral islands.

Participant Institutions in the Programme

(1) Lakshadweep Administration.
(2) Indian Institute of Technology, Madras.
(3) National Institute of Oceanography, Goa/Cochin.
(4) Regional Research Laboratory, Trivandrum.
(5) Central Salt and Marine Chemicals Research Institute, Bhavnagar.
(6) Coir Board, Cochin.

Education and Health

Prior to 1956, education in the Lakshadweep Islands was limited to teaching of Kuran in the Madrassas of local Mosques. The first high school was established in 1960-61 in the Amini Islands. Progress of education in terms of schools, pupils and teachers as on June 1986 is shown in Table 4.

TABLE - 4
STATUS OF EDUCATION IN THE LAKSHADWEEP ISLANDS AS ON JUNE 1986

Number of Primary Schools	20
Number of J.B. Schools	18
Number of S.B. Schools	4
Number of High Schools	9
Number of Junior Colleges	2
Number of Pupils	12,695
Number of Teachers	640
Teacher - Pupil Ratio	1:20

Arrangements are made for higher studies from the Islands in the colleges and professional institutions of mainlands. A sum of Rs. 233.70 lakh was spent on education in the Lakshadweep Islands during Sixth Five year Plan period. The Seventh Plan outlay for education is Rs. 405 lakh. Twenty centres for National Adult Education Programme have been established in the Islands. It envisages to cover the entire illiterate population in the age-groups of 15-35 by 1990. Decade-wise percentage literacy achieved in the Islands is shown in Table 5.

TABLE - 5
DECADE-WISE ACHIEVEMENT OF LITERACY IN THE LAKSHADWEEP ISLANDS

Year	*Achievement of percent literacy*
1951	15.5%
1961	23.57%
1971	43.66%
1981	55.04%
2005	By neutral forecast should exceed 80%

Prior to 1956 the medical and public health activities of Lakshadweep Islands were controlled by the District Medical Officer of Malabar and South Canara. After the formation of Union Territory, the health care came under the purview of Lakshadweep Administrator. In April 1972 the Director of Medical Health Service took over the charge of health care. Principal diseases in the early days in the islands were cholera, small pox, leprosy, dysentry, tuberculosis, malaria, and filariasis. Most of them are controlled to a large extent. Nutritional disorders, anaemia, eye infection are the most commonest disease. Considerable advances have been made in the health service facilities in the recent years. At present there are 2 hospitals, 7 primary health centres and one first-aid centre. At Kavaratti there is a 50 bed referal hospital with facilities for dental, maternal and paediatric care. Minicoy has a 920 bed hospital. There are two Ayurvedic dispensaries, one at Kavaratti and another at Andrett. One Homeopathic dispensary was started at Amini during April 1986. A Health Education Bureau was started in Kavaratti in 1983 and one centre in each island was established in 1984-85. Medical stores from Cochin supply medicines to the Island hospitals. Till recently clear health data are not available for the islands. Table 6 shows the health status of people of islands for the periods 1967-74.

Suggested Areas for Further Evaluation

(1) Establishment of Navodaya Vidyalayas in the Islands.

(2) Vocationalization of education by establishing technical schools to impart training in boat building, house building, coir making, etc.

(3) Equipping all hospitals in the islands with adequate specialized facilities, doctors and paramedical staff.

(4) Strengthening of family planning and public health activities.

Participant Institutions in the Programme

(1) Lakshadweep Administration.

(2) Medical College, Department of Medicine, Trivandrum.

TABLE - 6
STATUS OF HEALTH PARAMETERS FOR PEOPLE OF LAKSHADWEEP ISLANDS DURING 1967-74

Parameter (per thousand population)	*1957*	*1968*	*1969*	*1970*	*1971*	*1972*	*1973*	*1974*
Birth rate	41	37	43	42	37	39	35	34
Death rate	13	12	12	12	16	14	11	8
Infant death rate	102	82	100	97	77	69	72	70
Maternal death rate	8	17	5	3	3	1	1	1
Still birth rate	50	53	45	28	34	36	41	36

Transport and Tourism

Lakshadweep Islands are suitable for promotion of both domestic and international tourism. Kavaratti is the main disposal centre for the tourists. There are one guest house, some tourist huts and dak bungalows available at Kavaratti. Other islands like Minicoy need such facilities to be developed. Bangaram, an uninhabited island is good for developing a beach resort. Foreign tourists are permitted to visit Bangaram provided they get permits from the Ministry of Home Affairs. The Liaison Offices of Union Territory at New Delhi and Cochin also issue permits to the foreign tourists. Table 7 presents a picture of growth of inflow of tourists to the islands despite the limitations imposed by lack of infrastructure.

TABLE - 7
TOURISTS INFLOW TO LAKSHADWEEP ISLANDS

Year	*Domestic*	*Foreign*	*Total*
1982-83	490	470	960
1983-84	930	160	1090
1984-85	1200	41	1241
2000-01*	5000	10000	15000

* (estimated on the assumption that requisite infrastructure including airport is developed)

Opening of islands to tourists and introduction of a few automobiles have necessitated the development of roads for intra-island movement. Smallness of the islands (area of biggest island 5 sq. km.) coupled with loose sand soil and nonavailability of native construction materials have imposed greatest constraints on the growth of road length. There is only 153 km. of road available in the islands of which 37 kms. are surfaced. Most of these roads are only cycle tracks and whatever a little road available for vehicular traffic are having 3m width without shoulder. Inter-island transportation is only through use of odams, speed boats and ships. It is reported that about 15,372 people have travelled in ships between islands during 1984-85. Passenger traffic between mainland and islands and vice versa is increasing year after year. However, there are only two ships being operated for the purpose. Table 8 shows the volume of passenger traffic back and forth of Lakshadweep Islands.

TABLE - 8

VOLUME OF PASSENGER TRAFFIC INTO AND OUT OF LAKSHADWEEP ISLANDS

Year	*Mainland to Islands*	*Inter-Islands*	*Islands to Mainlands*	*Total*
1982-83	12,244	13,341	13,057	38,642
1983-84	15,541	15,690	17,674	48,905
1984-85	16,011	15,372	17,808	49,191

Lakshadweep Islands do not produce anything except coconut, copra and fish. All essential commodities needed for survival are obtained from the mainland. It was recorded that 7635 tonnes of goods traffic moved to the Islands from the mainland during 1985 of which 65 per cent way rice alone. Table 9 gives year-wise two-way goods traffic in the Islands.

TABLE - 9

GOODS TRAFFIC RECORDED FOR THE LAKSHADWEEP ISLANDS

(tonnes)

Year	*Export*	*Import*
1983	1967.1	6466.3
1984	1647.3	6906.6
1985	590.9	7636.3

Passenger transport in the Intra-island is likely to increase from 15,000 person trips in 1984-85 to 29,000 person trips in 2005 AD. The Islands traffic attractions potential from the mainland is likely to go up from 16,000 person trips in 1984-85 to 30,000 person trips in 2005 AD. The cargo movement from mainland to Island is likely to increase from 7636 tonnes in 1985 to 15,516 tonnes in 2005 AD.

Suggested Areas for Further Evaluation

(1) The island is connected with mainland by air base.

(2) More shipping facilities into the islands and transport and accommodation facilities in the islands is established.

(3) Each inland specializes in one type of tourism like sports and recreation to attract more tourists.

Participant Institutions in the Programme

(1) Lakshadweep Administration.

(2) Department of Tourism, Government of India, New Delhi.

(3) National Transportation Planning and Research Centre, Trivandrum/New Delhi.

Panel Discussion and Conclusion

It was recommended in the Panel Session to form a task group consisting of institutional experts in different sectors to draw feasible alternate scenarios for the development of Lakshadweep Islands in 21st century. The task group shall take into account the following points while preparing the action plan. A breakthrough for the development of the Islands shall come from the ocean and its resources and action shall be taken faster to catch up with time. High technology and large-scale programmes should be enmeshed with the interests of the people in the Islands.

The task group shall consist of expertise from the following institutions:—

(1) Administrator, Lakshadweep Administration.

(2) Director, Central Marine Fisheries Research Institute, Cochin.

(3) Director, National Environmental Engineering Research Institute, Nagpur.

(4) Director, Central Plantation Crop Research Institute, Kasaragod.

(5) Director, National Institute of Oceanography, Goa.

(6) Director, Housing & Urban Development Corporation, Bangalore.

(7) Director, Regional Research Laboratory, Trivandrum.

The task group shall draft sector-wise, first level report indicating possible S&T inputs for future development of Lakshadweep which will be circulated among the participants for further improvement. It is expected that the draft report reflects the views of institutional efforts in their respective areas of specialization.

ART AND THE FUTURE*

Satish C. Seth and Padma Seth

We believe that the concern for future is the concern to build a new society. We also believe that along with education, science and technology and management the "Arts" also hold the key to this developmental task.

The shifting scene in the world of art in every society — the developing and the developed — suggests that by and large that we are moving in the right direction towards the future. The insight of the artist in any society helps to create a larger world outlook. It makes one understand the past and the present. At the same time it offers a sense of direction—depicting harmony and conflicts and a synthesis—for the future.

We also believe that futurology, futures research or futurism whatever name we may accept is primarily the search of new ideas and new images for a better society. Likewise, the concern of art is also with imageries, new possibilities and new combinations. The well-spring of all creativity is the imagination, which manifests itself in the projection of images, new forms, new designs and new possibilities. An artist is continuously interacting with historical, social and cultural environment. He responds to it in the same manner in which a futurologist responds to the interplay of these forces. The common desire is to build anew; to search new possibilities.

The concern of a futurologist is with needs of today and of tomorrow. Likewise, the artist in his interaction with the society has a special faculty in that he can see, hear and feel aspects of the world around that one has never experienced before. Taken as a whole the concern of societal innovators and the concern of those who are dedicated to 'arts' at a given time and period, both

---

* Addressed by Ms Padma Seth (the then Executive Secretary of ICMF) at a Workshop of Art and Future at Jakarta, held from 8-15 July, 1978. Organized by WFSF and Academy of Art Jakarta and Art Centre, Balajseri Toya-bungkash.

usually demonstrate, a certain unity of direction. They are constantly searching the frontiers of a new society. A society of creativity; a society of possibilities; a society of fulfilment and a society of opportunity, where the basic human urges, aspirations and needs may be fulfilled—not for an individual but for every member of the society.

Futures research pursues a certain scientific methodology! The objective is the pursuit of truth. Unlike a scientist who analyses his material, isolates it and breaks it down to atomic size to study the objective world of facts and phenomena to search laws and relationships, the artist, in his methodology, does the reverse. He synthesises his material, assembles and builds, puts atoms and things together to create a subjective world of images and feelings. In this process he offers a unique experience. Cumulatively the artists strive to give form and substance to a worldview. As has been rightly remarked by Romain Roland.

> The political life of a nation is only a superficial part of its being in order to learn its inner life—the sources of its actions—we must penetrate to its very soul by way of its literature, its philosophy and its art, where the ideas, the passions and dreams of its peoples are reflected.

Thus, we will find that whereas scientific theories can be disproved, can have a brief life, the work of art, once completed, stands as a final-statement for all times. Art can be disproved by new forms and styles; but it cannot be destroyed. Art endures.

Out of artists subjectively built world, we believe, that he projects a moment in the world of objective values a fragment of infinity. The artist thus does something to make the moment last, to give permanence to the present.

Apparently, the artist, then is the only, victor in the man's—struggle against time. The work of art is the crystallization of a moment "a link between past and future, a bridge between individual and universal experience."

Art cannot be divorced from society. As a creative process, irrespective of its form or activity, it involves both the artist and the audience—the people. Every person is, in some way or the other, projecting a social image of oneself. But every person is not articulate or communicative enough. It is through arts that experiences of great richness and variety get articulated. The numerous images that the artist forms, like the futurologist's concern for future possibilities and future images, are but a reflection of asking numerous questions of life. Through these questions thus art offers several manifestations, expresses several conflicts, outlines several synthesis. As Lionel Venturi remarks:

> Ultimately what matters in art is not the canvas, the hue of oil or tempera, the anatomical structure and all the other measurable items, but its contribution to our life, its suggestions to our sensations, feelings and imagination.

In this world of variety the insight of the artist makes the past continue to exist as a living process and in a sense its arbitrary separation from present and future disappears. After all art in its most basic meaning signifies a skill or ability.*

Every society has a right to judge the manifestation of its ability in its quest to shape the future. We need to continuously make critical appreciation of the whole range of creative and imaginary possibilities in the field of art and other forms thereof in order to see its relevance or irrelevance to the development of a new society whether in India, in Indonesia or elsewhere, to judge, if we are moving in the right direction towards the future.

Most of the developing societies are old and new. They are multi-racial societies. They are with deep history, culture and

---

* The term more generally carries the connotation of nonutilitarian activities: the art of painting, poetry or music.

Liberal Arts include practical pursuits that facilitate freedom of expression in language (grammar), speech (rhetoric) and reasoning (logic) as well as studies which lend to understanding of main physical, social and cultural environment.

Fine Arts are cultivated more for their own sake and for the intensive pleasure they afford for the minds and emotions of those who experience them.

— the arts concerned only with the beautiful: see the French word beaux-arts.

The fine arts, in any rational view, however, must be broadened to include any aesthetically directed expression in visual, verbal or auditory images and symbols. The arts thus would include:

(i) architecture;
(ii) sculpture;
(iii) painting and related: usually plastic and graphic arts;
(iv) literature in its various poetic, prosonic and dramatic forms; and
(v) as well, dance and music.

civilisation. These societies offer an interaction, more intense, more dramatic, more creative. It is necessary, therefore, to see how we are going to move towards the 21st century. In doing so each society, in its own context, should pose certain questions and seek an answer which will indicate the future directions. We should ask for instance:

(1) Have our performing art and artists remained stagnant over centuries?
(2) Is our art routinised and stylised—hence non-innovative?
(3) What are the new developments in the folk and the traditional art?
(4) Will it be correct to assume that it has been considerably commercialised?
(5) What are the commercial characteristics and how they affect (a) creativity and (b) quality?
(6) Will it be right to say that today's art lacks in spirit, ideas and emotive expression which could encompass the future dimensions of culture, society and the quest for individual identity?
(7) Is performing art primarily an entertainment fix?
(8) Do our contemporary performing arts reflect a creative response to the changing value system?
(9) Will it be right to say that our art is considerably divorced from the people and their aspirations and ethos?
(10) What will be the new possibilities that our arts endeavour to acquire in order to usher in a new society?
(11) Have we identified the needs of our children and youth in relation to art and creativity and found adequate institutional response thereto?
(12) Do we have adequate teaching and training infrastructure available in the country to cope with the needs of the present and the future.

In search of an answer—several answers—to the illustrative—questions listed above (these questions can be multiplied) alone, we can find the elements and the directions for the future. The logic of future can be spelled out in terms of identifying:

(a) emerging needs (some of—our societies are large human systems)—hence the concern for numbers; (b) the concern for right choice of technology; (c) concern for right system of education and creativity (education not in its traditional sense but in search of new forms of non-formal systems—of learning); and (d) choosing and developing adequate management systems (we are still short of ideal delivery systems of 'goods' of welfare). All these alternatives can be multiplied as we look at society and the developmental compulsions in a scientific manner; having applied scientific process we have then to apply the creative process of synthesis of searching new design and new forms of serving humanity and thus ushering in a new society. It is a great challenge.

We are confident that in this very important conference-even though our deliberations here have been in the context of 'Art and the Future' in both its 'limited' and very 'broad' sense, we shall certainly arrive at that methodological process, posture and approach—not one but several—which will take our respective societies towards a better society and a happy future. Creativity ushers optimism. It is only with hope and faith that we can launch ourselves into committed and dedicated service of people, our society; so as to lay the foundations of a happier international order. Needless to add that in seeking our options and policy choices, we shall be well-served if we try first to look at a distant date, a long time horizon, a perspective which will only help us proceed towards future with confidence and preparedness. In short, art should be an instrument of choosing a preferred future. For better future we need to act today. Verily in a sense, future is today.

38

INDIAN COUNCIL OF MANAGEMENT AND FUTURE (ICMF)

Aruna Vasudev & Satish C. Seth

(I) ACTIVITIES ON PERFORMING ARTS (A REPORT)

The objective of our study is to examine: (a) the need element for creative endeavour in the Indian society today and by the turn of the century; (b) the relationship between the performing artists and the Indian cultural ethos and special milieu; and (c) to identify the contemporary trends and new possibilities in the field of music, dance, theatre and cinema.

Music, Dance, Theatre and Cinema: Today and Tomorrow

Suggested Areas for Further Evaluation

A critical appreciation of the whole range of creative and imaginative possibilities in the field of performing art and endeavour to relate its relevance or irrelevance to the development of a new society in India during the 21st century is needed as related to the following questions.

(1) Has Indian performing art and artists remained stagnant over centuries?

(2) Is our art routinised and stylised—hence non-innovative?

(3) What are the new developments in the folk and the traditional art?

(4) Will it be correct to assume that it has been considerably commercialised?

(5) What are the commercial characteristics and how they affect (a) creativity and (b) quality?

(6) Will it be right to say that today's art lacks in spirit, ideas and emotive expression which could encompass the future dimensions of culture, society and the quest for individual identity?

(7) Is performing art primarily an entertainment fix?

(8) Do our contemporary performing arts reflect a creative response to the changing value system?

(9) Will it be right to say that our art is considerably divorced from the people and their aspirations and ethos?

(10) What will be the new possibilities that Indian art should endeavour to acquire in order to usher a new society?

(11) What is today's quality, need and scope of entertainment that the performing arts today offer in our restaurants and hotels? What are the likely future trends?

(12) Examine the needs of our children and youth for teaching and training infrastructure available in the country to cope with the needs of today and the future.

(II)

A BRIEF REPORT ON THE "WORKSHOP ON THE FUTURE OF PERFORMING ARTS

As is apparent, the thrust of discussion on the future of the performing arts was set against a background of the relationship between society and the arts, and the future evolution of this relationship. It was agreed that the two are interrelated and that a changing society inevitably brings about change in the art form and even in classical tradition.

The tendency was to concentrate on the contemporary situation rather than project into the future. In the process, certain themes emerged which will influence future developments. The main one was universal acknowledgement that except for folk art which represents a spontaneous interaction between the people and local societies and customs, the performing arts in India were elitist both in presentation and in the composition of the audiences. Also, since support and patronage had always come from the princely and affluent land-owning classes, it was agreed that if the arts were to survive, they had to be patronized by the State, as there was no alternative source.

Within this framework, there were two main views—one staunchly traditionalist, and the other recognising that change was inevitable. The traditionalist minority held that the classical form had to be maintained without dilution and that audiences (society) should be educated to appropriate this. The more realistic view recognised that the arts emanate from society and therefore will change with it. Thus, even the folk arts will evolve as the horizons and requirements of the villagers expand. An extreme illustration was the gradual replacement of traditional tribal love songs by film music and evenAmerican popular songs like "You are my sunshine" (a forty year old favourite). This inevitably carries over into ceremonial music; as people change so will birth, marriage and death rituals and with this, the music for them. The extent of the change will depend on the variations of traditional life patterns.

The emergence of massive audiences seeking escapist entertainment is met by the cinema. The major art form of the twentieth century, having entered into the 21st century with even more following. Born of the technological revolution, it already influences the performing arts and will do so more extensively as income levels rise and audiences increase. Its music denigrated by classicists, is already more widely known both nationally and internationally than the traditional forms. Only the cinema can accommodate the immense numbers involved. It has the advantage of catering for specialist audiences, with the additional capacity of recording for the future, existing traditional art forms, hitherto dependent on memory and heredity.

The changes that have taken place in for instance music and dance are lost to posterity. Further developments in these and in other disciplines must be balanced in such a way that the classical form at least as we know now remains untouched. While experimentation must be welcomed and innovations or alterations (additions in presentation or technique) enthusiastically encouraged, these must not be presented under the name or the guise of the traditional version, for example, the Alarippu in Bharat Natyam must retain classical form, and the name Alarippu must not be used for any variation on it.

The role of the State Agencies was much criticised for inadequacy of effort, lack of vision, and ineffectiveness. It was felt that State assistance came too late in the creative life of the artist. Awards and honours are given to people at the fag end of their lives. A number of examples were given of leading classical artists breaking hereditary traditions and urging their progenies into fields unrelated to the arts. On a massive scale, folk arts and traditions (and even special instruments) are dying out for lack of encouragement. Tribal societies are denied spontaneous expression by puritanical interference and misguided efforts made to "improve" their customs.

Summed up, the view of even the present situation—and very little projection was done—was bleak. The essential problem was best identified in relation to the theatre for which audiences have not developed despite considerable increase in trained personnel, experiments in research into folk forms, and modern techniques of staging and production. The main constraint was financial, limiting presentations to plays with small casts, simple sets and inexpensive techniques. In spite of the admirable efforts of the National School of Drama and its recently formed Repertory Company, it is still virtually impossible for even dedicated people to make a living in the theatre.

A gloomy glimpse into the future saw little improvement in the present and anticipated a more extreme polarisation between the entertainment oriented demands of mass audiences and the struggle of a tiny elitist minority of performers and audiences to maintain quality standards. Throughout there was emphasis that a clear cultural policy was lacking. To meet this, it was suggested that advisory groups should be set-up to assist government in the planning and implementation of a cultural policy which would maintain the classic tradition and simultaneously encourage experimentation. It was also suggested that newspaper and magazine editors should be asked to give more perceptive attention to the arts and to change the somewhat subjective, sometimes ill-formed attitude of critics.

The three-fold objectives of the Workshop were in large measure realised in that the participants animatedly discussed the relationship between the performing artists and the Indian cultural ethos and special milieu, identifying clearly contemporary trends in the fields of music, dance, theatre and cinema. It was generally felt that new possibilities in creative endeavour would depend greatly on the direction taken by the evolution of society itself.

(III)
BOMBAY WORKSHOP ON FUTURE OF PERFORMING ARTS*

Deleberations
Satish C. Seth

Dr Seth initiated the discussions. He gave a brief resume of the key-questions posed at the Delhi Workshop and summarised the high points of the discussion as recorded by Dr Aruna Vasudev in her report. He then pointed out that the concern of future is to prefer the right kind of society that we would like to see emerge in the beginning of the 21st century. It is in this context that we have to identify the role of the performing arts and ask ourselves: What changes, if any, need to be ushered in the Indian creative endeavour to ensure that the performing arts contribute to the vitality and the early emergence of a better society? He also pointed out that the concern of future is with needs today and needs tomorrow. Are we accommodating future needs in our current day decision making process whether they pertain to the choice of technology, choice of management systems or choice of diversification in the pursuit of excellence? Will the classical forms of our arts and traditions continue to be the 'preserve' and the 'pleasure' of a few? Can we do something to share the excellence in the country, no matter from which quarter it emerges, with the rest of the society? Can we take art to the streets? Will our artists agree to climb down from their high pedestal to share their excellence with the masses? Of course, local authorities should provide funds for this. He wanted the group to examine if there is something stagnant in our performing arts? He also wanted the group to identify ways and means whereby Indian creative effort could be made integral to the Indian educational and learning process so that no child in the country is

* The Indian Council of Management and Future organised a One Day Workshop on "Future of Performing Art" on October 22, 1978 at New Delhi. The second session of this activity was held at the National Centre of Performing Arts (Courtesy: Dr Narain Menon, Director, National Centre of Performing Arts, Bombay) on February 3, 1979.

denied an opportunity to seek and pursue that art form which it wishes to seek. He wondered if the Indian social set-up, in the context of its poverty conditions, in the context of its being at the same time in agraria, industria and post-industria, and in the context of its institutions having failed to communicate with the masses, is really ripe to give to its people a different future. Nobody can predict future. We can only minimize the degree of uncertainty which goes with the future. We can also to some extent shape and influence it. Future is in that sense today. What we do today has great implications for the future. Can we, therefore, 'today' think how best we could catalogue a series of changes and offer concrete inputs which can help evolve a new national cultural policy?

Dr Narain Menon

Dr. Narain Menon pointed out that a great deal of ignorance prevails in the country as to what exists and is happening in the field of performing arts in the various regions of the country. It will be wrong to say that the classical dance and music is not known to rural folks. What is happening is that the patronage in these areas has changed. Today, there is not that big a gulf between the literacy, excellence and knowledge. The artists are no more ill-paid servants. Classical forms of dance in music have certainly changed and developed over the time. The process has not been hereditary. The present position is not too bleak. Of course, music and dance have not evolved like painting. Older traditions are still dominant. Like literacy, performing arts, hereafter, need not remain a relic of a certain social system. Let us not forget that music and dance have a tendency to please audiences. Let us also not forget that development of technology has a great impact on the performing arts. It will bring about a collective change in the performing arts over the years. Let us look forward to more logical developments.

Mr A. Padamsee

Indian performing arts are more stagnant *vis-a-vis* plastic arts, for example, painting. Cinema too has debased itself. Curiously enough, in many countries, for example, USA there is more investment in music than in cinema. Even though in India more people watch cinema and TV particularly on a Sunday, almost 35 million people a week watch cinema ("Possibly these are the same people watching over and over again" -B.D. Garg). However, the content of Indian cinema is still stagnant in nature. Let us not forget that when cultural forms begin to freeze and get mummified they don't remain art. Let us recognize the factor of alienation. To promote art shared background is essential. Art cannot be divorced from people. For example, in Calcutta there are five thousand little theatre groups. Here theatre is integral to the people. Let us not get anxious if youth, internationally, are identifying themselves with a certain kind of music. It is no danger to the indigenous traditions. We need to train professional managers in the field of art. There is also need to set-up a group of creative people to suggest what is culturally needed. We need a cultural directory listing individuals and institutions working in the field of performing arts in India.

Mr Murti

Today art stands divorced from life. Let us examine how and where? Is it due to economic factors? One can, of course, say that some local traditions are today nationally shared, for example, Kuchipudi dance from Andhra Pradesh. But what is happening to cinema. The art films are not getting an exhibition outlet. The exhibition cinema, as an important outlet has become a big bottleneck. Much needs to be done in this region. If you go to the funding authorities, such as, the Planning Commission, one is posed with a dilemma and a question: What should one choose bread or art: Food or culture? ("If Art can relate itself to society, people and regional needs and aspirations this dichotomy can be taken care of." —Dr Seth).

Mr K. Rathod

All art form basically are there to communicate. Yet cinema today is the largest media in the world to communicate with masses. The role of cinema needs to be strengthened.

Mr B.D. Garg

Undoubtedly cinema is a great media to reach masses yet we are reaching less and less people. This is where we should find out our strategies for the future.

Ms Tarla Mehta

Performing arts cannot be divorced from the question concerning patronage of art. Cinema may be an ideal media to reach masses. However, due to its impact, the folk forms are getting degenerated. Even television today is not able to accommodate or promote the viewing interest of the children. Where are the children films? I accept the viewpoint presented by Dr Seth that excellence in art should be taken to the streets and shared with people. Gujarati theatre and some others are slowly moving in this direction.

Mr Nissim Ezzikiel

It is high time that we stop thinking in narrow sectoral terms, cinema, dance, etc. Instead we should develop a national viewpoint relevant to evolving a national cultural policy. Let us not mystify art. Demystification is the need of the hour.

Mr Rama Pai

We need to support the creative efforts of the young persons. Let us recognize talent and creativity in performing arts at all levels.

Ms Uttara Asha Coorlawala

What is needed today is creation of ample opportunities, such as liberal grants-in-aid and funding by the various local bodies in the field of performing arts, as is the case in several foreign countries. Let us recognise non-conformism in our performing arts since it is integral to an evolutionary process.

Mr K. Sontakka

In the field of performing arts, both in its form and content, the decaying forms need to be resurrected. Of course, there still is the question of obtaining subsidies. There is need for more exchange of ideas amongst artists. I endorse the view of Dr Seth that the art should go to the people.

Mr S.L. Gujar

The classical training in music has become an imitative exercise. It is not a creative exercise. We need to have more appreciation courses.

Ms Kalpana Desai

Our performing arts must transform themselves in order to become relevant to the emerging Indian society.

Dr Prabha Atre

The classical form cannot resist change. It has to face new challenges. I agree, the art and its excellence, must be shared with the people. The art should go to the streets. All round coordination amongst the academies and other organisations too is inescapable for strengthening the social role of performing arts and artists.

Suggestions from Mr Alyque Padamsee

1. Training of managers (in Institutes and Polytechnics) in management of cultural institutions.
2. Calling of a National Workshop for evolving a Cultural Policy and its execution within a time bound plan.
3. Drawing up of a Directory of Grants available for culture, to be circulated to all through Press, TV and Circulars.
4. Special grants for performing arts among the underprivileged like patients in hospitals, prisons, slums, etc.
5. Open up TV freely to performing arts groups who have set standards.

Suggestions from Ms Tarla Mehta

1. A peep into the future can only be done by looking back to our past and assessing our present.

   I would like to do this as regards the theatre—the Gujarati theatre to which I belong. We are celebrating this year the 125th anniversary of the theatre in Gujarat. And while evaluating this period, one comes to some basic conclusions; which may be even true for the performing arts in our country. The evolution of the art activity tend to go round in circles. The basic *status quo* always remains. The revolutionary changes seldom occur.

   For example, the Gujarati theatre has remained entertainment oriented—catering to the urban middle-class tastes. The tendency to dish out the proven formulas in the proven formats—of course, with some superficial changes here and there always remain unshaken and firmly established.

The Gujarati films have a fixed pattern of pleasing the lower middle-classes/the rural audiences (with their mythological-legends and the social stories glorifying the age old value-pattern). This has more or less remained unchanged for the last 30-35 years.

2. Perhaps, the performing arts: The theatre, the Film, the Children's theatre/films, and the the TV with which I have been associated, has catered to the urban middle-class penchant for a set type of entertainment. Can one say escapist? They certainly do not reflect the contemporary reality, the problems, the aspirations, the feeling of the contemporary man and his children.
3. Can one explain away the situation by saying that the films and the theatre are a business. Big money is invested and the big sale is the need result.
4. But what about the children's theatre/and children film movement? With their State patronage what is their impact? Big cities lack good theatres for the children's entertainment. The rural reality is quite different. The *chapatti* versus the pencil and the notebook.
5. TV was supposed to be a tool for a change, as so one thought, not a *status quo* refrigerator. But we all know where it has ended up—being used as a middle-class toy.
6. Thus looking at the recent past and the present, it appears, unless and until a conscious effort is made to plan the performing infrastructure, the future is going to be non-innovative as ever.
7. Who can do that?

   The State with its patronage—yes. It can do much to preserve and patronise the rich art traditions both classical and folk.
8. Encourage the experimentations therein too. Perhaps, by keeping, preserving and using the rich conventions and techniques of these arts, the modern content can be expressed. Even the myths and legends can be reviewed from a modern-contemporary angle. Again it can help in popularising the folk arts—at least stopping the filmy vulgarisation seeping into it.
9. But more than that, the emergence of conscious artists,

committed to individual freedoms—the freedom of expressions. As some one has said "In our age, the artists are the eternal members of the opposition—opposition to the status-quoism."

10. The bright future of the performing arts lies in developing a band of the category. Committed artists have to emerge.

Suggestions from Ms Uttara Asha Coorlawala

A group discussion on the Future of Performing Arts, that met on February 3, 1979, at the National Centre of the Performing Arts, was well organised and presented by Dr. S.C, Seth in conjunction with Dr. Narayana Menon. The topic outlined in Dr. Aruna Vasudev's report were summarily noted. and the discussion moved on to the more practical aspect as what should be done to foster creativity and excellence in the Performing Arts.

Some useful suggestions and interesting observations were made. I sincerely hope that these will be acted upon, rather than filed away in some office corner.

Below, I have listed a few suggestions which may or may not be applicable, based on my experience both in the US and India, in my own limited field as a choreographer, teacher and performer of creative dance.

Ref: Dr Aruna Vasudev's Report

Since Independence, there has been a tremendous resurgence of interest in traditional Indian Performing Arts—as these are the living crystallized expressions of our culture. Socially, India is going through the upheavals of industrialisation, and Western influence is inevitable. All Indians, especially artists, are re-examining their values and should have plenty to say about this process. This is a crucial time in the development of the Performing Arts. In terms of creativity the future looks colourful and promising. It is not bleak.

'Elite', Performing artists always were and will be, numerically speaking, an 'elite' group. However, the performing arts in India have an audience potential that is far from being economically and socially elite. This evaluation of elitist applies only to esoteric classical arts outside their native areas.

May I quote an example: A village outside Puruliya (Orissa) which is probably exceptional, but not unusual. This village (like some others in India, that we may not know of) has for generations subsidised its own dance company. The resulting dance form and the performers have achieved a high level of perfection and excellence. All this with no government financing, just the love and support of the local community, which barely earns enough to feed itself.

Why cannot urban societies function similarly? Why cannot the large industrial houses (including the film industry), sponsor and develop projects of creative and cultural value. To a small extent, this is already happening with the Tata, Sarabhai, Shriram and other similar companies. But so few industrialists have an enlightened and responsible attitude to the cultural environments in which they function. Can we not make them an offer they cannot refuse, i.e., by providing incentives via the tax structure, such as tax deductible contributions to performing arts institutions.

The government can help by sponsoring and organising programs similar to those sponsored by the State Cultural Councils in the US and UK.

(1) Artist-in-Residence, or Artist-in-Schools programs. These serve the double function of (i) educating the public, and developing cultural awareness in the areas where they are placed and also (ii) help the artist.

(2) In village communities especially, an enlightened and discriminating policy of sponsoring folk dances, and folk dance festivals, should be developed by the States, in conjunction with the ITDC since the tourist trade is after all, a source of income and tourists will benefit by seeing 'authentic' dances, as opposed to vulgarized commercialized alternatives. Also tourist centres should be used as the venue for the presentation of performing arts, for example, the recent Khajuraho festival and the UNESCO-Air India Dance festival which arranged for Chhau dances to be performed in Aurangabad.

(3) Make accessible to performing artists such necessary and technical services as those of administrators, legal and financial advisors, light and sound designers, etc., for the

Arts. Is there a society of lawyers volunteering legal services for artists? All that needs to be organised is a list of specialists, willing to help, to be made available to those who require such help via an intermediary.

(4) The State should also organise courses and seminars to train managers and administrators for artists. Many artists simply rely on the help of their immediate family, who would greatly benefit from such training. However, such courses would also mobilize effectively the services of housewives in urban communities, who may have time to spare but are unable to take up full-time professions.

These suggestions are based on a forward looking approach. There is need that is very urgent at this time of terrific cultural and social change. This is to preserve the folk art forms in their present form, for this cultural heritage will not survive the barrage of influence now reaching and pressing the individual—I am referring to the following:

(a) the effects of mass communication—radio and film, on the arts.

(b) the effects of increased social mobility, for example, a sculptor's son will not be a sculptor, unless he prefers to—which is unusual in the lower paid handicrafts.

(c) the effects of increased geographic mobility, in response to industrialisation and the growth of urban culture. The folk arts developed out of a rural lifestyle, will be irrelevant soon—if something is not done to engender an atmosphere of appreciation and pride in the excellence, simplicity and purity of these cultural legacies.

Some of these folk arts will be irrelevant and change (as indeed they should) no matter what policy we follow. Should we then let them disappear, or try to preserve some audiovisual record of them for posterity?

Nothing is being done about this, though a lot has been said. I, for one, am eager to contribute my services in this direction as I see it as an urgent need.

Suggestions from Ms Ina Poddar-Theising

It was in a workshop on the Future of the Performing Arts under the impact of technological and societal change that the whole ambit of problems besetting music, dance, theatre, and cinema came up for discussion and scrutiny; and it was refreshing that they were not straightaway blamed on lack of funds, as one has heard once too often.

The inevitability of change and adaption to current needs and trends of even the most tradition-bound arts, music and dance, was generally accepted. The question of whether the urban youngster could still be interested in classical music at all, or whether he has already irretrievably fallen victim to the world-wide pop-wave was cut short by the assurance, he would take to it if exposed to it. On the strength of what evidence?

Art should be stripped of its halo and taken to the people. (We just had the open-air-exhibition of paintings in New Delhi, apparently a success with the artists and spectators opening a dialogue. That certainly blazes the trail into future). Yet, the gathering was perhaps a bit too blue-eyed about the accessibility of art in general and in a poverty-stricken society in particular. It was pointed out how art in the countryside is part and parcel of everyday-life and that performing peasant as well as his counterpart are not aware of anything extraordinary about painting, pottery, weaving or staging *tamashas*. That is no doubt true. But the very moment these native artistic creations are uprooted from the soil and exhibited in a museum (or on a lawn, for that matter) the exhibit stands aloof *vis-a-vis* a spectator. A piece of daily use or an ordinary concomitant of life thus turns into an artefact. Life and art have parted, alienation occurs.

Every country on its way from an integrated agrarian to a specialised urban society has to pay this price. If we want to learn about artistic creativity in a country as variegated as India, we have to fall back on exhibitions in urban centres and become spectators. The step from folkloristic activity towards art is not necessarily one towards perfection: but it changes the very essence of the object with the changed conditions of its presentation.

The artefact severed from its natural context faces spectators to whom it means nothing in terms of their experience. Either it evokes no response at all or the spectator responds aesthetically, i.e. to an inherent quality corresponding with his own sensitivity. How many persons in a society engaged in the struggle for survival can be expected to be susceptible to the radiation of a piece of art which is totally unfamiliar to them and unrelated to their immediate needs? It is a fallacy to believe that art and life are of the same stuff.

No doubt that government agencies are more inclined to shell out money for, say, a pesticides-spraying-programme than to subsidise art. The urban intellectual, however, challenges their priorities pointing out that the insight into the necessity of adopting new methods of cultivation requires a new outlook, the readiness to break with traditions. This "change of heart" can be initiated by the popular and persuasive medium of film, for instance.

In fact, both parties aim at societal change, but one accuses the other of putting the cart before the horse. For the participants of the workshop it seemed a foregone conclusion that only the enlightened mind paves the way to progress, whereas it is at least arguable that the feedback of a modern technology achieves the same result. The poorer the country the more suggestive the practical approach, ideally, backwardness should be tackled on either front. Only dogmatics dare decide whether the hen came first or the egg!

Such weighty problems by their very nature cannot be thought out within the framework of one seminar. All the more beneficial was the presence of practising artistes articulating the difficulties they have to cope with and suggesting remedial action. A stage-director stated in so few words how a centre of communication would help to cross-fertilize dramatic activities in all parts of the country, how badly a new kind of manager is needed who takes care of the financial viability of an outfit without losing sight of its artistic nature.

Delightfully revolutionary is the appeal of a seasoned musician to demystify the training of future musicians. The hallowed *guru-chela* relationship, with the disciple submitting body and mind to his master and "mounting" his art, ought to give way to a comprehensive education enabling the student to develop his personality, critical faculty and his own style

If only a fraction of the aspirations do get materialised the labour of the workshop would not be lost.

*The Workshop on "Future of Performing Arts" was held on 3rd February, 1979, at N.C.P.A., Bombay, organised by the Indian Council of Management and Future.

Suggestions from Dr Prabha Atre

PROFORMA WITH SUGGESTIONS FOR THE FORMATION OF A NATIONAL CULTURAL POLICY (MUSIC)

Listeners	*Artistes*	*Organisations/Organisers*
1. Prospective inspirer and patron of art—Music as a part of a fundamental education will provide an appreciative but stimulatingly critical audience. 2. Exposure of classical music on a par with film music through TV, Radio, Short Films, feature, commercial films with popular stars projecting themes, classical music. 3. Music programmes to be made available at economic rates. 4. Proper advertising with a	1. To prepare lists of the artistes at town, district and state level, under the following categories. a. i) Professionals ii) Semi-professionals iii) Amateurs b. i) Vocal ii) Instrumental c. i) Classical ii) Light iii) Film iv) Folk d. i) Performers ii) Accompanists iii) Critics iv) Composers v) Writers vi) Teachers vii) Instrument Makers 2. At least one State University and also college of	1. To prepare lists of organisations and organisers at town, district and state level under the following categories:- i) Government viz. AIR, ICCR ii) Semi-Government viz. Sangeet Natak Academy, etc. iii) Private Public/Music Circles and Music Festivals. iv) Private Organisations viz. ITC Academy, Bhulabai Memorial, National Centre for Performing Arts, etc. i) Govt. Organisations - Encourage talented young people to take music as a profession by assuring of minimum financial security. Artistes effective professional career being shorter than in many other occupations, recognition at

(Continued on next page)

(Contd.)

Listeners	*Artistes*	*Organisations/Organisers*
commercial get-up of new books, records and tapes, the prices being within the easy reach of the commoners. 5. To encourage mass musical activities at the temples. Ashrams and house through devotional music. 6. Areawise music teaching classes which could eventually turn into small cultural centres.	music at town level. Admittance on merit basis only. 3. Research Departments, libraries of books, tapes, records, instruments photographs, etc. Music periodicals in regional languages, authorities on music should be persuaded to write on various aspects for different age groups. To get songs specially written for music compositions based in ragas. Works of saints to be similarly explored. 4. Regular work-shops in music performances and appreciation at schools and colleges "artistes in residence" at Universities.	Govt. level should come when it is still not 'late'. Exchange of musicians across regional borders for performances, lectures, seminars for the benefit of rural and small town areas in addition to yearly State festival, regular musical performances areawise by individual artistes at town and district levels. Availability of good musical instruments at the social welfare office may be assured. Zonal Coordination Office should be set-up for zonal tours of the artistes. This will curtail travelling expenses towards artistes conveyance and artistes energy and time. Rates of advertisements for classical music conferences and concerts in newspapers, TVs and radios should be concessional as also the entertainment tax condoned.

Coordinated efforts of all the above three major components be achieved under a central guidance unit.

The Explanatory Note on the Formulation of a National Cultural Policy (Music)

The coming of Indian independence and the events that follow have made us realise afresh how, what happens in the political and social world affects, in an important way; the fate of art and the lives of artistes. We have seen the mergers of the old Princely States; the diminishing importance of dance, drama and music in the regular cycles of worship at the temples, the growing influence of Western ways in our lifestyles; the tendency of the wealthy and the elite to use their dealings with art and the artiste as status symbols; and the general inadequacy of public policy towards the arts and of the administration of such measures as attempted. These have tended to drive the arts to the common minds support for refuge. On the other hand, the new proud sense of national identity has extended also a warmer feeling for our classical traditions in the arts. The seeds of a new flowering in the Indian arts were here. Few will say that they have come to the fruition we might well have hoped for.

Now do I see the problems of our present situation?

I. There are the problems of the common man who is to provide both the audience and the support to the artiste (let me from now on be understood as speaking of the musical artiste). There are the problems of the artiste. And there are the problems of the institutions and associations that bring audience and artistes together.

The common man should perhaps come first, because he is the one who in some cases is going to develop into an artiste; he is the one who will in many ways influence the artistes' creative activity by appreciation or neglect; he is the one for whose sake one must suppose any national policy in cultural matters is undertaken in the final analysis.

If we regard him as the prospective inspirer and supporter or art, the common man's problem is in the first instance that he has an overload of economic and social problems in his personal life. In consequence, he is too often indifferent, uninstructed as to the nature of the arts, and therefore easily tempted to squander his poor resources of time and money on trivial entertainment. The form this state of affairs takes in regard to music is shown pretty clearly by his obsession with anything that goes under 'Film Music'. He simply has not had the opportunities, the exposure to genuine art, which are necessary for him to learn how to accept the comfort and the grace that sincere art can offer to his too often bleak life.

The artistes' problems might be said to begin with the opportunities of becoming one. We have distinguished exponents of classical Indian music, northern and southern, vocal and instrumental; but a national policy must surely take into account whether Indian conditions are as favourable as they should be for nourishing and continuing of our musical tradition. This must depend chiefly on how good the opportunities are for any young person of talent to receive the guidance and the training that will turn him into a mature artiste.

When a genuine talent has been matured into artistry, there emerge problems of the artiste and the man, who both have to coexist (to use that term characteristics of our generation-in the same envelope of flesh and blood). The artiste needs an audience that understands what he is trying to do; he needs a certain freedom from distraction and sheer worldly anxieties, he needs an acknowledgement that this pursuit is and honourable one. Concurrently, the man needs a reasonable livelihood, security in his chosen walk of life, hopes of a peaceful and independent retirement in his later years.

The institutions and associations that are to bring the common man and the artiste together both have and are problems. These are the thorny questions of the artiste's proper independence from government and organisational control. Existing associations have their economic problems, and these are too often the means of their passing unduly under the influence of patrons and organisers whose first care is not always the good of the art and the artiste of the good of the ordinary member of the listening public. When this happens, they become the means, in the hands of some expert organisers, to non-aesthetic ends, and the artiste has to learn the further art to securing a 'programme'. On the other hand, small associations of genuine music-lovers can run into difficulties with the travel expenses uncertain and extravagant demands for fees and facilities, and other vagaries of the artistes approach.

II. If this reading of the problems is a fair one, a very great deal needs to be done. What follows is, inevitably, a first sketch rather than a fully thought-out proposal.

Genuine classical music is never going to be altogether easy even to understand and appreciate, let alone perform; yet it is within the capacity of a vast number of plain folk, and once understood, its educative influence will go with a man throughout his life and tend to improve in general all musical forms, even those intended for pure entertainment. For the sake of this cultural and psychological value, then it ought to be given a secure place in our education. Syllabus and curricula designing bodies should be directed to regard it as a subject not for rare specialisation only, but as part of a fundamental education. This must tend to help the common man to appreciate good music and also to provide the artiste with an appreciative but stimulatingly critical audience.

In so far as the grown-up common man is hindered by his economic position, a very wide extension of the idea of State festivals of music seems necessary. An annual State festival is very inadequate. What we need is an arrangement by which at even district and town levels fairly frequent musical performances are made available at very little cost to the audience.

An excellent educative device would be to use film as a medium. The popularity of the cinema can use an actor to expose people constantly to non-classical uses of music; but it can be made to serve education towards a more classical taste by giving its vast audience an exposure to classical music. A comprehensive series of short films embodying good music, guidance towards its appreciation and introductions to famous schools and artistes should be prepared and released for showing as short films at the usual cinema houses as well as in educational cultural centres.

Another worth-while approach would be to publish literature on music graded by age-groups. Raga music would be the basis, and free use should be made of the compositions of our saints, which often lend themselves to dignified and chaste musical treatment.

Given the sort of extension of the educational base of music suggested, it becomes straightforward to prevail, at a later stage for those with special aptitude, courses and perhaps, in at least one place in each state, a university or college of music. Admittance to the latter ought to depend upon talent and merit and nothing else. These are the institutions that could naturally extend to well-equipped departments of research in music, both pure and in its interrelations with scientific concepts and social implications. This should meet the artiste's problem of becoming one. Evidently, artistes of proven distinction must be brought to involve themselves in this effort to preserve and prolong our musical tradition.

Methods used in other departments of education may be fruitful for this purpose too. Regular workshops in music performance and appreciation at schools and colleges and the institution of 'artiste-in-residence' at universities would provide foci of growth.

For the artiste who has definitely become one by avocation, the most important thing is a smooth and flexible system of relations with his audiences. Such an extension of musical performances as suggested earlier will create added opportunities; but care is needed to see that they are offered fairly and impartially. To this end a regularisation of both artistes' status and artistes' fees is important. Such a classification as the AIR has used might be elaborated and carried out for all practising artistes. This would in turn help organisers of musical performances and official cultural agencies in their planning.

Not only by these means but also by specific provision by the government, the artiste should be assured of minimum financial security. This must take into account the fact that an artiste's effective professional career is shorter than in many other occupations.

Another important source of financial support for the artistes will be the encouragement of records and pre-recorded tapes as objects of educational and cultural value. At present these are not commented upon widely in mass media as books and films are and the necessary record-player and tape-recorder are still astronomically beyond the reach of most Indians. Whatever may be the length of time necessary to bring these to support artistes effectively, they are valuable means of the general education in sensibility which we spoke of first.

In all this we have spoken of the committed artiste who lives by his art. There are unfortunately, 'amateur' artistes who have no real commitment to their art, but use it as an avenue to social prominence; and are able to get programmes where a serious artiste can not, in their normal lives, have the sort of connections which enable them to obtain donations and concessions for various musical associations. These must be carefully considered apart from the artiste whose needs are to some extent a social responsibility thus needed to preserve our cultural tradition.

Much of what has been suggested for the sake of the common man and the artiste must also benefit the musical organisations. A wider list of serious artistes to choose from an established set of categories and their appropriate fees and honorariums; and a greater range of recorded material will all obviously enrich and facilitate their work.

One definite suggestion is that a machinery should be provided by which associations can consult one another and co-operate in arranging the tours of artistes they are inviting; for the travelling expenses of artistes are a major part of their expenditure. If they get together and pre-arrange the route conveniently, this can be lightened a good deal.

The artiste apart from his education and his career need a certain freedom from pressure. This is a psychological need of the creative mind and even for artistes with moderate incomes this can be provided from time to time in special places maintained in quiet small towns.

Apart from economic support to the artiste, a considerable programme of recording good performances is necessary simply because much that is valuable may not be lost beyond recall. This has already happened at various occassions.

Incidentally, a great work of 'national integration' can be done by the government arranging for exchanges of classical musicians and music across regional borders. These exchanges should not be confined to performances but should include lectures and seminars conducted by competent students of the subject. These should be as far as possible in the local languages. These should be chiefly for the benefit of the rural and small-town areas that do not get the opportunity, very frequently, of hearing our own artistes.

Another marginal comment, but one of great potential importance, is that we have done almost nothing in special for music for children. May I, altogether, suggest that while we are aware of our rich musical tradition and have a feeling for it, what we actually do for music and the musician is both inadequate and un-coordinated. The government will naturally have much to do if these suggestions are to be given any effect; but all of us, artistes and members of the Indian social community, have our contribution to make.

Suggestions from Mr B.D. Garga

We love myths. One such myth relates to India's being the largest film industry in the world. Production aside, logically it should follow that cinema in India reaches the largest number of people. It doesn't. In fact, compared to its population—well over 660 million—the number of 35 million people viewing film weekly—is abysmally low. Worse is, that it is the same set of people, mostly urbanites, who view films over and over again. In terms of the spread of cinema habit/culture, the situation has remained moribund. And, our half a million or more villages/small towns have remained blissfully ignorant of the 'marvel of the country'. Sad, but it is also an exciting prospect for the communicator.

So, on one hand cinema—mobile, temporary, 35 mm, 16 mm, Super 8, whatever—must reach rural areas to entertain, educate and inform. On the other, we must create conditions whereby film making is made cheaper and easier as against the present trend of bigger and costlier production. (Bernard Shaw said that it is almost exciomatic that the more a film costs, the worse it is). This is one way to invite and nurture exciting new talent and raise the standard of film making in the country. Naturally, this would involve the setting up of 16 mm/Super 8 production/exhibition facilities which we must, sooner the better. We can delay or ignore it only at the cost of our future development—cultural, social and economic.

Last but not the least, for the spread of film culture, the government (and government alone) must provide funds to start serious film journals (at present not even one exists on a regular basis), and grant fellowship, etc., for research and other theoretical work.

Otherwise, the danger is that we will be swamped under gossipy glossy magazines which ill serve both the society and the cinema.

Technology with its cold, blunt and precise reasoning offers a kind of impact on the spirit of man.

Can art help to give a spiritual meaning and recognition to the inner human being seeking fulfilment on a completely different level? What are the pitfalls that await society on its march into future and how can they be avoided? What sort of cultural heritage do we plan to leave behind for the generation to come and how will it affect the world yet to awaken?

How can we create a dream, a hope, a faith both beautiful and meaningful that can be realised by our children? But perhaps most important of all, can we devise a means, a method whereby Art and Science can merge and intermingle in a happy union that may benefit society and awaken it to dreams of deeper and richer fulfilment?

The key themes of this conference are likely to be as follows:-

1. Art as a manifestation of Culture and Society.
2. Traditional, Modern and Contemporary Art in the present and in the context of the future.
3. Art and Education/Art and the child.
4. Art and the impact of Science and technology.
5. Art and Environment.

This Conference it is expected will contribute to the building of a new Universal Society that shall look and plan ahead and will aim at harmony and cooperation between various people and countries. We hope it will create an environment of peace and happiness besides shaping a common hopeful future through a new cultural policy.

INDIAN CHILD AND FUTURE

Satish C. Seth

The International Year of the child has invited attention on the welfare of the children world over. There are 1½ billion children under ten years of age in the world. It is acknowledged worldwide that children have special needs and that they are not being adequately met. It is a pet thought of many and the right one too—that the children are our future and that they are our most precious resource. The declaration of IYC, too specifically asserts that, "the quality of tomorrow's world—perhaps, even its survival will be determined by the well-being, safety and development of children today".

Coming to India and its children, we find that India is indeed a young country. About 44.2 per cent of India's population is below 15 years of age. We have, according to 1971 census, around 230 million children below and up to the age group 14 years, of which 81 per cent, i.e., nearly about 187 million children, live in the rural areas. Nearly 115 million children is below six years of age, of which 34 million are in rural areas. If 40 per cent of our population is living below the poverty line, which means that per person per head per day they have a spending capacity of Re. 1 each; then in this sector of our population there are 92 million children who are the victims of abject poverty. 9.2 million children in India live in slums. 2.8 million in the tribal areas. The average mortality rate of our children is 122 per thousand live births; rural 131 and urban 81. Of these 40 per cent of child deaths, however, are of those below five years of age.

It is apparent that the majority of the Indian children are the deprived children since they get born in homes which are poverty stricken and whose parents live in a totally hostile and vulnerable environment—an environment over which they have practically no control. Secondly, healthwise 60 per cent of our children, up to the age of six, suffer from high incidence of nutritional anaemia and calory-protein-malnutrition. This to some extent may even apply to pregnant and nursing mothers as well who too constitute a sizeable population of the country. (50 per cent of India's total population consists of women between the age group of 15 to 45 years).

The blatant fact we need to recognize is that one of the most handicapped section of the Indian society is that of our children. It is they who do not receive the fulfilment of their basic needs in three most important sectors : nutrition, health and education. Left to themselves and left to the care of their parents, they are totally vulnerable. In fact, the fruits of welfare hardly reach them. The classic example is that of major investments in the field of education. Notwithstanding the massive plan allocations for elementary education, out of every hundred children in Class I, 40 alone complete Class V and 25 reach and complete Class VIII level education. Less than 10 reach Class XI and only 5 go to the University. Curiously enough, the largest amount per head is being spent today on those few who manage to reach the top. The cost of educating one undergraduate student for one year has been assessed the same as for educating 22 children of primary school; while one M.Sc. student costs as much as 89 primary students.

When one looks at the numerous inequalities that confront a child, one finds that the Indian child suffers much more than others, say, by virtue of where he is born (rich or poor); by virtue of the values shared by the household in which he is brought up (9.2 million slums and 2.8 million tribals or 81 per cent rural); by virtue of education that he receives; by virtue of the economic status of the household; by virtue of the language with which he grows (English knowing child still has an edge over others); by virtue of the technological advantages that the environment offers (better hospital, better school, better transportation); by virtue of the media exposure (radio, TV or newspaper; its availability or lack of it; and finally by virtue even amongst fairly well-to-do households, by virtue of the lifestyles persued.

Thus we have, amongst the child population itself, in this country those who are being subjected to numerous inequalities in terms of unequal nutrition, unequal health facilities, unequal education, unequal exposure to knowledge, unequal social, technological and economic opportunities. This inequality is further compounded by other factors that promote social inequality. It is an irony of life that the Indian educational system too, amongst other factors such as income, property, status, etc., has become a potential instrument of spreading and strengthening inequality and organised social alienation.

The Indian child once it survives infant mortality and is enabled to participate in the schooling process which is usually subjected to a mode of socialization and upbringing which is highly negative. Several years ago a UNESCO study of the mother-child relationship in six cultures, pointed out that the most negative mother-child relations existed in India. Additionally, a child or even an adolescent in India has no idea of his or her future. Child's needs, desires, are invariably subjected to the parent's judgment, whims, fancies and decisions. It is they who do the thinking fo their children curbing their spirit of enquiry and initiative.

When such an Indian child of today enters the 21st century, if Indian conditions continue as they are, he will find a very strange world around him. He will notice that the industrialised countries have become post-industrial; that all progressive societies are knowledge-based societies with a vast information network; that people work and have in these countries several different careers in their life time; that society is encouraged to offer creative opportunities where people can innovate, experiment, differ and have the opportunity to diversify a thought, or a product or a system; that State's protection is available from cradle to grave; that technology has taken man into space colonisation giving them a new lease of life; that such societies are change-oriented; that they plan for a long-range perspective and not live from day-to-day or year-to-year; that there is leisure available to people of such societies and they have time to visit museums, gardens, theatres and centres of cultural excellence; and finally, that drudgery, uncertainty and the era of shortage have to a great extent ended for them.

As against some of these attributes of other societies, the Indian child may perhaps witness that even in the year 2000 AD, India is still living from crisis to crisis. There is a continuation of dithering in decision making; that in schools, in offices and in public life, initiative continues to be curbed; competition for survival has accentuated; cities have become over-crowded and have turned into slums, bereft of any mentionable quality of life; that mass-unemployment, mass-ill-health, mass malnutrition and rampant suffering still abounds; and above all, the society is still without a clearcut direction. Perhaps, some of this is true even today. Naturally, therefore, the Indian child if at all he survives death, even today acquires a split personality, and with the passage of time for him or her, it is clear, the identity crisis will deepen further.

If we thus look at the imperatives of future for India and examine the societal features of our country closely, then amongst other factors, the present growth rate of population with current day management of life and its needs, it is a apparent that if radical steps are not taken, the ordeal of managing even the basic needs of a large human system (630 million ± now : 960 million ± in 2000 AD) is going to cripple us totally.

We are 630 million people and it is our rough estimate that, if we continue to add people as we are adding them, because on an average we are adding a child every 1½ to 3 seconds, with this rate of growth we would be having approximately 960 million people by 2000 AD. Now if this fact has some relevance, then I think our starting point commences right here, since our concern is how we can offer a satisfactory living for 960 million people. How does one manage a large human system? Most of us will feel tempted — and perhaps rightly — to suggest that if Numbers be our problem, let us control our exploding population. Yes, we should do that. But there are one or two facts which we have to keep in mind. Firstly, in 1973 we had 104 million couples in the fertility zone. This number has since increased. Secondly, 44.2 per cent of India's population is below 15 years of age today. Thirdly, when one launches a population policy, it takes 25 to 30 years to have fertility equilibrium. It takes 30 to 35 additional years to attain zero population growth. Thus, the impact of our population policy based on coercion or persuasion launched in the seventies, now, will take place only towards the third decade of the next century. So by then we would have almost doubled up our population. This fact has then some serious implications. Take the educational needs of our youngsters. What is the nature of demand profile here? When the Indian Constitution was made for the first time in 1950's, the Constitution makers had offered their vision of preferred future for the children of this country. They have said in the Directive Principle of State Policy in Chapter III of the Constitution, that we should provide free, universal and compulsory education to children between the age group 6-14 years. They did not realize that the children in this age group almost counted to 50 million. Today we have more than 85 million children in this age group. By the turn of the century there will be 145 million children in this age group. From today onwards we must begin to worry about the educational needs of our children of today and tomorrow. We can't wish people away. They will be there. The important thing is to begin to take right decisions for investment for institutional arrangements now to accommodate future. Since it is a formidable problem.

How does one go about educating 145 million children ? In this context we have made a rough estimate that if we follow a conventional teaching method—a text book, a teacher, a class room, then we should start opening a school every tenth minute for 250 pupils for the next twenty years and employ today one per cent of India's population, that is about 6 million primary school teachers. Do we have adequate resources to do this ? If not, what alternatives are available to us ? It is in this way that we have to make right choices. What holds for children's education equally applies in the field of nutrition and health care.

If our quest is for change and total social transformation, we cannot ignore that our society faces the coexistence of value plurality; there are several centuries coexisting in each household, where the lifestyle of different members corresponds to different centuries. Add to this the diversity and uneven growth in different parts of India. We are simultaneously in the agraria, industria and post-industria. In addition we live with unique technological plurality. We are at the same time in the bullock-cart age as well as in the jet age. All this goes to complicate the determination of a right kind of future for our children.

What then, we may ask are the various possibilities ? Three scenarios, perhaps, clearly emerge.

The trend scenario indicates that even in the future, the Indian child will be in the middle of abject poverty, inequalities will persist, though many people would have moved from one economic class to the other.

Two other scenarios, both holding some clue for evolving a national policy, are based on differing policy postures. Firstly, if we opt for a decentralised social order, then, perhaps the management of the child welfare would be the responsibility of the community, which shall redesign life in its own way. For example, it may even usher a society which may altogether banish the schools. In this alternative apparently, the emphasis will be on too much individualism. The difficulty with this alternative is that it can possibly flourish only in a society which does not have a poverty line of the Indian type. The other alternative scenario would promote a centralized system which has perhaps greater relevance to a nation which has to deal with a large human system. It will be a system wherein high emphasis is placed on sharing and community participation and where child's welfare predominantly will be the State's responsibility. This alternative, however, has several value implications.

It is further obvious that all solutions for child welfare do not lie in merely developing different welfare programmes. They also lie in several other sub-systems, which fall outside the realm of the child or the child's world. The preferred future scenario, however, demands that we should usher the Indian child into the future to a society where the child is subjected to or suffers the least of the so many inequalities enumerated earlier. The preferred society of the future should be one which promotes creativity, cultural and social life in a manner, where no child will be denied the opportunity to pursue creative endeavours, and, is enabled to fully realize himself or herself to the maximum. In such a society each child would be a social asset. In such a society child's welfare, health, nutrition, educational and cultural growth and other needs will be met and shared by the parents, the State and India's organized sector.

Amongst many things that the country will do as a follow-up to the International Year of Child, it looks logical that the national policy should accommodate today ("future is today") an action plan, wherein, in a sense:

(1) We should literally nationalize the children who are below the poverty line up to the age group of 14 years and all the children who are handicapped. That is to say, it should be the State's responsibility to extend to them free education, free medical help (health services and nutrition).

(2) For others (i.e. those who do not belong to households, which are below the poverty line and those who are not handicapped--irrespective of the rural-urban setting) the State should subsidise the education, health and nutrition needs. For this category, the resources should be drawn and shared mutually by State, the parents, the industry and others in the organised sector.

(3) In order to promote emotional and national integration, we need to take several imaginative steps. For example, we can decide that our children, no matter where they go to school in any part of the country, shall wear the same uniform, made of the same cloth, for everyone irrespective of the economic status of the parents, or the character of the school (public or municipal). We can use khadi or handloom cloth for this. It will even promote employment. Such a small step, if imaginatively pursued and implemented, may not eliminate physical inequality but will restore a sense of psychological identification and affinity and also promote a sense of pride amongst children giving them a unique feeling of oneness. Several such steps will have to be taken which shall, amongst other things, constitute the bed-rock of the formation of a new citizenary of India.

(4) We should set-up in each district, centres of creativity, sports and social discipline. It should be obligatory for every school child to spend three months in the nearest such centre. In fact, sports and out-of-class field activities like, slum clearance, sanitation drive, afforestation, etc., should be made integral to the educational curricula and such activities should count towards child's assessment and grading.

Indian children cannot remain a neglected sector of our society. Instead they should be deemed as a privileged section of society. If child has to be the pride of our nation, we must take a long-range view of future and commence action today. Any delay will only hurt us badly. To achieve this, there is paramount need for a national dialogue amongst leading members of the political parties to evolve a twenty year long plan for the child welfare. This subject cannot be left to the vagaries of political viscissitudes, whims and fancies. A long-range plan is a must. Child welfare should be a political matter. Each Indian child should be treated and made a social asset and a creative member of the future India.

PART SIX

Corporate Futures

CORPORATE FUTURES: THE BASICS

Satish C. Seth

Is the Indian corporate sector planning for the future, say for the next 20 years (7,000 days plus or minus)? That planning, incidentally, has to be done in terms of (a) the changes in technology in different sectors, be it steel or textile, transportation or communications, etc.

I think it is now well understood by the Indian corporate sector chieftains that "technology" is the "cutting-edge" in a market oriented global economy. FICCI, ASSOCHAM, CII and other apex bodies must, therefore, develop long-range profiles for questions like:

Who possesses what essential metals/minerals and at what rate are they being consumed today? And if certain countries refuse to give these to us (remember the Canadian refusal to give Heavy water for our nuclear plants), what alternative do we have?

Secondly, having a few thousand MBA's is not the answer. We need level managers who are adept at future-scanning and work in organisations which *inter alia* believe in "Anticipatory Management". For this is the managerial culture of successful multinationals. Each day, these managers in every department, be it production, R&D, or marketing, ask the question: What next?

The Indian corporate sector thrives on collaborations. The indigenous R&D base is the weakest in the world notwithstanding the myth of our having the third largest number of science educated graduates and postgraduates in the world. Even the government-aided laboratories are crying that the best educated IIT technologists and scientists simply migrate and no one is interested in experimental science.

Has it occurred to the captains of our industry that they are operating with technologies what other countries used 20 years ago? Thus, the key question arises: Which of our organisations are doing a technology-scan? Which organisation/undertaking in private or the public sector is studying the patents of other countries—as the Japanese for instance do, year in and year out.

The building blocks of the future demand gathering of foresight information and a full time dedicated group to undertake "Technology forecasting". We have none of it either in the governmental or in the private sector.

Let us learn from the Japanese how they document in advance, the "product profile" which they will make by 2000, 2020 or 2050 AD.

Corporate futures are not built on seeking excise or customs concessions; they are built around visions of tomorrow.

Enter the Idea Industry

If one has studied carefully the multinationals managerial stance, one cannot miss observing that there are three pillars which make their industrial enterprise tick towards success. These are the HRD Manager, the R&D Manager and the Strategic Planning Manager. Of course, each one of them operates with a group and on a matrix basis to which the Indian equivalent would be the interdepartmental committee be it the Indian Public or Private Sector.

Let us look at the Indian corporate scene : The Indian HRD Managers in most companies are engaged to attend to recruitment and placement besides attending to quasi-training and quasi-elements of personnel management in the conventional sense. The HRD Manager is not conversant with his multinational counterparts training obligations. There are two kinds of managerial trainings :

(i) Skill development, like training someone, how to ride a bicycle;

(ii) Conceptual in character, coverning how to invent a new bicycle. The multinationals futuristic stance is on the conceptual plane which responds to the major western managerial philosophy and practise : What next?

The second pillar for the multinationals' prowess which Indian companies have yet to grasp fully is that R&D is not waste of money but level of new product development and, therefore, additional profits; and hence better rating on the market stocks. The Indian national record on the R&D front is miserable and pathetic since on the national level, it is not even 1.5 per cent of the aggregate capital investment in the industrial sector. Some companies have an outlay of 3 to 5 per cent investments as in the pharmaceutical sector or in any other, would be an exception in nature and a very recent phenomena due to collaborations and mergers.

The third pillar of incantational success which is ominously missing in the Indian scene is the strategic planning manager. The strategic thinking establishes in the western parlance, a date with the future. Culturally speaking, we Indians love to grovel in the past; whereas 'now and here' is more important, than generating ideas and entering the idea industry for and towards future. In my 30 years of close observations of the Indian industrial scene; firstly, there may be odd companies where there may be personnel designated as a strategic planning manager; in any case, he would have hardly been invited to attend the Board meeting.

Building Corporate Futures is entering the idea industry. If in the emerging Indian regime of globalisation and liberalisation, Indian industrial enterprise whether in the public or the private sector wishes to acquire a competitive edge, it better review the role and significance of the above mentioned three pillars of an undertaking/enterprise which would like to see success irrespective of the annual budget or public policy of 5 Year Plan since futuristic thinking for the corporate sector goes much beyond it.

Future Scan

Every MNC develops a strategic stance of the company's growth for the next 20-25 years. One of the futures studies institutes in California, for instance, is working on a research project to give a 20 years profile on US-Europe trade patterns. It is a 10 million dollars project. This is what future scan is all about.

There is no doubt that 'future' is that aspect of time which is uncertain and complex and not easily knowable. Yet today, a body of knowledge exists which enables us to develop future-oriented scenarios. There are a hundred odd methodologies—including the Delphi, modelling, simulation, cross-impact analysis and technology forecasting—which can, through statistical, mathematical and judgemental trend analysis, system analysis and scenario development and quasi-qualitative foresight wisdom. Foresight know-how is the anchor for the survival of a company because no company or an economic venture is set-up anywhere in the world for weekend pleasure.

Indian corporations have not yet developed a conscious and institutionalised mechanism to introduce an element of environment in the deliberations of a boardroom. In the government, 'perspective planning' is yet to be understood and practised. The private sector pays scant attention to long-term planning. The long run survival of a company demands rigorous future scan, something we can learn from the Japanese management ethos and practice.

The Japanese plan for decades in advance. Japan has entered into trade agreements to cut the grass on African pasture lands; they chemically treat and store the grass as cattle-feed for the future. Likewise, they buy coal over and above their immediate needs from Australia and other countries. They dump the excess into the ocean, which they will retrieve, dry and use as energy source sometimes in the future. The Japanese contract for Orissa's Iron ore is again a long-term one; and atleast a part of the imports Japan now stores for future use. The informations of the Club of Rome, was an attempt by five automobile companies of Europe, led by Mr Aurieio Pecci of Fiat, to understand the future global market for their cars in the event that hydrocarbon sources become prohibitively expensive. This was an institutional attempt at future scan. It is high time the apex bodies of Indian industry installed institutional mechanisms for future scan, to collect foresight knowledge sectorally.

How to make a Million ?

This indeed is the prime goal of those engaged in a business or an industrial enterprise. It is interesting that money comes in many ways. There must be at least a few thousand "Panwallas" (Betal leaf sellers) and "Chatwallas" in India who are millionaires and beyond.

They are shopkeepers par-excellence. They are responding to the conventional consumer need and, in a manner of speaking, to the market forces (of course, their merchandise is not on the stocks yet).

But when it comes to a Corporate player it is a different ball-game. Primarily, here one is in the manufacturing sector and secondly, in the service sector. Your success is judged by the quality of your "product" which enables one to cope with the national and international competition.

Indian Industrial scene is quite a paradox. Many Corporate players, for decades, have refused to grasp the meaning behind the slogan, "Diversify or Perish". There are two variants in every Indian Company : one the die-hard conservatives : they say : 'we are successful because we are conservative'. The second view is that 'the story of our company is that of missed opportunities. Either way "Future" stands discounted. However, those who have worked on their strength and diversified have touched billions. An Indian Tobacco Company going into Hospitality Industry is a case in point. And there are many others.

The key point is that "futuristic sense" exhorts and demands of a new Corporate stance which is bereft of "shopkeeper mentality". Tomorrows Corporate players have to go for tomorrows technology and tomorrows managers.

Dr Seth's Key to Make a Million

* Anticipate and manage: Dream a little. Enter idea industry.
* Motivation to change: (from past to future). You want to live in the past or you want to shape your future.
* Innovation versus imitation: invest some for the long-run.
* Leading new technology has commercial value. Whosoever adopts it first, shall beat the competition.
* Limited risk essential: Business as usual will not carry you very far.
* Information is the new wealth (capital): Like land/factory was in the past. How Good is your MIS System ?
* Old order changeth yielding place to new: Diversify or perish.
* New market opportunities are winners: Identify them. Be a bit adventurous.

* Future scan is an ongoing process: Not one time function, keep an eye on trends and systems and update your data/ information base.
* Organise your visions and dreams constantly since they can be realized.
* Research, development and design are essential corporate activities, it needs short-term financial capability, but leads to larger profits.
* Your success lies with others: Choose others carefully and be vigilant. Your good people can also get stolen.
* Organisations now need an Early Warning System. (EWS).
* Unstoppable benefits come from those technologies that do the most with the least.
* Don't invest in what you don't understand. Go for technology watch and technology forecasting.

Anticipatory Management

Modern developments in industry and the process of government demands a provision of the likely future threats and 'opportunities'. We have to constantly remember that,'technology' is changing and so are the markets. All systems, public or private, thus, in order to gain a strategic advantage should take recourse to understand the, 'future' (say, an assessment of the likely changes of the next twenty years time-span). They should 'anticipate' first in order to 'manage'. A thriving company hereafter would be one that consciously anticipates change in terms of technology material balance and markets. Based on this foresight knowledge, each undertaking should prefer their short-term and long-term 'Corporate goals'.

The managers of India do need to learn how to understand an elusive and unknowable period of time which, 'future' indeed is. The crux of Anticipatory Management, thus, lies in using sophisticated intelligence gathering techniques and in the setting up of the Management Information System (MIS) coupled with and Early Warning System (EWS). If such a combined group of professionals is further trained in Technology Forecasting and Future Scan Techniques, then it is possible to unravel, to a very large extent what the next 15-20 years future holds for a given corporate entity in their respective sectors. The identification of, 'Emerging Issues' is a basic task in this effort.

The current mentality of the Indian Corporate Sector to 'operate-in-safety', bodes ill for tomorrow. It inhibits choices for a diversified future. Better and relevant decisions for future get eliminated. The public and the private sector if they are not wise to the value of Anticipatory Management, they cannot seize the future opportunities.

Not only that, if their internal managerial culture for decision making process is based on precedence (past) rather than consequence (future), then it becomes a non-creative posture.

Managers lose touch with futuristic adventure and excitement instead of becoming innovative; they become adaptive in the R&D and in the search of new designs and new product range.

What is worse is that in our, 'operate-in-safety' managerial culture, unwittingly the industry and the government are turning their executives and undertakings 'tomorrows' into, 'yesterday'.

The Multinationals are constantly guided by the tenets of 'Anticipatory Management'. They try to encourage their managers to expand their horizons and self-confidence through scanning, monitoring and by conducting 'issues vulnerability audit' and scenario development techniques.

Thinking about the future is indeed a ticket for a better corporate tomorrow.

How long the Indian corporate sector with its fatigues and jaded functionaries will remain glued to the past and 'operate-in-safety', that too, while working with 30 to 40 years old technology? How can they make a powerful 'choice'? How can they develop a competitive edge? Or build a better Indian society?

It is high time our corporate sector took to Anticipatory Management and learnt the use of the futuristic analytical techniques; these techniques help determine alternative managerial paths to the future, taking into account the message and signals of future that emanate from the new science, new technology which are shaping the global journey towards the 21st Century milestone which is less than 900 days away.

We need to have an open mind to grasp the significance of external visible and invisible forces.

Anticipatory Management demands total managerial mind-set-overhaul.

Understanding Corporate and environment shifts is the essence of, 'anticipation'.

Change and uncertainty are inevitable; should our management style make it terminal? In anticipatory management, we have tools to know what, strategic stance to take, by whom and when, in order to realise a preferred corporate future.

RELEVANCE OF FUTUROLOGY TO INDUSTRY AND CORPORATE PLANNING

Satish C. Seth

Industries Commitment to the Future

The concern of futurology or future research is with preparedness and with the search of several alternatives to fulfil preferred goals. No industry is set-up for five or six years only; each industry normally exists and plays a vital role in the economy and development of a nation for decades to come. In this sense each industry is systematically committed to the future. Secondly, every corporate plan is simultaneously both a statement of industrial intent and, even if it gives only a short-term, say three to five years, perspective, of the activities that a company or a corporation is going to do, in terms of its product and marketing, it is systematically laying down the preliminary footsteps towards the future.

Thirdly, one of the major elements relevant to the future is the investment policy of the company. Every industrial venture has thus to examine: (a) the range of its products; (b) the nature of the technology or process to be employed and (c) the marketing strategies and management systems to be set-up. All these decisions are vital for the future.

In its unconscious date with the future, one has to realize that all decisions, here are primarily governed by the environment external to the company.

A company in its simplistic interpretation has to know, first of all, the market needs—things the prospective customers will need and buy.

Secondly, it has to look at the available technology: critical resources and the raw materials that are necessary to manufacture the products in question for which, for a long period of five to seven years, at least there should be an assured and uninterrupted supply.

Then it has to develop a management system and constantly readjust and revamp the marketing strategies.

The external environment to the company, however, can shape and influence such decisions favourably as well as adversely. Thus, the 'anticipation' of the factors, that shape of the external environment and which in turn affects the company's present and future, needs to be consciously recognized, analysed and interpreted in terms of their first order or second order consequences. But this important function is usually ignored, by more companies.

A long range perspective may not help influence external factors but surely it can minimise the degree of uncertainty that a company may face.

Anticipatory culture, which is significantly missing in the Indian industrial scope has to reckon *inter alia* with several parameters. For instance, governmental policies and programmes. Secondly, there can be resources and raw materials which it needs for which country is dependent on imports. Thirdly, there may even be technologies which may have a price, they may not be available indigenously; or they may have a prohibitive cost. Fourthly, it may need trained manpower which too may not be available locally. Finally, of course, there are other environmental factors on which industry has marginal influence. In fact, they can be labelled as threats—unseen fluctuations — both internal to a country or external such as, the frequent changes in the Government policy. The Government, for example, may, hereafter, say we are not going to manufacture synthetic fibre but shall only import it; or, it may say that all chemical industries will be allowed to exist only if they guarantee that the effluents thrown by them do not cause any environmental hazard; or it may like to nationalise some industries: or impose a ban on the manufacture of some items based on hydrocarbons.

Likewise, even though a company could hire the engineering and managerial personnel it needs from within the country, yet there can be areas where sophisticated and specialised trained personnel may not be available from within the country. The indigenous educational system may be deficient in providing such sophisticated training.

Also the customers, who too are a part of the external environment, may change their choice; they may seek new products or look for altogether different designs. Or due to inflation or low income levels, may decide to opt out of the purchase of certain commodities.

Finally, there may occur unforeseen events like floods, famines or wars which can completely upset or materially affect the production plans and marketing of a given company or industrial undertaking, in addition to the business fluctuations that internal or international market competition may produce. All these factors have a great relevance to the future of an enterprise and a nation's economic efforts in general.

And we need to have a mechanism where the likely future character and trend in these areas could be anticipated through an early-warning system. This process is Futurology. This is then the essence of preparedness. It is the hallmark of an alert and vibrant management and decision-making process.

Future research, if seriously undertaken, by the apex organisations of industry, such as FICCI, Associated Chambers of Commerce or sectoral societies such as Drug Manufacturers Association and others, on the one hand and Bureau of Public Enterprise or the planning units of each Public sector undertaking on the other can go a long way to keep industries afloat and not come to unexpected grief and shocks on its onward march towards future.

There are two relevant facts which needs to be appreciated here. Firstly, the top companies in India in the private sector are overwhelmingly committed to day to day obligations. The corporate plan hardly goes beyond three to five years—by exception seven years. The Air India, in the public sector, apart from BHEL, HMT and one or two other undertakings alone have a long-range perspective with them not as a matter of policy but under duress. For Air India, its fleet has a life span; after 15-16 years its air-craft needs to be grounded: hence, there is need to look ahead; for international coordination the volume of traffic needs to be extrapolated. BHEL and HMT are in the field of high and sophisticated technology where change is the order of the day; they have, therefore, to be continuously on a look-out for product-diversification. For some private sector companies such as Metal-box, ITC, Dunlop, Goodyear, a great deal of futuristic thinking is still done guided by their principles even in the field of designs, material substitution and market-trends they are with some exceptions, dependent on the information that their overseas principles may care to share with them. Such an information, in fields of sophisticated technology is actually passed on when it is out-of-date and worthless, so that dependency in its numerous aspects may and does continue to persist.

Secondly, the style of the Indian Company's functioning in terms of investment policy or diversification is largely dictated by the Government's five year or one year planning of the Rolling Plan. Then, for many, the annual budget is the first damper on the enterpreneurial spirit not by think in long-range terms. The import-export and licensing policies and their frequent fluctuations are yet another constraint.

But then the *raison d' etre* of business is to operate in the zone of uncertainties. It is the key job of all those working in an industry to employ such tools as shall minimise the degree of uncertainty which is associated with future.

It is not enough to make quick profits and feel complacent that we have a seller's market at home, and flourish when the going is good just because we may have some sway in traditional commodities abroad. For neither of these conditions prevail any longer. Indian buyer is increasingly becoming choosey. And as far as our exports in traditional items go, there is today stiff competition abroad. For instance, even in a traditional item like tea, India is fast loosing ground through the competition now being offered by such hitherto unknown countries, for this item, such as Indonesia and some East-African countries.

All this, amongst other factors, is due to lack of vigilance, non-availability of anticipatory futuristic analysis and information to trade magnets. To this, of course, one can add the contribution made by our feeble and non-aggressive and non-modern marketing technologies. To add to this there are illustrations from other sectors as well.

On the contrary, you see countries like the erstwhile Soviet Union and Japan whose every step was a long-range step. No planning was for less than twenty to twenty-five years in the former USSR. Interesting examples of Japan's concern for long-range arrangements, to safeguard the future, can be glimpsed from its bilateral agreements. Japan today buys coal from Australia over and above its needs. It dumps part of it in the ocean to retrieve it in the future. It has entered into long-range lease of pasture-lands in Central Africa for cattle feed. Its agreement with India for iron ore is too well known to be cited here.

Futuristic thinking is being employed world over in the industrial realm nowadays and is predominantly applicable in the field of marketing and Research and Development (R&D). For example, several American oil companies are spending billions of dollars on Solar-energy research today—all in anticipation to prepare oneself to an alternative energy source being made available in the future.

Both marketing and anticipation of R&D promote innovation and are equally geared to a long-range perspective. In India in an industrial *milieu*, where technology is predominantly an imported item from others, one can thus notice the non-emergence of a techno super-structure and moreso the industry—as glimpsed through its Board-room decisions—is not providing for that widest knowledge and information base which the complex and every changing technological network of future demands of it.

In fact, most successful corporations world over have realised that marketing and technology are the two sides of the success coin. Also, that the cost of innovation can be reduced because the time-scale of innovation can be telescoped; this in turn can reduce the invoiced price to the customer since the cost of the innovation has been lessened. Clearly, to install a futuristic and anticipatory input in a company both the 'marketing' and the 'technology' functions have to work together in full liaison and coordination—with a clearcut understanding where one's professionalism ends and where the professionalism of the other begins. The source of idea is not important. Its business and customer worthiness is. In this sense, futurology in search of new ideas. It is the new ideas which ultimately contribute to profits.

In the World Futurology Conferences one often meets executives from top multinational companies who have no specific function. They are the "idea-men". Their job is to provide their company with ideas—both in marketing and choice of technology. These are the genuine practitioners of futurology in industry.

The use of the techniques of technological forecasting are thus a must in any industry. They offer an important input in the corporate long-range planning, which is fundamental to the continuation and the success of any company.

Any effective cooperation between the technologies and the marketier, presupposes that such functionaries do understand implications of future and are trained in the field of anticipatory function in a management set-up which is geared to manage the known and the unknown industrial horizon. In Czechoslovakia, no industrial executive will get professional grading if he has not been exposed to the tool and techniques of technology forecasting. In Poland, all organizations, be they work related to in veterinary science, plasma physics, coal or electronics must have a twenty year long perspective plan.

Often one is asked what exactly is future? Future, after all consists of two kinds of events, events which we would like to see happen (more markets) and events we would like to see not happen (resource scarcity, non-availability of technology, etc.). Future is something on which, hopefully, we have some power. It is something there at a distance which, if we are precautious enough, perhaps, we could influence. A company, a venture, an undertaking can thus always choose or prefer a certain normative future for itself.

In short, what is needed is the training of our decision makers to learn such techniques that shall help them to know what the future holds in store for them; and what the effects of their decisions will be; in order that they might today evaluate the alternative courses of action open to them.

What one is advocating here is that this 'estimate-of-the-unknown' need not be made on a hunch or on a rule of thumb basis. It can be scientific activity.

Anticipatory know-how could be deliberately arrived at and specifically stated based on information, data, foresight and the use of forecasting techniques such as extrapolative approaches, the Delphi system, the morphological analysis, the statistical calculations and the generation of alternative technological routes arrived through scenario building exercise and tested through technological mission analysis.

Generation of futuristic knowledge in terms of market profiles, commodity profile, the resource profile, the technology profile, their availability or non-availability, is a function which has close links with international trade and industrial information network. Secondly, the pre-knowledge of the life span of a resource, its availability upto and date, or its non-availability after a given year internally, or the possibility of its availability from other countries, these are the prime considerations that go to influence and shape a country's foreign policy.

And all this should be one of the prime functions of industries apex organisations and their planning units. It is high time, one should hope, that in the private and the public sector we shall soon set-up highly skilled anticipatory groups, which shall interpret the futuristic trends relevant to an industrial enterprise's future, and provide valuable input to company's marketing and research and development units on the one hand and even many more futuristic scenarios to their respective board rooms. Such expertise should be set-up with immediate effect as, worldwide things are changing so fast that one does feel that time is against us. If, however, industry could give to itself a sound futuristic foundation one can confidently say, that more qualitative current day decisions will get taken and our corporate plans will be those that shall make passage, and adjustment to future challenges and opportunities less painful and more fulfilling.

One of the hallmarks of traditional corporate planning methods is that it continues to reinforce culture which makes an organisation less interested and much less to anticipate and respond to the changing environment. Important issues that may affect a company in the coming decade or two, do not seem to carry much weight, or even have a place in the board room discussions of the average successful company.

The emerging interdisciplinary science of futurology or futures research and systems analysis has some unique qualities. These not only help managements to identify and understand the issues that are likely to assume importance in the near and distant future, but can also help managements to implement responses to these issues as they arise. Anticipation of change and a management ability to adjust to changing circumstances ahead of the future competition, strengthens management and adds to corporate profitability.

In addition, futures research helps minimise future organisational risk or to use Alvin Toffler's memorable phrase, "future shock". Therefore, to say that each company needs to develop an early warning system is to state the obvious. Yet very few Indian corporate managements have devised such an early warning system whereas many top multinationals have developed not only successful information management systems, but they have also established monitoring and forecasting systems which enable their managements to frame a company's expansion and diversification plans.

Scanning Process

These monitoring and forecasting systems make it possible for corporate managers to detect, identify and incorporate change within divisions that are likely to be the growth areas of the future. By a process known as scanning, managers can consciously identify an immediate or future threat or an opportunity that may confront a corporate organisation.

Thus, monitoring focuses on the known, whereas the scanning anticipates the unknown. Monitoring involves study of the historical data, experience and enables managers to identify a pattern of growth or a trend, whereas scanning is based on the premise that important macronomic or environmental change does not take place without warning, just as a new industrial policy is not hammered out overnight. All new regulations are preceded by weak signals of social, economic, technological and political change and the rationale of new laws or policies are discussed in political party forums and in the media prior to being legislated.

An efficient and sensitive management attempts to understand what are the implications of such change for the company, even though many such judgements are bound to be of a subjective nature. In his article "Changing Responses to Change", James B. Smith states that:

> "Futures researchers have developed a class of analytical techniques that simultaneously allow for incorporation of a high degree of uncertainty and subjective judgement, yet

help structure relationships among both 'hard' and 'soft' variables. Each technique facilitates the asking of 'what if' questions; facilitates, that is, sensitivity analysis. And each can provide computer projections over time, of changes in the variables being considered. Among the techniques are—trend impact analysis, cross impact analysis, and cross impact simulation."

Developing Scenarios

Futures forecasting techniques are now commonly used by enlightened corporate managements the world over. Most of the applications of this developing discipline are to solve practical problems. Monsanto, for example, has successfully applied the 'principles of cross impact analysis' to a variety of future oriented problems including new product development and training of professionals to meet anticipated challenges. General Electric has incorporated trend impact analysis in its monitoring and forecasting system; and Pilkington Brothers Ltd., the British glass company, has used cross impact simulation to help it gain a better understanding of a pension fund issue.

Given the increasing importance of futures research and the rapidly changing business environment, top level Indian corporate managers require intensive exposure and training in the field of futures research and technology forecasting so as to monitor and forecast environmental trends, so that they are able—to make explicit assumptions about the future, to identify alternatives, to estimate the possible consequences of future developments and ultimately, to try to shape the organization to be ready to meet the challenges of the future.

Therefore, before the futures research and forecasting methodologies are adopted by indigenous corporate managements, the minimum that they can do is to begin the process with trend analysis and scenario building exercises. For this, the training currently being offered in this field by the Indian Council of Management and Future (ICMF) expertise is hardly being used by the Indian industry both in the private and the public sectors.

Briefly, trend analysis involves identifying events and policies which have long-term implications and have a historical perspective characterised by a line of development. A trend has direction, intensity and magnitude, for example, the continuous rise in the price of crude oil or the discovery of the new oil deposits and their impact on the sub-system. The critical aspect of analysis extends beyond the interpretation of a trend. It should relate more closely to understanding the impact of a given trend upon a company. This kind of analysis can help generate an early warning system whereby marketing strategies and product mix among other things can be recast and management structures changed.

Change Factors

Summing up, the key task of management is to identify the nature of uncertainty towards which a corporate entity moves as it moves into the future. Accurate or pin point forecasting is not the aim of futures research. An alert management is one which can make timely use of all the tools and techniques of futures research whereby it can identify the challenges of the coming decades and in its operations accommodate the long-range perspectives as identified in terms of change factors, be they demographic, educational, economic, organisational, technological or political.

The future holds in its bosom both crises and opportunities. Futures research can help forward looking business organisations to move with a sense of preparedness to shape, influence and even invent for themselves, hopefully, a relevant and profitable future.

TECHNOLOGY FORECASTING METHODOLOGIES

S. Mohan

The technological scene in the present day is evolving due to breakthroughs and advances in technology at a progressively accelerating pace. At the same time, many constraints have appeared, first in fuels and later in many materials. Social constraints on development are beginning to appear. In this environment, efficient planning for the future can be undertaken only if a systematic effort is made to understand the process of technological change, and to anticipate both the desirable and undesirable impacts. The disciplines of technology forecasting and technology assessment have emerged to fulfil this need. They will assist the planners, especially in the developing countries such as India, by providing a better basis for decision-making, to integrate technological advances more firmly into the national development process, and to rationally utilise limited resources by concentrating them on the most effective areas.

Scope of Technology Forecasting and its Role in Planning

Technological forecasting has been variously defined. Certain characteristics of Technological Forecasting (TF) emerge from the definitions:

(a) TF deals with the future of technological parameters, characteristics or achievements.

(b) It aims at predicting the extent and role of change of these parameters at different times in the future.

(c) It assesses the pattern of diffusion of such technologies through society and evaluates their consequence and impacts (The latter function is usually separately developed as TA).

TF, therefore, implies a systematic, quantitative and comprehensive analysis of future technologies. It is useful to the planner at two distinct levels:

(i) It tries to determine what technologies are likely to be available at what times as a result of the current trends in scientific and technical innovations (predictive function).

(ii) It can analyse what technologies are needed to the goals of development in a specific context (normative function).

A well integrated forecasting—planning resource allocation-implementation cycle is needed to overcome the problems of development. To fulfil its role in this cycle, TF/SA should do the following:

(i) Identify the limits beyond which it is not possible to go and establish the feasible rates of progress.

(ii) Describe all alternatives.

(iii) Indicate other possibilities which can be achieved if desired.

(iv) Provide a reference standard for the plan.

(v) Alert the decision-makers as to the possible dangers.

If used effectively, TF should enable underdeveloped countries to better close the lag between them and developed countries by "leap-frogging" over intermediate levels of technology.

Formulation of a Technological Forecast

Technology development does not take place in a vaccum. While technical development has an internal dynamics of its own, its function and growth are also heavily influenced by the social environment and competing technologies. Hence a technological forecast cannot be adequate without reference to the linkages, growth and change of the social forces that support and control the technology. The shifts in social value systems is also important, especially when considering long-term developments. Hence the forecast of a technology cannot be completed without adequate consideration of the technology delivery system.

A technology delivery system (TDS) is a social entity which is specialised to deliver a specific product, whether it be weapon systems or health services. The TDS consists of the institutions and individuals necessary to develop and control the ensemble of technical, legal, economic, political and social processes required for the functioning of the system. Connecting linkages between the components of the TDS are as follows:

1. Inputs to the system, including capital, natural resources, manpower, books information and value systems.
2. Institutional and organisational groups that play roles in the operations of the TDS or the modification and control of its output.
3. System processes by which interactions between the institutions are carried out, including consideration of external constraints.
4. System outcomes including direct and indirect benefits.

It is now possible to identify the components of a technology forecast.

1. Identification of the technology and its emergent level. Emergent level indicates the status of development of the technology. It is generally considered to consist of seven levels (a) Scientific knowledge, (b) laboratory trials, (c) prototype, (d) first operational or commercial use, (e) widespread adoption, (f) emergences of social and economic consequences and (g) future development and constraints (requiring the development of newer capability).
2. Technology description—a detailed analysis of the current status of all constituent components and linkages.
3. Specification of competing, supporting and alternate technologies.
4. Technology projection, including, if possible, projection of major competitors/alternatives.
5. Consideration of constraints.
6. Evaluation of the TDS (In normative cases, specification for formulation of the relevant TDS).
7. Social forecast, including evaluation of impacts and suggestion of alternatives.
8. Policy analysis, including action options for the decision makers.
9. Conclusions and recommendations.

Although the social and technological parameters form an integral component of a TF, it is often customary to consider the social impacts separately in TA. This has certain methodological and analytical convenience. It is also usually at the instance of the sponsors, who are often mainly interested only in finding out about the technical parameters of the problem, and are less interested in funding the social analysis part.

Many kinds of methodologies have been evolved for consideration of the technology projection and social impact analyses. They can generally be grouped under the following categories:

1. *Extrapolatory Methods:* Linear extrapolation, exponential extrapolation, growth curves, envelope curves, trend correlation, substitution techniques.
2. *Intuitive Methods:* Individual or "genius" forecasting, opinion polls, panels brainstorming, Delphi and its variants, scenario construction.
3. *Disaggregation Methods:* Relevance trees, perspective trees, morphological analysis, cross impact matrices.
4. *Models:* Analytical models structural and sensitivity models, dynamic models.
5. *Other Methods:* Technology monitoring, mapping, dimensional analysis.

In what follows, we shall outline the salient features of the major methodologies. However, it should be understood that the methodologies are not mutually exclusive. Rather, they can be used in an interactive and integrative fashion to highlight different aspects of the technology forecast. The genius of the forecaster lies in effectively combining the diverse techniques so as to be able to present the most coherent picture which can lead to implementable processes.

Extrapolatory Techniques

Examination of the historical growth of technology capability, such as, for example, in speed, power cost reduction, etc., reveals a surprisingly orderly development. Continuity of growth seems to be the norm, and discontinuities, the exception. Hence the recognition of the patterns of growth that characterise the behaviour of certain parameters or attributes can serve as a basis for forecasting.

Trend extrapolations assume that the factors which resulted in the growth of the technology in the past, continue into the present and the future. Hence the forecaster must be alert for the occurrence of discontinuities, whether caused by breakthroughs in competing technologies, or as a result of the alterations in the social, economical or political context. Limitations due to resource constraints or reaching natural limits (i.e., reaching 100 per cent efficiency) should be recognised.

Extrapolation techniques seek to represent the level of functional capacity, or performance of technology with time based or historical data. Functional capacity may be represented by a single technical attribute (a parameter) or a combination of such attributes (compound parameter). An appropriate parameter should ideally have the following qualifications:

1. Be capable of quantitative measurement.
2. Represent a measure of the actual functional capability, and account for the effects of possible design trade-offs.
3. Serve to represent functional capability for different technical approaches. For example, for lighting technology, lumens per watt can be used for devices ranging from candles to LED's.
4. Sufficient historical data on the parameter must exist for the trend to be established. This is the most important quality.
5. Be selected consistently with respect to the level of emergence of the technology.

When the appropriate parameter has been selected, and sufficient historical data gathered, the trend is established by plotting the parameter concerned against time on the x-axis. A variety of representations can be used:

(a) *Linear extrapolation:* The parameter is linearly plotted against time, and extrapolations made, e.g., food grains production of India.

(b) *Exponential trend:* When the growth is fast, the logarithm of the parameter is plotted against time. These semilog plots, which are frequently linear, are then extrapolated into the future to make forecasts, for example, decreasing costs of computer unit operations, world population growth, energy usage.

(c) *Regression and Curve Fitting:* Historical data, plotted against time, is fitted to an equation. Fairly large volumes of data are required. Where a linear trend exists, a straight line or first degree polynomial are used. Second degree polynomials are used where the trend is characterised by one bend, and higher polynomials for complex curves. A curve is fitted, if necessary by computer analysis, and the least square regression coefficients calculated. Confidence limits around the regression line can be established, and the line used for forecasting.

(d) *Envelope Curves:* When the parameter grows in a rather discontinuous manner, characterised by pauses or breaks with growth being resumed again, a line joining the peaks or troughs of the trend line can be used for establishing the boundaries for the variation of the performance parameter. This is called an envelope curve. This curve is characteristic of parameters for the performance from a variety of technical approaches that follow each other sequentially, each specific technology being characterized by its own growth pattern. An example could be given of aircraft speeds, as biplanes, propeller driven monoplanes and jet aircraft successively superseded each other.

(e) *Growth Curves:* Similarities between biological growth and growth of technologies has been noticed. Both are characterised by an initial slow phase, followed by a rapid burst of growth, as opportunities or ecological niches are grasped and competitors eliminated, followed by a flattening of growth rates as limitation of resources, saturation or other constraints appear. The equation characteristic of this growth is:

$$F = \frac{L}{1 + A - bt}$$

where, F = functional capability
L = upper limit of growth
A, B = constants

The curve (known as Pearl curve, logistic curve, or S-curve) has a lower bound of L/(1+A) and an upper limit of L. The curve is symmetrical, about its inflection point at L/2.

Many technological parameters, such as efficiency of engines, diffusion of a particular technology within a fixed population (such as colour TV sets in US houses) or substitution of one technology by another (steam ships replacing sailing ships) show such logistic growth rates.

$$F = Le \times p\ (-be^{-kt})$$

The growth in the initial stages is faster than the S-curve.

(f) *Trend Correlation:* In the case of many advanced technologies, the trend of a specific technical parameter may be complex and difficult to predict. In such cases, the trends of a related technology which leads or lags the parameter in question by either a fixed or a variable but systematic manner can be used as a basis for extrapolation. This method is known as trend correlation, e.g., speeds of transport aircraft from speeds of combat aircraft.

(g) *Substitution Techniques:* The substitution of one technology by another can be forecast by an equation:

$$\frac{f}{1-f} = e \times p\ A\ (t - to)$$

where, f = fraction of new technology or extent of substitution

A = constant

to = time when substitution is half complete

If log f/1–f is plotted as a function of time, one gets a straight line, which can be extrapolated into the future. Take over time is defined as the period between f=0.1 and f=0.9. If the time periods for the initial few per cent of substitution are known, the curve can be used to predict the extent of substitution in the future.

The equation has been successfully used for predicting the substitution of a wide variety of technologies, e.g., natural fuels by fossil fuels, natural fibres by synthetic fibres, Open hearth steel making by Bessemer steel, and so on.

Advantages and Disadvantages of Extrapolatory Techniques

Advantages

1. Simple, easy to use, and economical of time and effort.
2. Depends only on past performance, and not on subjective assumptions.
3. Contains the net effect of the interacting influences.

Disadvantages

1. Unreliable for longer term forecasts.
2. Unless based on reliable year-wise data, it can lead to large errors.
3. Does not explicitly identify the interacting parameters and hence cannot respond to changing environments.
4. Unreliable where discontinuities occur.

Intuitive Approaches

These are methods for utilizing the talents of experts. There are many aspects of a technology which are not easily quantifiable, but a constant picture based on the inherent dynamics of the technology and of its interaction with other areas may be present in the mind of experts in the technology, basic sciences or other interacting areas. Participants in the TDS can also have valid opinions about the opportunities, growth and costs of a new technology. The judgment and expertise of these people can be effectively mobilised for technology forecasting.

Individual Forecast

Unless one can get hold of a genius, this method will suffer from:

(i) lack of interdisciplinary perspective
(ii) individual bias.

Opinion Polls/Surveys

If the sample size is large and properly chosen the above errors can be minimized. However, any minority opinion will be drowned out, even if significant. Respondents get no opportunity to reconsider their views.

Although not very popular in TF, opinion polls or surveys are widely used in social forecasting and in impact analysis. There is a matter of finding out people's ideas, perceptions and attitudes about societal change, and surveys provide a valuable approach. The following points should be kept in mind:

1. Selecting a representative sample.
2. Constructing an appropriate questionnaire, keeping it reasonably short, with fairly simple questions. Open ended and ambiguous questions should be avoided.

3. Obtaining accurate answers, avoiding peer pressure and interviewer distortions.
4. Cost and administrative detail.

Panels

In this method, a group of experts interact across a table. Usually a group of experts in convened, given a time limit and a budget, asked to report on a particular issue. Panels are suitable when the subject under consideration requires discussion and analysis. The process is very valuable for identification of important problems, for initial assessments, and for policy analysis and evaluation. Multidisciplinary problems are taken care of by a suitable choice of the panelists.

Panels, however, suffer from the following major disadvantages.

1. Views not in line with majority opinion may get eliminated, due to the pressure to obtain a consensus.
2. The opinions of the most vociferous speakers, or the person with highest bureaucratic status will be given disproportionate representation.
3. In the same way, the views of non-dominant or lesser status persons may not be heard.
4. Many people are afraid of abandoning views expressed publicly even if they are wrong, due to fear of losing face.

Brainstorming

This is a modified panel approach, and one which is very suitable for exploring out-of-the way ideas.

The meetings are held in an uninhibited environment, with imagination being given free rein. The following ground rules are to be observed:

1. The session should be very free and informal. The formal atmosphere of organized symposia are to be avoided. Very frank and unorthodox views, some of which may be close to being absurd, are to be allowed.
2. The objective is suited clearly and only one objective is chosen at each session.

3. No criticism or cross questioning is allowed.
4. Feasibility and constraint are not considered in the initial session. Even ideas which might appear absurd at first-sight are to be considered.
5. Second or higher order implications of ideas are not considered.

When properly conducted, brainstorming sessions may yield a wealth of new ideas, which can be analysed later for feasibility and constraints. Although the great majority will be promptly culled out, worthwhile ideas might emerge. The technique has the great advantage of stimulating imagination and creativity. Brainstorming sessions are, of course, only the initial stage. They should be combined with formal assessment and forecasting methodologies later.

Delphi

Delphi is an intuition/expert opinion based method, especially designed to avoid the drawbacks associated with the other methods outlined above. Originally devised by Dalkey and Helmer in 1963, it has found widespread application in technology forecasting, social forecasting, impact analysis, R & D management and corporate planning. It can generate systematic thought about aspects such as possible technological breakthroughs which are difficult to treat by other means. The major features of Delphi are discussed below:

Delphi is an expert opinion survey with three special characteristics: (i) stentymity among participants, (ii) statistical treatment of responses, (iii) iterative feedback. A structured, formal and detailed questionnaire is given, by mail or in person. The different participants do not meet. The responses of the participants are analysed, combined, averaged and represented in quartiles and medians. Questions for the second round are now made, with modification if necessary (as perceived by the programme director or the participants). The averaged responses to the first questionnaire are provided to the participants. Apart from the original questionnaire, the participants may be asked to respond to scaled objective items, and sometimes to open ended responses. After scrutinizing the answers to the second round, respondents in the upper and lower quartiles may be asked to justify their responses. Further, iterations are continued if necessary, to some point where diminishing returns sent in a convergence of opinion often emerges but this is not forced.

Advantages of Delphi

Delphi can be used to forecast technological or social events and for policy analysis. It has specific advantages over panels and surveys in the following situations:

1. The problems are not amenable to analytical solutions but solutions could be found from a subjective group judgment.
2. Issues are controversial and there are serious disagreements among experts.
3. Issues are of such a nature (or due to organisation structural problems), that individuals are unwilling to take a public stance.
4. More individuals are needed than can effectively interact in a face-to-face meeting, and time and cost constraints make frequent meetings unfeasible.

Delphi also has the following additional advantages :

1. Individuals can express their true opinions, and can retract on stands already taken since anonymity is assured.
2. "Bandwagon" effects and domination by a single individual or groups of individuals is avoided.
3. "Salesmanship" effects are avoided.

Since Delphi can be used in a variety of situations, it will have to be modified according to the objective and the environment. Some ground rules, however, have to be kept in mind:

1. The respondents should be so chosen as to be representative of a wide spectrum of opinions. This is especially important for controversial topics.
2. Since many respondents might drop out after the first round, sufficient number of questionnaires must be disseminated initially so that the final number of participants is at least about twenty.
3. The questionnaire should be simple and straight-

forward. The total number of questions should be about twenty-five. If possible, the questions should be divided into five or six groups, each pertaining to a specific area.

4. Long and complicated questions should be avoided. Conditional statements, ambiguities and parallel and compound questions should be avoided. Such questions should be broken down into simpler, separate questions.

Although widely used, Delphi has been criticized on a number of grounds:

1. There is pressure towards convergence and this may suppress other valid perspectives.
2. The role of the director is crucial and subjective biases may be introduced through this route.
3. Lack of item clarity or common interpretation of scales and feedback may lead to invalid results.
4. It is time consuming and if the questionnaires are long, they may be fulfilled in a casual manner.

Variants of Delphi

In the Delphi, as originally envisaged, no data base was provided. The level of support needed for an event to happen at a given data was not indicated. The occurrence of supporting events, needed for the event in question to occur is not considered explicitly. It is possible to modify Delphi to avoid these defects. One such method is the SEER (Systems for Event Evaluation and Review). This method has the following features :

1. A data base is provided.
2. Only two rounds are undertaken. The composition of the panels is different for the two rounds. The first round panel is more widely based, and the second round panel consists of a small group of experts.
3. Each of the panels is asked to assess any additional events of importance and to indicate their desirability, feasibility, probability and timings of occurrence.
4. The function of the second round is not to produce convergence of results, but to identify interacting and supporting events. It has three main functions :

(a) Re-evaluation, refinement, assessment and extension of the results of the first round.

(b) Determination of possible interactions among the events likely to occur.

(c) Connecting and planning of the forecast events, including delineation of the pathways from the current state of technology to the future goals.

Computers and Delphi

The availability of computers, especially in an interactive and interlinked mode opens a great opportunity for improving the Delphi method. With computer terminals located in widely dispersed geographical locations, individuals can engage in an interactive Delphi by typing in and calling up comments at times and speeds of their own choice. Since all individuals are operating a synchronously, more information keeps track of discussions and comments, and acts as a data-base. Each participant will be able to contribute to the computer store, and will be able to interrogate and interact with the other people's stored materials, according to agreed upon rules, and with protection of privacy or security in information.

At present, Delphi is limited to verbally expressible opinions. With incorporation of the computer, and sophisticated programming, it will be able to utilize any form of information, such as algorithms and heuristic rules, models equations, analytical or synthesized data, and a variety of other devices. The participants will be able to have a "Cooperative modelling" of the problem. Opinions will be traceable to their premises, consequences of modes of action explored and a detailed understanding of reasoning obtained.

Scenario Methods

This method was pioneered by Herman Kahn and his group, first at Rand Corporation and later on at the Hudson Institute. The main purpose of scenario writing is to provide a self-consistent set of future events; generated from a postulated event or set of circumstances. Scenario method can present an integrated picture of the collective impact of a group of forecasts.

The relevance of scenario lies in the fact that it can easily incorporate non-quantitative factors. Political and economic implications of postulated technological changes can be explored in an imaginative manner. A scenario represents a possible future, and an examination of alternative futures could help to identify events that are significant, and help to steer the planning process accordingly.

A scenario, or a set of scenarios is implicit in every forecast. In this sense, all planning is concerned with constructing a desirable scenario, and finding out means of turning it into reality.

Being a very flexible, non-quantitative, judgmental approach, it is not easy to prescribe a set of recipes or tools by which effective scenarios can be generated. Construction of scenarios is an insightful blending of forecasting with imaginative story telling. An information base for a scenario should be generated, based on the best available forecast of the relevant factors. Such forecasts could be derived from other techniques of forecasting such as Delphi, technology monitoring, relevance trees and so on. A "Surprise-free" base line scenario should be first generated, and then the alternatives, based on technology breakthroughs, policy choices, probable future states of society, resource levels, interacting forces and so on. A minimum of three and preferably more scenarios should be generated, so that significant developments can be explored in detail. To be effective, scenarios must focus on significant differences. Explicit consideration of the topic definition, core assumptions and interpretations are very important and should be presented along with the scenarios.

Scenarios can alert users to critical policy issues, suggest areas to monitor and illuminate critical factors and their interactions and sensitize people to potential impacts of a development by means of a vivid portrayal. Although one of the most widely used methods of futures analyses, the scenario approach has often been criticised on the grounds that it is too populistic and simplicistic. Also, often it is difficult for a user to understand the implication of changes in key variables or major assumptions. The multiple nature of events and conditions of a scenario make appraisals difficult.

Disaggregation Methods

This approach breaks a problem down into its constituent components, tries to evaluate what changes can occur in each and reintegrate the changed parameters to yield a coherent picture. There are several methods in this group of approaches with varying degrees of sophistication. A distinction must be made between scanning and tracing techniques. Scanning methods make a direct, single step identification of significant elements. Tracing techniques, on the other hand delineate the structural relationships between the various elements.

Checklist

The simplest approach is a checklist, which is merely a description in detail of significant elements. The elements can be grouped in various categories. Checklist serves as an aid to the forecaster in identifying the elements to be chosen for further analysis, and to consider relative importance.

Matrix Representation

A matrix representation is similar to a checklist, except that two or more dimensions are needed for its representation. The added dimensions provide increased capacity to represent dependence and causal relationships.

Cross Impact Analysis

This is a means of utilizing a matrix representation to analyse interactions between probable future events, or between elements of particular technological events. Elements or events to be analysed for interactions are arrayed in the first row and column of a matrix. Interactions between the elements are represented in the matrix by means of a number which reflects the strength of interaction, probability of occurrence or other parameters of importance. The events, or elements can interact in three major ways:

1. *Mode interaction:* One event may enhance or diminish the likelihood of occurrence of another event, may advance or delay, enable or prevent, necessitate or deviate.

2. *Force interaction:* Influence can be strong or weak.
3. *Time interaction:* Influence might be felt immediately or after a delay.

Equations can be developed for describing the interactions, conditional or marginal probabilities and so on. Some computer assistance is invariably needed. A typical matrix could be 50x50, needing the evaluation of 2500 possible interactions.

Relevance Trees

Relevance trees are used in problems which have distinct hierarchical relationship. Basically, an objective is destructured into smaller sub-objectives and tasks with clearly identifiable goals, with specified techniques. Relevance trees are very effective in normative forecasting.

Objective
Sub-objectives
Tasks
Targets
Approach
Technique

Relevance trees are used to analyse a particular objective, delineating strategies and bottlenecks, which becomes the basis for planning and decision making. The planner works his way down the tree until specific goals can be visualized and approaches and techniques delineated.

At each node of the tree, a quantitative value is assigned to the importance of that branch in terms of its contribution to the hierarchically upper level. This can be done using interaction matrices, decision criteria and subjective probability assignments. Cross support and status and timing factors are also assigned numerical values: The information is made use of in deciding the optimal pathway for the solution of the problem.

Relevance Tree
Cross support — Optimality analysis
Status and timing

Relevance trees have proved to be very effective in R & D planning, project selection, and project evaluation. They have been very widely used in industry, corporate and state level planning, and in impact analysis. Many variants of the relevance trees approach have been developed for specific tasks, such as decision trees, logic trees, impact trees, perspective trees and so on.

In utilizing relevance trees, or in general, any disaggregated approach, there are three fundamental questions which have to be faced :

1. Can large number of complex, interrelated variables be broken down into simple decision factors such that these factors can be expressed numerically?
2. Can such numerical assignments be manipulated so as to arrive at logical conclusions without destroying the validity of these initial number assignments?
3. Can conclusions and extrapolation be made from an analysis of these numbers based on information that was inherent in their assignments?

The success of the relevance tree approach demonstrates that these questions can be answered in the affirmative.

Morphological Analysis

Morphological analysis is a combination of scanning and tracing techniques. Each problem is broken down into components that are structurally independent. For each component, a number of alternative possibilities are considered. The methodology is operated in six steps:

1. The problem to be solved, and functional capability or technology needed is precisely stated.
2. Characteristic parameters for determining the objective are identified.
3. Each characteristic parameter is divided into various cases, states or options.
4. Construct a "morphological box", a multidimensional matrix containing all potential solutions. If there are 5 critical components and 10 variants on each component, there are 5/10 possible solutions.
5. Evaluate all possible solutions contained in the box with respect to the purposes to be achieved. Some of the combinations would be unreasonable (e.g. an air-breathing engine to be operated in a vacuum) and hence would be eliminated.

6. The viable options are joined by pathways and then are further analysed as to the feasibility of the intermediate steps required to achieve the objective.

Morphological analysis could be used, at least in principle, in searching for the totality and the technological picture. Although unwieldy in practice, the method has the great advantage that when properly used, no potential solution goes unidentified. Hence, many solutions, some of them very creative and original, could be found. Morphological analysis thus stimulates the imagination, and is a systematic aid to creativity. It has been widely used in aerospace industry and defence planning.

Functional Level
(Systems)
Morphological
structure

Operational level (Needs) | Technological level (Techniques or products)

Models

When the elements of a technological system interact in a dynamic fashion with the environment and with each other, modelling methodology is used for predicting the time-behaviour of the system. Modelling has been extensively used for a wide variety of tasks in environmental management, economics, planning, resource analysis, technology forecasting, social forecasting, impact analysis and a whole lot of others. To cater to this wide variety of users, a large number of types of models have been developed, such as analytical models, causal models, sensitivity models, simulation models, hierarchical models, econometric models, structural models, system dynamic models and so on.

In a general sense, all forecasting proceeds from some implicitly, or explicitly assumed model. A model is defined as "any systematic interrelationship of elements and components in a system which is intended to parallel in structure, form or function some real world system". However, in the usual sense in which it is utilized, a model also implies a set of structurally interrelated variables which can be fitted into a set of questions and which then are fed into a computer. The variables chosen are those which quantify some aspect of technological growth. The cause-effect relationships are expressed by means of the equation, and the input and system parameters change with the time dimension. When the model is run in the computer, the changes in the output parameter are used for the forecasting. Models are run on an iterative basis. A model is based on some proposed assumptions and tested against historical performance of the system if data is available. If disagreement occurs, sensitivity analysis are performed and model revised till the actual past performance and model performance coincide. The model can then be run forward in time to obtain forecasts.

Modelling techniques give us an extremely powerful means of futures analysis. However, the great promise of this methodology is not without its own drawbacks. The following drawbacks of modelling have been pointed out.

1. The construction of a formal model, complete with software and data base is very time consuming and expensive.
2. The nuances of a complex issue will not be adequately represented in a model.
3. There may be a tendency to quantify factors which are intrinsically difficult to quantify.
4. The greatest danger is that the model may be used as a substitute for critical thought and its output accepted without analysing the factors that led to it, since modelling is a very sophisticated technique.

However, if the limitations of models are clearly understood, they can do very useful service, since they can make explicit the course of evolution of a system, analyse the effect of changing of parameters and core assumptions, and investigated alternate policies and implications in a systematic manner.

Other Methods

Technology Monitoring

Technologies do not burst upon us like a bolt from the blue, they emerge out of basic discoveries which are applied or tried out in modest form. Then through interactions among the economic, technical, ecological, social and political environment, some emerge as winners and are widely adopted. Hence during this process, various signals would be generated in these environments. It should be possible to monitor these signals which are the "heralds" of significant technological change. They would, naturally, be buried under much noise. It would be necessary to do a systematic sifting, through expert judgments. The activities can be grouped under four main heads:

(i) Searching the environment for signals that may be forerunners of significant technological change, through extensive analysis of basic research, patents, markets, political developments, and so on.

(ii) Identifying possible consequences if these signals are judged to be non-spurious and the trends suggest that they would continue.

(iii) Choosing the parameters, policies, events and decisions that should be followed in order to verify the true speed and direction of the technology, and the effects of employing that technology.

(iv) Presenting the data from the foregoing steps in timely and appropriate manner.

The forecaster tries to stay ahead of the game, tries to see the developments and implications sufficiently early. His contribution lies in providing early warning signals. He tries to understand not merely activities, but also attitudes and values. Threshold or determinant points, that would need to be crossed for a development to become significant, are also established.

Although more or less obvious from the way it has been presented, technology monitory is one of the most important of all forecasting activities. It is widely practiced in corporate planning. It is especially important for developing countries in order to make intelligent technological choices for development.

Mapping

Mapping is a means of interrelating technological predictions by means of a coordinate system. A set of forecasts about technological events provides a scatter pattern of events against time. These predictions could be mapped as to coordinate a system, using market information and other environmental factors. This would generate an overview of a whole region of technological interest and social impact. Mapping would make it easier to visualize potential technological alternatives and their consequences rather than a consideration of the item alone.

The first step is to delineate the boundaries of the problem to be analysed. This a divided into hierarchical levels. Exploratory forecasting techniques are used to develop a comprehensive list of anticipations, related to the subcategory under study. These are then used on "triangulation points" uniquely related to a specific category of the map such as engineering developments and the prerequisite scientific discoveries, applications of these in the form of products or services and either precursors or consequences related to other aspects of the environment.

The third step consists of the transfer of this data to the map.

1. Events, the occurrence of which can be anticipated at a particular point in time are represented by circles at the appropriate level.
2. Activities, which consume time and require the commitment of resources are represented by lines.
3. Dependencies between activities and events are represented by dotted lines.

From the map, the following information will emerge :

(i) A surprise-free, time-phased array of viable alternative options relevant to a particular area under consideration.

(ii) The sequence of scientific discoveries and engineering developments prerequisite to each alternative.

(iii) The environmental factors which may influence the choice among alternatives.

(iv) The consequences of each choice in terms of its impact on the rest of the environment.

Concluding Remarks

In the foregoing sections we have given an outline of the major methods of technology forecasting. There is no doubt that TF can be viable tool for policy planning by anticipating future developments. Nevertheless, it is not an infallible recipe, nor a substitute for reasoned judgment and critical analysis. The complexity of the real world will always be greater than can be handled by formal methodologies. It must be realized that there are many ways in which forecasts could go wrong. Over-optimism or pessimism, lack of imagination, failure to anticipate converging developments and supporting events, concentration on single systems or configurations rather than on total system macrovariables, over-reliance on a single technique as opposed to a spectrum of methodologies, preoccupation with the quantifiable, the illusion of over precision, failure to update, including update of the assumptions—these are some of the pitfalls of forecasting. Basic core assumptions, which are not derivable from methodology are the major determinants of forecast accuracy. If these are wrong, methodological sophistication adds little to the accuracy. Technology forecasting should be recognized for what it is, an aid to systematic thought.

REFERENCES

1. A.L. Porter, F.A. Rossini, S.R. Corpenter, A.T. Roper, R.W. Larson and J.S. Tiller "A guidebook for technology assessment and impact analysis", North Holland (1980).
2. P.K. Rohatgi, K. Rohatgi and B. Bowonder, "Technological Forecasting", Tata McGraw Hill(1979)
3. J.R. Bight and M.E.F. Schoeman, "A guide to practical Technological Forecasting", Prentice-Hall (1973).
4. R.V. Arnfield, "Technological forecasting", Edinburgh University Press (1969).
5. J.S. Armstrong, "Longrange forecasting" Wiley Interscience (1978).

INSTALLING ANTICIPATORY MANAGEMENT AND SYSTEMS ANALYSIS UNIT*

Satish C. Seth

The Objective

The objective of this research note is to stress that while formulating public policy, amongst other things, the inputs furnished by the scientific study of future should also be given their due importance. Wherever possible, such long-range perspectives and analysis of various issues and problems, should be incorporated in the current day decision making process and policies.

For this purpose, the ideal objective would be that in India we set-up a full-fledged "National Centre for Futures Studies" which can serve all the Ministries, both of the Central Government as well as those of the State Governments.

Pending the setting up of such a national organization and notwithstanding its creation, it is also extremely important that each ministry should also have its own Inhouse Futures Research Unit which can undertake future oriented scientific research relevant to the vital aims and objects and the corporate goals of the concerned ministry.

It is therefore proposed here, that the Ministry of External Affairs should set-up a future oriented Foreign Policy Anticipatory Analysis Unit: within its existing approximate network.

The functions of this Unit shall be:—

(a) Intelligence scanning,

(b) Imparting of periodic training in anticipatory management, and

(c) Promotion of investigative future oriented research relevant to international affairs.

The Concept and the Implications of Future

The historical data has its due place and relevance. So does the importance of understanding the future. The key message of

* Although here a special emphasis has been given to train the Foreign office managers, laid out are valid both for the public and the private sector undertakings and agencies.

the study of future lies in offering an intellectual challenge to explore the character of "uncertainty" which characterizes future. Our concern here, as against the private future, is with social futures which affect the life of millions of people of our society.

Future consists of two kinds of events: Events we would like to see happen and events we would not like to see happen. Methodological Preference today is not for prediction or forecasting, but for the normative goal setting and preferring events and future.

So far as the national and the global futures go they are vastly determined both by the national action as well as the international policies pursued by different countries. Such policies too, in a way attempt to minimize "uncertainty" so characteristic of future. Thus, international policies too, in a way try to promote and work towards preferred futures through international intercourse, exchange, understanding and amity, simultaneously, averting and solving threats and cries and the occurrence of other unwanted events.

Relevance of futuristic study and its inputs to a nation's foreign policy thus essentially lie in making a continuous and deliberate attempt to look "Beyond one's nose". Additionally, it consciously promotes the study not merely of the past but of numerous known and unknown systems which can help build "a new society". Futurism also exhorts and tries to impart a managerial culture which is anticipatory in nature. Through its nets, we can train our "managers of international relations" not merely to be cautious enough to wait to react to events, but to function and carry their duties, based on an investigative and anticipatory knowledge and information, based on long-range analysis, thus going beyond the concept of "Business as usual".

The study of future simply helps generate several alternatives and several new ideas. In this sense, the study of future, in a way, is also the study of the dynamics of change both national and international. Finally, it also teaches administrators both anticipation and "crisis management. Through it, one learns how nations can try to safeguard their long-range future interests through current day decisions. Afterall how can one miss the fact that many countries, like the erstwhile USSR and Japan built a future by entering, mostly, into long-range pacts and treaties which indeed were a futuristic approach. They realized that future could develop on them both as a crises as well as an opportunity and, therefore, they should be ready for both then and there.

In the Indian context, amongst other things, the message of future is that we must learn how to manage the basic needs of a large human system (1 billion plus all or minus, by the turn of the century) and ensure for all of them a certain quality of life in as little a time as possible, say by 2000 AD. The countdown to the 21st century has begun and each day thus becomes too important for socio-economic development and for improving the international relations.

It should also be noted that the developmental studies, the futures studies and the study of the foreign affairs and internationalism do converge, since they are all directed towards developing a better human society nationally and globally.

Finally, it must be emphasised that "future depends on today". Any decision taken today, any investment made today, any policy posture, adopted today has several long-range implications for the future. Most current day decisions which interpret our policies often become irreversible. Future should, therefore, be carefully studied in order to provide right and relevant inputs today while we are reviewing and redesigning our foreign policy.

Forecasting, Futuristic Modelling, Scenario: Generation and other Anticipatory Techniques

The next question is how do we anticipate future. There are several approaches whereby the national and the global futures can be studied. The societal issues and the international issues, in today's world, influence each other significantly. A continuing exercise in forecasting, Trend analysis, in strategic planning and Systems Analysis does constitute an important management resource to help review and formulate national and international policies.

This necessitates rigorous orientation and training in monitoring, internal and external consulting and communications as well as prognostics use of other analytical tools. This can be achieved only through a formal Inhouse futures research unit: that can be entrusted with the responsibility of constantly training, (batch after batch) our diplomats and other associated functionaries.

Scenario generation using Delphi and other methods based on part intuitive and part quantitative appraisal actively helps to "stretch our mind" to generate new alternatives, options and to make a fine-mapping of long-range possible events. All this goes to serve our national interest in the field of promoting international trade, or technology transfer or for determining steps of a purposive technological and sociocultural cooperation.

The national, the regional and the global modelling is yet another way to understand and influence the international systems and thinking, besides searching new ideas and approach for international reordering. No model developed for the international order is, however, foolproof. They are based on assumptions and quantitative data laced with technical details which can be questioned. Nevertheless, they do help open new vistas for international dialogue. Such future-oriented models do require on our part investigative and anticipatory assessment competence on the one hand and conscious ability for scenario analysis on the other. Several global models presented both by the experts from East and West including UN Models have generated several ideas and have, in some cases, even influenced the foreign policy and thought. Some such models, however, can be tendentious. They ought to be judged carefully.

We have, further, to acknowledge that the international relations are too complex to be encompassed in a computer model. At best a model can attempt to provide a language which may help to describe in comprehensive terms this complexity. It need not, however, be acceptable to one and all. Secondly, we must also accept that future oriented studies which are being carried out by more than 1000 professional organizations including governmental and non-governmental bodies including most UN agencies, are today, subtly, influencing international exchange of ideas and dialogues now being conducted at various international forums: The North-South dialogue being a case in point. We, therefore, need to train our diplomats to understand and interpret and even prepare and simulate Indian views and even offer Indian Global Models.

It is, thus, suggested that in our foreign policy review efforts, we should ensure the full play of an inherent ability to anticipate future and to see through its implications without which our decision making process will be an incomplete exercise. The question that is being posed here is : Can we say that, we do have an adequate set-up, within the existing administrative and organizational network of the External Affairs Ministry's Policy review division, which can help develop, undertake and enhance this additional anticipatory competence and future oriented managerial culture?

Organizational Aspects of Foreign Policy-Anticipatory Analysis Unit

If we do decide to create future orientation, then an In-House Futuristic Unit should have *inter alia*, competence for the following activities:

(a) Intelligence scanning
(b) Training in Anticipatory Management
(c) Promotion of investigative analytical research and interpretation.

Such an administrative structure broadly would undertake activities enumerated below:

(a) Intelligence Scanning
 (i) Installing of Early Warning System
 (ii) Setting up of a Resource and Materials Intelligence Unit
(b) Training in Anticipatory Management

1. To organize seminars and workshops in forecasting anticipatory techniques:

(a) Exclusive for the foreign office personnel and hold
(b) a "joint exercise" of the external affairs officials with the senior officials of other Ministries, such as Defence, Home (Security), Trade and Commerce, Industry, Science and Technology, Education and Culture, etc.
(c) Research Activities: Promotion of Future-oriented research studies to provide:
 (i) Thematic, and
 (ii) Region or issue specific position papers as an input for Foreign Review.

(*Note:* The personnel and financial aspects of developing such a unit have not been spelt out here).

We give here a set of questions, as illustrative and not exhaustive list of some training exercises and questions, answering of which can stimulate our administrators and diplomats to stretch their mind and get a preliminary feel of what is described as Anticipatory Management.

Questionnaire

Q. 1. (A) By the year 2000 AD the population of India would be around one billion people (plus-minus). Has it any implications for the formulation of India's foreign policy?

(B) If not, give your reasons.

(C) If the answer is in the affirmative, identify ten indicators which need to be deeply examined in order to search new elements for India's foreign policy.

Q. 2. In the country to which you are accredited, what new shifts you have noticed during the last one year which have long range implications for India. Examine the following shifts:-

(i) Value shifts

(ii) Educational policy shifts

(iii) International Trade shifts

(iv) Ideological shifts

(A) What kind of people or organizations/movements are behind the above mentioned shifts?

(B) Do you think that the host country is enriching this trend or resisting the same?

(C) If these shifts continue to gain momentum and strength, has it any special significance or implications for: (i) India, (ii) Indians, (iii) Our Foreign Policy.

Q. 3. Do you have the means to analyse the resource picture of the host country? Identify five critical minerals/materials in which the host country is in shortage and five such items that the host country holds in abundance.

(A) With which other country they have the largest trade in these items? (Export or Import).

(B) What is your rough estimate—how long these items will last with these countries at the present rate of consumption (or export wherever applicable).

(C) Where does India stand, *vis-a-vis* these resources and trade trends?

(D) Like oil, do you think any country can turn off the supply of their commodity and resource or use it as a political weapon affecting bilateral or International relations?

Q. 4. What are the new regional markets you see ripe for India?

(A) For exports.

(B) For setting up India owned trans-national ventures.

(C) For developing regional resource pool.

Will the present foreign policy support such a move. (i) Well (ii) Moderately.

State your answer with respect to China, Pakistan and Nepal, if so in which area?

Q. 5. What are the various ways apart from bilateral treaties to defuse hostility within any cluster of neighbouring countries?

(A) Can one generate common assets in the field of high technology manufacturing, so that they become a buffer in lessening tensions and threats?

(B) Identify various modes or various ways in which regional cooperation and resource sharing (other than cultural) can be developed in terms of trade, governmental R&D efforts.

Q. 6. State the present global arms sales picture.

(A) Do you think India should also enter in a big way, in selling arms to some friendly countries?

(B) Will such a step be consistent with our foreign policy?

Q. 7. (A) Relate basic needs of the Indian society with our foreign policy. Develop a global model of international cooperation based on basic-need approach.

(B) Develop a regional model of international cooperation, again, based on basic needs approach.

(C) Compare the key attributes of your model with one developed in 1976 at the Foundation Bariloche Argentina by A. Herrera and others.

(D) What are inherent limitations in the modelling methods (Global) which help little in reinforcing foreign policy of a country?

(E) If you disagree with (D) above then simulate a model and relate it with India's present foreign policy.

Q. 8. What are the various implications of the:

(i) *Japanese Global Model:* "A Vision for Development, by Y. Kaya and Others.

(ii) *The UN World Model (Input-Output)*, by W. Leontil.

(iii) The Globus Model.

Q. 9. What is your understanding of NIEO?

(A) Is it a Western ploy to weaken or strengthen the developing countries? If so, how? If not, why not?

(B) Outline ten or more guidelines to present an Indian point of view for NIEO.

Q. 10. What is Club of Rome? What global models has it offered? What is the message?

(A) Do you think Club of Rome is a front organization for certain western commercial and other interests? If so, what interests?

(B) Do you think that the Club of Rome has inner linkages with the NATO? Identify common personalities.

Q. 11. Is it a fact that NATO through Club of Rome, have taken a posture:

(i) Hostile re com con countries.

(ii) Or, are they bringing the Warsaw Pact and Western Countries to a common viewpoint, adopting what is known as the 'Theory of Convergence'.

Q. 12. Discuss various aspects of the Five levels of global militarism, namely,

(i) The Military-Industrial complexes.

(ii) The Arms race between the Super Powers.

(iii) North-South Arms Transfer.

(iv) Arms Race within the Third World; and

(v) Armed repression within Third World Countries.

(A) Relate your conclusions to India's Foreign Policy.

(B) Judge UNO in the light of your discussions.

Q. 13. Identify Five anticipatory major factors that shall affect: (a) India's present foreign policy, and (b) in which year that change will take place, spell it in two parts.

(A) National Factors.

(B) International Factors.

Q. 14. Do you think that India's foreign policy postures are fully reflect and are fully supportive to :

(i) The Indian Economic and Industrialization Policy.

(ii) Indian S&T Policy.

(iii) Indian Sociocultural Development.

(A) What consultative communication-active network our foreign office has with the:

(i) Indian Private Sector.

(ii) Indian Public Sector.

(B) If in 15 years, India has to triple its share in world economy. What developments ought to be commenced now. Identify a minimum of ten points.

(C) For (B) above : what shifts in India's Foreign Policy are needed.

Q. 15. Do you think a third world war is imminent? If so when?

(A) What will be India's involvement, if any.

(B) Develop two or three alternative scenarios on this subject.

Q. 16. What has been India's role in the UNCTAD deliberations.

(A) Catalogue key issues.

(B) Suggest special measures advantages of India.

(C) What conditions are basic to get measures outlined in (B) acceptable to the International Forum.

Q. 17. What new futuristic developments do you anticipate in the organizational and establishment context in handling India's overseas diplomatic responsibilities.

(A) In this context, discuss:

(i) Personnel

(ii) Information system

(iii) Technological inputs, and the

(iv) Fiscal aspects.

(B) Do you think our missions abroad have an anticipatory managerial culture? Make a detailed comment.

THE HARVA METHOD: A METHOD FOR FUTUROLOGICAL STUDIES WITHIN ORGANIZATIONS

*Olle Edelholm**

The Swedish Educational Association, in cooperation with the Swedish Board of Education, have, during the past few years, been focusing increased attention to the establishment of futurological studies. It is obvious that there is a growing need within organizations today to establish regular routines for studying and evaluating future prospects in order to strengthen their future action capacity. The method described here has been worked out partly to stimulate an active self-interest within the organization to start paying greater attention to futurological studies. It has also been construed as a practical example of how such studies can be organized.

This material has been compiled to give instructional guidelines to those who will be in-charge of administrating and leading such courses where the main goal is to study future and to make assessments that can be useful as basic material in connection with future decision making.

Introduction

Futurological studies are one way of strengthening preparedness and ability to solve future problems. If we can foresee the coming difficulties, or anticipate constructive opportunities, it will be a lot easier for us not only to avoid making mistakes but to be capable of creating further chances of success instead. Studies of future are, therefore, both beneficial and practical, something

---

* The author is General Manager of The Association of Adult Education in Sweden.

(1) There are ten Educational Associations in Sweden, all independent of the State and municipalities. Participating students have a decisive influence on the main lines of the activities. Most of the work is usually done in study circles, i.e. in groups of 5-10 people who study either some particular subject, or an entire subject field.

from which we can profit in the regular routine planning within organizations.

As a rule, most organizations draw up a working budget on an annual basis. Some of them also work out a schedule of activities but even that extends only a year ahead. Such plans are mainly based on the results from the previous year. Thus, the activities are being continued approximately as before. They are only "prolonged" for a year at a time.

We generally agree today that this form of planning is no longer sufficient. We must try to see further ahead into the future. We must try to guess what the future society will look like. What kind of people will the members of that future society be, and what kind of role can the educational associations be expected to play? Such guesswork can, of course, be done in many different ways. We have only worked out one practical method which will be described below.

Studies of future are optimistic in philosophy. We start from the belief that we can influence the course of the future development. We also believe that our ability to use such an influence will increase if we train ourselves to recognize and interpret, at a very early stage even weakly, discernible tendencies in the development. This optimism remains, even though we will have to concede, that it is not possible for us to train ourselves to the point where we could take full command of the steering functions. What we mean with development is a very complicated process, interacting relations between individuals and society, between different types of societies and so on. Many of the steering factors are also beyond the reach of our sphere of influence. Yet, we must not forget that many of these factors are, indeed, within our reach, and that we must do something to find them.

The methodology of futurological studies presents quite a number of problems. We have tried to compile a working model for such studies. We have also had an opportunity to test the model.

Problems Related to Futurological Studies

We have concentrated on the following problems :

(a) How can we detach ourselves from the problems and prerequisites inherent in today's situation?

(b) How far into the future should we try to look? Five, ten or fifteen years, or longer?

(c) How shall we set out to describe the future? What kind of variables in the development are we to describe? Which one of the variables are particularly important?

Naming our method was a much easier matter. A research method should have a name, so we christened ours as the HARVA-Method after the Harva estate outside Stockholm which is used as a centre for course activities. The conference which resulted in this work was held at Harva.

How can We Detach Ourselves from Today's Problems?

It has been repeatedly pointed out at conferences where the future role of the educational societies has been discussed that we are far too locked up with the present. We tend to start from the assumption that society from now on remains practically static. In view of this argument, we in our working group, set out to find a method which would facilitate our dissociating ourselves from today's problems and today's conditions.

We are clearly aware that it is hardly possible to become totally detached from one's everyday environmental reconditioning. We have our experience and it will inevitably influence our assumptions of the future. But we also feel that it is actually necessary to start from our own experience when we try to look into the future. What else could we use as a starting point? However, we have chosen to interpret the notion that "we are far too locked up with the present", not as an argument, but rather as an observation to the effect that all that is problematic today may only be so from a short-term view. From a long-term view, some other issues might be more important. Anything that is difficult from a short-term view must not be allowed to blind us from seeing the long-term view. How can we overcome this pitfall?

We have thus chosen to start our studies from a thinkable course of development in society. The participants of a study group start by discussing what society could look like in the future. They discuss issues like war and peace, the prospects of the economic development, energy resources, rich and poor countries, etc. To ground the discussion we have drawn up three possible pictures of the future which can be generally characterized as a negative picture, a neutral picture and an optimistic picture. With the aid of these three prototype pictures the participants can then develop their own views of the future society.

In our tests the material proved to work well. It seemed to serve its purpose as a starting point for the intended discussions. However, it also became obvious in connection with the tests that the participants tended to formulate a national (Swedish) picture of the future. They clearly leant towards the assumption that the national picture differed from the three prototype pictures of the world presented to them for discussion.

How Should We Describe the Future ?

It is important that we select the "right" variables both when we start describing the society as a whole and the individual educational associations. The only piece of advice we can give is as follows : when it comes to assessing pictures of the future, the participants will themselves be able to determine which variables are important in the context. When the participants are discussing the predictable future situation of, say, one particular educational association, there is no concrete example we could refer to them. On the other hand, we have included in the study material, a catalogue of a number of specific problem fields among which the participants can make their choice.

Time Perspective

For one year ahead, the future development of an educational association can be assessed with quite a great degree of certainty. Even two or three year assessments are still fairly easy going. But when the time perspective is increased to 25 years it is already practically impossible for us to assess to any reliable degree of certainty how the course of development will turn out to be.

The degree of certainty in the predictions, therefore, depends upon the length of the time perspective. We have chosen to place our "future" fifteen years ahead in time. This length of time perspective has proved suitable in connection with our tests. However, each study group can naturally choose the length of time perspective they prefer, or find most suitable in their context.

Diagram of the HARVA method

Picture 1 : The three different prototype pictures of the future presented to the participants as a starting point for their discussion. We hope that these prototypes will help the participants to free themselves from being too locked up with short-term problems.

Picture 2 : The National picture. It describes the Swedish society, the society where the educational association will be working in 1990.

Picture 3 : This is called the prognosis picture. This picture is described taking into account Picture 2 and partially even Picture 1.

Picture 4 : The Optative picture. This picture is formed on the basis of the actual wishes and evaluations of the participants. Only actual experience Picture 6 in the diagram — is taken into account in forming this Picture 4.

Picture 5 : This is called the Synthesis picture. This picture represents the adjusted picture obtained through weighing up the results of the prognosis picture and the Optative picture against each other.

How the methodology model can be used, appears from the following stage by stage instructions. As pointed out later on, the studies can be organized as intensive course of two or more days, or as a regular study circle over a longer period.

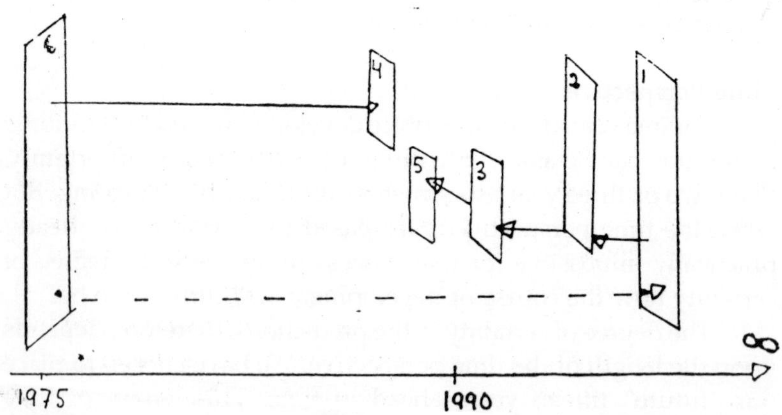

Fig. 1: Diagram of the Harva Method

Stage 1

The participants discuss the three prototype pictures presented to them. They must explain their attitude to each of the descriptions. Whether they are acceptable to them or not. If not, what adjustments would they like to make. From these pictures of the future, the discussion is then led to the subject as to what the Swedish society (2) in particular, will look like. It is important to try to achieve as detailed a picture as possible. This is a very essential part of the studies, since, according to our belief, the structure of the society will, to a very great degree, determine the conditions for future educational association activities. Before going on to the next stage, the participants should prepare a written description of the picture of the Swedish Society in 1990 they choose to start from.

Stage 2

The participants have now decided upon a certain kind of development in the Swedish society and made a written description of it. From this description of society (2) they must now proceed into working out the Prognosis picture (3). This picture is formed to show how the own organization will relate to the new society. At this stage it is important not to lose touch with Pictures 1 and 2.

The task is to remain "faithful" to the presumed course of social development, and on the basis of that, to make conclusions as regards the role of the own organization. It may prove to be trying to stick to this faithfulness, particularly if the Prognosis picture tends to become negative towards the own organization. The Prognosis picture (3) should be described as detailed as possible before the participants go on to the next stage.

Stage 3

The task is to describe the Optative picture (4) of the own organization.

Start from the personal evaluations and wishes (6) the participants have as regards their own organization. How many educational associations will there be ? Have some new ones been established? Have some mergers taken place? What about the municipal adult education? What kind of economic prospects are valid? What subjects are most prominent?, etc.

The Optative Picture should be written out in detail.

Stage 4

The participants should now start forming the so-called Synthesis picture (5). Should the Prognosis picture (3) and the Optative picture (4) coincide at this point, there may be cause to discuss whether such a result can reasonably be assumed to be probable. Very likely, it suggests some faulty conclusions. Most probably these pictures will differ.

The participants should then discuss what the Synthesis picture should look like, i.e. determine how they will weigh up the desirable and the predictably possible to form a new adjusted picture. The Synthesis picture should be that picture of the own organization that the participants find most realistic after weighing up all the different courses of adjustment. This picture should be described in very careful detail. It should provide background information for further discussions on the future of the organisation and be dealt with each time the organization is working out its annual schedule of activities.

The Synthesis picture should be revised yearly. This means that studies of the type described above should be carried on continuously within organizations.

Some Tips to the Course Leaders

Group Work

If there are more than 10 participants, it is advisable to arrange the studies as a group work. It is of advantage to have several groups, as it is probable that the various groups come to different conclusions. Such varying results can form a fruitful basis for continued discussion. None of the groups should have more than 8 participants.

Lectures

The courses can be started with a lecture of the goals, contents and methodology of futurological studies. Suitable lecturers can be requested from organizations or institutions which are doing futurological research work. It might also be advisable to have another lecture by some active futurological research-worker somewhere in the middle of the course. The participants have an opportunity to grasp the problems and will be able to present questions of their own.

Relaxed Atmosphere

Try to create as relaxed an atmosphere as possible. It is important that all points of view will be introduced and judged. Avoid grading in any way the points of view presented by the participants, for example, their being unrealistic, etc. Try to stimulate fantasy as much as possible.

Training of Course and Group Leaders

Those who will be in charge of leading the courses on the basis of this material should be given an opportunity for training in advance. The intensive two day courses mentioned before are perhaps suitable for this purpose. We would also strongly recommend that the programme should include some special incentive to promote good cooperation within the study groups.

We also recommend that, before the courses are started, the leaders will be invited to a conference where the laying out of the course programme and its contents will be dealt with.

The group leaders naturally have a great influence on the final results of the work.

GLOBAL FUTURES: THE EMERGING SCENARIO

Satish C. Seth

One of the most remarkable development of the post-Second World War period has been the increased understanding in the world of the aspirations of different people belonging to different countries and regions.

This has manifested itself not merely through the setting up of the United Nations and its auxiliary agencies but also by increased bilateral and multi-lateral aid, trade agreements of cooperation between different countries in the field of culture, science and technology.

Additionally, in spite of the fact that since 1945 there have been many instances of localized conflicts and wars in different regions of this globe, international efforts continue unabated to keep the international dialogue for increased global amity and cooperation.

The second most significant development has been the transportation and communications revolution which has shrunk the world considerably leading to a special kind of closeness, socio-cultural awareness and even togetherness for economic development amongst the people on this planet.

The third important factor consists of numerous extraordinary feats achieved in the field of science and technology: For instance, the landing of the man on the moon is a significant step, inasmuchas, it has on the one hand, given to the man an opportunity to fulfil a dream which the *Homosapiens* have cherished for centuries and on the other hand it has also shattered many a 'belief' and 'value' which mankind had held irrespective of where they were born and brought up including even their private or public views on matters spiritual and divine.

Fourthly, there is also a negative development, which too arises from the advancements in the field of science and technology, in the form of the vast acquisition of sophisticated arms including highly destructive nuclear capability. It is negative inasmuch as that some of the superpowers now possess destructive potential enough to destroy this world several times over. Of course, we cannot neglect the fact that nuclear power also holds vast potential to serve the ends of social economic development.

Fifthly, to the above S&T achievement one can also add developments in the field of genetic research and engineering on the one hand which unravels the mystery of the genetic code of a cell—the recombinant DNA—and yet if this knowledge is misused through 'cloning' some nations can create problems on this planet causing incalculable harm to the human life.

We, thus, stand on a strange threshold where the future of our globe stands precariously perched atop a crossroad wherefrom commence one path towards total destruction and the second path which can unleash a golden era of prosperity for the entire mankind.

Looking at the emerging scenario, it now looks that what constituted fiction a few years ago is becoming a grim—and at times—even a terrible reality of today and tomorrow. For example, long time back, George Orwell, wrote the famous book, entitled, *"1984"*. In that book, he had conceived of the world as divided into three superpowers and had made approximately 137 prognostications of various kinds. It so happens that many of these bizarre predictions have since come true. Prof. David Goodman has analysed the Orwellian predictions, such as:

> "The government of Oceania monitors Party members by means of remote sensor of human heartbeat. The sensors are located in the two-way telescreens built into every lodging, government office, and public square in Oceania. By turning in on a certain person, government police can detect when he is lying or engaging in subversive activity.
>
> Prof Goodman remarks: I am particularly interested in these sensors because I invented such a device and thus unwittingly helped to make one of Orwell's predictions come true.
>
> I was shocked to realize that "I could be an inadvertent collaborator with Big Brother. I continued reading *1984* and soon resolved to identify the predictions Orwell had made in the book and find out how many had come true. Several

months later, with my colleagues Gary Swift and William Sparks, I counted the predictions that Orwell makes in 1984. We identified 137 specific predictions, which we divided into two categories: (1) scientific and technological predictions, and (2) social and political predictions. We found that about 80 of Orwell's predictions had already (in 1972) been realised. In 1978, I returned to the list of 137 Orwellian predictions that we had compiled six years earlier. This time I found that over 100 of the predictions had come true. There is now no doubt in my mind that *1984* describes a future that is clearly possible."

Future Threats

The concern and study of the global futures have engaged the attention of world's statesmen, scientists, creative thinkers, spiritual leaders and futurists — all of whom after a careful scanning of the emerging trends, have shown their anxiety, amongst others, with respect to the following seven major global dangers that deserve international attention. These are:

(1) Food shortage in several parts of the world;
(2) High cost of energy and depletion of both renewal sources of energy;
(3) Mineral resources (Their exploitation and transfer);
(4) The degradation of environment;
(5) Nuclear war (The probability of nuclear war is one; it is not zero);
(6) Likely accentuation of International Terrorism and the piracy at sea and in the space; and
(7) Increased social fragmentation, youth unrest and value crisis and universally people being subjected to the cultural and the technological shocks.

Scientific Analysis for Searching Likely Global Futures

The efforts of the futurists in developing global models, in order to give to mankind several alternative options for national and international policies and programmes have thrown up many important scenarios captioning world trends which do recognize the above mentioned likely events but also suggest how the citizens of the "Global Village" can realize several positive opportunities and points of fulfilment.

Of the various global models the following seven are worth noticing:—

1. Limits to Growth : LIMITS
2. World Integrated Model : WIM
3. Latin American World Model : BARILOCHE
4. The United Nations Model : UN
5. Future of Global Interdependence Model : FUGI
6. The INFORUM Project : INFORUM
7. Integrated World Model : ILM

Some Model Characteristics can be seen in Annexure 1.

Methodologies

The methodologies used in these global models can be broadly categorized into three types:

(i) Systems Dynamics and dynamic modelling techniques.
(ii) Input-output accounting techniques.
(iii) Optimization techniques.

A major ground of criticism of the global models has been their inadequate reflection of institutional realities, at the world level. There exist no world level "decision and policy making" institutions that can take into account or implement the recommendations of the models. The institutions that do exist e.g., the UN agencies, OECD, EEC, etc., are those whose authority is akin to that of a "staff" function. Even as far as regionalization of the models is concerned, there has been little attempt to disaggregate on the basis of the cartels that exist—except in the consideration of OPEC countries. Further, most of the models assume international trade and aid to be routed through a pool to the exclusion of existence of bilateral relations. In this regard, the bottoms-up approach used by INFORUM seems to be a more comprehensive and useful approach, though more time-consuming and heuristic.

Even at the intra-country level, some of the models are quite unrealistic in terms of institutional realities — particularly unrealistic is Bariloche, with its assumptions of "autarky" and lack of inter-sectorial transactions. Though it is true that any quantitative model, in itself, is generally incapable of handling institutional designs, the global models do not seem to attach much importance to analyse them even qualitatively as constraints that exist when they make their recommendations, nor do they suggest the sort of institutional requirements that would act as catalysts. Wherever an attempt has been made to define them, however, rather broad and vague suggestions like "autarky" (BARILOCHE) "conflict-avoidance" (WIM) "far-reaching internal changes of a social, political, and institutional character" (UNM) are made, and little effort is invested in suggesting the mechanisms of such change. As we mentioned previously, the more quantitative projections with their aura of finality and authenticity, do not absolve modelling (if it has to be useful for development planning purposes) from the responsibility of analysing and suggesting implementational institutional alternatives.

It is clear that each of the models, in varying degrees, have their own limitations and merits but are capable of providing sound methodological grounds for consideration of sectors that have been hitherto treated as being outside the realm of casual modelling. It is also clear that their use as policy laboratories could be indeed great. Their use as educative tools, as supplements to mental models, and as initiators of both academic and public debate on policy issues have been quite high. There is no gainsaying the fact that, as tools of "prescription" at this stage of methodological development these models are constrained by judgements, biases, assumptions and eclecticism, but as tools of "genuine analytical content" their importance is tremendous. They are also evocative of an attitude that attempts to steer modelling, from certain esoteric quantitative preserves, to the model user. It is believed that economists have gained a greater sense of humility towards global modelling efforts, from their own attempt in the field. Also, tools such as computer simulation, and methodologies such as Systems Dynamics have come to stay. All these are tangible contributions made by the global modelling efforts.

We noted that the one major limitation of these efforts has been their lack of consideration of distributional parameters, that are, possibly, the policy parameters that assume greatest importance in the development context.

The North-South Dialogue[1]

Notwithstanding the futurologists global models and scenarios, the political and economic international relations, can also be glimpsed through a scanning of the foreign policies of different countries and the developments taking place at several international forums. These exchanges and efforts are now part of an international folklore or hymn encapsuled in the term, the "North-South Dialogue". The thrust of the North-South dialogue essentially lies in establishing a New International Economic Order. The economic institutions with which the world economy in the West (excluding Soviet Union and centrally planned economics) has run itself commences since 1944 meeting of Bretton Woods which lead to the creation of IMF, World Bank (IBRD) and subsequently with General Agreements for Tariff & Trade (GATT). The World Bank began giving money for projects to the Third World. They did not go into the questions of trade. In 1960, the World Bank was augmented by the International Development Association which was a kind of soft lending monetary "window".

It is only when the UNCTAD was held in 1964, the first North-South dialogue led to the formation of Group of 77 whereby the developing countries sought to promote their economic interests jointly. In the early seventies, the world economy was characterized by inflation, unemployment (less jobs), the balance of payment problems, fluctuating exchange rates, further augmented by the oil crisis arising due to quadrupling the price of crude oil in 1973-74 by OPEC. This was the beginning of crumbling of the Bretton Woods system and the universal need for a New International Economic Order.

It is at this stage that the Western view that the prosperity of North is of benefit to South and it enables the North to be more generous to the South began to shift from Aid to interdependence. The recent effort made by the Brandt Commission to come out with a report is one more step towards remodelling the Global Future. Essentially this report looked at resources and the commodity price stabilization and the reform of existing financial institutions. They emphasized on the principle of global inter-dependence economy and mutuality of interests between nations. In terms of basic thinking, the shift has been what let the prosperity of South help the North. The Brandt Commission refers to two poverty belts - one running from Africa, south of Sahara and the second through Asia and South- East Asia. This report is the result of an independent investigation by a group of international statesmen and leaders, headed by Willy Brandt, into the urgent problems of inequality in the world and the failure of its economic system.

The report takes its title from the belief that major international initiatives are needed if mankind is going to survive. For the hundreds of millions of people who live on the edge of starvation in the developing countries and the South, this is an obvious fact. How can these countries be ensured an economic environment in which they can cope with their own problems? The industrialized countries, the North, have not been willing in the past to go very far towards accepting the South in case the world economy works to the South's disadvantage. The report argues that today, in almost every field of the world's present troubles, a substantial number of the solutions depend on recognizing the mutual interests between North and South.

With striking unanimity, the eighteen members of the commission, coming from five continents, and different points of the political spectrum have agreed on a set of bold recommendations, including a new approach to international finance and development of the monetary system. They propose long-term reforms by the year 2000, priority programs for the 1980s and emergency action to avert an imminent economic crisis. Behind everything they have discussed the traditional questions of peace and war, and the massive expenditures on armaments which take resources away from urgent needs. This is a political report, and it deals with world problems politically, calling on all countries to make an imaginative response. It was also felt that there should be increased emphasis on global negotiations, increased transfer of resources, creation of an energy affiliate of the World Bank. The negotiations, it was felt, should be on the basis of consensus. The recent passing of the UN Resolution for global negotiations, the Concun Conference and now the Indian effort to hold a South-South dialogue in the third week of February 1982 in India. The US has, however, taken the view that UN should not interfere with the specialized agencies like World Bank, the IMF and the GATT. The American stance is one of retreat which does not auger well for NIEO. Some experts, however, opined that today the world economy, particularly, in the Western sector is heading towards conditions of recurrence of the depression of the 30s recession, high unemployment and escalating inflations in a way that there is a danger of these countries have *inter-alia* problems of servicing loans. Their foreign exchange earnings through exports and borrowings almost get spent in paying the interest and other debts services. If, therefore, there is an OPEC withdrawal of its deposits from the Western Banks, a scenario is presented that there may be a possibility of upheaval and exchange rates and failures of many banks leading even to conditions of a global war.

All this, all the more, points out increasingly for the need of North-South cooperation on the basis of national equality and mutual interest. The future rests in how well developing societies can generate surplus, managerial skills and get a rationalized trade and economic relations with the developed world. The need is not of more financial transfer but of local, regional and global mobilization of resources and technology. Sharing both regional and international resource holds the key to global development.

The world is today unquestionably poised at a crucial point in this search of rationality *vis-a-vis* the visible display of prejudice and power.

International rationality will, perhaps, come if the world will unite. In the words of Kenneth E. Boulding, Chairman, The Global Seminar on the Role of Scientific and Engineering Societies in Development, "Science as usually conceived is part of a larger human enterprise of the search for scholarly knowledge, which includes the humanities and the arts. The study of languages, literatures, human history and records, music and the arts, is just as much part of the world scholarly community as is the study of physics, chemistry, and biology. The professional communities which apply scholarly knowledge — engineering, medicine, law, business and government administration, and so on, are also part of this world community. The world scholarly community derives ultimately from the fact that increasingly, at the level of scholarly knowledge, the world is becoming a single system. A thousand years ago it was many isolated systems, even at the level of scholars. The scholars of Mayan civilization knew nothing of the scholarship of the old world; even those of Europe, China, India and Japan knew very little of each other. Today, however, the periodic table of elements is found in every country. There is no such thing as communist chemistry or Catholic chemistry or

Buddhist Chemistry, even though the reward structures for chemists in different societies may differ a little. The differential calculus and set theory know no national boundaries. The teaching of history, literature, and the social sciences will have different emphasis in different places, but a large core is common to all. Even at the level of custom, fashion, culture and the arts, the world is increasingly one. Beethoven and blue jeans, coffee and coca-cola, chowmein and curry, saki yaki and sausages, are found in almost every city of the world. There are political attempts at cultural isolation, perhaps even for good reasons, for we do want to preserve cultural variety, but these seem to be increasingly hard to sustain as everybody seems to want to join the human race.

Local differences will, and should, remain, Monoculture in human life, values, and behaviour is as dangerous as it is in agriculture. There is real danger in the development of a single world system, simply because every complex system has some probability, however small, of moving into unfamiliar and improbable states which can bring about collapse and "system death". The life expectancy of a single organism is much less than that of the ecosystem of which it is a part, expectancy of a single ecosystem is much less than that of the whole evolutionary process. It is adaptability that is the key to long-run survival, not a mere rigid adaptation to existing environments. The adaptable, though perhaps less well adopted mammals, survived the castastrophe of some 65 million years ago which destroyed the well adapted, but less adaptable dinosaur.

This principle, however, reinforces the conclusion that the development of an active world scholarly and scientific community is of vital importance in extending the life expectancy of the human race, and even of the evolutionary process in this part of the universe, for it is precisely that part of human culture which promotes adaptability. Just as the "one world" of land, water, and air supports a vast variety of different organisms and ecosystems, so one world of science and scholarship could support a great variety of human persons and cultures in coexistence. Without this underlying unity of a scholarly and scientific community, however, the political, religious ideological and cultural diversity of the world instead of being an enrichment of human life could savagely destroy it.

ANNEXURE 1
MODEL CHARACTERISTICS - A COMPARISON (ILLUSTRATIVE LISTING)

Model	*Authors*	*Sponsors*	*Methodology*	*No. of Sectors*	*Time Horizon*	*Current Status*
LIMITS	Meadows et al	Club of Rome	Systems Dynamics	4	1900-2100	Completed
WIM	Mesarovic/Pestel	Club of Rome	Econometrics Input-Output	22	1950-2100	Continuing
BARILOCHE	Hererra et al.,	Fundacion Bariloche	Econometrics, Optimisation	5	1960-2050	Completed
UNM	Leonitief et al.,	UN	Input-Output Systems	45	1980-2000	Completed
FUGI	Kaya et al.,	Japanese Govt.	Systems Dynamics Input-Output Optimisation	14	upto 1985	Continuing
INFORUM	Almon et al.,	US Pvt. Industry	Econometrics, Input-Output	200	upto 1985	Continuing
IWM	Kile/Rebehl	Aid Assn. for Lutherans	Systems Dynamics	19	1968-2018	Continuing
BACHUE	Rodgers/Hopkins	ILO	Econometrics, Input-Output	9	upto 2000	Continuing
WORLD BANK	Gupta et al.,	World Bank	Optimisation	—	—	Continuing
SARUM	Roberts et al.,	UK Govt.	Systems Dynamics Input-Output	—	—	Continuing

NOTES AND REFERENCES

1. The North includes two rich industrialized countries south of the Equator, Australia and New Zealand. The south ranges from a booming half industrial nation like Brazil to poor landlocked or island countries such as Chad or the Maldives. A few southern countries - mostly oil exporters have higher per capita incomes than some of the northern countries. But in general terms and although neither is a uniform or permanent grouping, North and South are broadly synonymous with rich and poor, developed and developing. Most of the North-South dialogue has been between the developing countries and the market economy industrialized countries."

   "The nations of the South see themselves as sharing a common predicament. Their solidarity in global negotiations stems from the awareness of being dependent on the North and unequal with it; and a great many of them are bound together by their colonial experience. The North including Eastern Europe has a quarter of the world's population and four fifths of its income the South including China has three billion people-three quarter of the world income in the North, the average person can expect to live for more than seventy years; he or she will rarely be hungry and will be educated at least up to secondary level. In the countries of the South the great majority of people have a life expectancy of closer to fifty years; in the poorest countries one out of every four children dies before the age of five, one fifth or more of all the people in the South suffer from hunger and malnutrition; fifty per cent have no chance to become literate." (From Brandt Report).

ATOMIC AGE AND THE FUTURE OF MAN

Satish C. Seth

In a way the Atomic Age actually commenced when a crude Prototype got tested in the New Mexico desert on July 16th, 1945.

However, it was on the morning of August 6, 1945, a little after 8-15 am, when the actual gruesome moment came, which shook the earth and raised a mushroom cloud over the city of Hiroshima, which "in no time became a mass "funeral pyre".

Whether or not the memory of that destructive event, which took place on the blackest of black Mondays, 40 years ago, haunts any one today is not so important. The gruesome fact that remains is that, today, we have on the planet Earth, the thermo-Nuclear weapons, which possess such destructive potential that a single Thermo-Nuclear Bomb can have an explosive power greater than that of all the explosives used in all wars since the Gun-powder was invented.

The explosive power of the nuclear arsenals of the world is now about five thousand times greater than that of all explosives used in the Second World War. Man's future in a way, is thus linked with this dangerous product produced by man himself.

Whereas the Atom Bombs of the type used in Hiroshima and Nagasaki represented an increase from tons of TNT to the Nuclear Weight of thousands of tons (kilo-tons: Kt), Hydrogen Bombs, developed about a decade later, represented an increase from Kilo-tons to millions of tons (mega-tons: Mt).

In this Atomic Age the planet earth now possesses nuclear weapons whose estimated total capacity is nearly 20,000 Megatons, if not more.

The Atomic Age is thus characterized by a unique feature in which, in order to ensure a secure existence of life on the planet Earth, man has created such powers of mutual destruction which if used can destroy the Earth six time over.

In this context, the first few legitimate questions that we need to ask are:

What does the Atomic Age portend for the future of man?

And whether man can still exert some measure of control over his Future?

And if so, to what end? And, in this context', how do we redefine and achieve for all Wisdom, Creativity and Progress?

What does Atomic Age Portend for Future?: The Nuclear War Scenario

Let us first look at a sceneria for all-out death and destruction, should a Nuclear War ever take place?

The detonation of nuclear weapons gives rise to:

(i) blast wave
(ii) thermal wave
(iii) initial radiation (neutrons and gammarays)
(iv) local radioactive fallout
(v) global radioactive fallout
(vi) electromagnetic pulse
(vii) atmospheric disturbances

These phenomena produce physical or biological efforts or both, almost all of which are directly detrimental to human health.

Whatever be the nature of the Nuclear War Scenario, 'limited' or 'all-out', the rule-of-thumb procedures developed for conventional warfare and civilian disasters would not be applicable in situations where the number of casualties could run into millions.

If such an event ever took place, the hospitals and other care centres would be mostly reduced to rubble; fires would rage; survivors would be panic-stricken or, as in Hiroshima, reduced to a state of stupor and help, if available at all, would be prevented from reaching the people who needed it by the omnipresence of radiation and this would further lead to the collapse of the existing framework of society.

The lack of food, the disruption of health services and damage inflicted on the environment will lead to the destruction of sources of energy and the breakdown of communications and we shall have a paucity of water and high levels of radioactive contamination.

The spread of infection and outburst of diseases, burns and injuries amongst the surviving population will be widespread in nature.

What is true with the short-term effects of a nuclear war, the long range effects, though more difficult to predict, may be equally devastating in character. A WHO report points out that, 'a population which gets exposed to explosion or local fallout, for them, cancer risks would increase by about a fifth in such population.

It further says: "It is a tragic irony that, whereas the warning time and action and reaction in nuclear warfare have shrunk to hours and minutes, the detriment to health it could cause would continue for years, decades and generations".

The report finally adds, "The immediate and the delayed loss of human and animal life would be enormous, and the effect on the fabric of civilization would be either to impede its recovery or make recovery impossible. The plight of survivors would be physically and psychologically appalling. The partial or complete disruption of the health services would deprive survivors of effective help."

This scenario can thus give a peep into man's future, "Should man abandon the path of wisdom".

Man's entry into space age and the star-war scenario

The atomic power and other developments have made men enter the space. In this context, a development, allegedly, presently confined to research and christened as, the Strategic Defence Initiative (SDI) leading to 'Star Wars Scenario' portends even worse kind of future for humanity. In this option for seeking security, the superpowers are now trying to pollute the space. Around the planet Earth the nuclear powered Satellites and Systems have begun to increase. There are already 2000 Military Satellites, many of which are functioning with Nuclear power reactors. To add to this the use of Beam Weapons and a variety of lasers, the man is adding to destructive power. With laser, it is possible to destroy the enemy while sitting anywhere in the world. The CO_2 laser can tear thickest steel as if it were made of paper. The X-Ray laser can send missiles at an enormous speed. This laser can also silently destroy satellites of other countries in the space.

These developments do complicate the future of man on the planet Earth.

Cosmic Perspective of Man's Future

In a perceptive paper entitled," A Cosmic Perspective on Man's Future", Ralph Wendell Burho, using an imaginary story technique, points out how the, "Earthlings are now in the position of the Sorcerer's apprentice". Now scientific procedures provide vast powers for human use. He describes an imaginary assessment of the Planet Earth by visitors from Planet 'X' of the star 'Y' giving their new analysis of the Earth situation. The assessors from planet 'X' point out:

"On earth, *Homo* is the only creature who significantly possesses the cultural level of divine information to structure his behaviour. Nevertheless, we have reports that *Homo* has in the past century been observed to succumb to such disorderly, entropic forces as planet-round (1) suicidal actions in which use is made of recently found atomic-weapon technology, (2) pollution of the ecosystem on which his life depends, (3) cancerous growth of his own population along with-depletion of its ecological support base, (4) Psychosocial disruptions and disorientations consequent to planet-round dissolution of the former cultural institutions that had reasonably well transmitted *Homo's* values, purposes, duties and proper hopes for evolving creatures within the divine cosmic order. Recently, we have observed some of *Homo* take their first trips away from the Earth to its small satellite and we have wondered if they are preparing to escape the holocausts threatening on Earth, and if this may be a contemporary acting-out of one of their earlier myths about an Ark to save them from a great flood.

They further say", what makes matters worse is that, while in our history on Planet X, the arrival of scientific technology was an opportunity for transcending our previous stage of cultural evolution, for *Homo*, lacking a sense of his need to know before the transcendent sovereign reality determining his destiny, the new powers of scientific technology may shortly deem him. He has come to assume that the powers God gave him by grace of his prior evolution are somehow Independent of that history and its present reality. *Homo* has tended to take a more existential view of himself, as given without a long history and destiny utterly dependent upon the realities of an essentially infinite spacetime of the cosmic ecosystem".

"Scientific technology, they say, did not arise on Earth to give *Homo* significant powers until about a century ago. It was at about this time that his religious cultures began to wither from their inability to maintain credibility or beliefs in the reality of the Gods, and thus to shape *Homo's* behaviour in fitting ways to that reality. As a result, the new applications of blossoming scientic myths in new technologies to fulfill man's unsacralized wants have so transformed the Earth that the total ecosystem may become unviable, not only for *Homo*, but for any forms of life that are found there now moreover, it is these new powers of application of scientific knowledge in technology that have sold science to countless groups of Homo who use the technologies with little Capacity to restrain themselves to the proper uses of its magical powers that are ordained by the cosmic ecosystem as it operates in Earth's societies. Thus, earthlings are in the situation of the sorcerer's apprentice, who does not know the proper words to stop the machinery he has set in motion".

The above account succinctly sums up man's predilections 8 dilemma in the Atomic age.

The Emerging Scenarios

If man doe" not take to the suicidal course, we have hope, in as much as that, the Science and Technology developments of our times, in terms of the Bio-technology revolution, the micro electronic and computer revolution, the partial conquest of Ocean and Space and the expending horizons of more knowledge and information and his applied sense do suggest that the Planet Earth has become a global village which can enrich the cultural and the intellectual life of the Homo sapiens. Herman Kahn, a renowned futurist, has given an inkling of what other future possibilities exist for man. (See Appendix A) The truth however, is that the split between the subculture of human values from the subculture of new Science and Technology threaten the future of mankind including the possibilities of total alienation of the precious element of the life on the Earth's eco-system, features which look man several billion years to build and which, 'till this point in Earths history has something of a cosmic significance".

The Question remains, will man in his onward march towards

future be creative enough to resolve his earthly differences and share equitably his resources with fellow homo sapiens. This still persists as an unanswered question and it constitutes a problem to all thinking people to react to innovatively, creatively and with Wisdom. If we fail to find an answer, then whatever else may be a matter of 'speculation' or 'Conjecture', man's 'progress' does stand compromised.

The Global Threat Inventory

In the Global Threat Inventory there are many other problems that Man faces besides the fear of Nuclear Holocaust

If we closely look at the existing world problems that mankind faces, it is apparent that these problems as we move towards the future will "get much worse before they get better" both globally or in the context our own country, India. Some of those threat that need to be taken into account seriously are the following:

(i) The problem of world hunger and malnutrition
(ii) The energy crisis
(iii) The Non-availability of potable water for millions
(iv) The Wide-spread illiteracy
(v) The Mass migration of people from rural areas to cities
(vi) The increase in unemployment both in the developed and in developing world.
(vii) The growing pressure of expanding population
(viii) The Environmental degradation
(ix) The social fragmentation and youth unrest
(x) The increase in terrorism on earth, ocean and in space
(xi) The inflationary trend in economy.

The points mentioned above are self-explanatory.

It is clear that today we live in a world of great contrasts in human condition. 'Affluence' and 'poverty' exist in many countries, side by side. Some of us have the opportunity to realize the full potential of a human being, while a majority of us cannot even touch the 'Basics' of life. What is needed is that we should work to 'create' a world order where every one can realize his full potential. Which approach can do it is still a matter of further interdisciplinary study. All systems need to improve and work for societal re-design. This is the challenge that calls for wisdom and a creative response.

It is the Atomic Age, and several Science and Technology revolutions that are changing our future. Notwithstanding, what is and what is not within man's reach to make a strategic use of technology to bring about a dramatic improvement in human conditions both locally and globally. The way India has conquered the food problem, is a case of judicious use of technology, to serve basic human needs. Such creative and experimentation needs should be multiplied, for human welfare.

In addition, for human welfare, we urgently need both locally and globally, new values and a new social ethic. It involves a sharper and focussed definition of what many have called 'New Humanism and new harmony' of man with nature and his environment at all level.

We also have to ensure an end to all kind of discrimination racial or that of sex leading to oppression of women and ill-treatment meted out to the children. Some of these points of course are easier said than done.

The geo-political forces, the international super-power rivalries and inequitable command of global resources are the disturbing hallmarks, of the Atomic Age.

Everyone today recognizes what are the key issues pertaining to the human welfare. But the human nature has not yet found a viable answer to new global priorities, new global institutions, new levels of global cooperation.

Locally, too inequitable lifestyle, the rural-urban divide and unequal access to economic and financial gains have led to marked increase in social tension, Intergroup rivalries also cause decay in 'morals' and general 'morality'.

How to improve the quality of life of the society handicapped and how to use 'technology' for elimination of 'poverty' and how to develop a 'new and political man internationally' still remains the unresolved problem of our times.

Lester R Brown, President World Watch Institute, discussing "issues of Human Welfare, once observed," Future requires a commitment to society in its totality, and the numbers so committed must expand rapidly in order to reduce the damaging impact of special interest groups.

APPENDIX - A

Reflections through Editorial Comments (1970-1990)

India Towards 21st Century

The entire nation today stands enthused and feels invigorated in every sector, to take such steps, which can fulfil the Prime Minister's exhortation that, each system in the country, should speedily usher itself into the 21st century.

What does this really imply? The first thing that "India towards 21st century" implies is that we should view "future" more seriously than, as a tradition bound society, we normally do so.

After all, majority of us will be living in the 'future'. Majority of us individually, collectively and as a nation will be achieving things in the 'future'.

The question therefore arises, do we know what kind of future we as individuals and as a social collectivity are seeking?

The second thing that the slogan "India towards 21st century" implies is that, if we have an individual or a corporate view of future, then we better begin to prepare for it from today onwards.

Thus, all corporate entities have an obligation to undertake long-range planning.

At the individual level it is a 'call' for becoming an inventive and a creative person.

In terms of managerial culture, it means that we need not constantly be backward looking. We need not wait for events to overtake us, or to hit, while we are unprepared for the future crisis, or future 'opportunity'. In short, all systems should, from today onwards, commit resources based on a long-range view of the future.

The third important implication lies in developing professional groups who know how to 'scan' and 'interpret' future. They have to be trained to pay full time attention to scan the future.

Undoubtedly today, some such activities are being carried out by half a dozen public and private organizations in India. But not all functionaries carry out or use right forecasting methodologies and techniques.

The first basic requirement of looking into the future is to broadbase and reorganize the information and data base in a given organisation, what we now call the Management Information System (MIS).

The second thing is that, each organization should set-up a group consisting of persons who are well versed in interpreting data, carrying out Trend Analysis, who know how to apply statistical methods against a time-frame. This group should also be well conversant with Systems Analysis and Forecasting and Programming. Such a group would constitute an Early Warning System (EWS).

The combination of MIS and EWS then ideally constitute that professional unit which can help an organization to draw perspective plans and to identify, sector by sector, the real building blocks on which each sector can intelligently, conscientiously, and in the context of preferred future, move towards the 21st century.

In the Governmental sector, its planning process provides the only vehicle of change through a five-year plan.

Apparently, when the Prime Minister suggests that all systems should think in futuristic terms and should move speedily towards the 21st century, he in no unmistakable terms, is demanding that the professional world of this century, sector by sector, to set-up:

(a) future scanning groups;
(b) draw long-range perspective plans; and
(c) the Indian educational and training network should have educational courses to train and develop forecasting groups for different organizations.

All this also implies that the current day investments, be they for an Annual Plan or a Five Year Plan, should be made only after sufficient effort towards environmental scanning has been undertaken.

In other words, in the public administrative context, the options for the Seventh Five Year Plan would have to be based on a 'vision' and full awareness of the expectations of a given system for its likely expansion and growth for the next 20 years to encompass the time-frame of the Eighth Five Year Plan, the Ninth Five Year Plan and the Tenth Five Year Plan. The four five year plans for the period 1985-2005 AD, do constitute the major period for "transition". Each plan should become the foundational building block for the succeeding plan to enable the nation to realise a certain preferred future for India.

Secondly, it also implies that considering that our national resources are finite in nature, we need to draw up a material balance statement to examine our national requirement, to develop the infrastructure and to gear all systems to work to fulfil the tomorrows needs of a billion Indians, who will be with us in less than 700 days.

Finally, to conclude, whatever, else may be important for those who swear much too much by past and day-to-day current obligations, no dynamic and alert system can survive without paying attention to future.

A nation/all sectors has to work in a systematic and a planned manner. The time has come that a massive effort should be launched for three things:

Firstly, in our schools and colleges, in our universities, we should introduce formal or non-formal education in technology forecasting, technology assessment, and future related studies.

Secondly, all systems, as in Poland and in many other countries, must draw their Perspective Plan, for the next 20 years. The current choice for physical and fiscal outlays should emerge out of such analysis.

And, finally, systems which have become too rigid and inflexible, must promote a great deal of experimentation and invention to encourage creative efforts at the individual and collective levels within the broad national guidelines.

If this is done, one should sincerely feel, that we should have taken the first few necessary steps in our long march of ushering India towards the 21st century with strength and pride.

India Surges Ahead

We welcome the onset of emergency. It has ushered days of national discipline and has brought new commitments on the part of citizens, workers, administrators and managers all alike. The declaration of the economic reforms is indeed a turning point in the history of India. It has brought the prices of essential commodities down. Constraints on increased production have either disappeared, or are disappearing, what with availability of more power and raw materials and improved industrial relations. There has been a distinct reduction in crime, violence and other anti-social activities. A greater sense of discipline has emerged. Punctuality has become the order of the day everywhere. Efficiency has gone up and the nation is geared to the task of implementing national objectives. People are cheerfully working harder. Life is normal. Thus, India marches ahead towards modernization.

Administration is now geared to put an end to smuggling, to bring tax relief for middle income groups. Laws will soon be announced for the socialization of urban properties. With the abolition of bonded institutional credit to landless labourers and to small farmers and artisans, it is proposed to establish about 50 regional banks in rural areas to serve the rural population.

As part of the total strategy of resisting inflation and reducing prices, the Prime Minister's 20-Point Economic Programme lays stress on increased production. Government has called upon all sections of industry to work tirelessly to increase production further. Labour, management and the Government have made some concerted moves to create a better climate for work, in which there should be little room for lockouts, strikes and go-slows. Meetings have been held between Government and representatives of public and private sector undertakings. Major manufacturers have given the assurance that they would step up production of essential commodities including controlled cloth, tyres for trucks and scooters, essential drugs and other items of mass consumption.

They have agreed to reduce trading margins and packaging costs and to cut down the number of intermediaries to ensure fair and reasonable prices at the retail level, particularly in the interior.

Public sector enterprises have been called upon to improve their performance still further, so as to attain new production targets. Production targets are to be revised. upwards. Recent measures taken by the Government have produced encouraging results. The steel authorities have been directed to provide essential commodities to workers at reasonable prices and to set-up workers welfare committees. Such steps have been taken to ensure workers participation in the production cost effort.

Workers' participation in industry at shop-floor levels was particularly stressed by the Prime Minister Mrs. Indira Gandhi in her 20-point programme. Legislation has been suggested to enforce workers participation in industry in the private sector.

To ensure the welfare of workers, a special deposit scheme has been formulated to benefit more than 10 million workers by providing them non-Government provident fund, superannuation and gratuity funds at 10 per cent rate of interest. This scheme has been decentralized for the benefit of all and accounts can be opened at any nationalised bank in which the authorities have their funds.

We hope that these reforms will be matched with relevant administrative and managerial reforms. Once this is done, India will emerge as a great country. We join millions of others to work with greater dedication to strengthen the hands of the Prime Minister to make the future of this country secure, purposeful and strong.

Managing Rural Development

It is unmistakably clear that the task of rural development cannot be looked upon in isolation from the total exercise of national development. Rural development and urban development are intimately connected, notwithstanding the interest of professional organizations to adopt villages and districts for an integrated development. We have to recognize the importance of numerous management facets of the problem. The key task of rural development lies in diminishing its level of poverty. We have to do things whereby the income level of people increases. We have to, thus, create work for them, and it should be by one of the products which is marketable. Thus, a judicious application of science and technology on the one hand to the rural setting, supplemented by a marketing outlet, would be the bare minimum for any agro-industrial activity. This calls for a great deal of management, apart from being an interdisciplinary exercise, in which there is a participation by scientists, technologists, engineers, economists and other professionals. It may, however, be admitted that the diversity and the vastness of Indian setting does not attract a single omnibus solution. We are still a country where social statistics is not available in its fullness, and therefore any effort to plan for people would be an incomplete exercise. We have to ascertain what people actually need. People's involvement in a developmental process is an inescapable necessity. This calls for a Herculean effort; besides, we need to establish correct interface between the voluntary agencies and the governmental bureaucracy engaged in rural uplift.

Appropriate technology and appropriate management combined with ample people's participation is the key to integrated rural development. The sooner this is realized, the better will it be for all. It is a challenge in identification of social responsibility of science and management.

The International Women's Year

The year 1975 has been earmarked as the International Women's Year all over the world. It is indeed important in so far as most nations will focus attention on the problems faced by women world over. Many countries have indeed produced able women managers, scientists, engineers. There have also been gifted women artists and exceptional women politicians. Nonetheless, women workers have to work in a world which is dominated by men. It is therefore not enough to give women merely a right to vote. Nor would it suffice to bring forth legislation to protect their social interests. A great deal more needs to be done which goes beyond legislation. Much of the benefits that women can get from life in different societies would come from the radical change that can be brought about in the local customs. Still better benefit will accrue if the men around them change their traditional attitudes towards women. Be it as it may, the condition of the working women in India is still far from satisfactory. Sundry job-opportunity or vocational training course would not make women better managers. Equal pay for equal work is important but is not the ultimate to improve the conditions of service of women executives or women workers. In so far as the women labour force is concerned, the less said the better. In most parts of the country, their conditions of work need to be literally overhauled in several ways. A woman as a member of the family, and also simultaneously a member of the working community in the professional sense, usually stands torn between two worlds, apart from being a minority community in the organized sector in any society. The question that needs to be debated is: Should not there be reservation for employment for women to give them enhanced job-representation. Perhaps, this may require basic change in the laws of the land in some countries. So what? Also, is it not important that women should have a right to demand part-time employment with proportionate compensation. No change would make educated women in India happier than the acceptance of their right to seek and get part-time employment. In so far as the working class is concerned, the social security, free medical assistance, institutional care of the children, and a modest roof over their head, among other things, are the basics that the State should provide to them. We only hope that the socio-legal aspects of reforming women's status will alone not be the dominant theme in the International Women's Year. There is an urgent need in India to set-up a Commission which should examine and suggest how the conditions of the working women, whether they are at the managerial level, or at the worker's level, can be ameliorated. This we consider could be *inter alia*, a modest step that can be taken in order to bring about a touch of quality in the life of women, who today serve the society not merely as housewives but also as active agents of development and social change.

Management of and Towards the Future

The concern for future is the concern to build a new society. Management is the key to this developmental task. The shifting scene of managerial practices both in the Government, in the private sector and in the public sector, suggest that we are moving in the right direction. If we look at the 50's and then at the 70's. We can see that the emerging scenario of the year 2000 is one of hope as well as that of ample fulfillment. This is not to say that we do not face any crisis points. Management of India's resources, the management of man and material and the development of science and technological inputs hold the secret to our future prosperity. We are today 608 million people. We may be around 960 million in the year 2000 AD. This vast humanity can be our asset. The capacity to organize ourselves and to manage our affairs well, can guarantee and provide the right strategies for survival and to ensure a certain quality of life.

In building up the scenarios for the year 2000, one cannot escape the temptation to say that Indian managerial force has the necessary vigour, capability, and expertise to prepare for a secure future which guarantees a state of affairs, where the right man is working at the right job, with the right techniques to ensure conditions in the country where food is available for everyone; and our people possess appropriate skills; can get employment as they are and where they are, can generate wealth in its numerous forms; and with the discrete use of known technologies both indigenous and those which characterize a post-industrial society are able to instal right management systems to deliver the goods in time.

When we look at the emerging management profile of India, three things become clear. Firstly, the new managers, the manager of today and tomorrow, would have to be one who is intellectually well-informed, not only in the national context, but is also familiar with the international data in the area in which he specialises, be it in the field of exports, marketing, production or resource planning. Such a knowledge on his part would be needed in addition to his general knowledge and creative ability. At the minimum, he shall have to possess the ability and means to acquire international data and information. Secondly, the responsibility of the Indian management is primarily one of managing "a large human system", be it in the field of education, transportation, health or whatever else one may think of. The Indian need element as it gets accentuated and aggravated by ever increasing population would make tremendous demands on our management capability, accountability and timely delivery of the services in numerous areas. Thirdly, in the context of these emerging responsibilities and the qualitative demands that they put on the management; any management, be it public or private — the paramount need of tomorrow and for that matter even today is that of resource management. No matter how much we advance, there could always be a live crisis, that our resources could fall short of what we need, to provide to the people a bare minimum standard of living not without a certain touch of quality about it. This would then be an additional task, a heightened challenge and indeed the paramount duty of each manager to think of those innovative social systems whereby even with minimum level of resources we may be able to ensure 'maximum happiness to the maximum people'. All this would demand a management system which is less alienated from the Indian social milieu, a management system and a managerial style, where concern for others and the concern to deliver goods should take precedence over traditional norms of procedures, rules and regulations and the formality of the process prescribed for due accountability. This could be the case with every management function, be it prevention of disaster, or be it pre or post-disaster service

The emergence of a mature self-governing, self-sustaining, self-relevant society calls for a new management style. The ability to analyse facts, formulate alternatives, take a decision, implement it to its minutest details, is the essence of modern management which is information based and at the same time is indicative of a creative endeavour.

The paucity of resources, trained personnel and insufficient community participation are three obvious crisis points that characterize futuristic scenarios. We need to take every conceivable step to overcome the same.

Community participation with the management and an Indian version of 'social self-management' in the form of citizen participation with administration, in the form of industrial democracy or in the form of participative decision making process. Whatever be the form in which the community action could be organised, it would, one is compelled to consider, hold the key to new organizational forms and decision making process for the future management system.

Feudalistic structures thus have to yield to a participative management culture. And an intense state of active competition shall prevail, hereafter, not only to get hold of and employ a well-informed manager, but the organization will have to struggle hard to retain his or her services.

In order to produce a good manager—a creative and bold decision maker and executive—we shall have to begin his training earlier than is the case today. We have to make management and educational discipline to which our children have to be exposed from the very beginning of their learning experience, right from the school age. This is a great educational responsibility.

Human resource development is the most important task for a nation as vast and great as India is. Management is an important input in this entire process. Management for 2000 AD clearly indicates the immediate tasks of today which can turn our population into a 'resource'.

The management for and towards future will be one which is less alienated and is non-elitist in character. The need for modern management is not of large organizations alone. The small industry and the small farming operations equally need the advantages that can accrue from sophistication. In fact, they still are a neglected sector. We have tried here to spell out concrete areas in which massive work should commence be it organizational development or the emergence of non-hierarchical, data based innovative and task force oriented administrative action. Mere advancement in technology would not make the society more modern, until and unless the men who handle the new technologies are well trained and are basically result oriented managers. Without a participative management culture which permits freedom for initiative and innovation to all functionaries, big or small, we would not be able to go very far. The management culture needs to be freed from the 'feudalistic'-cum olerical' negativism.

The management of the future clearly indicates the need for the emergence of such a participative culture which is creative and at the same time has that innate strength which turns the seeming catastrophey into a great opportunity of immense fulfilment and generates that unique 'euphoria' which one gets when a job is done well. Indian Management, one fervently hopes, will swiftly move in this direction.

Management for the Needy and the Poor

It is an incredible experience to see the management system that characterizes the work of Mother Teresa and her associates. The sustained devotion and the dramatic touch with which millions of sick and helpless are cared for in the various homes run by Mother Teresa, display something more than the characteristic qualities in modern management. "India's problem is not lack of riches. It is one of ignorance. We are ignorant of ourselves and of others. What is needed is self-knowledge and care for others. It is through love that we can extend ourselves and help others", Mother Teresa points out. Apparently, the key characteristics of her management style are knowledge, love and service. Asked about her management practices, she observes, "We manage from day to day. It is through God that we get the strength to move over from one day's commitment to another. The secret of our management lies not in working for rewards or money. But working for joys and happiness that each dedicated person who works in these various homes receives from their involvement and actions. This is the action of love and of God". She adds, "In touching the dying persons I feel I am touching God himself. It is through him that our strength comes". Mother Teresa is confident that science and technology can help her endeavours a great deal. She points out, "There are some people here who are almost paralysed waist downward but they can use their hands for sometime. Thus, some work has to be found for them so that they can use their hand and fill their time usefully and gainfully." The trouble with most professionals, she points out is "that they have forgotten to get down and lie more on their knees and pray." Here do lie some gems of thought worthy of deep reflection of sustained practice on the part of our workers manager and administrators, particularly those engaged in disseminating "welfare services" to the needy and the poor.

Training Bureaucrats for 21st Century

Who would have even thought that only a year or two ago, even the cabinet secretary of India who is the topmost civil servant, could be compelled to go, at least, for a day, for training. Well, times are changing fast even in the steel-frame of the top echelon of the Indian bureaucracy. The cabinet secretary, a few months ago was at Poona for full five days enjoying an enforced stay of training with several other younger colleagues of his ilk—the Indian Administrative Service.

Prime Minister, Rajiv Gandhi, has indeed enforced the movement of a Four Thousand and odd most privileged bureaucrats, amongst the Indian Civil Servants for being re-exposed to a class-room setting in two parallel programmes of a five days and a month's duration in different Institutions, Universities and other Management training outfits in India.

The first point that we need to closely look at is the difference between (a) the skill generation, and (b) the broadening of the mental horizon of the trainees. These are two entirely different institutional training obligations and training inputs.

The "skill-formation" input of training is akin to teaching people how to ride a `bicycle', whereas, the "broadening of mental horizon" mode of training input is to make trainees reflect how to design, improve or re-invent not only a new `bicycle' but to go into the morphology, sociology and engineering associated with "mobility" as an essential need of mankind. Besides, they need to learn to associate these "reflections" to the current policy related to this "area" in a quest to seek, "ways and means" of realizing "new possibilities". This process helps identify loopholes and the inadequacy of the current policies on the one hand and also helps outline and generate numerous alternatives for the"policy-shifts", if any.

It should be obvious, therefore, that (a) the skill formation mode is a process of transmitting, the body of knowledge accummulated in the past, whereas (b) the broadening of mental horizon, is an exploration into "future", the future possibilities of ways and means of doing this anew. In short, it is an enquiry into several facets of "change". At this stage we shall not enter into a debate as to which is more important "the past" or the "future". The prime questions that arise here would be somewhat as follows:

(1) Whose (which Institute's) job it is to train awareness in "skills".

(2) To what level of officer and in which kind of programme the emphasis should be a "skill". Awareness or on the "Re-awakening, analysis, enquiry and probe into change"?

(3) And, above all, the key question would be: In the present context, when each sector and system is being exhorted to move with a fresh vigour towards the 21st century, what exactly should constitute as the "product-mix" of a given training programme?

If the training programmes, to state a simplified version of a complexity, could be reduced to the:

(i) Awareness and familiarization aspects (how to do it learning process); and the

(ii) Reflective creative process (where one probes deep into a problem as a philosopher and as a designer, like an engineer, or, a technocrat), then one would have no difficulty to see through the trap in which our training institutions are caught. By their very constitution-genetically speaking, they are overloaded with the skill formation function, in order to cater to a rigidly prescribed mandate of that official agency, which funds a given training institution be it railways, income tax, police or telecommunications. The core-staff of these Institutions are the repository of the skills; and they do a good job to run through their equally rigid syllabi, within a time-frame, acquainting their clients with the "Process"—(the rules, regulations and prescribed governmental procedures); the functional training—a grand exercise of imparting", How-to-do-or-not-to-do "Knowledge", which is the essence of the skill Awareness training.

In such a training programme, questions of "change" do not, and cannot possibly figure.

In order, to keep up with the geneses and to display an Institute's own awareness to the new developments in the theories of Management education and practices, these Institutes, do bring in outside speakers to give an odd lecture, on organisational development (OD), Behavioural inputs, Sensitivity Training, Transactional Analysis, etc. All these lectures constitute, firstly mere, added "awareness", contributing little to the second component of "training" where one can expect to train people to open up trainee's mind and inspire the trainees to learn to "look beyond their nose", to reflect to search creative and innovative ideas concerning himself, his colleagues, the process and purposes of his organisation and its work.

Secondly, the exposure to non-prescriptive syllabus—through lectures, whether from an insider or an outside speaker—contributes very little to the skill armoury of the trainees, since none of these new ideas, are understood well enough by the trainees to be able to take them back for use on their desks, or in their work situation. The Training Institutes hardly feel sorry for that; they have a well specified job, a time frame and a limited budget. The question of deviation does not necessarily arise. These institutes are trainers of the "known". They are not concerned with reflections about the "unknown", "change", "innovation", or "creativity"—all these elements being integral to the realm of "unknown", the "tomorrow", in fact, the future the so called 21 century.

Since these later concerns are not a part of the "mandate" or "syllabus" of the official training institutes, one need not blame them for ignoring it. The question that needs to be posed to Training-Policy Makers who should be squarely asked: should it be so?

Yet another question, at least theoretically, can arise. If "probe into the future" is not the prime job of an established training institute, then where should bureaucrats be sent to probe and explore the nature and characteristics of the "unknown". Do we then need a new academy for training which dabbles in disseminating the knowledge of the "unknown" (Future)? Can the setting up of such a body be justified? Or do we "futurize" the existing institutions?

One need not emphasise this point that it is only such nations, who had cared and dared to know and do the unknown, have added to the body of knowledge now available in the field of creativity, forecasting and human resource development and in achieving some of the current and future marvels in Science and Technology. Their endless quest (a) to know the unknown and (b) to constantly ask: What next? Is now further adding knowledge of the planet earth beyond the Oceanic regime and in the steadily increasing conquest of the space. After all these are Management victories too.

One need not, therefore, wonder if, Non-Conformism, and going beyond the given boundary—conditions, ought to be pursued to search excellence and rationality—*inter alia* it does constitute, the hallmark of a new managerial culture which can help, shape and influence "change", "development" and "future".

In the present context, the significant points associated with "unknown"— if, it is to be expressed in terms of the `familiar' then, it obviously would be better "Research" activity—which is an organised exploration of "unknown". The pity is that Ninety-Nine per cent of the Indian Training Institutions (those that operate in the Public Administrative System) do not have any auxiliary Research mechanism associated or incorporated with the training bodies. Consequently, training knowledge does not quite flow from the `probe' into `live date' comes more from the dated books and manuals and is regularly supplemented by the foreign text-books. Our libraries are full of knowledge contained in the journals belonging to Harvard, Rochester, Columbia, the Wharton School and the Ox-Bridge systems—but on `Research' of enquiry has been codified: How the Indians—the Tatas, Birlas and others managed things to generate so much wealth without going to any training academy—whether Indian or foreign.

Besides, even in terms of the indigenous literature and theme there is a plethora of unprocessed and unedited indigenous reservoir of reports and allied literature available which is seldom used as a training aid. We also need to reflect why no funding is possible to a training institution for creating research posts and whatever goes with it. We need to further reflect that when we keep using foreign text-books, we are acquainting ourselves only to an alien theory, principle and practise. It is always good to know how others manage things. But it is more important to understand our own situation, its components, its failings and its strengths.

The training function as far as possible, should not be divisive or restrictive in character. For the past fifteen years we have been advocating the need to impart training to composite groups. And, therefore, the best part of the recent move, with respect to training of the officers of the Indian Administrative Service, lies in having them as a composite group of officers of differing seniority.

In India, unlike in some other countries, training has also been treated as if it is a special way of giving the trainees an administrative reward. This feeling is much more so with respect to the Overseas training. The authorities sometimes show resentment first by not sending an officer on training or by constantly keeping him out. I remember a case where training was used to keep a 'difficult' officer away; he was constantly being sent to one training programme or the other, since his superior felt that he is less of a nuisance to the Department when he is out!

Be it as it may, we would like to further highlight three aspects of training: Firstly, let us avoid wastage in training. Often we train personnel for 'X' speciality but, on return we transfer them to a responsibility which does not require the kind of training he or she got. This certainly is an avoidable wastage.

Secondly, let not training raise unnecessary hopes amongst officers who go to be trained. The trained officers often carry a chip on their shoulders and treat it as a 'premium' or 'gate-pass' for promotion. Training should instead be treated as an on-going learning process.

Thirdly, any training, whether for "skills-generation" or for "mental awakening" could yield richer dividends—if it is linked also to organisational change—be it of the structure or of developing a new managerial attitude and culture. Currently, this is not at all happening in the Indian Public Administration.

To sum up, therefore, if we have to build managers for tomorrow we have to realise a fundamental fact that the "training" function is only a reinforcing input. The prime thing would be the research of a new administrative philosophy and a new work-ethics. An organisation is the structural aspect of a `Philosophy', while administration is the implementation of that Philosophy. Here too, the purpose of `management' and `training' is neither to tend nor to tame men and women; its purpose is to release the power of `men and women'? Let's then ask once again if our Training Programme are precisely doing this or not?

Science Fiction and Creativity in Science

Science fiction and fantasy can be considered as part of a Surrealistic fiction. It consists of events, against certain background social or scientific, that does not exist today, nor has it existed in the past either. However, many unimaginative writers, through a liberal interpretation of what scientific advances we can make, have certainly enriched a new branch of literature known as the science fiction. Such writings also include examples of even items such as time travel, faster than light velocities, and so on.

Of course, it will always happen that many such changes do not become visible in an individual's life time.

Isaac Asimov has pointed out that the advancements of Science and Technology, however, are of a cumulative nature. Each advance tends to encourage a more rapid further advance. Eventually, the rate of change, and the extent of the fact of the change, on society, becomes great enough to be detected in the space of an individual's life time.

In this sense, fiction becomes a fact and a new creative phenomenon of science and the future is for the first time discovered.

The essence of science fiction lies in developing a perspective of 'change' through 'technology'. As Asimov points out 'it is change, continued change, inevitable change that is the dominant factor in society today. It is indeed true that our decisions today have to take into account not only the world as it is, but the world as it will be. Hence we should welcome different perceptions of even bizarre possibilities that creative function lies behind the development of Science and Technology.'

Some of the earliest writings in science fiction have been more in the nature of extraordinary voyages. Others have now talked in terms of the population control; emergence of the world Government; search for a permanent energy source; weather control; robotics; computer and artificial intelligence; computerised education; mass transference through radiation; setting up of a global village;

clonning; Bionic human beings; Genetic Engineering; control of evolutions; immortality; telepathy; inter-stellar travel; black-holes; galactic empires; time travel; alternative time paths and so on.

On these dreams and fantasies, Isaac Asimov remarks, "The Futuristic and, possibly predictive aspects of science fiction are indeed many. Some of these dreams such as gravitational control or time travel, are probably impossible even in theory. Others, such as the use of the black holes or a mass transference or galactical empires or telepathy, would seem to be unlikely in the extreme. Some dreams are mutually incompatible, for if we develop complex society of space settlements, there isn't much reason to indulge in terraforming". He further adds: "Almost any dream can turn into a nightmare. A world government may become a universal oppressive dictatorship. Immortality may produce a boring world of sameness that completely stultifies humanity. Control of evolution may produce a race of mediocrities. Computers may reduce human beings to helplessness or even obsolescence. Telepathy may end the last vestige of privacy". "Nevertheless, what is life without dreams"? Asimov rightly concludes.

Whatever be the philosophical fact, the most popular question usually asked is, "Do some of the dreams of the science fiction writers ever come true". The answer perhaps is both yes and no. We can perhaps pick a book and examine the facts for ourselves. For example, if we take George Orwell's book *1984*, it can indeed be an interesting case-study, where, out of 137 predictions more than 110 have come true.

Some Scientific and Technological Predictions Form 1984

Predictions in Military Science

1. Think tanks where experts plan future wars.
2. Improved missiles and bombs.
3. Planes independent of earth.
4. Lenses suspended in space.
5. Floating fortresses to guard important sea lanes.
6. Germs immunized against all antibodies.
7. Cell-propelled bombs to take the place of bombing planes.
8. Earthquake and tidal wave control.
9. Soil submarines that could bore through.
10. Efficient detonators that could be spread over wide areas.

Predictions in Police Technology

1. Data banks containing detailed personal information.
2. Rapid access to and retrieval of data.
3. Two-way, flush-mounted televisions.
4. Remote sensor of heartbeat.
5. Tone-of-voice analyzer.
6. Sensitive omnidirectional microphone.
7. Police patrol helicopters.
8. Large telescreens for public viewing.
9. Memory holes for rapid destruction of information.
10. Scanner to detect and analyze human thought.

Future Scan and Perspective Planning: The Indian Thrust

During the last two decades in India, the study of futures has acquired a special significance. It is now being recognised as a powerful tool of development. Futures Research influences policies and inspires all systems to look for creative and innovative ways of fulfilling their prime and strategic objectives. It is mostly in the field of science and technology and socio-economic development that futurology has found its highest application. However, not all sectors in India, seem yet to recognise this.

It is an established fact that 'future' is a state of uncertainty. Nevertheless, this time-phase alone holds all the opportunities as well as a few threats. In fact, 'future' is now treated by alert societies as one of the prime 'resources'. Futurology, which is an interdisciplinary subject, has three key components: Technology Forecasting (TF), Social Forecasting (SF) and Technology Assessment (Long range impact of technology on man, nature and society). India, however, has yet to start any serious formal educational programme in futurology so as to build a strong foundation of futures-consciousness for the educated Indian and other professionals.

It is common knowledge that Technology Forecasting makes it possible to identify several directions of change. The 'future-scan' methodologies help us a great deal. Futures study is, thus, a two stage process: (i) Specification of goals and (ii) Specification of plans. The anticipatory techniques provide us tools of intense analysis which is achieved through studying System-behaviour and by developing 'long-range scenarios'—a sequence of events. Future-scan is thus the basis for the environmental scanning and further helps us to draw up the perspective plans. A perspective plan is not an activity calendar. It is first data collection, then rigorous analytical work; then forecasting ability and finally, generation of several choices be it for Research and Development (R&D) work; or, for achieving the future goals (normative). Today no scientist or planner can afford not to learn the alphabets of Future-Scan, Systems Probe and Perspective Planning, more so, in the Indian context, where the Prime Minister of India has now directed that all Public funded systems should prepare perspective plans. There, thus, exists a need to usher in a massive training programme in forecasting to all planners and policy makers.

In India, the Department of Science and Technology is the nodal Ministry for 'Futurology' and it is through its activities that the real thrust has come for futures consciousness and the advent of a Forecasting culture in the Indian management. The DST's main programmes include: (i) Long-range regional Science and Technology perspectives, (ii) Towards 21st Century: Futurology Awareness lecture-cum-Seminar in Technology Forecasting and Technology Assessment, (iii) Training of Civil Servants in Technology Forecasting, (iv) Research Projects in Technology Forecasting and Technology Assessment, (v) Special thematic workshops, such as, Water Futures, Ocean Technology for 21st Century, Food Futures, etc., and (vi) Extension Service in Futurology.

The impact created by these programmes include the spread of (i) Enhanced Futures Consciousness (ii) the widening of its Futurology workshop's participants in comprehension of the importance of the inter-disciplinarity and inter-sectoral aspects and (iii) the understanding of the long-range impacts of Science and Technology developments on Man, Nature and Society (TA).

In most of the above stated programmes the DST encourages inter-university participation by academics and young scientists and other professionals to partake in DST Sponsored Futurology workshops. This step has, to a large extent, led to the emergence of a Futurology Network in the country. Earlier in 1986 the UGC had also invited the Universities to reflect their interest in 7th Five Year Plan profile should they like to introduce some programmes/ courses on the subject of Futurology. Nothing concrete has though yet come out of it. Even though the DST's Futurology workshops, Research projects and extension services, it is expected, will help the emergence of a broad-based futurology network in India: yet the Indian Educational system, the Indian Public Sector Undertakings and the Indian Research and Development Network too need to demonstrate their interest and institutional response to Future-scan and perspective planning. The setting up of Technology Information Forecasting Assessment Council (TIFAC) under the Department of Science and Technology, one can hope, will certainly provide the much needed critical thrust to Futures studies. Still a formal directive on this from the highest concerned quarters will indeed be welcome.

Futuristic Thinking and Socio-Economic Change

Futurology/Futures, Research and systems analysis/Futuribles or Futurism is primarily the study of the interplay between resource and demand. We are also concerned here with technological and social prognostics. When we are looking for new alternatives and options for the future of India, we have also to take into account the needs, the aspirations and the lifestyle that our people wish to have, both in the rural as well as in the urban areas. Such an exercise, thus, eventually acquires a normative character since we have to provide a wholesome answer to the question: What kind of society are we going to create in the year 2000 AD?

The relevance of futuristic studies essentially lies in our deliberate attempt to look "beyond our nose" to study numerous known and unknown limits to growth, to establish systems which will help build a new society based on a philosophy of development which goes beyond the concept of "business as usual". Any single view or a combination of different views of future that we may foresee does, however, imply that action on them should commence now. In this sense, one can aptly say what shall happen in future starts today. Thus, a concern for prognostics is not entirely an utopian exercise. It is intimately tied to a nation's efforts for "preparedness".

What is the Message of Future?

The message of future lies in offering a challenge to mankind to explore the character of uncertainty that characterises it. Future consists of two kinds of events: Events one would like to see happen and events which we would like to see not happen. Thus, the additional challenge for us is to so plan the national life that we are able to realise the "futures" that we prefer. In so far as the global and national futures go, three things are certain:

(1) Future of every nation is intimately linked and will directly correspond to its advancements in the field of science and

technology. It is through science and technology alone that poverty can be eradicated; ill-health conquered and a quality of life ensured. Therefore, it will be an erroneous step to have an ambivalent attitude towards 'science and technology'.

(2) Future lies with those individuals, organisations and nations which are heavily drawing upon information which promotes a knowledge-based society and which has trained manpower and human resource on the one hand, and a vast pool of information on the other. This will definitely help any nation to meet the future with ease. Apparently, therefore, heavy investment in the field of data collection, information retrieval and information processing for current day decision making processes will go a long way to safeguard our future interest.

(3) The third message of future is that the future lies with the strong, be it an individual an organisation of a nation. Weakness has no place in the life of a society. The strength, however, does not indicate possession of an arsenal of armaments. The strength of a society emerges from its social resilience to change. If we have an adaptive and participative culture and, if we are an open society, we then definitely have a bright future.

Indian Societal Features

In the Indian context the implications of future arise from our paramount concern for the welfare of a large human system. (630 million plus or minus now and 960 million plus or minus by the turn of the century). Besides, the second parameter to be taken into consideration is the fact of value plurality. Indian society simultaneously coexists in several centuries. In the same household, different people have different value frames, both in the horizontal and in the vertical sense. In India we have to deal with multiple technology. Uneven growth of Indian society and the fact that India simultaneously also lives in the state of agraria, industria and post-industria, we are compelled not to cut-off any technology from use. Here no technology goes into disuse; we are thus simultaneously in the bullock-cart age as in the jet or space age.

The Key-Question

The key question pertaining to India is: How does one change and open up a traditional society which has centuries old customs and which is socially highly fragmented? We may thus ask, Do we have, here in India, a theory of social change? If so, what is it? One also asks if we are non-change-oriented? Are we the masters of status quo? Is our administrative system designed for how not to change? And if it be so, then how does one open up this society? How does one reach millions of people with this message of change. Or, how does one inspire them to change, to look for new values and new designs for life? Besides, one would like to know-how can this be done through force? Or through persuasion? What technological approach needs to be adopted to reach millions with the right message? One feels baffled when we have seen that both force and persuasion have met with a failure. Our efforts in the field of family planning and welfare being a case in point. What then is the third alternative?

India is a unique society in as much as the agraria, industria and the post-industria simultaneously coexist here and shall do so for centuries to come. However, our poverty, the paucity of resources, the population explosion do deny an equitable satisfaction of needs. On a per capita basis, we may not be able to satisfy human needs for a long time to come. And, therefore, one of the most important criteria for assessing any technology in the Indian context, in the context of the welfare of the millions of people of this country compels us to opt for the 'technology' which satisfies the needs of 'many' rather than a 'few'. Whereas factors like environmental degradation and other well-catalogued consequences of technology—now familiar enough—should be studied through Indian research in this area is still negligible. What is needed more is that Indian education, industry and Government should take a very long-range vision in choosing those technologies which can collapse time, bridge a gap of decades and be of use for large sections of society. The welfare and service criteria should take precedence over the "scale" and sophistication that characterizes "technology".

In conclusion, first we must categorically reject toying with the romantic ideas of a return to a pastoral living and a life of idyllic happiness. The times have changed. The logic of world history indicates the direction towards which we should be speedily moving now. India has once missed the 'Industrial Revolution'. India cannot afford to miss the 'Technological Revolution'. We cannot turn away from technology. What we need today is to learn and institutionalise a system to decide how best we can 'choose' and 'manage' our affairs for the 'maximum good of maximum number' ensuring the basic 'needs' today and ushering a better 'future' tomorrow.

Where does one start solving India's problem? It is almost like asking how does one eat an elephant. We may bite it anywhere and yet we can merely scratch it here and there. A total reorganisation, if not a revolution, can release human energy to work for regional and local developmental programmes. This is itself a great management task, a challenge both for the present and the future.

The Threat Inventory

There are many important threats that face us but five of these are significant indeed and deserve attention :

Biological Decay

First, in terms of futuristic thinking the future of our children stands heavily compromised. Scientific evidence exists to suggest that the present state of nutrition available to the vulnerable section of society could, by the turn of the century, bring forth 60 per cent or more of India's population as that of mentally retarded people. It could usher a genetic loss.

The Energy Crisis

Second, is the energy crisis. It has to be seen both in terms of the escalation of the price of oil and scarce availability of the middle distillates like kerosene and diesel ; and secondly, it has to be looked at the nonavailability of the domestic fuel particularly for the vulnerable sections of society. This can cripple our industry and precipitate civil disorder.

Institutional Redundance

The third crisis arises from the mismatch of 19th century institutions to the 21st century challenge. Many of our institutions today, which were good enough to serve the interest of a few, seem redundant when it comes to place on them the demand and interests of many. With the present work style, these institutions cannot serve the interests of the millions of people. The educational institutions are a classic case in point. They serve, for instance, only 30 per cent of our population. Such institutions have thus become stagnant and do not promote creativity and change. Their management style only support the 'process' and not the 'substance'. Most of them are anyhow elitist in character. These institutions, if not drastically overhauled, will fail to usher better social futures for India.

Non-Participative Culture

India is still a non-participative culture and its organized sector feudalistic in character. Without people's participation, the effort made by the Government cannot today reach, with the fruits of welfare, to millions of our countrymen. People's participation takes many forms, it involves community action and joint participation of the people with the governmental programme. In the industrial sector it takes the shape of participative management and industrial democracy. This is an area which deserves an innovative look. Failure to serve people and to introduce participative element will cripple administration and managerial efforts.

Crisis Arising from Short-term Planning and Lack of Anticipatory-Management Culture

Short-term planning leads to short-range decision and yield merely short-range results. Resources once committed, investments once made all these spring from decisions which are irreversible in character. And this commits us towards future without providing for it. Our planning should accommodate future needs today. Thus, without taking recourse to long-range planning we would be steadily compromising our financial investments and fail to cope with the demands of future.

The Need of the Hour

It is apparent that we need to generate a massive awareness within the country to arouse future consciousness. People on the one hand and the organised sector on the other, should think of all those areas where they can make a quantum leap into future.

We need to invent future in every walk of life.

Since time is against us, we cannot afford the luxury of slow march towards future.

Structural changes will have to be brought about and social systems introduced ensuring long-range investments in the basic need areas.

In our schools and colleges we shall have to create a new innovative and creative culture whereby our children and our youth acquire a vested interest in the future since they are going to be the beneficiaries of such an outlook.

Future rests on political goodwill and understanding and consensus. Ultimately, however, all decisions have a political character. It is high time that the interest of Indian society and its future brings forth a political dialogue amongst all concerned to evolve a national consensus on policies and programmes, at least, in the basic need areas, to ensure water, health, education, energy, clothing and housing to the vulnerable sections of society.

Patch work reform will not help this nation. We are a large human system. We need to make a radical break from the past.

If we wish to safeguard future, it is high time that all those who are running government, bureaucracy, education and industry and are thus concerned with creativity and change took a second look at their style and evolve appropriate work-methods upholding the new norm of promoting creativity and total change, if not a revolution. It might help us a bit from preventing India turning into a disaster area even before future arrives.

To sum up, people's participation is an inevitable, overall governing factor which should determine the new institutional arrangements. Too bureaucratic, hierarchical and power oriented institutional apparatus would not help to manage such a large human system. Secondly, we must usher ethos in every walk of life whereby innovation, experimentation and creativity is given primary importance and organisational recognition. Finally, in every organised sector activity need to search our current day options, choices and decisions based on a long-range assessment of human needs. Thus, Futuristic viewing of things will go a long way to augment and strengthen our developmental programmes and make the society face future with ease. Are we prepared for it?

Creativity Change and Future

One of the missing elements in the India educational and organised sector is the absence of creativity. It is understood that all education has talent in its elements of creativity. It is equally believed that any industrial production is necessarily a reflection of creative endeavour. However, both these opinions are partly erroneous. Creativity can be understood in many ways: it is to create to make; it can be inspiration; innovation; improvisation; colour pattern; awareness; sensitivity, beauty, truth, an arrangement; satisfaction or fulfilment; a bridge; horizon or an effort to touch new heights; growth; development; quality not quantity; a composition; a combination, say of sounds, words; or re-design; softness; a beautiful manoeuvre; a tackle or a harmony; it is also personality development; it could be concentration; an experiment; an effort for learning; a brilliant execution; originality; analysis; reaction and response to environment; projection of the self; unburdening of one's soul; portrayal of visible and invisible; contemplation; a dream; a vision; a method; a system; unearthing or description of relationship of sub-systems in a system; a new approach; a new idea; a shining patina; objectivity incarnate; subjectivity of a higher order; formal education; non-formal education; informal education; free expression; a right to differ; the total system; right to challenge; confirmity expressed a new; non-conformity; a function and product of training; an interpretation, ability to evolve new modules; the methods; and learning process; a human ability; a change of attitude; an opportunity; or, reflection of continuous encouragement.

Like this, we can endlessly search social indicators which shall define creativity. Ultimately, however, creativity is a function and product of liberalised, innovative experimental training on the one hand and approximity to future, on the other. It is the hallmark of a change process; and since it is the search of new ideas, and new alternatives, this is what is the concern of future also.

Likewise, turning to change one should first ask what is change? Is it to be something different? Is it a fulfilment: a goal; a target; a clue; a state of flux; a movement, a method; a system; or mobility; an aggregation or disaggregation, bundle of fears; security; insecurity; crisis; hell; paradise; a challenge; thesis, anti-thesis or synthesis; disorder; or progress; growth; and development; or, is it resistance and desire to be different; a decision; agreed solution; a democratic design or a dictatorial fiat; a manifesto; a document; a desire; a wish of one or many. Or, is it the shape of things to come? In this sense, change is essentially the future.

What is future? Future consists of events —uncertain events. But some of these events we would like to see happen; such as 100 per cent literacy; 100 per cent employment, food for all, health and educational facilities for all and so on. Then there are events we would not like to see happen, such as unemployment, disease, hunger, poverty, flood, famine and war, etc. To arrive creatively to a changed life, that is, the future. It is necessary perhaps, to prefer events that we desire to take place.

It is also necessary, that we understand the logic and imperatives of the future for our society; in the light of which we shall have to evolve a 'criteria' for creativity, change and progress.

In the Indian context the implications of future arise from our paramount concern for the welfare of a large human system. (630 million plus or minus now and 960 million plus or minus by the turn of the century). Besides, the second parameter to be taken into consideration is the fact of value plurality. Indian society simultaneously coexists in several centuries. In the same household different people have different value frame; both in the horizontal and in the vertical sense. In India we have to deal with multiple technology. Uneven growth of Indian society and the fact that India simultaneously also lives in the state of agraria, industria and post-industria, we are compelled not to cut-off any technology from use. Here no technology dies or goes into disuse; we are thus simultaneously in the bullock-cart age as well as in the jet or space age. Considering these factors what then should be our criteria for creativity and change?

It is clear that creativity and change can be ushered only through educational interactions, management interventions and technological interventions. Apparently, therefore, the real norm to judge whether or not an activity or action purports to creativity and change shall depend on its consequences whether that action or activity firstly promotes a society which is knowledge and information based and secondly, whether it helps usher in a participative culture. And finally, an action is creative and is promoting change, if it serves the welfare not of a few but of many.

Obviously, the crisis that India faces today is basically an institutional crisis where institutions are consciously obstructing creativity and change and which are primarily catering to the needs of a few—elitist or otherwise. And thus, essentially, they have already become totally redundant to usher in better social futures.

If we wish to safeguard future, it is high time that all those who are running Government, bureaucracy, education and industry should get concerned with creativity and change and took a second look at their work system and style and evolve an appropriate work — methods, upholding the view of criteria promoting creativity and total change — if not a total revolution.

Futures Research Indicates Need for Institutional Surgery

Futurology or Futures Research, in the context of accumulated body of knowledge, is apparently a recent phenomenon going back to 20 or 30 years. Undoubtedly, concern for future has been expressed by individuals and visionaries from time to time in different societies and culture. But looking at future in a scientific way not on a hunch or a rule of thumb basis, but making assessment of estimate-of-the-unknown scientifically to the extent it is possible is essentially a rational and knowledge based process.

Anticipatory know-how could be deliberately arrived at and specifically stated based on information, data foresight and the use of forecasting techniques such as extrapolative approaches, the Delphi system, the morphological analysis, the statistical calculations and the generation of alternative technological routes arrived through scenario building exercise and tested through technological mission analysis.

Notwithstanding these possibilities, a general cynicism prevails against forecasting and futuristic analysis. A part of this is notably caused by the conditioning of the past and frustration and dissatisfaction with day-to-day problems of the present which makes people, by and large look away from future. They generally express disappointment with those in authority including our public policies, conditions of work, and total purposelessness of the Indian life and the lack of direction to pursue relevant national goals responsible for the current day mess which leaves little scope to reflect on future.

All this naturally leads to non-thinking and rejection for concern of future and futuristic considerations. This can be seen by the very fact that the well-off section of our society today stands aloof and could care-no-less if more than 300 million people of this country experience non-fulfilment of their basic needs in terms of food, water, shelter, health, education, energy, etc.

A simplified reaction to this state of affair would be to generate greater consciousness and awareness both of the current day-to-day life and of the numerous crisis and opportunities that the future holds for us. It is not easy to give a single theory or formula whereby people can be exhorted and motivated not to be fearful of change but seek change consciously. Concern of future does not seek theoretical responses. Concern for future is a concern for preparedness, of providing valuable policy inputs. Future, after all, consists of two kinds of events. Events which we would like to see happen (food for all, 100 per cent literacy) and events we would like to see not happen (famine, widespread malnutrition, resources scarcity, etc.). After all, future is something on which, hopefully, we have some power, it is something there at a distance, which if we are precocious enough, we could influence. In fact, one can invent future. The real impact of futuristic thinking apparently demands certain new parallel developments, amongst others, at least in four major systems. These are:

(1) Sociocultural System;
(2) Educational System;
(3) Management-Technological System, and
(4) The Policy and Political System.

All the four above-mentioned systems, at least in the context of India, are characterised both in terms of values and institutional network by 19th century and early 20th century wisdom. A system which is not anticipatory in nature. The sociocultural response of people in these systems towards events is one, where they wait for the event to arise to react. Such a social ethos is one which responds through reaction as against anticipation. In short, ours is not an anticipatory culture. Thus, the anticipatory process whether in terms of anticipatory management, in terms to anticipatory technological choice, whether in terms of anticipatory policy postures or in terms of anticipatory delineation of politics, national goals and targets, does not draw inspiration from the future—at least the long-range future. The concept of 5 years planning is indeed too short a time span. It can hardly accommodate serious implications of future which can be anything beyond 15 to 20 years depending on ones capability of scientific anticipation, it definitely eludes provision for Tomorrow's Technology.

The futures research movement, thus, clearly indicates that there is need for major social, educational, cultural, managerial, technological and political reforms which the present institutional system and work methods do not provide for.

We in our educational system usually say that we are educating our children so that they may get prepared for their future life. However, any scrutiny of our text-books would clearly indicate that 90 per cent of the information that they contain is about the past and not future.

In the cultural fields we talk of preservation of the national heritage. But any growth in terms of creativity demands experimentation, innovation and non-conformity which we shall not permit.

In the management field, the basic need is to take recourse to long-range planning, since socio-economic development, demands gestation period and uninterrupted growth climate. Whereas we have a system wherein terms of administrative policy and in terms of political set-up administrations change every fifth year or earlier; and this hurts both the investment pattern, programme choices, targets, goals and achievements.

In national interest, it is apparent, the futures research, which generates alternatives and points out to the likely and impending crisis and likely opportunities has become a meaningful new developmental input, and it should be so recognised.

A massive awareness to usher an anticipatory culture on the one hand, in spite of a multi-party system, a hard core of national-apolitical consensus, at least, in the basic need areas, on the other hand, is an inescapable paramount necessity.

Agricultural growth, industrial development, emergence of skilled and trained manpower, fulfilling of the basic needs, such as, housing, clothing, food and water and even energy—all these demand anticipatory thinking and a socio-political climate characterised by national consensus.

In turn, these are new challenge areas, for reform and national debate. If India is going to be a country with one billion people in less than 20 years, it is high time that we look hard at future and its implications and make necessary changes in the present day institutional set-up and managerial practices, be they in the field of education, science and technology or the political system. Without such concomitant changes, futures research will remain an ineffective tool to enable the Indian society to provide the basic needs for all and begin to search and ensure for them a quality of life at least in the 21st century.

Environment Thought and Management: Need for Setting up of an Anticipatory Group

In the nature of things environmental concerns are long-range concerns. They are inextricably interwoven with the concern of nature and social designers. As a futurologist has to build his scenarios based on historical heritage and preferred dreams for a better way of life, likewise, the environmentalists, are also required to scan both the past and the future. It would, of course, vary from environmentalist to environmentalist as to what he focuses at, generally speaking, however, in the context of environment for and towards future, the following four dimensions need to be looked at critically, which are: (i) Environment and Socio-Economic Development (say for the next 20 to 25 years); (ii) Environment and Nature (the likely changes in land, water, forest resources and wildlife over the next 25 years); (iii) Environment and man and his living conditions (here long-range concern will be with poverty, habitat and quality of life), and (iv) Environment and the frontiers of the future (This will include developments in space and ocean and their consequent impacts on the life of earthlings).

Against these four parameters, we have to develop the environmental thought and take decisions for management and managerial innovation through using technology forecasting, social forecasting and technology assessment method, that is the various waves with which we can ameliorate environment and contain unhealthy trends and turbulence within safe limits. The difficulty, of course, arises because of India's limited Five Year Plan framework. Happily from the 6th Plan document, one can see that a new trend in Indian planning has since commenced in as much as the perspective plan efforts upto the year 1995 figures in determining the choices and options and investments in the 5th Five Year Plan. This calls for the setting up of an Anticipatory Group for "Environment Thought and Management" which shall examine several futuristic developments using the known methodologies of futures research in the above given four areas, based on which a body encompassing environmental thought and new management systems can be developed.

The difficulty with the current day environmental thought is that it is going on the beaten track and is duplicating subordinate formation and a traditional and familiar organisational form many of which originated way back in the 9th century. These are purely regulatory agencies. If future scanning is done, it is quite conceivable that the future Environmental Management Institutions shall be participatory instead of regulatory though regulation has a place by itself. Likewise, the environmental concern as expressed through national policy can be made to emerge out of a two-way communication where ideas from the grass root level also feed the thinking of the national brains trust which involves national environmental policies. An environmental communication network thus, will fulfil this better to enable millions of our people—by means of multi-media national forums—to understand and pursue a number of environmental goals and programmes not under duress or imposition, but through a voluntary inborn desire to protect and enrich one's environment.

If an Anticipatory System Analysis Group is set-up it will need an infrastructural support of the following five mechanisms: (i) Environmental Intelligence Scanning Unit; (2) Environmental two-way Communication Network; (3) Training and Educational Unit to spread environmental consciousness; (4) Developmental and Materials Scanning Unit; and (5) Technology Assessment Unit.

In a large country like India, in order to create a genuine impact, the environmental concern will have to acquire the dimensions of a movement. Apparently, its focus and operational networks should be spread far and beyond the web of the bureaucratic pyramids.

On Management of Creativity for the Young

The Silver Jubilee Celebrations of the National Bal Bhavan at Delhi, inaugurated by the Prime Minister of India, who has been actively associated with this Society for the past 25 years, is a landmark in the field of promoting creativity amongst children. Mrs. Gandhi has expressed satisfaction with the consolidation and diversification of numerous programmes that the movement encompasses in creating awareness and providing an opportunity for self-expression in diverse realms, such as, science and technology, performing arts, physical education, museum activities and specialised programmes dealing with experimentation and innovation in the field of electronics, photography, aero-modelling, recycling of waste and futurology, etc.

The Prime Minister has also desired that this movement should spread far and wide in the country. Presently, there are seventeen other Bal Bhavans in different States which are inadequate to meet with the aspirations of millions of children in this country. An excellent step has been taken by the Delhi Bal Bhavan to augment a rural complex and to set-up new Bal Kendras, 15 in all, in different parts of the city of Delhi to cater to the creativity needs of children from lower income groups and slum areas. Considering the galloping population of India, this movement will have to prepare itself to spread its infrastructure to meet the demands for creative learning centres of 300 million children upto the age of 16 within the next 20 years throughout India.

The future oriented planning for creativity thus has to directly derive its inspiration and programme-articulation in response to three factors:

(1) How to cater to a large human system;

(2) How to establish adequate linkages in order to reach different sections of the society and minimise the disparities that go with the rural-urban divide, and

(3) How to meaningfully interact and persuade the Indian

school educational system to formally integrate in this curricula, the various aspects of creativity and opportunity of self-expression as against the educational programme which is more related to memorisation; which offers very little choice and options at the school stage and is, by and large, examination and competition oriented. The Bal Bhavan Movement is an out-of-school activity and it avoids 'competition'.

Unfortunately, very little emphasis has found its place in the Indian educational system in general to enable the young people to become experimenters, innovators and creative persons. Rigidity, and inflexibility are the basic tenets of our education system that governs the growth of the manifold potentials of the children and the youth in this country. Whereas, the educational system does proclaim that education is meant to prepare a child for their future life, the educational curricula is, however, totally silent about future. Its total emphasis is on the past as can be seen from the scanning of any text-book on any subject. Moreover, little effort is visible of correlating education to society and to future.

Today 50 per cent of India's population consists of children and youth who are ill-equipped to cope with the challenges of the 21st century. The message of education is to establish the image both of the social reality and also to establish the image of the future. Thus, both education and the concept of future are powerful organisational concepts for change. And this is precisely what our present educational system denies them. In particular, our school educational system, has no place either to create awareness for 'change' (learning how to bring about change and not be overtaken or shocked by it) or 'society' (learning to help and care for others in society and appreciating a lifestyle which is socially relevant) or for 'future' (learning to anticipate and plan for future and be prepared to cope with crisis).

These three elements should, in fact, be the key reference points for an educational overhaul. And once inducted in our curricula, they can offer ample scope for young people, to become a creative person and a new kind of Indian citizen. Will this ever happen? Our educational system continues to provide education only for unreality. The result is that already, the current educational structure, at least at the higher level of education seemingly stands rejected by the youth; Here there is a visible collapse of teacher's authority and there is a strong feeling both amongst the students and the parent-community that the time spent in schools and colleges, even if it is leading to a passport for a job, still by and large remains a period of "boredom, painful humiliation and psychological degradation". Such negativism is bound to grow and, if not prevented, is bound to overtake the school and secondary level education also. The story of the "drop-outs" at this level is too familiar and unfortunate as to be recaptured here.

Since any total overhaul of our educational system and educational prophets who are vociferous reactionaries, shall not experience a change in any visible time span. But Bal Bhavan movement in the life of the schooling period of our youngsters can play an important creative, learning, experimenting, innovating, socio-educational role. This is a movement which thus needs to be strengthened and dovetailed and integrated with the school education in its formal, non-formal and informal modes.

For such an integration of the Bal Bhavan movement with the school system, it is necessary that all those connected with the short-range or the long-range educational planning in India should sit together and work out how this important linkage can be achieved not merely for infrastructural or curricular redesign but also for the formal pedagogic recognition of "creativity" as against the back-breaking monolithic weight of present educational syllabus. Any time lost in delaying this very important exercise will be a deliberate act of sociocultural-cum-educational suicide.

India is now on the threshold of becoming one of the most powerful countries in the world. It needs a new crop of citizens. In order to reinforce this endeavour and to accelerate the process of modernization, we shall have to take off the current day 'pedagogic shackle' off the Indian child who remains, today, a helpless prisoner of the current day educational system. He needs to be liberated from it. We shall, thus, have to deliberately reject such 19th century wisdom which ill-prepares our children to cope with the emerging world of the 21st century.

The Bal Bhavan movement has been the part and parcel of the twin emphasis on 'science' and 'creativity of its founder Jawaharlal Nehru, the architect of Modern India. It was Nehru who inspired the setting up of the National Bal Bhavan and the Jawahar Bal Bhavans in some of our States. His love for children and their growth is too well-known. We have to change the school education drastically to achieve Nehru's vision for our children's future.

The time has come when we should, like in some other countries, begin to treat our children as that privileged section of the society, for whom we should do much more than is the case today. Thus, the Bal Bhavan spirit which today basically is an out-of-school activity should also be made an 'in-school' activity to enable children to acquire learning to get acquainted with the "peaks of excellence" in a less painful and much more innovative way. Such a move shall be a socially relevant step in the right direction to build a stronger India. Let us deliberately permit our children to freely go through the process of self-actualisation for the good of our great nation.

Management Education For and Towards Future

It is now universally recognised that management is the key to all development. However, management styles and practices have, of late, as a body of knowledge, and a repertoire of skills, at the command of managers, draws its inspiration from three distinct sources which are as follows:

(1) Global developments in management systems;
(2) Body of knowledge on management as it has grown from a single discipline to a multidisciplinary subject; and
(3) Culture specific management practices, values, attitudes and styles.

If one carefully looks at the management systems, one can see that most systems are increasingly becoming global as well as increasingly becoming region specific and culture specific. As a body of knowledge, in terms of management theory and management thought, management education has from time to time received several inputs beginning from the engineers, economists, psychologists, sociologists and now futurologists.

Management education has also been influenced by developments in organisational structures, personnel policies, emerging technologies and national and international information and communication systems. Apparently, in terms of a particular country's emerging profile of management education, even if it may show a great many global similarities, nevertheless it rightly retains a country specific character. And within a single country too, there could further be a variety of management styles and practises depending on the ownership of an enterprise whether it is public or private. This fact also will influence both the management thought (as it could be obtained from management schools, colleges, universities or special institutes), as well as the use or non-use of skills and styles peculiar to the sector to which the manager belongs. A manager in the Government, thus, would need, over a time, inputs which are not totally identical to the inputs that the manager in industry is required to possess and constantly update.

The management education, to the end of this century, or in the beginning of the next century will primarily, *inter alia* be an education that shall help managers (a) to understand the logic of change, and further help (b) to understand how to manage that change.

The management education as a total package has a great deal to do with the anticipatory process. This anticipatory process alone can help managers understand the emerging phenomena in the following context:

The Global Perspective

Here the managers of today and more so, of tomorrow have to have an indepth grasp of the international economic relations. It requires future scanning of aid, trade, debt-servicing, the role of multinationals, the regional groupings, cartels, etc.

The Material Perspective

Here a manager has to know how various resources are being consumed today and what shall be their future in terms of their availability or non-availability. He needs a fore-knowledge of the substitute materials, etc.

The Technological Perspective

Here the managers of tomorrow have to grasp the role of research and development and science and technology. These are vital in as much as a manager has to learn to anticipate tomorrow's technologies today and make it possible for his organisation/undertaking/company to possess it at an earliest point of time, either from others, or through indigenous effort. Technology is the key to all progress, though it can also, if not carefully understood, or in case of being misused, harm society.

The Social and Organisational Perspective

A great deal of managerial decisions and response of tomorrow will be determined by the client and social groups interest or disinterest in his organisational products or services. This is what constitutes the social group or market external to an undertaking. On the other hand, there are special pressure groups in a society that motivate group behaviour of the elements internal to an undertaking. Their aspirations and motivations too need to be understood, forecasted and more than anything else they deserve timely management response. Failure to anticipate and grasp them leads to human failure in making harmonious industrial relations or retaining of personal loyalty, etc.

The Information and Forecasting Perspective

Management to the end of the 20th century needs also to set-up a good information and research base with people trained in anticipating facts, analysing facts and such trained groups, who can act as an Early Warning Network to a company to enable it to (a) take anticipatory decisions and (b) feed the top management with alternative courses of action.

Management education for tomorrow, thus, needs to reinforce managerial know-how with respect to the above-mentioned or additional management perspectives. The management for and towards future is the management of discontinuities/crises/high speed change. It needs managers who can make timely response towards society, its goals and needs.

The emerging management education programmes will thus need to redefine the knowledge-mix for different levels and different functionaries combining the traditional body of management knowledge with the knowledge pertaining to anticipating and inventing ideas to let management survive and grow in a highly turbulent and change-oriented future. For this we may have to (a) redesign current courses; (b) set-up new training institutes; (c) make training non-elitist; (d) cut down its cost which currently is acquiring alarming proportion and (e) dovetail all management education and management training to the needs of socio-economic development.

Technology Assessment

The Term 'Technology Assessment' (TA) in India is still a relatively new term and even raises questioning eye-brows? Globally, however, now a TA community exists both amongst the experts and the citizenary in societies characterised by an high incidence of technological culture. The public is beginning to demand some voice in decisions regarding technology. As Melvin Kranzberg has succinctly put it, "After all, people want more say over their own destiny and because technology has so much to do with that destiny, they want some control over it. Hence a new and powerful trend in public policy, called Participatory Democracy, is beginning to invade technology and is attempting to democratize its professional activities and direction."

An important institutional response came from the initiative of Emilio Doddario, a former Congressman, who introduced, legislation that led to the establishment of the Officer of Technology Assessment (OTA) in the US Congress and worldwide interest in Technology Assessment. In India, it was the NOST Panel on Futurology located in the Department of Science and Technology which emphasised the role of Technology Assessment in Futures studies. However, barring the department of atomic energy and one or two public sector undertakings, besides the newly created department of environment, the term TA rouses little, if any, enthusiasm in the Indian Industrial World. The recently set-up Planning Commission's Committee under Lovraj Kumar is indeed a welcome step in the right direction. It rouses hopes towards emerging inputs that shall lead to creative Futures Planning and Public Policy and identification of an Indian TA paradigm. All this, among other reasons, is needed to determine the "use", "choice" and "application" of technology for creating a desirable long-range future, rather than, as Governor Russewl Peterson put it: "Simply providing technological fixes to immediately pressing problems". When and how in India, we shall have a citizen involvement, "which can bridge the gap between factual technical analysis and value-oriented policy analysis", is hard to say. We in India, still remain a unique third world arena, where Indian elite, literate and articulate people lavishly participate in bogus debates, whether "small is beautiful" or "large is bountiful". Ninety per cent of the semi-literate have hardly any say so far. Part of the Indian dilemma not to understand the logic, the imperative of technology and its relevance to build a new India lies in part historic myths and part in a failure of the policy maker. A majority still believes that Gandhiji was against "Technology" and "Machine culture". Later perhaps, 'Yes' but former definitely 'No'. Gandhiji alone, in the form of spinning wheel (*charkha*) introduced 'Technology' in every home as a measure of "Social Good". All we need to do is to update Gandhi, as Japan has done by turning Electronics into a Cottage Industry. As for policy, the technology policy statement, made by Prime Minister Indira Gandhi is only a three year old phenomenon. In terms of legislation, except for 'Drugs and Pesticides', etc., India is still a 'free and virgin' land where only specific kind of Technology (Some indigenous and some imported) can have free play. Sober industrialists, privately do confess saying, "we do know some of our products (say detergents) have some adverse social costs. But can we withdraw out product? What is the guarantee that our competitors would do the same. We can surely, unilaterally, not commit an economic suicide" One does not have to catalogue products and drugs which many countries have put a 'ban' on but which are still in use in India for whatever reason—the use of DDT being a case in point. Many products, coming from Modern Synthetic Chemistry—the source of a variety of "Staples", for example, plastics, solvents, pharmaceuticals, and agricultural pesticides, certainly have benefited contemporary industry. Yet sufficient research based evidence does exist to show that "the residuals of some of these products themselves — have been major pollution vectors whose accumulation pose grave threats to the health of human and eco-systems". What "automobiles" are doing to 'Urban centres' and 'highways' is a well known 'environment' and 'safety' hazard for which less said the better.

In nut-shell, the concern of the TA community is with the long-range, the first order, the second and the third order consequences of any technology on man, nature and society. In managerial terms, we are concerned here with several aspects of "Contemporary Technological Decision Making". To spell it in terms of an empirical paradigm, we need, first, to view the following aspects:

Problem	*Question*
A. Strong Coupling between Technology and Development.	Have we taken a: (a) Systems view (b) Examined the future imperative
B. The compelling view of Scientists and Technologists.	Have we considered and allowed (1) Lay Man's view; provided for (2) People's Participation to at least, understand and "alternative reality perception"
C. Imperatives of Quantity/Measures (GNP), etc.	What about the qualitative aspects the so called "quality of life"?
D. Narrow Short-Term Considerations (Automobile has added to mobility, speed, etc.).	What about "bad", long-term consequences (Pollution, energy question, new lifestyle cutting. across socio-moral fabric such as sexual permissiveness).

Whereas the Policy makers will certainly evolve the relevant 'paradigm' as an aid to technology oriented decision making, what is needed much more, is universal technology orientation and education in the Indian sub-continent. Technology ushers change. But oriental societies live in the past and, by and large, majority of 'people', at least in India have a basic 'fear' of change. Besides, it is hard to accept that India has technological culture. In fact, our society is highly characterised by Value Plurality and Technological Plurality. Heterogeniety has its attractive side, but we need to carry the totality of our 'people' with us in our search and zeal to make a quantum jump towards better future for all.

Whatever may emerge in our concern for Technology Assessment in terms of policy inputs for industrial policy or import-export stance, the need to educate people cannot be ignored. Technology consciousness and familiarity should commence in the kindergartens, nurseries and schools. This is where the 'national stock' is nurtured. This is where we develop the future of a society. The concern for future is thus not an escape function. It is, and should be, as is the case in Japan, USA, USSR and other countries, integral to school syllabus and a major educational input in the graduate and postgraduate education of our youngsters. Is it not strange that concepts like Technological Forecasting, Social Forecasting and Technological Assessment are conspicuous by their observe in the educational system.

Yet, simultaneously, we need to take another step to usher, informally and formally, TA consciousness in the educational realm. "Peoples" participative role for TA can truly emerge from there.

Training: The Missing Element

One of the most remarkable developments in the Indian Management scene both in the private and the public sector, has been an increased emphasis on and spurt of training programmes at all levels.

There is now visible a mushroom growth of both in-house and the institutional training activities. Most of these training programmes, however, fall in three broad categories: Programmes that help towards (i) Skill formation (technical), (ii) Function specific training (personnel, finance), and (iii) General management programmes which will help widen one's mental horizon.

Different functionaries, who go for a dose of training, however, draw dissimilar advantage of the training opportunity. Their motivations and aptitude are different; and so are their levels of ability for absorption of training received by them.

In fact, in all training programmes there is a lot of wastage. It comes from two directions: Firstly, it comes from the ill-utilisation of the trained personnel. In fact, it happens to be the prime contributory factor of wastage for not using a person at a job, for which he or she, has been trained.

Another aspect of wastage is unimaginative transfers to the job which do not require the kind of training one has received.

In short, without the pre-existence of a career and growth oriented personnel policy, much of the training is a bit wasted effort—something that happens perhaps all the time in the public administrative system.

The second wastage occurs, primarily, at the middle or the higher levels, when the training does not contribute anything to the work style and the managerial culture of an organisation. The new language that training imparts to the trained functionaries, today barely adds anything to the effective functioning of the trained person. Amongst other reasons it is so for want of inbuilt structure and heirarchical insulation and an attitudinal complex.

For example, you train a person to learn to draw long-range

plan or to undertake 'Systems analysis' or to learn to take initiative in decision making; nevertheless, he or she cannot do either of the functions independently since the work culture, the lack of appreciation, the lack of delegation, in fact, the entire system and managerial culture remains a stumbling block. Often the fault lies at the very top who prevent a natural blossoming of the seeds, germinated by training. The trained person, in fact, often becomes an 'Odd man out'.

Percolating 21st Century Message to Masses

Now that India is poised on all fronts to meet the future squarely and boldly, it is suggested, that let not this message remain only an elitist concept. The new spirit invoked by Shri Rajiv Gandhi, Prime Minister of India, needs to be taken to all sections of the Indian subcontinent not merely as "yet one new news from the Indian Capital", but as a new national commitment irrespective of the Centre-State and Rural-Urban chasm. Clearly, therefore, the prime obligation rests with the organised sector to think long-range both in the public and the private sector. It is yet not clear why this is not being made an obligatory requirement for all undertakings and companies in the industrial sector to compulsorily draw a twenty year long-range plan indicating their directions of growth and technology upgradation, raw-material and energy requirements and indicating what percentage of domestic and import demand would they be able to meet by the end of the 7th, the 8th, the 9th and the 10th Five-Year Plans.

The second obligation rests with the Educational and Training networks of India, who should in all educational programmes, right from the primary school to the highest level in the university education, curricular or extra-curricular, organise programmes about 'future', 'change' and 'perspective development.' Such activities should be made integral also to adult education and technical education both in the formal and the non-formal systems. The 21st century consciousness should also figure prominently in all executive development programmes in a big way. Formal training in Technology and Social Forecasting and Technology Assessment too amongst others is a must for the Defence, R&D and Corporate sector functionaries, concerned with planning.

Finally, it is for the media, the voluntary organisations and the Apex Industry and Trade Associations to set-up inter-disciplinary groups to act as Management Information (MIS) and Early Warning Systems (EWS).

India and many third world countries have sufficient historical evidence that the "trickle-down" effect has not worked in the past. Be it as it may, the time is ripe to think of ways and means to let 21st century consciousness percolate to the grass-root level. The sooner it is done the better will it be to, usher India with strength, into the 21st century.

Technology Forecasting as an aid to Future-Scan and Perspective Planning

Many a developments on the planet earth have been a function of technology. And as we move towards the future and as new technologies continue to emerge in different sectors, we should be seeing in future a different world strange achievements and equally great threats and unforeseen opportunities. Future has thus become, today, an important area of enquiry, since it is full both of expected and unexpected changes and yet it remains shrouded in mystery. All this demands of individuals, systems and organisation to acquire a new preparedness in order to cope with the sudden onrush of changes as they are being generated by the technological revolution. Those who are not ready for the future, as it shall come to the world soon enough, it is quite possible that it may plunge many of us into the state of 'future-shock' mainly because of our unpreparedness.

Thus, future-scan today is not a matter of sheer individual curiosity and urge to probe futures uncertainty but a time has come when all administrative, industrial and productive systems and all the executives, scientists, technologists and planners working there should learn the use of anticipatory and forecasting tools and techniques so that a scientific probe into the future may become possible and 'systems' may be able to withstand the challenge of sudden change. Such an attitude alone can help us to be ready in advance to overcome future crisis as well as to grab the future opportunities. In this respect, 'forecasting' acts as an important instrument of planning since technology forecasting (TF) has many advantages. Jim Bright has catalogued a few uses of technology, forecasting, which are:

1. Selecting in the planning of research programmes, the amount, direction, scientific skills needed and so forth;
2. Guiding engineering programs towards the use of new technology and the adjustment to new technical demand;

3. Identifying areas where product improvement will be needed and revealing the need for new products;
4. Setting quantitative performance standards for new products, processes, and materials;
5. Helping to establish the timing of new technology;
6. Assisting and identifying the economic potential and impact of technological progress;
7. Guiding technological planning and its contribution to long-range planning;
8. Helping to identify major opportunities and threats in technological environment;
9. Identifying the social impact of technological progress on employment, skills, educational needs, etc.;
10. Identifying possible political developments arising out of technological advances. There are more than 100 odd techniques of technology forecasting.

They need to be combined judiciously since no single technique of anticipation, by itself, is fool-proof. All productive systems ought to go for long-range perspective planning. They should study the future using scientific methods of probing and anticipating future. At least a few managers can thus become anticipators and experts in future scanning. All organisations today do need to develop an anticipatory managerial culture. The study and application of technology forecasting can enable us to achieve this.

The problem with the Indian scene, however, is that neither in the Engineering Education nor in the Scientific Research network it has any full time dedicated group in the Field of Technology Forecasting. Similarly, the Field of Technology Assessment is equally barren presently. Besides, the Indian planning process is done too hastily and defensively. It lacks indepth analysis and is bereft of systems-probe covering inter-sectoral aspects. Part of this, of course, is due to data-gaps and partly due to the lack of training and commitment on the part of the Government and corporate planners. They have yet to learn to make use of tools and techniques of anticipation and to go in for the analytical mode before they generate their long and short-range planning options. The current situation, in fact, needs to be radically corrected.

Much of this can be achieved only if the Indian Centres of Excellence and its University Network starts several appropriate educational modules on the one hand and encourage research in the field of Technology Forecasting. What mechanism Technology Information Forecasting and Assessment Council (TIFAC) set-up by the Government of India will eventually evolve, is yet to be seen. Undoubtedly, India sooner or later has to emerge as an advanced technological nation. Our achievements in Agriculture, Space, Atomic Energy, Electronics and Defence are commendable indeed. If all this progress is any indicator of our future, then with a modified learning system, one should hope, that Technology Forecasting (TF) shall certainly emerge as an useable tool for "Future Scan and Perspective Planning."

Futures Networking: The Need of the Hour

The Scientific Study of 'Future' is today an international phenomenon. Its growth and spread, achieved, during the last two decades, now embraces more than sixty countries and nearly two thousand professional voluntary bodies working as, 'think-tanks'. The work done by the World Futures Society (WFS) in the USA and the World Federation of Futures Studies (WFSP), an International Apex Organisation in this field, is indeed commendable. In fact, for the last thirty years, a shade better emphasis has been given to this interdisciplinary subject. In the Soviet Union and the Warsaw Pact countries it falls under the head, 'Prognostication'. Each year many more countries, both at the 'Official' and the, 'Academic' level are realising the importance of 'Futures Study' and of its numerous allied applications. Entering only a decade ago, the Republic of China, which albeit was a late entrant, shall this year, in early September, be holding the World Futures Conference in Beijing.

The Indian efforts in this field also display a fair measure of success. Starting with the rudimentary work of the Operations Research Group of Baroda; and the so-called 'Second India Series', that came out during the early Seventies, thanks to the funding from the Ford Foundation in India; and along with the pioneering work done in this field by the NCST Panel of Futurology, under the Department of Science and Technology of the Government of India, all these early studies do constitute the first few preliminary, but important, steps in this field.

Regionally, in India, even though some State Level Futurology Panels were got set-up, yet barring the initial good work done by the Maharashtra Government Panel on Futurology, five or six such groups in other states, literally, faced soon an administrative extinction. This sad situation surely needs to be reviewed. Thus, in India, there is hardly any visible regional or local effort, but for the documentary encouragement, through its English language publications, that is being consistently offered by the 'Indian

Council of Management and Future', yet considering the size of India and its language plurality, it is quite sub-critical and has somewhat a low visibility. Apparently, in India, the Futures Networking, has not yet quite emerged.

The heartening feature of the Indian efforts come only from the programmes being carried out by the Department of Science and Technology, the 'Nodal' agency for Futurology, in the country. Through IITs, the Universities, the CSIR Laboratories, it has since organised, funded and guided a little over 150 Awareness and Thematic Futurology Workshops during the past fifteen years. Even assuming that 30 odd participants attended each of these workshops, even then, it is obvious that, in a population of 800 million people, the message of Futurology has reached only less than 5000 odd enthusiasts, drawn from the educational, governmental and the industrial sectors. This obviously is not enough.

The Research and Teaching aspect of, 'Futurology' and 'Forecasting' studies in India is too insignificant to be commented upon. It is primarily because the scientific leaderships and the sciences community has felt too shy to encourage it. The plus point, although, remains in that a great deal of Futures consciousness, though backed up by cursory institutional acceptance, has certainly emerged in the Academic and the Corporate sectors of India. Pitiable as the fact remains, the high priests of the Indian schools and the college educational system, have yet to understand the need and importance of this discipline in any significant way; except for the Bal Bhavan, a GOI Ministry of Education project, Networking in India, where the prime emphasis of its activities has been on creativity and where the children do discuss and debate the 'images of the future' in their 21st century clubs, the concerns of future in the Indian learning system have been and indeed are, more with the 'past' than with the 'future'.

In future, the real thrust to the Futures studies, one should hope, will come if, the Prime Minister of India's, directive for preparing Perspective plans, is followed, in each organisation in the public funded system, scientifically and through analytical mode that characterises Futures Studies and Forecasting.

One should also hope that the emerging emphasis on the district level planning may even inspire our planners to motivate people's debate, in which millions of our villagers, tribals and other citizenry, may gear their thinking to develop creative futures perspectives for the local aspirations.

Let us hope that the government and the articulate people of this country shall give the due importance to "Futures" in order to generate confidence and faith in the Nation building activities. One should further hope, that all such steps shall be taken to enable our people's thinking to become optimistic and to give it due precedence, over the current gloomy and cynical viewing of the Indian politics, economics and societal developments.

It is our belief that a deliberate, healthy and widespread futures consciousness in the world of the Indian Industry, Education and Governance, at all levels, alone can establish a new vision and optimism to enable us to achieve the 21 century miracles for India. In a sense, 'Future is Today' verily, therefore, Futures Networking, perhaps, is the most important need of the hour.

Nehru, Science and Future

India, in the year 1988, is busy with the Nehru Centenary Celebrations. We too join millions of Indians to remember, him, as a Futurist and a visionary.

Pandit Jawaharlal Nehru was indeed a visionary and a futurist who ardently believed that until and unless we develop Science and Technology in India, we cannot lay any sound foundations for the modern India. He once remarked, that: Science is a different way of looking at things. It takes nothing for granted and has, or ought to have, no dogmas. It seeks to encourage an open mind and tries to reach truth by repeated experiment. The Scientific method, he further adds, seems to be the only correct way of approaching a question. Science today, has lost all the arrogance and self-sufficiency which it had during the nineteenth century. It is proud of its achievements, and yet it is humble before the vast and everwidening ocean of knowledge that still lies unexplored. However, he never for a moment forgot that, "Science needs to be harnessed for the service of the nation." While addressing a convocation of Allahabad University way back in December 1947, he said," I am myself a devotee of Science and I believe that the world will ultimately be seen, if it has to be seen only by the method and approach of Science.

Pt. Nehru believed that the geographical boundaries cannot govern or restrict Science & Technology. He said: "Science and Technology know no frontiers. Nobody talks or ought to talk about English Science, French Science, American Science, Chinese Science. Science is something bigger than the countries. There ought to be no such thing as Indian Science. So also with technology. This great business of looking at these questions in a narrow nationalist way will ultimately lead to the narrowing of your technology and your work itself. This business of evolving special terms which are known neither to the general public, nor to anybody else in the wide world, really means that you are isolating yourself from the general drift of knowledge and at the same time dissociating yourself from your own people who do not understand your technical terms and thus you convert yourself into something which nobody understands and nobody cares for"

In Nehru's mind, even though Science and Technology was an international phenomenon, yet he knew that to build a new future for millions of Indians who still have much to learn and much to do, especially in the application of science to problems of social well-being in India. He, thus, observed "We have gained political freedom and the urgent task before us today is to improve rapidly the economic conditions of our people and to fight relentlessly against poverty and social ills. We are determined to apply ourselves to these problems and to achieve success. We have the will and the natural resources and the human material to do so, and our immediate task is to harness them for human betterment. For this purpose, he believed that it is essential for us to have a period of peaceful development and cooperation with other nations"

It is remarkable that he felt Science as the major contributor to cultural growth as well as becoming an instrument where, it would put an end to superstitions, rituals and dogmas. This he called as "essentially the work of scientific spirit". "The progress of Science and its offspring technology," he said, "is changing the way man thinks of himself and the world. He wanted this power to be used for the good of all, if wisdom governs action; but if the world is mad or foolish, it can destroy itself just when great advancement is within its grasp"

Thus, to Nehru the development, in the field of Science and Technology had also to be the harbinger of peace, on the one hand and the supporter of the moral standards and ethical values on the other. Referring to the advent of atomic energy, he once asked, "Are we all living in a disintegrating world, where standards have disappeared, moral values have been bidden goodbye, and the people think more and more in terms of power over nature. It is obvious that all this technological and scientific progress in the world, unless it is balanced by some kind of moral standards and ethical values, is likely to lead to destruction. That is why, we are so concerned over the basic question presented by atomic energy. Use it for evil, and it will destroy the world, use it for good, and it will raise the world to unknown standards of progress and happiness."

Finally, to Nehru, Science was also the key instrument for planning. Any country which is tradition minded in regard to various matters, including administration, he observed," is doomed in a rapidly changing world. Scientific methods by the collection of data and statistics of all kinds, help one to assess the forces in action, to watch and control them and to stop and remedy what is wrong. In fact, the scientific methods mean planning. Planning is Science in action: Planning has to be flexible; it has to be wide awake and alert. That applies not merely to the industrial process but to the administration as well." "Administration has to adapt itself to the changing phases of society" he added.

Nehru in fact, in his efforts to build a new future for India gave to it in the form or our National laboratories and through various public sector undertakings, a unique network and institutional base. He was clear in his mind that "if India has to advance it should advance with Science and Technology and India should use the latest techniques, always keeping in view no doubt, that in doing so, the intervening period, which always occurs, must not cause unhappiness or misery." He always cautioned us to be careful in choosing our future path of Science and Technology and progress. He once said, "it is no progress which brings suffering and misery in its train."

Nehru has to be remembered also because, he was conscious of the fact that a new future for the Indian people can come only through a scientific temper and the method of science. Indian advent into the atomic and electronic and space age and our later day breakthrough in Life-Sciences and Agriculture are indeed the notable achievements and the fruits of the seeds that Nehru had sown, as the architect of modern India.

Nehru's rationalistic vision, that the spirit of Science should permeate not only in the Science and Technology institutional network but in every other walk of life be it administrative or societal and cultural to save and ensure a higher quality of living standard will be a valid guideline to build further the future of India.

Nehru's remarks made at one of our Indian Science Congress' indeed reaffirms his humanistic outlook. He observed," Scientists too will have to be not merely scientists but human beings as well. This applies also to all of us and especially to those who work in the Secretariat. As a person intimately connected with the administration of the country and concerned with the welfare of the people of India, I want scientists to help me to rid the country of its poverty and ignorance and give the people the good things of life and indeed for a different future to millions of our countrymen." Let the vision of Nehru for the Future of India be achieved. Towards that goal, let our Science and Futurology and administration strive hard.

> Sometimes as I reached a gathering, a great roar of welcome would greet me: Bharat Mata Ki Jai—'Victory to Mother India'. I would ask them unexpectedly what they meant by that cry, who was this Bharat Mata, Mother India, whose victory they wanted? My question would amuse them and surprise them, and then, not knowing exactly what to answer, they would look at each other and at me. I persisted in my questioning. At last a vigorous Jat, wedded to the soil from immemorial generations, would say that it was the *dharti*, the good earth of India, that they meant. What earth? Their particular village patch, or all the patches in the district or province, or in the whole of India? And so the question and answer went on, till they would ask me impatiently to tell them all about it. I would endeavour to do so and explain that India was all this that they had thought, but it was much more. The mountains and the rivers of India, and the forests and the broad fields, which gave us food, were all dear to us, but what counted ultimately were the people of India, people like them and me, who were spread out all over this vast land. Bharat Mata, Mother India, was essentially these millions of people, and victory to her meant victory to these people. You are parts of this Bharat Mata, I told them, you are in a manner yourselves Bharat Mata, and as this idea slowly soaked into their brains, their eyes would light up as if they had made a great discovery.
>
> I felt they had vast stores of suppressed energy and ability,

and I wanted to release these and make them feel young and vital again.

Though outwardly there was diversity and infinite variety among our people, everywhere there was that tremendous impress of oneness which had held all of us together for ages past, whatever political fate or misfortune had befallen us. The unity of India was no longer merely an intellectual conception for me: it was an emotional experience which overpowered me.

—*Jawahar Lal Nehru*

Rebuilding Bureaucracy for 21st Century

From time to time efforts have been made to bring about reform in our administration which has inherited a lot from the colonial concepts of governance. Of this, the Central Administrative apparatus in India, has strictly followed the British model of Public Administration, characterised by the Functional separateness and Accountability. The first led to the portfolio system; and the second to the Parliamentary Committee System and the Audit overseeing of the policy implementation. It is common knowledge that all policy approvals do have their political bias, but the programme implementation takes place through the professional, the clerical and other operational hierarchies. Whereas in the colonial period, and the then available means of communications, could justify delays and the languid manner in which all bureaucratic functioning operated, whether at the grass-roots or at the apex level, but today, we do expect, quite the opposite values and performance standards from our Public Administrative system and its numerous agencies at all levels. Yet, another interesting contrast comes as regards the relations between the 'generalist' and the 'specialist' civil servants. Whereas in the colonial days the British philosophy of administration laid higher emphasis on keeping the 'generalist' on the 'top' and keeping the 'expert' on the 'tap'; today, there is a demand and a visible reality, whereby, the generalists and specialists, to a large extent, enjoy, equal status, even though it has not quite so happened in terms of emoluments and promotion policies and allied conditions of the career growth between the two distinct hierarchies — one encompassing the functional, professional and scientific stream, and the other retaining the generalist cadre of the successor service to the Indian Civil Service (ICS) of the British Raj in India, namely, the Indian Administrative Service (IAS). The proliferation and induction of scientists, professionals, engineers, technologists and others is not confined to the Central Government alone but in the Public Administrative system, in the States too, to a very large extent;

they too have set up various specialised cadres. Finally, notwithstanding the several administrative reforms committees and the commissions of the post- independent India, today, we, do see many visible changes in the recruitment, training, classification and placement policies. We also have a semblance of a faster socio-economic delivery system. We can, thus, count many a healthy changes. But most of them are still cosmetic in effect. We have yet to achieve many a revolutionary changes in our administrative ethos in order to strengthen people's faith in the management of public affairs. All this is needed in order to cope with the 'uncertainty' and 'complexities' of the 21st century which is now less than 4000 days away.

When it comes to count the real issues of "Management in Government" — we still hear each day, increasing noise being made concerning the role and relationship between the 'generalist' and the 'specialist. There is even a greater hue and cry for the simplifications of procedures and of the control and the coordination to gain decentralisation, delegation and Mission oriented new work environment which should be more participative than hierarchichal. An equal outcry exists for the introduction of a variety of new available office gadgetry and new means of communication, for which even though it has the wholehearted support of the top management, yet its adoption and adaptions is still tardy. This is more so, amongst the lower level staff perhaps more due to the belated advent of the word-processors and computer literacy in the public realm.

And thus as we move towards the Future, witnessing changes in the character of the State and the global environment, which are affecting the composition and role of the bureaucracies, world over, it is obvious that more remains to be done if we have to wake up to a new mood and mode of overhauling itself. This is necessary so that the bureaucracies can play a meaningful role in the development of their respective countries in the 21st century.

What kind of new changes in the functioning of the bureaucracies do we really need, particularly, when we cannot get away from the fact that both 'hierarchies' and 'bureaucracies', whether they are manned by specialists or generalists, have to co-exist. The truth of the matter is that we are passing through many a silent revolutions which are virtually affecting qualitatively the organisational men and women. First of these happens to be the Information Revolution. Today we have a hundred-fold more data and information available on any matter. Information Networking, is today, the basis of good and alert management, a dynamic executive today has to be one who has access to new information. Either this information is available to him or her readily, or, he or she should be in a position to reach that source of information as early as possible. Thus, to become an effective instrumental power, a new type of qualitative information is what the bureaucrats and any Government needs for the decision making systems. Today, all "Environmental Scanners" unanimously point out that dead data or repetitive references to the past would not give any bureaucracy the kind of thrust it needs to tackle and cope with 'today' and 'tomorrow's complexities.

The second important awakening has come from the belated recognition of the fact that events and things happen or do not happen, not merely through a linear expectation; but they have to be precipitated by working in a zone and a mode of nonlinearity. And this emerges through the system interaction be it internal or external or both. This realisation has thus heightened the importance of understanding how systems interact and behave. How they are supplanted and supplemented; and how they impinge upon other internal sub-sets; and in turn, get impacted upon by extraneous factors. In practice it has now become evident to our administrators that the policy-shifts to improve, let us say, agriculture would simultaneously also demand some policy-shifts, in its systems context — internal and external — be it in the agricultural practices or in the water and irrigation policy, the industrial and the technological policies, or for that matter, in the changes needed in the energy sector or in people's food habits and lifestyle.

We now know that Systems phenomenon happens to be a non-linear phenomenon as against the linearity of the conventional administrative ethos so characteristic of the portfolio system, where the inter-ministerial contact lies more on the surface for coordinative purposes, whether it is at the referral mode of the middle management level or at the collective thinking of the

Cabinet level. This fact makes a demand for a sea change be it in the referral procedure of the decision making process or of developing the five year plan options.

The recognition of the non-linearity in our administrative ethos, in our bureaucratic culture, can be made a meaningful input in decision making, provided we teach our bureaucrats to learn: how to understand the systems phenomenon on the one hand and how to pre-figure system dynamics for sectoral policies in terms of emerging times.

In short, this requires on their part a great deal of understanding of judging "systems turbulence" on the one hand and of a "future scanning" and "perspective delienation" on the other. All this calls for a new bureaucratic attitude, down-the-line, where decision making, is not an instrument for 'fixing' things for the moment or a mere fire fighting activity. Instead, our management has to be totally geared to the 'analytical', 'forecasting' gears. This instrumentality can help them identify the long-range perspectives. It shall also help in determining the long-range preferred goals in a given sector, thus, imparting a new realism to our planning process. All this further calls for the installation of a new functional-work culture and work ethos where decision making by bureaucracies is not a precedent (past) oriented function: but instead, it is also a consequence (Future) oriented outlook and work methodology. Obviously, this would further require a new kind of bureaucratic training, wherein selectively bureaucrats and planners are trained not merely to learn the conventional administrative 'skills' but they also get trained to learn how to think and how to determine the, "directions of change" in a given system, sector or function, besides learning to assess, in advance, the likely impact of a given decision or plan option on Man, Nature and Society?

Whereas the Indian administration took to planning much earlier than many other countries of the Third World, yet it is only recently that, in India the long-range planning and perspective development work have begun to receive a higher emphasis. Today, all public funded Governmental organisations, operating at any level, are obliged to develop their long-range perspectives. This is an important and new element in the public domain which if carried out in its logical fullness and sway, would make it necessary that the planning work pertaining to the socio-economic development should be preceded by the setting up of a new organisational group. It will act as an ongoing Management Information and Forecasting Unit. It has to be an interdisciplinary group, which can provide the Management Information Service (MIS) — and also act as Early Warning System (EWS). This group shall also act as the Think-tank in the respective sector. These groups, it is clear, would be the natural collectors and repositories of information and data (MIS). They will also be acting as a Master analysis group. They will go for modelling and simulation studies; develop sectoral future oriented scenarios against different assumptions. It is through these analytical efforts, the trend analysis, the systems, probe and the morphological studies, etc., involving the use of the tools and techniques of technology forecasting, social forecasting and technology assessment—that the non-linear considerations can get integrated, in a purposive way, to develop and enrich the emergence of qualitative plan options and alternates.

It ought to be remembered that a sound and creative perspective can emerge only from hard, on-going analytical work. A perspective plan is indeed not the cataloguing of someone's hobby horses. Nor is it a crude and hastily drawn up 'activity calender'. Perspectives have to be drawn out of hard analytical work, based on Systems probe, modelling and forecasting. Also, it is not a one-time function: it continues to be an on-going activity. We should hope that the Indian Administrative system, at all levels,will have such inputs available to it. It is indeed the need of the hour.

Many new changes in the bureaucratic organisation in the government shall come in, as fast as it accommodates in its rank classification, the elements of functionalism, specialism and wherever possible, the modern mode of classification. The hierarchichal structures, of course, shall still continue to be the backbone of the administrative pyramids for work distribution and responsibility, but a significant development, which could emerge as a mega-trend in the bureaucratic work culture, would be the emergence of 'Participative Management'. This new work-ethos demands that the command-obedience work style (a feudalistic mode), has to yield to the participative-work-style wherein the hierarchichal levels and authority shall have to consult and respect the collective thinking, unmindful of considerations of rank or pay levels. Such changes will considerably alter our conventional perceptions of authority and delegation in the decision making process. It shall also influence the recruitment, classification, training, placement and career growth norms features and practices. Foresight studies (Futurology) can help decision makers avoid surprises that the future may bring.

Historically, during the life tenure of a few thousand officers of the All India Services, namely, the Indian Administrative Service (IAS) and the Indian Police Service (IPS), the Indian Bureaucratic system at the Centre and in the States periodically shares these officers. This system has withstood the test of time. However, the Federal Government does need to ensure the success of its plans and programmes even if they be eventually implemented and handled by the State Governments. What is needed is a new coordinative thrust to ensure the speedy implementation of the developmental tasks. Does this, then demand a new bureaucratic reorganisation? Does a need exist for a new federal force. In the mid-sixties I had suggested to one of the task forces of the Personnel Administration (Chairman Sh. K. Nagarkati, ICS) of the Administrative Reforms Commission (ARC), the idea of setting up of a Federal Civil Service of India. This task force did accept the suggestion but changed the caption to "the Civil Service of India". In my writings, I had pointed out the need of Federal overseeing. In early 1980's, in the context of the implementation of the '20-point programme' too, one of my articles, published in *Yojana* of the Planning Commission, I had floated the idea of setting up of 300 Federal task forces which could facilitate and oversee the implementation of 20-point programmes. The then, Prime Minister of India, Smt. Indira Gandhi, liked this suggestions and got it implemented.

Future Images: Redesigning Women's University

In India we have five Women's Universities. Thus, we have already five different designs/alternative models of stepping up learning centres which have to have a special orientation towards helping the quality of education of the women of India.

One of these Universities was set-up before independence. It was a period when women were not supposed to step out of the house, even though any such restriction did not prevent many women from participating in the freedom struggle that India was waging against the British rule in India. Under the influence of Gandhiji, several courted arrest and went to the jails. In those days, the motivation of the Founding Fathers/Mothers—the Founders of this University *inter alia*, was to set-up an educational centre only for girls so that the parents of the young ladies who wanted to be educated could be brought to a "Safety Zone" that a Women's University could offer. It was also a period when not many women went to work. Most professions like Civil Service, Police, Engineering, Railways and others except perhaps the Medical profession, it was only men's world all the way—at home as well as outside the home.

The post-independence period saw two distinct changes. To begin with, two of the premier women's colleges, got upgraded as deemed universities.

The Fourth Women's University too has grown around a women's college. The Fifth University has been recently set-up and has to expand into new areas of learning beyond the postgraduate programmes in women's studies.

The second development, of course, is that today out of 180 odd universities of India, more than 40 universities have introduced special departments dealing with women's education and this way, it is quite on the cards, that between now and the turn of the century many more women's universities may emerge in India.

The key question to be asked here is: Are these Universities going to be a duplication of the other Universities with minor exceptions of programmes, here and there? Are these going to be exclusively for women students? Or does not a case now exist to give a new orientation to these women's universities, in terms of their charter/corporate goals/syllabus/course content, methods of 'earning and above all, for a wider reach to cater to different women clients, living both in the rural and the urban areas? And won't they go beyond the conventional subjects like the Home Science, the Nutrition education and the child-care education or the teacher training programmes for B.Ed. and M.Ed. courses?

Future Obligations

We also need to look at the imperatives of future in two ways:

Firstly, if we look at the Indian setting we have to recognise the following societal features:

(i) India is a large human system;
(ii) The poverty factor;
(iii) The unhomogeneous development of India (Agraria, Industria, Post-Industria);
(iv) Value Plurality (Whose perception? Which direction of change?)
(v) Technological plurality.

Secondly, if we look at the Futures, in terms of the mega-trends, it is apparent, that the world of tomorrow is an era of:

(i) Science and Technology;
(ii) Proliferation of the service sector;
(iii) The age of self-employment and enterpreneurship;
(iv) Greater assertion by women of their legal rights;
(v) Higher participation of women in the professions which were hitherto the preserve of men only.
(vi) The increased emergence of the participatory and activist role of women in society, as it gets visible in issues and movements, such as, the Environmental concerns (Chipko movement) and other societal concerns (Anti-Dowry and Anti-Sati movement), etc.

The key question, therefore, is to see whether a new conceptual and structural design for Women's University in the context of the above mentioned Indian-societal features and the global mega-trends all pertaining to future, should, or can help decide a new focus of learning in the Women's Universities. There are two more points which we should keep in mind:

Firstly, any new dispensation should satisfy the client of women's education, irrespective of their urban or rural background, age-group, their family income, occupational interests, etc.

Also, the new focus has to squarely meet the eternal social handicap of the dual role that the women have to play.

Secondly, we have to remember that any change in general education pattern must be evolved along with the country's planners, and fund giving bodies, whether at the Centre or in the States. They too have to think in "identical terms of changes for and towards future," that we may envisage.

The Conceptual Change

The conceptual considerations for a new thrust of a Women's University committed to the 21st century, has to be sought around the prime needs of the client. This involves many a facet pertaining to women's security considerations; both social and economic.

In a random sample opinion poll, it was found, that education for women was constantly deemed as an instrument to gain her social and economic strength. "Education is not a degree or a job. Education should give the women the confidence and give her some economic independence. Education should help her in her moments of crisis. Education should bring about to her a new awareness of her rights, particularly her legal rights. Education should take her beyond the hold of tradition. Education should help her to learn how to cope with anxiety, how to deal with people particularly with strangers, in her day to day life. If education is concerned with social change, then in the light of future, education must impart all that will help her to seek a meaningful adjustment to the emerging and all pervasive industrial culture, that shall characterise future."

One does not get much of a new insight from these views except a heightened emphasis to the well-known fact, that, in India, for a very long time to come, education's key goal remains one, where it enables women to become self-supporting. The educational programmes in its new format too will have to have a direct relationship with economic opportunities that society can offer to women in the socio-technical context. We have to ascertain what kind of new job opportunity shall hereafter, be opened to women. We have to look at the societal stratification and the societal constraints that can be eliminated or circumvented by "new education" to be imparted by the 21st Century Women's University.

The Structural Changes

If we are looking at the structural alternatives we have to do all that can make the future Women's Universities take a new, bold and non-conventional orientation even in the operational strategies. There can be several approaches here. I would advocate the following model:

(i) The future university should shed such under-graduate and postgraduate teaching that can be handled by Autonomous colleges.

(ii) The future universities should act more as a major resource centre and an apex focal point to build an all India or regional network.

(iii) These Universities should have a very large Research and Development base where they are developing new modules which can be client specific, i.e., rural, urban, occupational; science and technology orientation, etc.

(iv) It is very clear that the future women's university shall have to take recourse to distance education in all its modern format to have a wider reach and to lead to the "societal learning equity". Distance learning has to acquire a network mode and can more or less develop Indian network like that of "Commonwealth of learning" that was started in Vancouver Session of the Commonwealth Conference. As Shridath Ramphal, Secretary General, Commonwealth points out, "This is one of the biggest things the Commonwealth has ever done. Literacy in Five Years Time. A youngster in the village of Gujarat working through the Indira Gandhi Open University could be doing a commonwealth degree in accountancy or physics or whatever, pooling in all the tremendous distance learning materials that exist in the

> commonwealth using English as a working language, and, of course, using television and satellite," "This will mean," he adds, "in actual terms a tremendous enlargement of the capacity of the younger generation to get technical and vocational education. It will mean the closing in the knowledge gap"... We have seen the end of the era of campuses and concert buildings. We are entering a different era of education when we have to be very creative if we have to close the knowledge gap. If we are to bring the new information as well as add to the basic University knowledge to the new generation.

To us in India, the future implications are crystal clear."We need to link here the twenty odd metro-cities and its knowledge and learning resources with the six hundred odd villages and cater through a flexible knowledge and information menu, to millions of men and women, as they are and where they are.

Conclusion

A time has come, when campuses exclusively for women or men have to go. It is high time perhaps and creative challenge to all as to how the Women's University in future may also have programmes to educate men, who ought to learn to look at women with sympathy and concern. They need to go through an attitudinal change and to learn to better appreciate the dual role in women's life.

We have to further see that the formal and informal education mix should be designed in such a way that education to women be available in her own context and traditions on the one hand, and may enable her a higher mobility outside the conventional expectations, on the other.

Ultimately, our success will largely depend on our innovation and creative effort, with which, without sacrificing much of the pedagogical principles of yester-years, we can build new bridges and approach routes to mix the domain of formal to the domain of non-formal— and the two to the domain of being (the future). We need to have a finer appreciation of the emerging era of science and technology and its attendant societal impacts and value-shifts.

As to what such an education could be, I am tempted to offer an empirical definition, wherein, I consider: Education as a learning process that carries with it the best of the past and responds fully to the best of the future. It is a synthesis between culture and technology.

In seeking our conceptual and structural changes; we have to correlate education, society and the future. The gap between the social reality of today and tomorrow can be bridged by a future oriented education which would require three things:

(a) Change in Curricula;
(b) Change in the internal structure of the educational institutions; and
(c) Linking up of education to the external and emerging environment and community needs and aspirations (see *India the Next 7000 Days* by Satich C. Seth).

Let the new format of the Women's University be one which is capable of readjusting itself to the changing times and can offer a fulfilling experience to its four key beneficiaries (a) the individual student; (b) the society as a whole; (c) the institution of education; and above all to, (d) the teachers, educational planners, technologists, policy planners, communicators—the entire lot of the "changing educational personnel".

To Sum up

Ultimately any change will rest on how intensive our future-scanning is and how bold and imaginative we are, or can afford to become. We agree with Alvin Toffler, a futurist, who wrote. "All education springs from images of future and all education creates image of the future."

The Crumbling Pyramid

The trouble with hierarchy is not that it encompasses far too many levels within its confines. It lies in the fact that as one climbs down the ladder in an administrative pyramid, one is invariably descending from the zone of too-much-power, to almost nothingness. It certainly was a rational order, as typified in the Weberian model of bureaucracy, until the members of an organization discovered that prolonged stay at any level in a hierarchichal set-up did not automatically make its incumbent the repository of the skills and the technical know-how that, the job, so held, required of its holder. And by the same token, the rank so held, was least indicative of the incumbent's individual brilliance and potential capabilities.

That no organization, however, inventive, unstructured and free it might be, can do without some sort of hierarchichal arrangement, is a fact, that nobody can ever refute. What, however, needs a penetrating analysis, more so, in the context of India, is the questionable validity of the faith with which we have been trained here to worship and adhere to all hierarchies — social, political, administrative or legal — with almost a religious obeisance and ardour!

Of course, the reasons for such servile acceptance and semi-feudalistic organizational structuring are both social and historical. Socially, we in India have always shown respect to age, which in the administrative context, is synonymous with the length of service or seniority. Our joint family tradition where, age was given the ultimate right to take decision, must have come pretty handy to the builders of the Nineteenth century administrative set-up in India. Indeed, they firmly planted a rigid hierarchical order, which was considered as the principal guarantor of organizational discipline and administrative success. This inflexible master-servant relationship that a hierarchical set-up supported and kept alive, also blended well with the then Western style of organization in which the hierarchical roots, went deep to the military and the ecclesiastical orders, wherein the superior-subordinate relationship had acquired a visible divine sanction.

Notwithstanding all the mumbo-jumbo of hierarchy and heiratics, the fact remains that a rigid hierarchical order establishes an administrative and managerial system in which the transaction of the affairs of an organization tend to be slow and tardy. It is much-too-much command-obedience oriented and takes little, if any, notice of the professional and human relations aspect that today characterizes the management of men and the timely realization of the organizational ends. If it were only this, perhaps, we in India though, we proclaim to be a nation in hurry, could have afforded to remain supremely pleased and complacent with our pace of administrative and managerial reforms. The truth of the matter is that even though a hierarchical order alone establishes the internal administrative structure by identifying the different, levels of responsibility and work-difficulty, yet, simultaneously it also affects the entire philosophy of personnel management adopted by an organization, and the two together, that is the rigid master-servant internal set-up and the personnel philosophy which upholds such a work relationship in an organization, can precipitate certain pernicious side-effects in the management of an organization. For instance, it can breed high and low feeling in bureaucracy, create promotional blockages, give uneven power to the incumbents in a hierarchy and stultify adequate career development and professionalism. In short, if the personnel management in a given organization is conducted in terms of Douglas McGregor's Theory 'X' as opposed to Theory 'Y', it could easily kill all initiative and enterprise on the part not only of a bright and upcoming individual, but the entire bulk of the employees serving it. Such an administration will have poor standards to measure men: to punish them, if they are slack or unproductive, or, to reward them adequately for their merit. Moreover, in such traditionally run hierarchy routine and *status quo* will get perpetuated for ever.

It is here, that we can look for reasons why notwithstanding, all administrative virtuosity now sung and danced about our top heavy administrative pyramids, we are increasingly becoming aware of the steady decline in the administrative and managerial motivation and morale. We need instead to recast the existing hierarchical values which make our management practices totally insensitive to our turbulent and interdependent environment and make our work-force full of feudalistic managerial deadwood. This bureaucracy has to be rebuilt in order to prepare it to cope with the challenges of 1990's. It has to be restructured keeping in view the needs of increased specialism in management, by offering equal opportunities both to generalists, administrators and specialists on the one hand and adopting the modern management techniques where 'Management by objective' and 'Management by participation' will be the order of the day. Some of the urgent and pertinent questions before us therefore, are: How long will we run a precedent oriented machine where every executive wishes to operate in a 'zone of safety'? In short, when shall we really become achievement-oriented? Who should occupy, which job in our administrative hierarchy? Should the higher echelons in administration be allowed to become a preserve of a privileged few generalist administrators—a system inimical to the growth of specialists and technologists — in the same way, as the cult of high casteism, undermined and hurt the rest of the Hindu social order. It took us nearly a century's struggle to reorder the Indian social structure and that too with limited success. How long shall we have to wait for a change in the administrative and managerial realm? Perhaps, we can take some courage from the following radical pronouncement of Mrs Indira Gandhi, the Prime Minister of India, who while addressing a successful Engineering Graduates' Convocation, as far back as 1967, declared:

> It is odd that greatest Doctors and Engineers in the country who could be rated as the leaders of the profession and who save lives or add permanent assets to the nation, can rarely hope to receive the pay or status of Secretaries of Ministries. The brightest of our young men and women choose engineering and medicine. If they happen to go into government, they are very soon overtaken by the general administrator. This must change and I am trying to change it. The Administrative system must reflect an

individual's contribution to human welfare and economic gain.

Apparently, the aforesaid objectives have yet to be fulfilled. For in that surely lies the beginning of the crumbling of the administrative pyramid, on the debris of which alone, a modern and effective super-structure of managerial competence, can be raised.

Revitalizing Bangladesh Administration

The pattern of Public Administration in most of the developing countries has followed the structure, organisation and work-method of the government administration in the West, particularly in the United Kingdom. It is a top heavy, bureaucratic, procedure-bound and legalistic administration. It is a style of administration which is more concerned with process than with substance.

Since the developing nations are in a hurry, their administrations have to be achievement oriented. Two important factors which these administrations have to take into account are "large population" and "abject poverty". They have thus to cater to the needs of large masses and all welfare services have to be extended to a people, who do not enjoy even the bare minimum of economic security.

The administration of Bangladesh, which is another developing country, will also have to take into account these aspects apart from the fact that, in the first instance, their administration would have to bring back normalcy speedily in a turbulent society which has been devastated by an oppression of over two decades and by the recent war. Immediately, therefore, three major administrative tasks seem to face the Bangladesh government, namely: (a) The restoration of law and order administration; (b) The formulation of Crash Plans and Programmes for speedy socio-economic reconstruction; and (c) The recruitment and redevelopment of a body of dedicated civil servants through a number of training programmes.

In order to achieve quick revitalisation of administration in a relatively short time, it is necessary that the entire administrative structure and practices be reshaped. First, the policy making bodies which shall draw out plans and programmes should be compact and small instead of being hierarchy ridden monolithic departments. These policy making compact functional bodies should also directly oversee and supervise the executive agencies which would be entrusted in the respective fields—such as health, education, agriculture, etc., with the responsibility of implementing the plans in the far-flung territories of the country.

The second problem is that of developing the manpower particularly, when Bangladesh has lost so many able administrators and intellectuals. Naturally, the administration, like the 'Mukti Bahini' will have to rely on the young people to man the various administrative bodies. Here, it will be useful if the young people are given strictly occupation-oriented education in the schools and colleges. Secondly, as far as the government is concerned it should recruit very young men as 'administrative cadets' who could then be trained for governmental chores through several short-term training courses and by the work on the job. This would be an ideal and inexpensive way to cope quickly with the staffing needs.

The essential step to make administration an effective instrument of quick change, would be to encourage public participation with the administrative programmes, particularly now when the public is enthused to co-operate with the national leaders. Here what is required is the establishment of the community squads.

The community squads would be a combined task force consisting of the administrators and those people in whose areas these task forces are required to carry out welfare and other programmes.

The essential aspect to these programme-oriented community squads would be that they would not be mere bureaucratic bodies. Instead, they would be a performance-oriented and programme committed band of dedicated administrators and the concerned leaders of the community.

In order to achieve the maximum results, it would be essential that, in each district, a number of community squads should be formed. These community squads would have to be given an orientation according to the nature of the task they have to perform. For example, take the work of rebuilding of the communications. For this work, the community squads would need the services of the experts and technically trained people belonging to the concerned branches of communication, be it the construction of bridges, or the restoration of the telecommunication services.

We believe that small and compact policy making bodies directly overseeing programme execution, the recruitment and training of the young men and women as civil servants, and the increased use of 'Community Squads' as the official agent of welfare and extension of the socio-economic services, will go a long way to earn early prosperity to the young and energetic, freedom loving seventy-five million citizens of Bangladesh.

"Quality is never an accident.
It is always the result of an intelligent effort.
There must be the will to produce a superior thing."

John Ruskin

Rural Energy Policy Alternatives

Any study of the future of energy, be it for rural or urban consumer, is intimately connected with the standard of living that the people can afford. Additionally, it is also an index of a certain lifestyle in particular, and the quality of life of a society in general. In so far as energy alternatives go, there is enough thought, knowledge and corresponding technologies known. What still remains to be studied and discussed at length is the whole question of 'Management of Energy' for both the conventional and the non-conventional sources. In the Indian context, an equally unexplored area in the energy sector is the paucity of data about inter-sectoral relationships of energy, like food and energy, industry and energy, transportation and energy. We need to update both the quantitative aspect of this data on the one hand, and to develop future-related energy scenarios (sectoral and inter-sectoral) on the other. Any study of the rural energy futures will have to be based on an indepth study of the rural sociology. Such study, and the alternative energy options that they will attract, will have to be "need-based" and have to be culture and region specific.

In this connection, many points can be highlighted. Firstly, the rural energy needs attention predominantly in the following five sectors:

(1) Domestic lighting and cooking fuel needs;
(2) Agricultural needs (Irrigation, Ploughing);
(3) Small industries needs (Mechanical Power);
(4) Transportation needs (Mobility), and
(5) Community needs (Street Lighting, Drinking Water).

In so far as the average energy consumer in the rural area is concerned, the question of energy is intimately connected with the presence or the absence of poverty on the one hand, and the presence or the absence of a given technology on the other.

Examine the following facts:

(1) Whereas the world has gone through several new sources of energies (they seem to have come nearly sixty-years, internal

coal-electricity-atomic energy), the average denizen in many areas of the rural India, has remained stuck with the energy input belonging to the ancient man, using wood waste and cowdung as his prime energy source. Many a Science and Technology revolutions, including those for energy, seems to have by-passed the rural India.

(2) The other sources of energy, such as coal and electricity, touch the rural poor only marginally.

(3) 60 per cent to 70 per cent of the rural poor and the urban poor have no consumer personality; since their per day spending capacity is only Rs. 2 per head, per day to meet their basic needs for a cycle of twenty-four hours.

(4) Therefore, the rural poor, at least for their domestic needs, require energy at a "Zero-Private-Cost" basis.

(5) The question of energy cannot be divorced from the question of lifestyle—which is the product of planner's capability and response to the national resource utilization in order to meet people's aspirations.

(6) Rural people will not long accept duality in our dispensations and lifestyle. They may not have the capacity to pay, but they want the same things as an urban dweller needs. Time is not far away when they all will loudly say: (What is good enough for goose should be good enough for gander?)

(7) The energy question is to be looked at in an integrated manner. (It would be wrong to think in terms of segmented energy policies: one for the rural and the other for the urban).

Energy Policy of India presently emphasises the following elements: (See 6th Five Year Plan document).

(1) Accelerated exploitation of domestic conventional energy resources, i.e. oil, coal, hydro and nuclear power.

(2) Management of demand for oil.

(3) Energy conservation.

(4) Development and exploitation of renewable resources of energy like bio-mass to meet energy requirements of rural communities.

We need to explore new ideas to make this policy deliver tangible goods. A long-range future perspective should provide us with better plan-options to implement such a policy posture.

A new concept that needs to be debated is : Should Energy Generation be primarily a public-sector activity? And how do we work towards "Zero-Energy-Import"?

It is submitted that a success of any policy posture can be further strengthened by strengthening their allied sectors. Since a logical nexus exists here.

A. For example, if a person is employed, he has an income. If he has an income, he has a consumer personality. If he has a consumer personality, he can share the energy packet to the corresponding extent of his purchasing power.

B. Likewise, there is a direct connection between population-growth-energy-quality of life (environment, forest wealth, etc.), for example, if the demand for fire-wood is nearing the sustainable yield of local forests, even a 10 per cent increase in population and demand will lead to consumption of the resource base itself. In such situations, slowing of the population growth, though necessary and laudable, is not enough. Failing to halt population growth before the critical threshold if crossed will lead to fuel scarcities fewer hot meals, and a decline in the quality of life and as some futurists have observed "it may result in fuel famine and fuel riots.

The principle being advocated here is that the energy policy should give due importance to non-energy sectors. Much of the success in the energy sectors will directly or indirectly come from the inputs that go into non-energy (non-oil) sectors. A systems-view and analysis is absolutely essential.

Implications of Future

Future scanning in the Indian context indicates two possible scenarios: (1) Marginal change scenario, and (2) Optimum change scenario. (See Appendix A).

We should opt for the latter. In optimum change scenario, we: (a) make quantum jump into future and (b) try to turn our population into a resource. If the rural India can skip a few generations and has the skills and ability to participate in the production process, "as they are, where they are". This can help alter the Rural energy perspective.

To give a meaningful energy future to the rural or the urban poor, we must first work to turn population into a resource. To this end, we need to develop many scenarios and policy alternatives. An illustrative suggestion is to develop a Power-grid as given in Table 1 below:

TABLE

A POWER-GRID WHICH CAN TURN INDIA'S POPULATION INTO A RESOURCE AND A POWERFUL NATION

Food and Water	for	Physical Power
Communications	for	Skills and Intellectual Power
Nuclear and other sources of Energy	for	Mechanical Power
Management	for	Organising Power

On a priority basis, India should concentrate and plan intensively for the key-sectors of this Power-grid, giving them funding weightage. (25 per cent more to these four sectors over and above other sectors). Besides, as far as it is possible, the plan schemes of other sectors should be built around these four sectors to reinforce the fullest realisation of the Power-grid. In these four sectors we should also make a quantum jump in choosing our technology.

It is submitted that once we opt for the best available technology in the world, and, on a selective basis, even take to "tomorrow's technologies" today (technologies which essentially belong to the post-industrial society), it should be possible for us to respond to the needs of a larger segment of our society in a relatively shorter time. Our efforts in space, to cater to India's communications and educational needs is a case in point.

The development forces unleashed by this grid can help turn our population into a resource. It shall create work opportunities for our people "as they are, where they are". It shall thus liberate them, to a large extent, from the grinding and dehumanising poverty that still keeps crippled, the life of more than 60 per cent of the Indian population.

In the context of management of rural energy futures, the following concrete recommendations emerge:

(1) We need to work for need-based energy planning. The technologies response will have to be a combination of various

systems. Wherever possible we should "leap-frog" into future, skipping traditional steps of technological development in the energy sector.

(2) To achieve a meaningful energy future for the rural sector, we need to introduce both sophisticated and less sophisticated technology sub-systems into the socio-economic and cultural system of the village. This should be done in a phased manner. It should further be backed-up by the local (district or block) Energy Maintenance Centres.

(3) Finally, in the short-term, our aim should be to augment the rural energy dispensations, at least, in the domestic cooking fuel sector in a way as to provide to millions of people, domestic cooking fuel at near "zero-private-cost-energy" basis.

(4) The managerial and management aspects in the energy sector need further research in the: (a) socio-organizational (b) the horizontal transfer of technology, and in (c) Lifestyle and energy nexus. (Are we managing lifestyle or energy?)

(5) Energy sector deserves an indepth long-range futuristic planning based on sectoral and inter-sectoral systems analysis besides introducing Anticipatory Management.

(6) Choices for the next 1825 days (7th Plan) should be based on scientific future scanning of the next 7,000 days.

Performing Arts: Some Emerging Issues

In most culture, the passage of time, vitally affects the tradition and mode of cultural and creative expression, recognised as the performing arts, as this heritage, gets passed from one generation to another.

The classical tradition of the Performing Arts in India has to some extent retained its own colour and durability. Our dance and music in particular do reflect an unbroken continuity which people rightly like to see in its purity. However, one cannot rule out the fact that even if such a tradition has sprung from the people, today it serves only the elite and, in particular, only a minority in the society both urban and rural (mainly Southern or South-Eastern).

The classical tradition in dance, drama and music has already undergone a considerable change in many ways. Firstly, the social strata which provided artists before, has now changed for the better in as much as today, well-to-do sections of the society do not consider their daughters or sons partaking in Performing Arts, as something demanding. In fact, the so-called well-to-do families today encourage their children to take to theatre, dancing or music. By exception the meritorious amongst them are even permitted to pursue this art as a life long career.

The mode of patronage, however, has since altered. The patronage that earlier came from the princely courts and landed aristocracy, today, comes from the departments of culture, State academics and the business houses—and to a very limited extent from the people.

The drill of getting to the "Stage" too has changed. A performing artist today has to first seek for an adequate platform which means two things : (a) either seek the patronage of some organisations, or (b) arrange a programme on one's own resources and strength. This would then mean collection of funds either from an 'Academy' or from a 'Business House'; that too if one has good connections or one is lucky. One has then to hire a hall, print a souvenir and run around to collect advertisements for the souvenir; take several steps towards publicity; collect further funds to pay the accompaniants; arrange volunteers for the days of performance, and so on.

In essence, it means that if you cannot get patronage of an official agency, you have to then go to a business house and their cultural societies or PRO's who do not hesitate to use the artist and the occasion of the performance for advertising their products, which can range from Horlicks to cigarette. And finally, if you are lucky and have the right connections, you need to get a VIP/a Minister to grace the occasion. Not to mention that such a drill is not a very satisfying an exercise. Far from it, it is a torture — a vicious and painful experience indeed. Now do we have a State mechanism or a National Centre for Performing Artists, where every budding artist has a chance to present his or her creative effort? Also, do we have a policy to eliminate the dominance of senior artists in sharing the State's patronage. Performing arts need not be equated to horse racing where all bets are laid only on a few.

The character of performing arts is, however, changing world-over. And thus all artists must grasp. Today, art has moved from solo performance to an orchestra or to a mode of many artists performing together presenting an eye-filling spectacle. Individualism has yielded place to pluralism. The eye of the audience now gets filled by a creative stage which communicates with the audience with enhanced communication as it emits out of a fuller stage — as against soloists. Much of this has, undoubtedly, been achieved through technology and the emergence and use of the contemporary themes. In such a changed context, if we now go to a programme, we sometimes see a dancer, who undoubtedly is a great artist in her own rights, who has full command not only over the "Shastra" of her dance, but is still busy in depicting the "Makhan Chori" through traditional "Abhinaya". Perhaps, artists can today use their artistic strength to portray more modern themes. Additionally, on a huge stage, such an artist (the soloist) is now no more affecting a thrilling spectacle for the eye. In fact, sometimes it is even noted that the accompaniant musician creates far more powerful an impact on the audience, as much as that, it makes the dancer play the second fiddle. Though good musicians, as soloists, have, however, still, a place of their own.

In fact, Indian performing artists have yet to learn and grasp the advancement, made in the field of technology, as it is related to the Performing arts. They do not know how to reinforce their art to the maximum advantage both for the organisers and artists on the one hand and for the satisfaction on the other.

Enjoyment of Performing arts apart, one feels very concerned for the future of classical Indian music/or dance or theatre in terms of its relationship with people and society. Whereas the society is changing so fast, our performing arts have not yet related themselves to it well: the classical tradition is becoming somewhat exclusive; as if it is only for a 'few'. And also to be given to and enjoyed by a 'few'. And, likewise, the folk tradition has also been somewhat exclusive. Such a situation is not what one could call rational—in its all pervasive sense. One does not yet see a meeting ground between these two traditions all over the country in a way whereby this richness and beauty becomes integral to an average Indian's listening experience and appreciation.

Undoubtedly, Radio has done a lot and, perhaps, to some extent even the films have taken part in the spread of our musical heritage to our people. But a few programmes held here and there and that too at such a cost do not satisfactorily meet the real creative needs of our people and society.

The second anxiety is the inadequacy of the education in the performing arts in India. When we look at our society, particularly our children and young people's interest and training needs in performing arts, whereby they could first acquaint themselves with the best of the classical and the folk tradition and, secondly, if they have aptitude and creative talent, they could partake in acquiring the excellence that lies behind the rendering of either classical or folk music.

Administrative Image and Gigoism

Through many decades of British rule, the millions of this country had come to fear and respect the administration. They looked upon it also as the main source of their hope and happiness. Though a new vista of development and progress opened with independence, raising expectation of overall prosperity, citizens today have started doubting if the administration has all the capacity it needs to deliver the goods of welfare. Now and then the critics say that, with respect to administrative efficiency, a point has been reached where both the governed and the governors should take a timely note of it.

What exactly is the nature of this doubt? We are told that it manifests itself in many ways. It can be seen in the all-round inefficiency in the various administrative bodies, such as the railways, the customs, the public health agencies, the taxation machine, and the posts and telegraphs. In fact, all these departments which have to deal with the people, which by the nature of their organisation offer public utility services, whether they are helping with respect to transport, electricity or milk bottles, there is a consensus of opinion, according to which, not everything is well with the performance of such agencies. Very often it is the individual frustration that actually goes to blur the good image of these bodies.

People blame the administration sometimes for valid reasons, but mostly because they have no one else to blame. The administration somehow becomes an easy target of public condemnation. Today, the country has more schools and colleges than ever before; more roads, railways, and health facilities; and notwithstanding the state of unemployment in which sixty-thousand qualified engineers find themselves, even greater job opportunities. And yet in all these, something is lacking. Railways are overcrowded, milk supply is scarce, malaria has raised its naked head once again. Advancements in science and technology have taught that these are emergencies which can be taken care of by timely and imaginative administrative measures. And yet, misery, deprivation and death start taking their toll, droughts recur leading to near famine conditions, like God's wrath.

With roads developing deeper hollows, electricity failures becoming more frequent, traffic accidents continuing to increase, insanitation growing worse each day, this is the time for the nation and its leaders in every walk of life—political, commercial and administration—to reflect seriously and urgently what has gone wrong, with whom, and how? When people, both literate and illiterate, suffer under the cruel bludgeoning of the rising costs of living, when the number of jobless swells by thousands, it is not unnatural if, the people begin to wonder, if anything like a welfare state really exists. And under such circumstances it is the supreme responsibility of one and all, to improve the administrative image, since the experience of other country reveals that blurred administrative image is an open invitation to chaos and anarchy.

The image cannot be restored by a mere survey of administrative measures already taken, or by initiating a few far reaching reforms in new fields. It introduces a much bigger task. To make the nation one homogenous whole, and carry it together with the help of various administrative and other means to achieve progress and welfare sooner than the public has come to expect, requires, the building up of a national apparatus, as much as keeping it in full operational trim. It is, thus, a question of continuous measurement. Administrative image is but a reflection of the nation's adherence to standards. And this applies both to the public as well as to the private sector.

It is not all cynicism if, we are told, that today, the Indian administration, at all levels, has been lacking the sophisticated instruments of measuring men, matters and performance. Even the top political leaders have admitted so, at least in their private and some times, in not so private utterances. The Indian society needs yardsticks badly because by the very nature of the people's cultural attitude it is more prone to accommodation. We accommodate everything. We have accommodated both good and bad, perhaps more of 'bad' than of 'good'. Measurement, therefore, alone can show what steps we should take to convert the 'bad' into 'good' and how can we reject mercilessly what is rubbish and garbage.

Good administrative image, therefore, is the product of various factors, of which the most important is the process of rejuvenating men and material. This image could be built through education. Thus, the real need is to install instruments of training and testing. We must have only such people as administrators, who have received training for their jobs, who know what to do and how to do it efficiently. The administration would suffer greatly if it does not introduce this twin system of training and testing from top to bottom. If we do not do this we shall simply be turning 'garbage in and garbage out', and indulging in the wasteful exercise of "GIGO" to use the abbreviated term. That is how computer works. It gives back what it is fed with. If we feed it with garbage it will give us back only garbage. Therefore, the lesson is manifest. If we with to improve the image of the Indian administration, we must try and escape from gigoism. We are certain that our people do have the strength to do so.

Rebuilding Bureaucracy: The British Style

The Fulton Committee's Report on the reorganisation of civil service in Whitehall has narrowly missed being branded as an organised tirade against the cult of amateurism which makes the Whitehall tick ! In the process of calling a spade a spade, it has earned for itself an enviable position amongst all those Royal commissions which the British government had, during the last couple of centuries, set-up to suggest administrative reform. The pith of the Fulton Committee's report lies in a sound and familiar but little practised advice: "The Service must continuously review the tasks it is called on to perform; it should then think out what new skills and kinds of men are needed and how these men can be found, trained and deployed". This is as good a principle as any. In so far as it constitutes an administrative aphorism, it is also a universal touchstone with which every administrative performance and innovation could be tested. Then again, the Fulton Committee's recommendation to replace the various classes by a single unified grading structure covering all civil servants from top to bottom and all non-industrial workers in the British service, is not only admirable but is verily a bold and imaginative step forward. It will be futile to lament that here American influence has been involved. It is obvious that national and scientific attitudes do not brook national barriers. What, perhaps, is surprising, is that Britain should have woken to the need of `job evaluation' and of `development of greater professionalism both amongst specialists and administrators' now. While, to take the commonwealth countries, Canada, way back in 1919, has already taken the first few preliminary steps in this direction. If anything, these steps should have been taken up in Whitehall a long time ago. It would be begging the question to ask if Fulton Commission's recommendations have any relevance to the task of remodelling bureaucracy in India. Perhaps in no field has the British and Indian history profited from each other's experience more than in the field of public administration. And this is as true in the time of Fulton as it was in the days of Macaulay. It would be wrong to anticipate the administrative innovations which the Indian Administrative Reforms Commission has thought of to renovate the civil service structure bequeathed to India by the British. But, if there are some lessons to be learnt from the Fulton Report, then, our reformers would do well to pay attention to two simple facts: civil service reform calls for hitting the nail at the head of the vested interests who keep themselves well protected under the myriad of rules and regulations; secondly, it ought to be based not only on sound `research' and `perspective projections' but in order to succeed, it needs to be progressed with the full support of politicians as well as of the civil service without much palaver from either side.

> We argue about public and private enterprise. The real fact of the matter is that its success comes from the efficient administrator whether in the public or private enterprise, like dubbing public or private does not make much difference except in the consequences and the outlook. But the actual thing depends on the administration of that enterprise.
>
> *Jawaharlal Nehru*

I do not envisage a necessary antithesis between business and bureaucracy either in respect of their attitudes or interests. In the context of Indian economic development properly conceived, their functioning ought to be mutually supporting even when their roles are not similar as indeed they are over a large area.

S.G. Barve

Let Government remove a whole host of controls and regulations; let the few that must be retained because of shortages, such as foreign exchange, be simplified, so that they can be operated smoothly and swiftly; let Government take a few calculated risks instead of attempting the impossible task of plugging all loopholes; let Government not overlook the simple fact that patriotism and honesty are not the monopoly of any section of class of the people and are to be found amongst all professions.

H.M. Patel

Working out a Top Man's Bonus

Top Man's Bonus =

$$\text{Achievement Bonus} + \text{\% Salary Qualifying}\left[\left(\frac{\text{Service Provided}}{\text{Budgeted Service}}\right)\left(\frac{\text{Budgeted Cost}}{\text{Actual Cost}}\right)-1\right]$$

When Merrett and White contrived the above formula as a sequel to their analysis of Incentive Payment System, they little thought that the modern taxation system for the high bracket income can make a nonsense of any kind of top level income. However, the substance behind this apparent mathematics is a simple administrative maxim that : `Any system of management remuneration which is not, in effect, highly performance related, must be one in which inadequate executives are overpaid and exceptional executives underpaid'. Their main premise is equally pertinent in that administrative costs with respect to categories such as, advisory head office departments, accounting, personnel, etc., ought to be controlled according to well-defined standards, this being the essential prerequisite of determining any bonus system. Clearly, costs as large as the profit margin itself cannot be left to be determined by chance or unsystematized initiative on the part of the individual executive. Notwithstanding the size of the company, it sounds reasonable that administrative costs need not remain a neglected entity in cost control and thus there are good and sufficient reasons to design Performance Related Remuneration Systems (PRR). Amongst other things, it is bound to secure high levels of efficiency, particularly in this cost area.

The latent element of this familiar management philosophy eventually boils down to an increasing use of 'Efficiency Audit' on the one hand, and a consideration of, 'Specific Duties' of all employees irrespective of the level at which they are operating, on the other. The work of any Managing Director would not, therefore, be beyond measurement. If he is able to maintain a high level of 'profit-oriented efficiency' in all the functions of the company, and if he could raise the level of efficiency of the Company to some new high standards, surely, in doing so, he is performing well, the Chief Executive's responsibility of bringing about a consistent improvement in the company's earnings per share. In general, if earning per share fails to improve, the share price of the company will either remain at a highly unsatisfactory level or fall. And possibly, it has been suggested, other board members and support staff, who are generally not covered by bonus payment scheme related to their functional performance might as well be given a percentage of salary equal to some multiple of the improvement in earnings per share.

Whether or not, such an arrangement gets accepted, the merit of developing objective criterion of performance—in the light of outside experts or directors—is essentially the touchstone of both good management and something basic to the shareholder's interest's, who would then not object to give their executives, the option of taking their bonus in the form of capital.

In so far as this formula is concerned, it is supposed to determine the bonus for particular administrative functions. Here, "the achievement bonus" is the bonus (as a percentage of base salary) which would be appropriate to the executive simply attaining the budgeted profit or cost standard he has been set for the year. The level of this bonus would be decided on when, the year's budget is first accepted, and should depend on the extent to which the bonus is thought of as representing an exacting standard of achievement. Thus, a highly demanding budget might qualify for a bonus of 20 per cent while a merely acceptable budget would qualify for a bonus of only 10 per cent. The formula also has a straightforward cost element, the ratio of "budgeted" to "actual" cost of providing the administrative services in question.

The other criteria of performance, "service provided", divided by "budgeted service" is inevitably to a degree subjective. But it should be based on an annual numerical rating by the departments concerned. For example, the personnel function should be rated by the heads of major departments so that "satisfactory" level of service (having regard to the budgeted standard) would represent 100 per cent, or 1 in the context of the above formula. All this constitute its mechanics. The world of 'practicels' is, however, a far cry from the world of `theory'. But every good theory has its field day too. If, for no other reasons, than for this above, the Indian businessmen and public sector enterprise Directors, can pay some attention to this provocative thought without losing anything, anyway.

Administration Swedish Style

The fact that Sweden is a small country of eight million has not dampened the enthusiasm of other countries in accepting some of the administrative innovations which started first here. It has surprised the Swedish people to find the institution of Ombudsman, which has existed with them for over a few decades now, as the most popular abroad. They never even once thought that it could be an exportable commodity.

The smallness of the country should not, therefore, diminish the need for a study of the working of the Swedish administration in some details. It has both familiar and unfamiliar sides to it. Sweden is as good a parliamentary democracy as any. It accepts the notion of a Cabinet Government and that of parliamentary accountability. Its administration is well regulated by law and is conducted in the 'full light of public'.

There are some oddities as well which curiously enough have been the strong points of Swedish administration. One such notable characteristic is the 'Fact of Legal Security' whereby not only the courts but also administrative agencies are open to safeguard the rights of private citizens as well as the rights of the States. The Ombudsman acts as the arch guarantor thereof.

Secondly, in its personnel policy, the 'security of tenure', is guaranteed by the Constitution itself, and, in practice, it is maintained far beyond it. Even the highest officer, who could be constitutionally removed 'at will' by Government, will almost invariably retain his position even if he finds himself opposed to the wishes of the Minister concerned or to the whole of Government. This relationship between politics and administration may apparently look odd to an outsider but the Swedish experience clearly indicates that the administrative policy and the general political policy can both work well to realise the goals of welfare, even if it has to be independent of each other.

Once general principles have been expressed, they have to be applied by autonomous organs freely and the political heads are thus not concerned with the day to day administrative decisions. The Swedes don't get a shock to find that sometimes their public servant can even be a Member of Parliament sitting in opposition to the Government. Whereas this may not be a thing worthy of being implemented in India yet, near total non-interference from politicians in day-to-day administration certainly merits some notice.

One of the fundamental principles of administration in Swedish system lies in the duty of all public agencies to cooperate directly without necessarily passing through a common superior. This practice is even embodied in the Constitution itself and in actual fact, it is applied daily. How lucky can we be in India if, administrative cooperation and inter-agency coordination, could be brought to work here at all levels of administration, more as part of one's administrative habit and not as a reflex to administrative compulsions.

Perhaps, the important point for us would not lie in the form of government but in the nature of administrative behaviour. Whereas it would be irrelevant in our system to encourage civil servants to start disagreeing with the ministers, except where public interest explicitly demands an expression thereof, yet the Swedish practice, which makes both the politicians and the civil servants totally accountable to the people, does call for a serious probing on our part. This is in fact is the essence of true democracy. As a practical step, we could also take a good look at their administrative custom, whereby, all official documents are open to public for inspection except what can be called working material, in use during the preparation of a decision. Nobody has to show cause why he wants to see a public document. Perhaps, if this cannot be made possible with respect to the internal documents of the Central and the State Governments in India, at least, the working of the city governments in this country can be carried out in full and complete public gaze of every citizen. It is worth considering if, under certain circumstances, the people in India, should not likewise have a right to inspect the official records of the local administration?

To Public Services

"We should root out the former mentality, according to which the be-all and end-all service was to earn money and feed fat".

Mahatma Gandhi, on the eve of Independence of India.

"Tomorrow's India will be what we make it by today's labours. I have no doubt that India will progress industrially and otherwise; that she will advance in science and technology; that our people's standards will rise, that education will spread and health conditions will be better, and that art and culture will enrich people's lives. We have started on this pilgrimage with strong purpose and good heart and we shall reach the end of the journey, however, long that might be".

Jawaharlal Nehru

APPENDIX - B-I

Introduction of Future Studies in the Indian Educational System

The Modular Draft Syllabus for M.Phil/ M.Tech Course Drawn up by the UGC. Expert Committee (1988)

The Department of Science and Technology of the Government of India is the nodal ministry for the item 'Futurology'. Recognising the importance of introducing Futurology in the educational system in India, a few years ago, the Department of Science and Technology had set-up a committee under the Chairmanship of Dr Madhuri Ben Shah with the author as its member secretary. The committee recommended that, at all appropriate levels, the study of the 'futures' should be introduced. In response to this report the University Grants Commission requested all Universities in 1986 to reflect their interest in this subject integral to their Seventh Five Year Plan Profile. Recently, the UGC has once again requested a select number of universities, who have since evinced interest in this subject, to give details of the syllabus/course content, etc., with which they wish to introduce 'futurology' in their respective Universities and the affiliated colleges. Presently, it has been noticed that futurology can be introduced without taking recourse to any major institutional change, as electives and at the M.Phil level. Also future related fullfledged papers can be introduced in any given subject. Besides, it is also possible for some Universities, who have already acquired an 'inter-disciplinary system' to set-up either a School on Forecasting and Perspective Planning or, a

Centre of Futures Studies, or Futurology or that of Forecasting and Anticipatory Management, etc.

In 1987, under the auspices of the Department of Science and Technology, the Government of India has also set up the Technology Information Forecasting Assessment Council (TIFAC)—an agency, which besides technology monitoring will also carry out itself or shall sponsor research studies in technology forecasting and technology assessment. Moreover, the Prime Minister of India has also directed all the organisations, within the Indian Public Funded System, to draw up their respective perspective plans for a period of 20 years. Thus, today, a new demand has emerged in India, to provide for education and training programmes in the field of futures studies, technology forecasting, technology assessment and the long range perspective planning and anticipatory management—a concept coined by the author to interest Indian Industry in technology forecasting and futures studies.

Recognising this national need to introduce futures studies at the appropriate level, the University Grants Commission of India had set-up, early last year (1988) an expert group, of which the author also happened to be a member. This group, has now developed a Modular Curricula which has since been circulated by the UGC to all universities and the autonomous colleges, who can now pick and choose the appropriate module, and, if need be, alter it to best suit to their local requirement. This draft syllabus for M.Tech/M.Phil is as given below:

One year Postgraduate Course-Draft Syllabus for M.Tech/M.Phil

A Model Curricula for Future Studies

(Prepared by the University Grants Commission Expert Committee)

M. Tech. (Futures Studies) : 3-Semester Programme: 50 Credits

M. Phil. (Futures Studies) : 2-Semester + Summer Programme: 42 Credits

Semester 1 (15-16 Weeks): (Common for M. Tech/M. Phil)

1.1. Introduction to Futures Studies: Concepts, Techniques, Research Methods and Applications: 3 Credits (3-0-0).
1.2. Systems Analysis and Methodology: 3 Credits (3-0-0).
1.3. Data Processing and Computation: 3 Credits (2-0-2).

1.4. Technological Forecasting and Technological Assessment: 3 Credits (3-0-0)

1.5. Elective: 3 Credits (3-0-0)

- 1.5.1. Study of Indian Futures-Rural Development
- 1.5.2. Urban Society-Future Trends
- 1.5.3. Population Growth: Future Scenario
- 1.5.4. Industrial Futures
- 1.5.5. Social Futures
- 1.5.6. Econometrics and Economic Forecasting
- 1.5.7. Social Research Methods

1.6. Minor Project 1:2 Credits (0-0-4) (Field Oriented)

Total: 17 Credits
(20 hours)

1.1 Introduction to Futures Studies: Concepts, Techniques, Research Methods and Applications: 3 Credits (3-0-0)

Futurology— Its meaning and scope; Technology;

Forecasting— Social Forecasting; Technology Assessment.

Concept of Future; Characteristics of future; Lifestyles; Analysis; System analysis; Social Accounting; Social dynamics; Social change studies on Future; The future of the futures; The use of futures studies.

EWS (Early Warning System)—Threats and Opportunities; extrapolative and normative futures.

Types of Scenarios— Business, Moderating enhanced (Energy or Quality of Life) Scenario, National Socio-economic Development Scenario - Seth Harva Method : A Scenario Building Methodology; Uses of Scenario Writing.

Methodology for Futures Scanning

1. Brain Storming
2. Trend-Extrapolation
3. Delphi
4. Simulation Modelling
5. Cross Impact Analysis
6. Scenario Building

Management of change— Future oriented management planning; Specification of goals and specification of Plans; Long-range planning; Strategic planning; Corporate strategic planning; Corporate goal setting; Generating alternative.

Research-Philosophy and Meaning; Need for scientific research; Approaches to research; Interdisciplinary, trans-disciplinary, multidisciplinary; Trends in research in Social Sciences.

Identification of the fields and sub-fields, themes, problems of study.

Concepts; hypothesis; theory; law-role of models.

Statement of the problem, topic, formulation of hypothesis; testing of hypothesis; methods of testing.

Research Design—Collection of data; Sources of data; Primary data; Secondary data; Structuring the data; Data transformation and maps, charts; Diagrams and tables; Planning for thesis; maps and diagrams.

Sampling Techniques

Simple quantitative techniques used to analyse the data; Co-efficient of Correlation; Regression, Linear Programming; Component analysis.

Library research-Bibliographical cards; Glossary; Appendix, etc.

Thesis writing-Language-Presentation-Chapterization-Review of works done in the field-Review of books and journals.

Project-Proposal; Budgeting; Staff pattern; Report writing; Presentation of research papers; Presentation in the Seminar and Symposium; Abstract of synopsis writing.

1.2 System Analysis and Methodology: 3 Credits (3-0-0)

Overview of Art of Systems Analysis

Introduction to general concepts in systems; Definition of systems, subsystems, general systems approach; Organism, analogy and vitalism; The nature of general system laws and various schools of thoughts; General, physical mathematical system theories; An outline of the approach to general system theory; Concepts, definitions, classification and system perspective; Computer aided planning systems; Introduction to information theory and cybernetics; Law of medium numbers; Law of requisite variety.

Methodology of Systems Analysis

Methodological framework for systems engineering, value system design. Comparison and evaluation of alternative frameworks for decision making such as investment analysis, cost-effectiveness analysis, multiattribute impact assessment.

Techniques of Systems Analysis

Modelling techniques-interpretive structural modelling; system dynamics; econometric models; input-output models; physical systems modelling for joint scale systems via component-to-subsystem-to system modelling techniques; transfer functions and state variable models; linearisation of non-linear state equations. Response evaluation of linear continuous time and discrete time systems.

Qualitative Analysis, Synthesis and Design

Stability, sensitivity, controllability and reliability of linear time-invariant systems; Forecasting techniques; Synthesis and design techniques; Optimization technique; Performance index; Optimization without and with constraints; Linear programming; Dynamic programming; Experimental and simulation techniques; Illustrative examples from different disciplines and publications.

1.3 Data Processing and Computation: 3 Credits (2-0-2)

Basic components in computers and data processing. Remote control/communication systems; Data-entry/Information response, Information devices; Storage, Computer systems and application software; Programming process and long-waves; Structured-design concepts; Systems analysis and design tools; Data processing through COBOL; Elements of a chosen high level programming language (FORTRAN/TASCAL/S), and numeric and non-numeric computation in that language.

1.4 Technology Forecasting (TF) and Technology Assessment (TA): 3 Credits (3-0-0)

The Need for Technology Forecasting

The rapidly changing technological scene and the need for competitiveness; The normative approach to developmental planning and the role of TF in it; TF as a tool for social strategy; TF as a tool for corporate strategy; Stages of innovation; TF for research and developmental planning. Brief history of TF.

Methodologies of Forecasting

Extrapolation Methods: Linear extrapolation, Exponential Extrapolation, Growth curves, Envelope curves, Trend correlation, Substitution techniques, Regression methods, other methods for time series data analysis.

Intutive Methods: Opinion-polls and surveys, panels, brainstorming, Delphi and its variants, scenarios.

Delphi: Advantages and disadvantage of Delphi; The Delphi Procedure; How to frame the Delphi Questionnaires; Precision and reliability of Delphi. Selecting of panel members; Guidelines for conducting a Delphi. Computer-interactive Delphi.

Scenarios: Generation of scenarios; advantages of the scenario methods; Individual variations; Integration of scenarios with other methods; Evaluation of scenarios.

Disaggregation Methods: Check-lists, matrices, relevance trees, morphological analysis, cross-impact analysis.

Computer Modelling Techniques: Simulation models, structural models, hierarchical models, etc.; Sensitivity analysis for models.

Other Methods: Technology Monitoring, Dimensional analysis, networks and casual loops; Forecasting for breakthroughs.

Combinatorial Methods for Forecasting

Technology Assessment: Basic Features Assessment Objectives—Validity, Utility. Types of assessment. Distinction between TA and other studies; Distinction between TA/ETA; Types of TA/TIA/Other Impact Studies; TA as a map for alternate futures; TA as an educational tool; TA as an adversary tool.

Components of an Assessment: Problem Definition; Technology Description; Technology Forecast; Social Description; Social Forecast; Impact Identification; Impact analysis; Impact evaluation; Policy analysis and options; Communication of results.

Bounding an Assessment: Areas for Bounding; The Bounding micro-assessment.

Analytical Strategies: Process and content dimensions; Selection of Techniques.

The Technology Delivery Systems: Components, linkages, indicators, impacts.

Environmental Impact Analysis (EIA): Procedural Issues; Substantive Issues; Identification of ecological parameters/Land/Air/Water/Noise/Radiation/Other; System Linkages.

Social Impact Analysis: Identification of Impacted population/interested parties; Social Impact Parameters: e.g. in health, living standards, lifestyle; Cultural impacts; Psychological impacts; Community values; Religious, Historical and other interests; Construction of Social Impact Profile.

Limitations of Technology Forecasts and Assessments: Some common forecasting errors; Limitations of the techniques; Core assumptions; Environmental and personal factors; The human factor; The need for multiple perspective and an integrated approach.

Presenting the Results: Who are the users? What do they need? Credibility and usefulness of the forecasts.

Case Studies and Examples of TF and TA.

1.5 Elective : 3 Credits (3-0-0)

1.5.1 *Study of Indian Futures-Rural Development*

1. Modern trends in the caste structure. Caste Relations-Present and future. Impact of social legislation relating to caste in the future society. Rural women: Their status in 21st century. Changing patterns of family.
2. Land ownership. Future of Agriculture labour-Impact of technology in rural areas-Land reforms.
3. Rural Administration: Patterns of rural administration in 21st century. Forecasting the rural factionalism for future.
4. Rural Education. Future Social constraints on education. Impact of adult education and functional literacy for future. Pattern of education for future.
5. Rural Health: Techniques and tools to improve health and sanitation in villages. Mode for better rural health. Means and ways to decrease epidemic and communicable diseases. Ways to increase health knowledge.

1.5.2 *Urban Society: Future Issues*

1. *Basic Concepts*— Urbanism, Ruralism and 'urbanism'. Future urban society. The relationship between urbanization and industrialisation in the future society.
2. *Structure and Growth of Indian Societies*— Trends of growth of Indian cities (Intensive study of one metropolitan city).
3. *Urban Planning*— Long-range urban plans, Determinants of effective implementation of planning.
4. *Urban Characteristics*— Future characteristics of Indian cities. The relationship between different institutions. Neighbourhood relations.
5. *Urban Problems*— Future trends of urban work, unemployment, urban recreation, housing, health problems, problems of transportation and communication in urban area.

1.5.3 *Population Growth: Future Scenario*

1. *Optional*— Nature, Scope and importance of study of social demography. Role of population in future society. A comparative study of population and machine.
2. *Population Theories*— Malthusian theory and Post-Malthusian theories. Application of these theories in the future society.
3. *Components of Population*
   (a) *Fertility*— Impact of biological, social, psychological and Economic factors on fertility. Future trends.
   (b) *Mortality*—Health and mortality levels infant and maternal mortality. Changing patterns and future trends.
   (c) *Marriage*—Age at marriage, Widowhood and Divorce in future.
   (d) *Migration*—Impact of internal migration in future society.
4. *India's Population Planning.*

1.5.4 *Industrial Futures*

1. Industrial Sociology in 21st Century.
2. Industry and the process on industrialisation in India. Industrial expansion. Industrial consequence. Industry as a major force of social change.
3. Work and leisure. The place of work in the future society. Leisure and its role in the coming society.
4. The industrial organization. Formal and informal organization. Management of industries in the future society.
5. Labour Relations in industry. Future trends in Absenteeism, Industrial disputes, etc. Labour problems.

1.5.5 *Social Futures*

1. *Caste*— Traditional caste system. Changing caste patterns, emerging patterns.
2. *Tribes*— Tribal India. Problems of Tribes, Social legislations. Future of tribes in India.
3. *The family*— Hindu joint family, it's characteristics. Disintegration of joint family. Nuclear family. Future of family as an institution in India.
4. *Marriage*— The Hindu view of life. Hindu marriage. Modern trends in marriage. Marriage as a social institution in the next century.
5. *The Village Community*—Organization, structure and changing role of villages. Polity and economy for future rural India.

1.5.6 *Econometrics and Economic Forecasting*

Transfer of indicators and forecasting techniques of social processes. Problems of adoption and validation trend. Projections versus discontinuous forecasting, development of alternative scenarios. Historical (retrospective) or prospective projections. Dynamic models.

1.5.7 *Social Research Methods*

Concepts and indices. Analytical and formal aspects. Hypothesis formulation and testing strategies. Design of applied empirical research. Measurement and interpretation of social data. Social statistics (non-parametric).

Note: Different Institutions desirous of introducing Futures Studies at any level can pick all or a few "Modules", of this curricula which is flexible and only illustrative in character.

M. Tech Semester-II (15-16 Weeks)

II.1 Science, Technology, Society and Futures: 3 Credits (2-1-0).

II.2 Operations Research and Decision Theory: 3 Credits (2-0-2).

II.3 Modelling and Simulation: 3 Credit (2-0-2).

II.4 Elective 1: 3 Credits (3-0-0).

- II.4.1 Large Scale Systems
- II.4.2 Economic Growth—Models and Strategies
- II.4.3 Management Information Systems
- II.4.4 Computer Aided Design
- II.4.5 Systems Design and Analysis
- II.4.6 System Dynamics Modelling and Industrial Applications
- II.4.7 Intelligent and knowledge based systems

II.5 Elective II : 3 Credits (3-0-0)

- II.5.1 Energy, Ecology and Environment
- II.5.2 Economics and Planning of Energy Systems
- II.5.3 Urban and Regional Transportation Systems
- II.5.4 Science Dynamics
- II.5.5 Alternative Futures
- II.5.6 Technology Alternatives for Rural Development
- II.5.7 Planning and Management of Human Resources

II.6 Minor Project II : 2 Credits (0-0-4) (Field-Oriented)

Total : 17 Credits
(20 hours)

M. Phil. Semester-II

II.1	:	3 Credits (3-0-0)
II.2 or II.3	:	3 Credits (2-0-2)
II.4 or II.5	:	3 Credits (3-0-0)
II.7	:	Major Project/Dissertation in Futures Studies Pt. I:8 Credits (0-0-10)

Total : 17 Credits
(20 hours)

II.1 Science, Technology, Society and Futures : 3 Credits (2-1-0)

An interdisciplinary exploration of the mutual interaction of science, technology and society, with insights drawn from anthropology and philosophy and sociology of sciences, history of science and technology, and the changing formations of modern society.

II.2 Operations Research and Decision Theory : 3 Credits (2-0-2)

Introduction to OR, history, nature, scope and phases. OR and decision theory. Structure of decision strategies. Decision-making under certainty, risk and uncertainty. Pay-off matrix for decision strategies. Decision trees. Decision under competitive situation. Theory of games—pure and mixed strategies. Types of models in OR. Guidelines to modelling an OR project.

Linear programming: Formulation and solution methods, Quality. Deal-simplex methods. Transport and assignment models. Post-optimality analysis. Complications in LP problems and resolution. Goal programming. Concepts in non-linear and chance constrained programming. Waiting line models and their industrial applications. Industrial appreciation of mathematical programming. Introduction to dynamic programming and network analysis. Monte-Carlo system simulation.

II.3 Modelling and Simulation : 3 Credits (2-0-2)

Models and their applications. Common types of mathematical models used for engineering and non-engineering systems. Derivation of models from physical relations. Model determination from input-output observations.

Basic principles of simulation. Systems dynamics simulation. Analog and digital simulation techniques. Some common simulation languages.

II.4 Elective I : 3 Credits (3-0-0)

II.4.1 *Large Scale Systems*

Modelling theory for physical systems: Component and interconnection models. Formulation of composite system transfer function matrix and state-space models in continuous and discrete time modes. Computer-aided decomposition and reconstruction techniques based on graph theory. The Dentzig-Wolfo decomposition principle. Model order reduction techniques with particular reference to dynamic aggregation. Study of aspects such as sensitivity and stability of interconnected dynamical systems. Applied systems analysis case studies for industrial control systems, power systems, and socio-technical systems.

II.4.2 *Economic Growth-Models and Strategies*

Theories of development. Underdevelopment in contemporary economic thought. Capitalist and Neo-Marxist. Growth economics-the Harrod-Domar model. Neo-Keynesian distribution theory and growth. Ingredients and types of equilibrium. Factor substitution and neo-classical growth. Two sector growth model. Technology and growth.

II.4.3 *Management Information Systems*

Concepts in MIS. Role of information in decision making. Effect of poor quality, reliability and availability of information on quality of decision-making. Decision-making without information (under uncertainty). Information needs for various kinds of management. Distinction between physical system and information system. Information flow. Periodicity, form and storage. Design of MIS. Basic steps in identification of information, cost and revenue centres. Choice of source, sequence, frequency and form of information flow. Computer packages for various functional areas. Systems entropy, concepts and information. Selective information management.

II.4.4 *Computer Aided Design*

Computer aided design philosophy. Systems definition. Software requirements specifications. Computer method of linear and non-linear systems analysis. Sensitivity models for computer-aided design. Optimisation methods in systems design. Automated system design. Computer aided probabilistic design. Data structures and data base management. Numerical considerations, Graphics.

II.4.5 *System Design and Analysis*

Systems—their models and representation. The design process and methodology. Inventiveness, analysis and decision-making. Engineering houristics. System components. Interconnection of system elements. System reliability. System layout. Feasibility studies. Optimization of systems. Man-machine relationships. Sensitivity analysis.

II.4.6 *Systems Dynamics Modelling and Applications*

Introduction to system dynamics. Causal-loop diagramming. Flow diagramming. Positive feedback structure. Negative feedback structure. S-shaped growth structure. Delays.

Applications in planning and policy design for production systems. Dynamics created by interactions with company suppliers, labour, customers and competitors. System dynamics models to evaluate financial performance of organisations. Dynamics created by capacity expansion and professional resource expansion.

II.4.7 *Intelligent and Knowledge Based Systems*

Production systems, search strategies, predicate calculus and resolution, rule based deduction systems, semantic networks, frames and scripts. All system architectures. Knowledge acquisition. Hardware/software support for IK 85. Expert systems.

II.5 Elective II: 3 Credits (3-0-0)

II.5.1 *Energy, Ecology and Environment*

Origin of the earth. Earth's temperature and atmosphere. Sun as a source of energy, nature of its radiation. Biological processes, photosynthesis. Food chains. Marine ecosystem. Ecosystem theories. Auctecology. Sources of energy, classification of energy sources, quality and concentration of energy sources, characteristics temperature. Fossil fuels-coal, oil, gas, geothermal, tidal and nuclear energy. Solar, wind, hydropower, biomass. Resources of energy and energy use pattern in different regions of the world. Environmental degradation, primary and secondary pollutants. Thermal and radioactive pollution, air and water pollution. Micro-climatic effects of pollution. Pollution from stationary and mobile sources. Biological effects of radiation, heat and radioactivity disposal. Pollution abatement methods.

II.5.2 *Economics and Planning of Energy Systems*

System Economics: Basic concepts. National accounting framework. Criteria for economic growth. Model types and philosophy. Production functions. Input output economics. Macro economic growth models. Econometric models. Policy options and budgetary implications, some illustrations of econometric research for identifying demand functions, supply functions, cost functions, production functions, utility functions and Energy curves. Dynamic models of the economy and "simple" theory of business fluctuations. Multiple linear and non-linear regression analysis. Energy per unit monetary value of consumer needs and services. Energy efficiency, cost benefit risk analysis. Environmental repercussions and the economic structure. Conflict between energy consumption and pollution. Systems design and quantitative economic policy with particular reference to energy. Econometry in the context of multiple objectives, conflicting goals and decision under uncertainty.

II.5.3 *Urban and Regional Transportation Systems*

Components of transportation system and their interaction. Dimension of the widening role of urban transportation system planning. The planning process and use, and transport system models. Comparison and evaluation of various models. Transportation impact study methodologies. Strategies for the evaluation of alternate transportation plans and plan implementation. Regional analysis and development concepts. The role of transportation planning in the overall regional system. Methodology and models for regional transportation system, planning, implementation framework.

II.5.4 *Science Dynamics*

Theories of knowledge. Scientific revolutions. Normal and extraordinary science. Scientific method. Introduction and verification. Propper's falsification. Logical problems in time, space and quantum mechanics. Science and technology. Industrial revolution. Limits to growth. Appropriate technology. Appropriate case studies for the above topics.

II.5.5 *Alternative Futures*

An introduction to approaches and techniques in developing preferred futures for nations in the making, with emphasis on normative value elements.

II.5.6 *Technology Alternatives for Rural Development*

Concept of technologies appropriate for rural India. Social economic and environmental consideration. Rural-urban and organisational industrial conflicts. Appropriate technology for energy, agriculture, inputs and tools, housing, textiles, water supply and sanitation, health care, transport and small-scale industries. An integrated approach to the use of alternate technologies. Issues of technology transfer. Farmhouse and overland management, dairying, some case studies.

II.5.7 *Planning and Management of Human Resources*

The approach to human resources management. Social aspects. Problems of selection, training and placement in diverse organisations. Planning of human resources. Manpower planning. Manpower development. Utilisation of human resources. Industrial relations and personnel management functions, legal aspects, factories acts, etc. Training needs and planned refresher programmes at various levels for updating skills. Evaluation of training.

M. Tech. Semester III

III.1 Major Project/Dissertation in Futures Studies: 16 Credits (20 hours)

Total : 50 Credits

M. Phil. Summer Term (9-10 weeks)

S.1 Major Project/Dissertation in Futures Studies Pt. II. : 8 Credits (20 hours)

Total : 42 Credits

APPENDIX - B-II

*Syllabus for Futures Studies for Schools**

(As an Elective Activity undei Work Experience)

Preamble

Looking to the potential that Futures Studies offer for development of special qualities in the students and the competence it cultivates to analyse, anticipate and project the future and find solutions to many of the problems that the mankind may face, the Board has decided to introduce Futures Studies as one of the components of study under Work-Experience. It is being done with the hope that the CBSE schools, progressive as they are, would take up this area as a new challenge and initiate their students in a new way of thinking and looking at the things so that they grow into intellectually introspective and thoughtful minds, sharing the concerns of mankind and provide various alternatives on a more rational basis. In this context Futures Studies or Futurology has been conceived as the study of the processes of 'change' and of Environment. Of long-range images and perspectives at the individual, societal and global levels. In this interdisciplinary subject, we conceptualize, identify and design for alternative futures and possibilities.

The key aim here is to have an indepth understanding of the environment and systems: social, economic, political or developmental and their interactions in the context of a given society.

Here, we also study the questions of alternative lifestyles, value, shift and the emerging cultural configurations.

---

* This syllabus was designed by ICMF expert group, led by Dr Seth. It was accepted by the CBSE. It is reproduced as a reference material for teachers. (Courtesy: CBSE/ICMF).

Such a future probe naturally depends upon the intelligent use of information, relating to different sectors, their interaction including the ever changing role of new science and new technology that is impacting upon, not only the various systems but also on day to day life.

Thus, Futures Studies teaches how to scan and analyse, information of data-bases, in order to identify emerging 'trends' and the 'patterns' and 'shifts' for and towards future.

Futures Studies is also a powerful instrument of foresight, knowledge of planning, of developing policy designs and management of our normative 'Goals'.

This course, therefore, besides helping the youngsters to become more imaginative, also enables them to learn to scan future and many aspects of uncertainty.

It helps them further to relate themselves to long-range complex problems and issues of the wider world and to understand the current and emerging local and global problematic issues.

At the level of children and youth, the Futures Studies enables them to develop meaningful 'Images of Future'. It sharpens their creative skills.

To summarise, through this course the students should be able to:

— Understand the processes behind change and the different aspects of time: Past, Present and Future.
— Understand the term 'Futures Studies' and appreciate the necessity for future related thinking, since they will be stepping into it in time to come.
— Have an understanding of the systems-how dynamics behave and their dynamics in terms of time, in terms of likely threats and opportunities.
— They also learn to distinguish between short-range, medium-range and long-range perspectives for and about future.
— Think laterally, creatively and analytically.
— Generate ideas and images of future and learn to prefer future possibilities and develop a critical and scientific attitude to human problem situations, as well as to

plan and manage the realisation of their preferred options for future.

— Search for new goals and directions of changes and to face future, creativity with confidence and a sense of responsibility.

— Identify individual future needs and lifestyles and resilient enough to adapt to emerging work ethics and social values.

— Above all, to learn how to explore and appreciate the joy of 'knowing the unknown'.

DETAILED SYLLABUS

Class IX

THEORY

1. *Concept of time*
    - 1.1. Past
        - 1.1.1. Meaning
        - 1.1.2. Nature
        - 1.1.3. Recollection of past
        - 1.1.4. Recounting of experience
        - 1.1.5. Lessons learnt/drawn
    - 1.2. Present
        - 1.2.1. Meaning
        - 1.2.2. The bearing of the past on the present
        - 1.2.3. Survey of the state of art of the present
        - 1.2.4. Assessment of the present
        - 1.2.5. Time to plan
        - 1.2.6. Time to decide
        - 1.2.7. Time to act
        - 1.2.8. Future is today
    - 1.3. Future
        - 1.3.1. Meaning
        - 1.3.2. The influence of past on future
        - 1.3.3. The influence of present on future
        - 1.3.4. Linkage of past, present and future
        - 1.3.5. Future is change
        - 1.3.6. Preparedness for change

2. *Futuristic Thinking*
    - 2.1. Explanation
    - 2.2. Need
        - 2.2.1. For individual
        - 2.2.2. For society
        - 2.2.3. For nation
        - 2.2.4. For world
    - 2.3. Usefulness
        - 2.3.1. To improve quality of life
        - 2.3.2. For coexistence
        - 2.3.3. Purposeful and meaningful life
        - 2.3.4. Creativity

3. *Process of Future Scanning*
    - 3.1. Meaning
    - 3.2. Read
    - 3.3. Advantages

4. *Future Events*
    - 4.1. A fulfilment (opportunity)
        - 4.1.1. Meaning
        - 4.1.2. Private and Societal
    - 4.2. A Crisis (Threat)
        - 4.2.1. Meaning
        - 4.2.2. Private and Societal

5. *Future Oriented Thinking*
    - 5.1. Private Futures
        - 5.1.1. Meaning and scope
        - 5.1.2. Individual efforts and contributions
        - 5.1.3. The need and necessity
    - 5.2. Societal/Public futures
        - 5.2.1. Meaning and scope
        - 5.2.2. Collective efforts
        - 5.2.3. The need and necessity
    - 5.3. Private and societal futures
        - 5.3.1. Interdependence
        - 5.3.2. Individual family-society-nation-world
        - 5.3.3. Global mind and citizenship

5.4. Dominant factors influencing futures
- 5.4.1. Science and Technology
- 5.4.2. Value Systems and Culture
- 5.4.3. New Complexities and uncertainties.

ACTIVITIES AND EXERCISES

A: Illustrative Activities and Exercises

1. General readings in Futures Studies with emphasis on Science fictions (Please refer to the list of Reference Books and Materials provided at Appendix II).
2. Activities to promote imagination, speculative writing and lateral thinking:

   Illustrative topics
   - 2.1. Loss of a house key
   - 2.2. A sudden surge of population in a small city
   - 2.3. Teachers replaced by computers
   - 2.4. Religionless society
   - 2.5. Power cut
   - 2.6. Population explosion
   - 2.7. Depletion of natural resources
   - 2.8. Environmental pollution
   - 2.9. Natural calamities
   - 2.10. Saturation limits reached in food production
   - 2.11. Scarcity of raw materials
   - 2.12. Traffic congestion and lack of parking facilities, etc.
3. Project work in the class room (The following topics can be conveyed in terms of essays, models, exhibitions, dramas, paintings, etc.)
   - 3.1. Use of computers and field work
   - 3.2. Collect data and analyse patterns with reference to immediate surroundings:
     - 3.2.1. Population
     - 3.2.2. Education
     - 3.2.3. Housing
     - 3.2.4. Communication
     - 3.2.5. Garbage
     - 3.2.6. Energy
     - 3.2.7. Pollution vs Industries

3.2.8. Any other

3.2.9. Planning an exhibition on population scenario in 2001

3.3. Thinking and predicting alternative futures of:

3.3.1. Communication

3.3.2. Employment, etc.

3.3.3. Any specific small unit/energy. Transportation, Entertainment/Problem relating to these may be chosen.

3.3.4. Prepare images for 2020; on any aspect

a. Cosmopolitan city

b. Space conquest

c. Agriculture

d. Education

e. Environment

f. Sports

3.4. Develop a futuristic scenario on:

— Writings

— Learning

3.5. Identifying resources for an individual relevant to the emerging lifestyles in 1995, 2001, 2025, 2050.

3.6. Visualize future forms of the following:

3.6.1. Public telephone

3.6.2. Public park

3.6.3. Market

3.6.4. Hospital

3.6.5. News broadcasting

3.6.6. Ration cards

3.6.7. City water-supply

3.7. List out the likely threats

(a) for you

(b) for society

arising out of the following:

3.7.1. Traffic noise

3.7.2. Traffic rules

3.7.3. High speed driving

3.7.4. Auto exhaust

3.7.5. Rapid transit system

Class X

THEORY

6. *Types of Future Environment*
    6.1. Deterministic
        6.1.1. Meaning and scope
        6.1.2. Examples
        6.1.3. Utility
    6.2. Normative
        6.2.1. Meaning and scope
        6.2.2. Examples
        6.2.3. Utility

7. *Preferred or Desired Futures*
    7.1. Meaning
    7.2. Need and necessity
    7.3. Usefulness

8. *Perspective Planning*
    8.1. Planning: Short range, Medium range and Long range
        8.1.1. Meaning
        8.1.2. Need
        8.1.3. Types of Planning
        8.1.4. Methods of perspective planning

9. *Tools and Techniques of Forecasting*
    9.1. Forecasting : Definition
    9.2. Needs and necessity of forecasting with special reference to technology and social forecasting and technology impacts.
    9.3. Types of Forecasting
        9.3.1. Qualitative Technological Forecasting. Opinion-polls and surveys, panels, brainstorming, Scenarios, Seth indicators method, Delphi. Use of social indicators
        9.3.2. Quantitative methods
        — extrapolative methods, relevance
        Tree Technique, Cross-Impact Analysis
        Computer Modelling: Simulation System Analysis

9.3.3. Technology Assessment (Impact study)
Meaning, scope, need and relevance, simple exercises

10. *Anticipatory Management*
   10.1. Meaning and scope
   10.2. Examples
   10.3. Need and necessity
   10.5. Early warning system

ACTIVITIES AND EXERCISES

4. Exercises on technology assessment:
Scientific and technological discoveries and their assessment in terms of positive and negative outcomes and short-range and long-range impacts on people and environment at large (physical, cultural, societal)
   4.1. Calculator
   4.2. Automobiles, TV, Computers
   4.3. Automation at home/office
      — Washing machine
      — Dishwasher
      — Vacuum cleaner
   4.4. Electronic gadgets
   4.5. Futuristic cooking
   4.6. Natural resource depletion
   4.7. Satellite communication
   4.8. Starwars
   4.9. Computer-aided instruction
   4.10. Uniform
   4.11. Countrywide class room programmes
   4.12. Computerised ticket counter
   Electronic typewriters
   4.13. Traffic signal indicators
   4.14. Underground drainage
   4.15. Street lights
   4.16. A public library
   4.17. A moped
   4.18. Information technology
   4.19. Diet

5. Activities to promote identification of issues, local, national, global and discussions around them.
   - 5.1. Education for all
   - 5.2. Employment for all
   - 5.3. Transportation
   - 5.4. Urban renewal
   - 5.5. Mass communication
   - 5.6. Future village
   - 5.7. Future of marriage as an institution
   - 5.8. City/village
   - 5.9. Man and woman
   - 5.10. Society
   - 5.11. Environment
   - 5.12. Entertainment
6. Discussion on
   Technology society nexus with reference to likely changes and shifts in customs, tradition, social practices, alternative lifestyles.
7. *Development of long-range scenario on*
   - 7.1. Nuclear family
   - 7.2. Interpersonal relationship
   - 7.3. Problems and prospects of youth in 21st century
   - 7.4. Work and career
   - 7.5. Work ethics

B: ADDITIONAL ILLUSTRATIVE EXERCISES

Note:

A. These discussions are to be held in the context of change, society, value and systems.
B. These can also be given for class practical work, assignment. This work can be considered for assessment.
C. Recollect an incident/situation that happened last year.
D. List out the possible reasons that led to that incident/ situation.
E. Note down your experiences.
F. Write down the lessons you have learnt.

1. *Suggested Areas (for Break-casting and Trend analysis)*
   - 1.1. A fire accident
   - 1.2. A dowry death

1.3. Street violence
1.4. A road accident
1.5. An aircrash
1.6. A theft
1.7. Bus breakdown
1.8. Late arrival of a train

2. a. Identify a happy occasion you had last year.
   b. Briefly narrate the occasion
   c. Note down your experiences
   d. List out the bearings of that occasion on you today

   More Suggested Areas:

   2.1. Birthday
   2.2. A Wedding
   2.3. Visit to science exhibition
   2.4. Watching a TV serial
   2.5. A Film show
   2.6. A debate
   2.7. Your school day celebration
   2.8. Your school sports
   2.9. Visit to a circus
   2.10. A school excursion

3. *The State of Art of the Current On going Systems and Emerging Principles*

   3.a. Single out a present condition/facility, etc.
   3.b. Find out its relevance to the past
   3.c. List out plus and minus points of the conditions/ facility
   3.d. Assess whether you are satisfied with the present condition/facility

   3.1. Suggested Areas
      3.1.1. Campus cleanliness
      3.1.2. School bus
      3.1.3. Class room facilities
      3.1.4. Class discipline

   3.2. a. Visit to the place identified
      b. Is it now as it was last year?
      c. List out the plus and minus points
      d. Assess if you are satisfied with it
      e. Suggest some ways of improvement

Suggested Areas: Transportation Systems

3.2.1. A railways ticket counter
3.2.2. Railway canteen
3.2.3. An historic place
3.2.4. A bus stop
3.2.5. An auto stand
3.2.6. A medical shop
3.2.7. Pen
3.2.8. Your garment
3.2.9. A magazine
3.2.10. Your wristwatch
3.2.11. Your daily routine

3.3. a. Identify a thing
b. Imagine its state of art in another five years hence
c. List out the likely fulfilments you may have
(i) for yourself
(ii) for society

Suggested Areas

3.3.1. Fair price shop
3.3.2. A health centre
3.3.3. A petrol pump
3.3.4. A general election
3.3.5. An overbridge
3.3.6. Underground subway

3.4. a. Identify a thing/place
b. Imagine the state of art in another five years
c. List out the likely threats
(i) for you
(ii) for society

Suggested areas

3.4.1. A level crossing
3.4.2. Street holdings
3.4.3. Cinema crowd

3.5. a. Imagine a situation
b. How would it be likely to go about in three-four years? List
c. How will it help/affect you? List
d. How will it help/affect your society? List

e. Establish linkage between the two

Suggested areas

3.5.1. Personal cleanliness
3.5.2. Punctuality
3.5.3. Observance of road rules
3.5.4. National integration
3.5.6. Communal harmony
3.5.7. Saving habits
3.5.8. Cautious driving
3.5.9. Competitive Examinations
3.5.10. College admission

3.6. a. Imagine general future of an identified thing/situation.

b. Note down your preferred future of that.

c. Analyse why to prefer that kind of future.

Suggested Areas

3.6.1. Education today
3.6.2. Examination system
3.6.3. School fees
3.6.4. Medical checkup in school
3.6.5. Public meetings
3.6.6. Inter-school tournaments
3.6.7. Character building

3.7. a. Identify a thing/situation

b. How would you prefer it to be in the next four-five years?

c. How will you go about to achieve that? List.

d. What plans do you have in mind? List.

3.8. a. Imagine achieving a preferred future for a thing/situation.

b. List out the possible indications that the preferred future you envision may go wrong/well.

c. Reason out the possible hurdles/pitfalls you may encounter in achieving the preferred future.

d. List out your plans to manage to face/cope with/overcome those hurdles.

Suggested Areas

3.8.1. Cent per cent literacy in your area.

3.8.2. Free education for all.
3.8.3. Eradication of road accidents in your town.
3.8.4. Co-education in schools.
3.8.5. Abolition of caste system.
3.8.6. Inculcation of values.
3.8.7. Compulsory games in schools.
3.8.9. Fair valuation in examinations.
3.8.10. Removal of corruption.

4. *Conduct Brainstorming Sessions*
   Suggested Areas
   4.1. Indian cricket
   4.2. National Cadet Corps
   4.3. Small savings
   4.4. Community service
   4.5. Adult education
   4.6. The influence of TV on open school children
   4.7. Drug addiction
   4.8. Newspaper reading
   4.9. Air travels
5. *Using Seth-Harva Method, Build a Scenario for 21st Century*
   5.1. School boy/girl
   5.2. Job placements
   5.3. Housewives
   5.4. Mass media
   5.5. Leisure time activities
   5.6. Air pollution
   5.7. Town improvement
   5.8. Sanitary conditions of your town
   5.9. Food habit
   5.10. Religion
   5.11. Future warfare
   5.12. Future of international relations
   5.13. Social security
   5.14. Women welfare
   5.15. Future work career
   5.16. Future Business travels and direction
   5.17. Leisure usage
   5.18. Currency

5.19. Space colonies
5.20. Inter-stellar voyages
5.21. Food from ocean
5.22. Child development
5.23. Future health care
5.24. Future education consultant
5.25. School less society
5.26. Disaster management
5.27. Future management
5.28. Artificial intelligence

Note to Teachers

1. Theory part should be completed before suggested activities begin.
2. The suggested areas under each activity are only illustrative. The teachers could identify many more similar areas to suit to the local conditions and potential of students.
3. Futurology provides more scope for mental/intellectual activities than physical/manual activities.
4. Reporting and discussions thereafter on each activity are essential.

INTRODUCTION TO FUTURES STUDIES

Introduction

The National Policy on Education, 1986 and the Acharya Ramamurthi Committee which reviewed it, recommended that in order to make education relevant, purposeful, meaningful and useful, new programmes could be introduced in the uncharted are, courses of studies on interdisciplinary basis. In this context, with the unprecedented knowledge explosion in all fields of knowledge and in the wake of enormous advancement in science and technology, in its manifold applications, Futures Studies, as an academic discipline, deserves great merit, serious attention and due recognition at all levels of education today.

All educational systems are designed to help children to prepare them for adult life. But it is quite unfortunate to find that even though we prepare children, through the educational system for their entire future life, down through history, most educational systems have shown a remarkable capacity for excluding the present as well as the future.

They have all looked backward praising the wisdom of bygone ages rather than awakening curiosity and interest in what goes round in society and what lies ahead of them.

If anything is important, it is the future. The past has gone and the present exists only as a fleeting moment. Everything that we think and do from this moment onwards can affect only the future, since it is in the future, that we shall be spending the rest of our lives.

What needs to be done now is to give students an understanding of the most important issues, problems and opportunities they may face in the future and to teach them the skills they will need to continue to look ahead with confidence, and prepare themselves to cope successfully with the crisis, stresses and rapid changes that lie ahead. To impart this kind of strength of character and intelligence to our children, youth and others who partake in the educational system, it is essential that our education becomes an instrument to create a continued awareness of the future in terms of various needs, resources, demands, objectives and institutional innovation for their fulfilment to achieve human happiness for all. Therefore, awareness of societal needs and more effective utilisation of national and global resources is an inescapable ingredient of future-focused educational learning. Educational institutions are the means by which traditions of a country—intellectual, artistic and ethical and the technical skills are transmitted from one generation to another. This learning process contributes towards the progress of any community. We deal here with human beings and try to help them realise their full potential to cope up with the future. Education is aimed to developing man in his wholesome nature— to enable him 'to think, to feel, to do and to be'. These are the aims which a Futures Studies teacher would set before himself. Without thought, in the absence of new independent thinking, nothing great can ever be achieved.

Futures Studies: A Historical Perspective

No one knows who taught the first course in Futures Studies. It was, however, in 1943 that Prof. Ossip Flechtheim wrote an essay recommending that future be taught as a subject. It was Alvin Teffler who taught one of the first courses on future in 1966 at the New School for Social Research in New York City. Today there are more than 500 formal courses available at different levels of education in the United States. Similar educational programmes find place in the curricula at different levels in the Soviet Union, West Germany, other European countries of the East and the West. The societal needs and more effective utilisation of national and global resources is an inescapable ingredient of future-focused educational learning.

Future: Its Relevance

Future is full of breaks and discontinuities

Attributes of Future

— Future is a stage in the flow of time
— Future is where things shall happen
— Future is a state of uncertainty
— Future is change
— Future will not just happen with just wishes
— Future is assessment of tomorrow's needs and current decision to accommodate tomorrow
— Future requires decision now
— Future imposes risk now
— Future requires action now
— Future requires work now
— Future requires our direction of change

Why we study Future?

(i) It helps us to prepare ourselves for it.
(ii) We can and we should influence and control the times (Future) we wish to live in.
(iii) It gives us the sheer joy of knowing the unknown.
(iv) All our opportunities will come to us only in Future.
(v) It is a tool for planned, purposive and creative existence.

Futures Studies : Nomenclature, Essential and Scope

Nomenclature

Futures Studies is called by different names in different countries. In the erstwhile USSR it is popularly known as

Prognostics; in France, as Futuribles, in Western Europe as Future Research, in the United States as Futurism and in India as Futures Studies, Foresight Studies and Futurology. However, today Futures Studies has come to stay as the accepted term all over the world in the academic parlance. The word Futures is used because it is concerned with not of one future but of several alternative futures.

Essence

Where were we?
↓
Where are we now?
↓
Whe hall we be?
↓
Where shall we prefer to be?
↓
How are we to achieve it?

Scope

Futures Studies is an emerging area of transdisciplinary knowledge. It is scientific study of future which offers unlimited scope and potential to tackle many a global as well as local problems both on long-range and short-range basis. Whatever be the area—Education, Housing, Environment, Population, Energy and the like—it deals largely with drawing lessons from the past events and experiences, surveying the state-of-art, identifying future threats—events which we like to see happen, choosing a preferred future, preparing a blue-print for the desired future and finally chalking out an action plan to fulfil and achieve the preferred future. It lays great stress and emphasis on perspective planning and anticipatory management for fulfilling and achieving the desired future. It is more concerned with the choice of alternatives than with a mere prediction.

Futures Studies: Major Components

Social Forecasting

Social forecasting relies on techniques of social science research and use of social indicators.

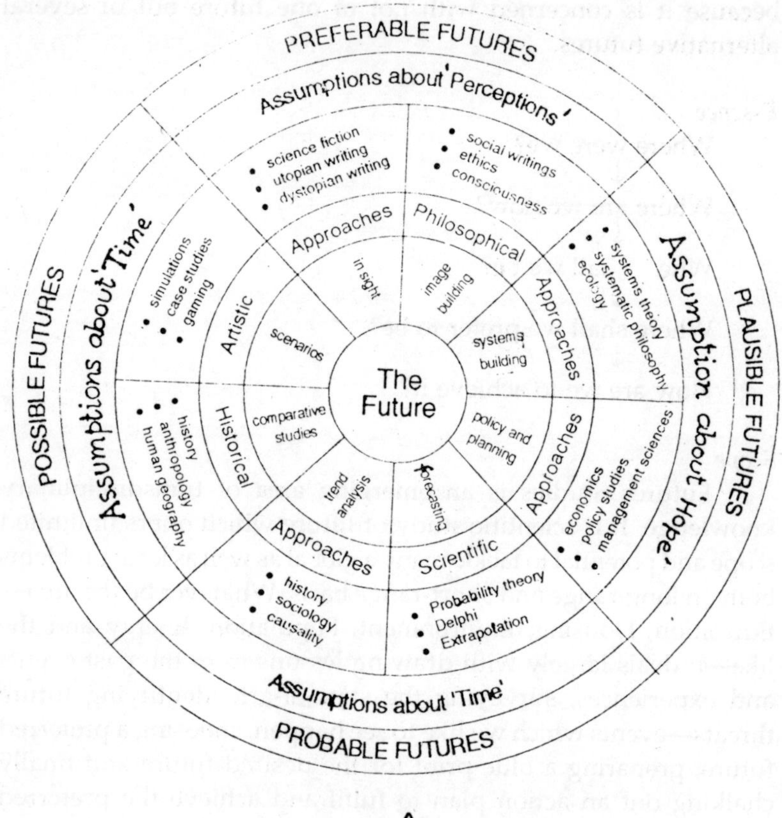

A
Model for studying the Future
(HENCHY'S MODEL)

Technology Forecasting

Technology forecasting, at the policy planning level is the clarification of scientific technological elements determining the future boundary conditions for corporate development, at the strategic planning level, the recognition and comparative evaluation of the alternative technological options or the preparation of the technological agenda at operational or tactical planning level and the probabilistic assessment of future technology transfer.

Technology Assessment

Technology Assessment is a thorough and balanced analysis of all significant primary, secondary, indirect and delayed consequences or impacts present or foreseen of a technological innovation on the society, the environment or the economy.

Futures Studies: Uses

— helps us to prepare ourselves for future.
— offers analytical tools to scan and map out future.
— is a powerful tool for management.
— provides immense input to planning by generating ideas and alternatives.
— gives the joy of exploring and knowing the unknown, and
— serves as a mechanism for planned, purposive and creative coexistence and promotes confidence and creativity in life.

Futures Studies : Role Playing

A student of Futures Studies is

— A divergent thinker
— A visionary
— A forecaster
— A planner
— An anticipatory manager
— A trouble shooter
— A confidant
— A creator of new ideas and policies, and
— An asset to the country.

Course Objectives

The course has been so designed as to achieve the following major objectives:

— Understand the processes behind change and the different aspects of time: Past, Present and Future.
— Explain the term "Futures Studies" and appreciate the necessity for "Future related thinking" since they will be spending the rest of their lives in future only.
— Know about systems—how dynamics behave and their dynamics in terms of time, in terms of likely threats and opportunities.
— Learn to distinguish between short-range, medium-range and long-range perspectives for and about future.
— Think laterally, creatively and analytically.
— Generate ideas and images of future and learn to prefer future possibilities and develop a critical and scientific attitude to human problems situations as well as to plan and manage the realisation of their preferred options for future.
— Search for new goals and directions of changes and to face future, creatively, with confidence and a sense of responsibility.
— Identify individual future needs and lifestyles and be flexible enough to adapt to emerging work ethics and social values.
— Attempt to explore and appreciate the joy of "Knowing the unknown".

Immediate Instructional Objectives

It is hoped that by taking this course under work experience, the students shall be able to:

— Understand the meaning of the Past, Present and Future
— Establish the linkage between the Past, Present and Future
— Accept the need for change
— Develop futuristic thinking
— Envision future events in terms of threats and opportunities
— Scan future
— Think of private and societal futures
— Differentiate between normative and deterministic futures

— Build scenarios on futuristic topics
— Prepare perspective plans
— Learn about anticipatory management
— Participate in simple forecasting exercises
— Attempt any exercises in technology assessment, and
— Appreciate Futurology as an interesting and useful subject.

LEARNING OBJECTIVES AND TEACHING STRATEGIES

The objectives of the course have been broadly defined above alongwith the major areas of content which should be helpful in the realisation of those objectives. An attempt has also been made to delineate the perspective which the Futures Studies at the school stage should develop. Teaching of content alone can not be expected to bring forth the desired results; more particularly in Futures Studies which is forward looking in its outlook. This is more a way of looking at the things, as such it is imperative for the educational planners and teachers that they should be able to visualise such competencies and capabilities and would cultivate in the students of Futures Studies, a sense of confidence in anticipating future with its varied ramifications. In the successive paragraphs some of these competencies have been identified and further spelt out in more operational terms so that the teaching-learning process may be organised more fruitfully. It would be advisable if the teachers also could do a similar analysis in their own way and come out with many more such attributes or their elaborated forms to make teaching a more scientific and realistic exercise. Such an exercise will also be helpful in understanding mechanism of learning in Futures Studies and gearing the process of learning accordingly.

Objectives

1. Existential (Life and Living)

Adaptability (Conquest of Change)
(Why Futures Studies?)

1.1. To sensitize students about change and its effects on individuals, communities, organisations and society.

1.2. To prepare them to recognize, understand, analyse and manage change.

1.3. To impress upon students that the main purpose of futures studies is to make, by means of identifying or imagining several possible futures.

2. General Problem Solving and Decision Making (group/individual)

Skills:

(What to do?)

2.1. To show that adaptability to change can be developed through harnessing general problem solving and decision making skills.

2.2. To orient students towards group decision-making.

2.3. To train students to evaluate alternate futures and specify corresponding actions for each possible future. This constitutes adaptability.

3. Mental Orientation

(How to do?)

3.1. Creativity/Lateral thinking

1. To encourage students to practice divergent (or lateral) thinking.
2. To foster creativity in terms of ideas and images of the future.

3.2. Systems Perspective

1. To orient students towards systems thinking, with special reference to time-space perspectives.
2. To expose students to concepts of connectivity and complexity in systems structure.
3. To sensitize them to systems behavioural characteristics such as:
   * Linearity vs. Non-linearity
   * Absolute change vs. Marginal Change
   * Continuous change vs. Discrete Change
   * Order of interactions between elements.

3.3. Open Mindedness

1. To develop qualities such as
   * Willingness to participate in discussions (date/information/knowledge)

* Readiness to receive informations
* Tolerance towards dissent or disagreement
* Flexibility in forming opinions
* Neutral disposition towards any decisions and outcomes.

3.4. Values Specificity/clarification.

1. To guide students in clarifying value dilemmas
2. To enable students to identify value options
3. Recognition and acceptance of alternatives without being threatened.

GUIDELINES FOR THE TEACHERS

A: Class Room Dynamics

1. *Lectures*

A straight talk or exposition possibility using visual or other aid but without group participation other than through questions at the conclusion— (Ministry of Labour's Glossary of Training terms).

2. *Discussion*

— may be free or led

— short, structures, purposeful 'buzz sessions' with small groups (on the same specific questions) followed by reporting to the whole class.

The Teacher's Role in a Class Room Discussion

1. Provides a discussion statement and sets a time limit for the discussion.
2. Uses 'open ended' questions to stimulate discussion or to refocus the discussions on the topic when participants' listening skills decreases.
3. Facilitates group discussion by using effective listening skills.
4. Avoids giving information or opinions.
5. Avoids making evaluate or judgmental statements.

3. *Team Teaching*

Panel discussion type (with members supplementing, interacting and also discussing with the class)

4. *Demonstrating and/or Experimenting*

Live demonstrations using models, prototypes, recorded demonstrations.

Experimentation both verification (practice after theoretical background) and investigation (practice before theoretical background).

5. *Project*

— (Studies, experiments, production or any other purposeful and planned activity)

— Forms

(a) guided individual projects (with a project brief giving details)

(b) guided group projects

(c) independent individual projects (thesis/dissertation)

— suited for development of cognitive, and effective skills where almost all the behavioural outcomes of learning are involved.

6. *Supervised/Independent Study*

Development of good habits/skills of study, personal traits, value, higher order intellectual abilities.

7. *Use of Structures/Self Paced/Programmed Instruction Materials*

Structuring- (Bibliography, P.I. Materials)

8. *Assignments (Term Reports)*

Forms

(1) class (development of application, evaluation, synthesis abilities)

(2) home (development of copying, presentation)

(3) laboratory (development skills)

(4) field (development of research skills, communications, expression)

9. *Seminars*

— Forms

(1) paper presentation seminar

(2) symposium type
(3) panel discussion

— suited for development of application, evaluation, synthesis, personal traits, interests, attitudes, values, communication.

— controlled by teacher/expert.

10. *Case Study*

— useful to examine a real or contrived event or problem and diagnose reasons which lead upto it or purpose remedies for solving.

— useful for practice in solving 'human' problems and for attitude development.

— suited for development of research skills and inference ability.

11. *Role Playing*

— act or play the role for which they are being trained (teachers, salesmen, interviewers)

— suited to build up personality traits, personal skills, attitudes and values.

12. *Syndicate Method*

— Students, in separate small groups, arrive at solutions. These are then presented to the whole group.

— Suited to build up personality traits, social skills, attitudes and values.

13. *Business Games*

Students play the roles of managers in company the details of which they are given. The effects of their decisions are relayed back to them by a team of assessors and they take further action in the light of these effects.

14. *Workshop Method*

Combining theoretical presentation/discussion by teachers, use of appropriate aids, group discussion and work, productive effort, group presentation and general discussion, review, etc.

15. *Brainstorming*

It is an elementary approach wherein groups can be inspired to conjure images for future on any topic followed by discussion how to realize the same.

16. *Delphi*

Assessment of future based on intuitive knowledge and judgment of a matter in hand, through a confidential group field feedback process of exports geographically distantly located to determine consensus, if any. It is an improvement on the Committee system.

B: How to Design a Training Session Or Class

Any instructor can guarantee improved effectiveness by reducing his plan for class to a one-page outline that answers the following questions:

1. What is the performance objective of this class?
   Just what am I trying to accomplish?
   What do I want the participants to be able to do at the beginning? (What behaviour at what level of competence?)
2. What materials are required?
   Arrangement of room? (chalk, blackboard, tape, etc.)
3. What is the most effective way of structuring the session?
   Should the participants work alone, work together, or compete?
   Having decided that, which technique is most appropriate (lecture, demonstration, visit, project, individual work, game)?
4. What are the key points to be looked for?
5. Approximately where should the class be and by when?
6. What would be the most effective way to end the session?
   Verbalisation of any learning both clarifies and reinforces the learning.

Theory without Practice is Sterile:
Practice without Theory is Blind.

INDIVIDUALS/PERSONS

GROUP DISCUSSION TASK | INTER-ACTIONS | CHANGE AND GROWTH

GROUP/COMMUNITY

CONTENT

PROCESS

FUNCTIONAL BEHAVIOUR

DISFUNCTIONAL BEHAVIOUR (Self-Orientations)

TASK ORIENTED BEHAVIOUR (Group Task roles)

PERSON ORIENTED BEHAVIOUR (Group Building and maintenance roles)

TASK ORIENTED BEHAVIOUR	PERSON ORIENTED BEHAVIOUR	DISFUNCTIONAL BEHAVIOUR
Initiating	Encouraging	Being aggressive
Information	Expressing group feelings	Blocking
-seeking		Competing
-giving	Harmonising	Clowning/Joking
Clarifying or Elaborating	Consensus testing	Seeking sympathy
Sharing	Setting standards	Dominating
Analysing		Silence/withdrawing
Evaluating		Disagreeing beyond reason
Summarising	Gate keeping	Whispering

COMMUNICATION

AIDS (that build relationships)

BLOCKS (that destroy relationship)

LISTENING AND RESPONDING

ATTITUDES	SKILLS	BLOCKS
Empathy	Acknowledgements	-Giving advice
Respect	Door openers (Drawing out)	-Criticizing
Trust	Content paraphrase	-Rediculing
	Active listening	-Sympathising
Genuineness	Non verbal observation	-Moralising
	Silent listening	-Questioning

Group Development Level

From	*Towards*
Surface discussions	- Depth discussions
Intra-group competitiveness	- Intra-group collaboration
Guarding information	- Sharing information
Denying feelings	- Expressing feelings
Undercutting other members	- Supporting other members
Being unaware of group process	- Being aware of group process
Using a few group resources	- Using all group resources
Win/Lose conflict resolution	- Win/Win conflict resolution
Resistance or Apathy to group goals	- Commitment to group goals
Self-enhancing behaviour	- Contribution to group action.

> "In an atmosphere of acceptance, trust and love, a caring and growing community of learners will experience true fulfilment and a sense of belonging.
> Therefore encourage one another and build one another up."
>
> *Albert Associates*

C: How to be an Effective Participant

Not only the leader but also the participants share the responsibility for the progress of a discussion. To make a meeting more productive and satisfying, remember the following:

1. There are three questions to ask yourself in every meeting:
    (a) Are you satisfied with the way the meeting is going on?
    (b) If not, what do you feel is causing difficulty?
    (c) What can you do to improve the situation?
2. Make your remarks as concise as possible. Brief, to the point. Contributions are both appreciated and influential. Think before you speak and relate your remarks to what has been previously contributed by others.

3. Follow the Prep. Formula. This is a very effective way of participating. Briefly, the way you should present your contribution is this:

    State your Position (P)
    Give the reason or reasons for your position (R)
    Give an example to illustrate your position (E)
    Restate your position (P)

4. If the discussion is going off the track or proving fruitless, bring it to the attention of the Chairman tactfully.
5. Do not think merely of what you can do to get out of a discussion; think also of what you can contribute.
6. Listen attentively to what each member has to say. You should be able to summarize the position and reasons of each speaker.
7. If there is a call for volunteers for a committee and you feel you are capablc, volunteer. You grow by taking responsibility.
8. Do learn to disagree agreeably.

Special Traits of a Futures Studies Teacher

1. A visionary
2. A divergent thinker
3. A forecaster
4. A planner
5. A motivator
6. An anticipatory manager
7. A trouble shooter
8. A creator of new ideas and policies
9. A confidence booster
10. A catalyst for change
11. A comprehensive priverce
12. An objective critic

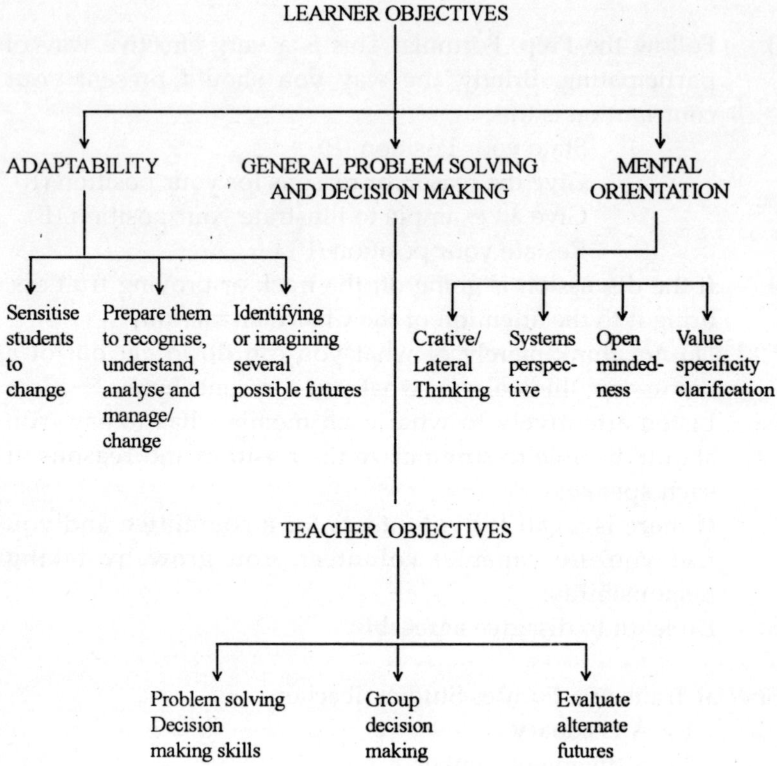
LEARNER OBJECTIVES
ADAPTABILITY
GENERAL PROBLEM SOLVING AND DECISION MAKING
MENTAL ORIENTATION
Sensitise students to change
Prepare them to recognise, understand, analyse and manage/ change
Identifying or imagining several possible futures
Crative/ Lateral Thinking
Systems perspec- tive
Open minded- ness
Value specificity clarification
TEACHER OBJECTIVES
Problem solving Decision making skills
Group decision making
Evaluate alternate futures

TABLE 1

LEARNER OBJECTIVES AND CORRESPONDING TEACHER OBJECTIVES AND RELATED ACTIVITIES

Learner Objectives	*Teacher Objectives*	*Activities*	*Suggestive Examples*
1. ADAPTABILITY	To impress upon students that the main purpose of Futures Studies is to make them more adaptable by means of identifying or imagining several possible futures	Individual: • Term Paper • Project	1. Transport: The students must present in text or through models/audio-visual aids. What forms of personal and public transport they imagine to be available at different times in the future.
	To sensitise students about change and its effects on individual, community, organisation and society	• Lectures • Field Visits • Team Teaching	1. Population and its effects on individual society 2. Water availability to socially under priviliged or rural women 3. One-day cricket and its effects on organisation 4. Computers and their effects
	To prepare them to recognise, understand, analyse and manage change	• Led Discussion followed by • Group Discussion • Case Study	1. Find treasure when you dig your ground 2. Depletion of natural resources 3. Traffic conditions 4. Price rise 5. Land use
2. GENERAL PROBLEM SOLVING & DECISION MAKING	To orient students towards group decison making	• Syndicate Method • Seminars • Workshop Method	1. The task could be–you are the representative group of your school. We are planning to change the timings of the school from 8-1.45 to 10-4 p.m. Your group must give your consensus on the issue. The decision will be based on your group's suggestion. Give the group about 30 minutes time.
	To train students to evaluate alternate futures and specify corresponding	• Assignment • Case study	1. Yours is a middle class family. you want to do medicine. It may be difficult for you to get through

(Continued on next page)

Learner Objectives	*Teacher Objectives*	*Activities*	*Suggestive Examples*
	actions, for each possible future		the merit quota. Your father has just now taken a loan for buying a house. Think of possible solutions and what other alternate careers you can go for?
		• Project	2. Education today or Examination system or Leisure activities.
3. MENTAL ORIENTATION	To encourage students to practise divergent thinking	• Group work • Brain storming • Syndicate Method	1. Task: The word given to the group is Youth a fluent thinker gives the following alternatives: Swami Vivekananda, Michael Jackson, Adhi Shankara, Jesus Christ, Tom Boy, Genious, Beautiful, Smart etc. (All the above related to the person/personality) A divergent thinker gives the following alternatives: Michael Jackson, Disco, Marina, Ambitious, Smart, Competitive, Fashion, Beautiful. (The above words relate to persons, place, things, emotion, nature, etc.)
	To orient students towards systems thinking with special reference to time-space perspectives	• Dance-Drama • Syndicate Method • Project • Mock Delphi	1. (a) Identify a thing (b) Imagine its state of art in another five years hence (c) List out the likely fulfilments you may have (i) for yourself. (ii) for society. 2. Fair Price shop 3. A Health Centre 4. A petrol pumps 5. A general election 6. An overbridge 7. Underground subway 8. (a) Identify a thing/place (b) Imagine the state of art in another five years (c) List out the likely areas (i) for you (ii) for society 9. A Level Crossing 10. Street hoardings 11. Cinema crowd

(Continued on next page)

Learner Objectives	*Teacher Objectives*	*Activities*	*Suggestive Examples*
	To sensitize students to system behavioural characteristics such as linearity/non-linearity, absolute/marginal change, continuous/discrets change	• Lecture • Discussion	1. Discussion on child development
4. OPEN MINDEDNESS	To develop qualities such as willingness to participate in discussions/tolerance towards dissent or disagreement/ flexibility in forming opinions/neutral disposition towards any decisions and outcomes, readiness to receive informations	• Role Playing • Games Group Discussion • Buzz	1. Use of Computers 2. Pollution vs. Industries 3. Society in the year 2001.
	Value Specification		
	(a) To guide students in clarifying value dilemmas	• Group Discussion	1. Single parent society 2. Nuclear family
	(b) To enable students to identify value option	• Role Playing	3. Mercy killing
	(c) To aid students in the prioritization of articulation and values	• Syndicate Method • Drama • Workshop	4. Honesty vs. Personal progress 5. Discipline in class

D: Some Illustrative Examples for Activities (Exercises)

1. *Adaptability*

Sensitize students about change and its effects on individuals, communities, organisations and society.

Exercise 1

Instruction to Teacher:

The above topic can be conveyed in the form of discussions, debate extempore speeches. Follow the following steps.

Step I

Ask students individually, to list five major changes that have come within a short span of 6 years. Give a specific time limit of 10 minutes.

Step II

Ask the students, at the end of 5 minutes to list the chosen changes from each person. Have a writer from among the students to write them all on board.

Step III

Glaringly some of the changes will be repeated over and over again in all the lists. Choose five of them.

Step IV

Divide the class into five groups. Give one change sighted to each group. Instruct students to discuss the effect of such a change on the above mentioned facets: namely, on individual, community, organisation and society. Allot a few minutes. Help the group to choose its own coordinator, moderator and secretary to record outcomes.

Step V

At the end of 5 minutes ask for a feedback by the secretaries of the groups to write the report on the board.

Step VI

Throw it open for general discussion on each of the controversial points if any.

NB: (i) If time permits, Step IV can be extended to include, classification of the outcomes or effects as Positive, or Negative and Natural.

(ii) The above can be also extended to think as what will be the impact of certain developments in the long run. (A time span of 10 years or 20 years).

Examples of Topics

1. Satellite telecasting
2. Artificial intelligence
3. Nuclear family
4. One child norm

To prepare them to understand, analyse and manage change.

Exercise 2

This could be dealt with as an extension of exercise or could be dealt as an individual exercise.

Strategies: Individual and Group work or Group Work alone.

Step I

Choose five examples of change and list them on the board. Instruct students to discuss in their groups. This 'change' in terms of

Understand: Define and redefine 'the change' occurred; clarify the meaning of it.

Analyse: Ask why/how and by whom has this change occurred.

Effects: Study the effects or the impacts of such a change on individual, community, organisation and society.

Manage: Put forth clarifications of whether the impact is an opportunity or threat.

Step II

Make the secretary of the group present the report.

Step III

Allow the class to agree, substantiate or refuse. Record suggested/accepted changes. Allow the students of the group to defend their outcome also.

Step IV

Summarise 'the change'.

Examples

1. Single parent society
2. More competition and the merit quota narrowing down with reservation
3. Surgery by robots
4. Non-allopathic and natural cure gaining importance
5. A turn towards more of Indian culture and tradition

Step V

The above problems can be extended to identify possible trends/effects emerging after 10 years, 20 years analysing multiple futures.

Step VI

Changes required in individual, community, organisation and society in order to cope up with such futures.

2. *General Problem Solving—Future Related Decision Making (Group/ Individual)*

General problem solving and decision making skills.

1. Fox Trap Model problems.
2. Given the same kind of situation ask all the students to write down possible suggestions of tackling the same.

Exercise 3

Situation (1)

Yours is a middle-class family. You want to do medicine. It may be difficult for you to get through the merit quota. Your father has just now taken a loan for buying a house.

Situation (2)

Plan and prepare for a future studies and career.

Step I

Identify factors and subfactors of a problem

Step II

Identify information gaps if any

Step III

Foresee blocks or impediments in the process of solving the problem

Step IV

Suggest the best possible means and ends

Step V

Decide your priorities

Situation (3)

Simpler task :

You want to keep a pet

Factors :

1. Animal : dog, cat, monkey, rabbit, horse, etc.
2. Breeds
3. Cost
4. Place

5. Food
6. Habits
7. Sex
8. Age

Sub-Factors:

Cost - 1. What is the investment?
2. What is the natural expense?
3. Is it worth making this expense/can it fit into our family budget?

Food- 1. What types of foods?
2. What should be avoided?
3. What is the time interval schedule?
4. Who will feed?
5. How to feed?
6. Vegetarian/non-vegetarian?

Exercise 4

Problem = Objectives + Obstacles – Crisis management

The Desert Survival Problem

The Situation:

It is approximately 10.00 am in mid-June and you have just crash-landed in the Thar desert in Western Rajasthan. The light turn imagine plane, containing the bodies of the pilot and the co-pilot and a few passengers has been completely burnt. Only the air frame remains. None of the remaining passengers, of whom you are one, has been seriously injured.

The pilot was unable to notify anyone of his position before the crash. However, ground sightings taken before the disaster, indicated that you were 105 kms off the course that was filed in your VFR (Visual Flight Rules) Flight plan with flight control authorities. The pilot had indicated before the crash that the plane was approximately 120 kms south-south-west from an oil exploration.

The whole area is flat, completely sandy and except for an occasional cacti, it appears to be quite barren. The last weather report indicated that temperature would reach 45 °C means that the temperature within a foot of the surface will hit 55 °C. You are all dressed in light weight clothing—bush shirt, pant, socks and sandals or sari and sandals. Everyone has a handkerchief. Collectively, your pockets contain Rs. 2.83 in change, Rs. 85 in notes, a pack of Charminar and a ball-point pen.

The Problem:

Before the plane caught fire, your group was able to salvage the 15 items listed. You have all agreed to stick together. Your task to rank these items according to their importance to your survival, starting with '1' the most important, to '15' the least important. You may assume that the number of survivors is the same as the number in your group.

Step I

Each member of the team (10 mins.) is to individually rank each item. Do not change your ranking once discussion begins.

Step II

After everyone has finished proceed to rank as a team, use the column step 2 (30 mins.).

Difference Between steps

Difference between Steps	1	2
	&	&
Survival Experts Ranking	3	3

Problem: List of 15 Items Salvaged from the Aircraft

Sl. No.	*Item*	*The team's Ranking your Ranking*	*Step 1*	*Step 2*	*Step 3*	*Step 4*	*Step 5*
1	2	3	4	5	6	7	8
1.	Torch/Flash light 4 battery slice						
2.	Pen knife						
3.	Sectional air map of the area						
4.	Plastic rain coat (large size)						
5.	Magnetic compass						
6.	First-aid kit with gauze						
7.	45 Calibre pistol (loaded)						
8.	Parachute (red & white)						
9.	Bottle of salt (1000 tabs) Tablets						

(Continued on next page)

(Problem Table Continued)

1	*2*	*3*	*4*	*5*	*6*	*7*	*8*
10.	2 litres of water per person						
11.	A book entitled-Edible Animals of the Desert						
12.	A pair of sun-glasses per person						
13.	2 litres of 180 proof vodka						
14.	1 overcoat per person						
15.	1 cosmetic mirror.						

Score

Your Score (Step 1 – Step 3)

Team Score (Step 2 – Step 3)

(*Courtesy:* Xavier Institute, CGKN, Jamshedpur).

A rational approach to decide best alternative for future.

The main elements of a rational approach to decision making are given below. The decision maker should :

(1) identify, scrutinise and put into consistent order those objectives/values which he believes should govern the choice of a solution to the problem;

(2) comprehensively survey all possible means of achieving those values;

(3) exhaustively examine the probable consequences of employing each of the possible means;

(4) choose a means that will achieve the best results.

This rational approach assumes that it is desirable, that decision makers possess both intellectual capacity and the time. It overlooks the fact that the information regarding consequences is at best only partial.

Examples

1. Fox Trap Problems
2. Give situations or case studies involving group decision.

At School level:

Step I

Select a group of volunteers of 5 or 6 students. Brief them the task in secret.

The talk could be—you are the representative group of your school. We are planning to change the timing of the school from 8 am - 1.45 pm to 10 am - 4 pm. Your group must give your consensus on the issue. The decision will be based on your group's suggestion. Give the group about 30 minutes time.

Step II

Ask the key group to design the questionnaire in order to collect various informations like location of residence, financial background, distance to be travelled, mode of travel, frequency of transport, crowd pattern, extra/co-curricular activities of the individual, etc.

Step III

Analyse the pros and cons of existing schedule and that of change proposed. Help the group to evolve on the basis of the information collected to come to a consensus decision.

Step IV

Make the key group to present the process and the decision to the class. Allow the class to question, clarify and fill any missing information. On the basis of this process help the entire class to come to the final decisions on the change in timings.

3. *On Lateral Thinking Skills — Any Given Situation or Idea*

Fluency of ideas		*Flexibility of ideas*	
Linear Thinking		*Lateral Thinking*	
Explore	Analyse	Challenge	Create
Personality	Identify	Ask why	Think of newer avenues
Things connected	Seek missing information	Predict possibilities	
Places			
Emotions	Ask when, where, what, who, how	Assess alternatives	Create idea in form of essay, painting, picture, model, poetry, skit, story, etc.
Activities Environment Symbols or emblems used		Classify as positive negative or neutral	

Exercise 5

On Divergent or Lateral Thanking

Step I

A class is divided into several groups (4 to 7 per group)

Step II

Each group is given a word, for example, Youth, Marina, Politician, Poverty, Lady, Fashion, etc.

Students are asked to choose 20 words having remotest connection to the above word.

The words are given in secrecy to the individual groups. The time allotted for the selection of relative words is 10 minutes.

Step III

Each group is asked to call out the related words except the word given to them. The rest of the class is allowed to guess the good word.

The group that has the longest list of words related given before any guess can be made is the divergent thinker.

Example

The word given to the group is 'Youth'. A fluent thinker gives the following alternatives:

Swami Vivekananda, Michael Jackson, Adi Shankara, Jesus Christ, Tom boy, Jenas, Beautiful, Smart, etc. (all the above relate to the person/personality.)

A divergent thinker gives the following alternatives:

Michael Jackson, Disco, Marina, Ambitious, Smart, Competitive, Fashion, Beautiful. (The above words relate the persons, place, things, emotion, nature, etc.)

What is Openness?

Open and Closed outlook of Future - The Perspective.

Some people believe that luck or chance of a predetermined act of forces (closed) are responsible for the outcome of the events. Others believe that the events are affected by human effort and personal decision making (open). Futurists believe that while there are many natural laws and limitations to which we ultimately conform, there exists a great deal of human freedom to affect and select the course of personal and social events.

A closed outlook comprises:
(1) In attention to the future
(2) A view that many things are possible
(3) A belief that we have any in what happens.

These are considered to be conducive to the social-psychological development of an individual and to becoming a good futurist.

Value Specifications

Values			
Means		*Ends*	
Instrumental means and Mode of conduct		Terminal (end) and states of existence	
Moral	Competence	Personal	Social
Guilt-responsible, Forgiving, Honest, etc.	Broad minded, Capable, Logical, Intellectual, Imaginative, Independent, etc.	Freedom Happiness, Wisdom, Security, Comfortable	World of peace. Equality, Justice, Co-existence

Reference

The Nature of Human Values, Milton Rokeach, The Free Press, 1973.

Albert Associates

Exercise 6

Task: Listed below are some of the major concerns of the human race.

* Terrorism
* Population Explosion
* Energy Crisis
* Unemployment
* Urbanisation
* Economic drive
* Environmental degradation
* Value crisis/Death of morality
* Programmed education
* Nuclear war
* Communalism

* New disease
* Losing control over technology
* Future shock
* Depletion of non-renewable resources
* Loss of identity/individuality
* Increasing violence/crime (global)
* Illiteracy
* Racial discrimination
* Famine
* Pollution (global)

Step I

Ask the students to select any five concerns of importance to him/her.

Step II

Ask the students to arrange the selected five in the order of priority.

Step III

(1) Make them relate the omitted choices to values.

(2) Ordered priority also would be related to underlying value they stand for.

Step IV

In the light of the above reselect if necessary.

Exercise 7

Visualise development of one technology at the threshold of the Twenty-first century.

Technologies	*Illustrative Answers*
Car	(e.g. Electric-Battery Operated hovercraft)
Plane	(e.g. VTOL supersonic plane)
Telephone	(e.g. Radio-Video telephone like TV)
Refrigerator	(e.g. Solar battery-operated fridge)
Camera	(e.g. 3-D Polaroid colour instant picture camera or infrared camera for fast photography)
Bomb	(e.g. Fusion bomb)
Computer	(e.g. Speech translation computer)
Television	(e.g. 3 D colour television-holograph)

Future is:

Possible	Impossible
Probable	Improbable
Controllable	Uncontrollable
Known	Unknown
Predictable	Unpredictable
Certain	Uncertain

4. *Prepare two contradictory scenarios about the following:*

(i)	Food in India	(a)	By 2000 AD enough food for every mouth: big revolution in food. Production, better inputs, better methods, alternative sources of food exploited like marine food, synthetic foods in common use, food habits greatly changed.
		(b)	Man conquers hunger, no need to take conventional food, Metabolic requirements supplied through tablets, injections, etc. No intake, no excretion.
(ii)	Warfare	(a)	Purely on computer, the winning party takes over administrative control of the losing party.
		(b)	Atomic warfare resulting in partial to complete loss of human race.
(iii)	Energy	(a)	Solar energy fully tapped, new methods of energy like tidal, geothermic, fully exploited resulting in energy surplus and pollution free.
		(b)	All sources fully depleted great shortage of resources.
(iv)	Indian Village	(a)	Village is self-contained economy, full employment potential to its people, population controlled, simple living style, same as now family system.
		(b)	Village extinct, urbanisation takes over, production/consumption centre remote, all facilities of services centralised, telephone, TV provided.

(v)	Pollution	(a)	Pollution fully controlled, all industry compatible to environment.
		(b)	Air, water, environment fully polluted by noise, gases, etc.
(vi)	Sex/ Marriage/ Family	(a)	Institution of marriage not required. Procreation by choice, artificial insemination, incubation possible, sex purely for enjoyment sake. The children purely state's obligation. Free "breeding". No father, no mother to be needed. The sex relationship purely on transient basis.
		(b)	Family and marriage bonds very strong, birth rate checked for zero population growth, all pervading prosperity, large family back in fashion for emotional reasons.
(vii)	Indian Population	(a)	Total annihilation due to warfare, pestilence and disease. Only few people who are the decision makers left to start all over again.
		(b)	Teeming population, over 1200 m by 2000 AD unchecked growth continues resulting in dire consequences, misery and hopelessness.
(viii)	Transportation	(a)	Superfast ground transport through jet propulsion supported by small VTOL planes for short level services.
		(b)	Road transport by buses, cars, overwhelmingly slow and rail transport dead.
(ix)	Management	(a)	Totally bureaucratic, centralised, computer controlled.
		(b)	Decentralised participative at all levels.

5. *Prepare a fantasy about:*

(a)	Machine	A self-thinking regenerative machine.
(b)	Death	Ability to die at one's own sweet will at a known point of time.

(c)	Mother	Test-tube and incubator
(d)	Sewage	Processing of sewage into edible food.
(e)	Management	Management of people purely through remote control ordering without any personal contact whatsoever.
(f)	Trees	Computer controlled trees for photosynthesis conversion of solar energy into foods.
(g)	Stars	Manipulation of star surface say by triggering explosions of certain kinds to get mineral resources.

6. *Analyse*

(a) History never repeats itself: (Yes, it never does, because the fourth dimension of time is irreversible, incompressible and inextendable).

(b) There is a straight line to the future: (No, there can not be: The discrete events at any random time will alter the course of future).

(c) Events are shaped by leaders: (Yes, they do. The dropping of two atomic bombs on Hiroshima and Nagasaki lead to complete surrender of Japan in World War II).

(d) Geneses changes the course of History: (Yes, they do. For example, Einstein's theory of mass conversion into energy lead to discovering of fission and hence atomic bomb).

(e) There is a rhythm to be unfolding of time: (The statement is vague. Probably yes, time is linear in concept, diverging to infinity).

(f) Future is dialections of thesis and anti-thesis: (Perhaps, yes or no).

(g) Time does not wait for anybody: (True, it does not, otherwise nothing would have happened, there would have been no past).

7. State Whether

Statement	*True*	*False*	*Do not Know*
(a) Life in future will be catastrophic			
(b) Man will overcome difficulties in time			
(c) Technology will destroy and conquer man			
(d) Technology is the best friend of man			
(e) At present changes are too fast for man			
(f) Today's changes are disrupting the equilibrium of the society			
(g) Modern man lives in uncertainty, conflict and, tension			
(h) Time moves at an exponential speed			
(i) One day man will be able to control time			
(j) Tomorrow never comes			
(k) One day is worth two tomorrows			
(l) Destiny determines future			

8. *Future is:*

(A storm; a melody; a brook; a sneezing girl; a singing elephant; a galloping horse; a cooked potato; a sleeping great grandmother; a revolution; a winter cloud; a forest; fire; jelly fish; moving ants)

9. *India in the year 2000 AD*	*Select (in millions)*
Total population of India	450, 950, 13,001, 500
Urban population of India	110,. 250, 350, 500, 750, 900
Food production (in tonnes)	120, 160, 200, 250, 350, 425
Energy requirement for domestic purposes (million tonnes of coal required)	85, 150, 275, 325, 425 550, 675, 775, 900
Housing requirements in India (million dwelling units)	50, 150, 200, 275, 350 400, 450
Per capita income (rupees at 2000 AD prices)	500, 750, 1000, 1250 1500, 1750, 2000, 2500 3000, 3500, 4000
Life expectancy (years)	40, 45, 50, 60, 65, 70, 75, 80

10. *Forecasting Techniques*

    (There are several ways to forecast about the future. Explain and show the limitations of each one of the following techniques when applied to Futures Studies).

    (Analogy, Intention, Projection, Simulation and Gaming, Delphi, Cross Impact Analysis, Trend Extrapolation, Scenarios Building, Model Engineering, CEA, Normative Analysis, Extrapolation).

11. *Identify 5 major inventions in the following fields in 21st Century*

    Medicine, Transportation, Agriculture, Housing, Energy, Sex, Education, Communication, Space.

    1. Large-scale medication for entire population through water supply and air control for combating virus epidemics.
    2. Communication— Development of ESP (Extra-Sensory Perception) as a means of communication.
    3. Sex— Control of sex urges through pills to get if off and on prolonged duration.
    4. Housing— Floating cities on sea and air.
    5. Education— Fast learning through computer, using hypnosis for data an information transfer.
    6. Agriculture— Special farming in space using computers.
    7. Space— Satellite cities for common people.
    8. Transportation— Propulsion through magnetic discharge.

12. *Make social psychological scenario in 21st century concerning the following: Family, Marriage, Child bearing, Friendship, Old age, Work, Recreation, Conflict, Management, Government, Crime, War and Peace, Religion, Caste, Leadership.*

13. *What do you understand by Utopia? How do you relate Futures Studies to Utopia? Explain what do you understand by desirable Future? Is a desirable future constant or changing? Prepare a scenario of an Utopian society you would like to envision for the 21st century.*

Exercise 8

If wishes could come true ....

List ten wishes in preferential order corresponding to each spatial entry given below.

1. You
2. Your Family
3. Your Neighbourhood/Your Work Place
4. Your Community
5. Your Nation
6. Our World (If you take the 'Y' out of Your, what results is Our)

Which of these wishes do you feel will be fulfilled.

(a) Immediately
(b) During the Next Few Days
(c) During the Next Month
(d) During the Next Half-Year
(e) During the Next Year
(f) During the Next Five Years
(g) During the Next Decade
(h) During the Next 25 Years
(i) Sometime in the Future

This exercise is completely open-ended. You may state any wish you have. As regards the second part, your judgment is called for. Please indicate the earliest time horizon/period during which you feel there is a clear possibility of your wish coming true.

The purpose of the above open-ended exercise is to bring out some of the underlying issues that require consideration while performing futures analysis and research. These issues are:

— the dilemma of choice
— space-time conceptions, and
— the tyranny of the majority.

Now, of the 6 × 10 = 60 wishes you have made, can you call out the top ten preferences?

Exercise 9

Given below are a few descriptions of the future. Arrange them in some order and explain the basis of your arrangement.

* Future is now
* Future is change
* Future belongs to fools
* Future is unforseeable
* There is not just a single future ahead of us, but many futures
* Future is but a reflection of the past
* Future is that period of time in which our affairs prosper, our friends are true and our happiness is assured
* Future cannot be remembered
* Future requires actions and decisions now
* Future is a state of uncertainty

Modes of Assessment

1. *Weightage*

The process of evaluation of the Work Experience has two major components: (i) Continuous assessment of classroom activities and (ii) Summative evaluation of the Project Work. The weightages given for the classroom activities and the Project Work are 50 per cent and 50 per cent respectively. The total marks for this activity under Work Experience are 60.

2. *Components to be evaluated*

2.1. The evaluation process for pupils' performance in the classroom activities and the Project Work has been so planned that the evaluation becomes continuous, comprehensive and holistic. While adopting the proposed evaluation process it should be borne in mind that whenever there are value judgments, there is subjectivity. A little subjectivity occurs even in the most objective measurement and in Futures Studies there is more room for subjectivity to creep into the evaluation process since there is no answer for the likely problems of future. This can be overcome by keeping an open-mind to the pupils' responses and allowing considerable margin in the assessment of pupils.

2.2. To enable the teachers make the assessment as objective as possible, the components to be evaluated are spelt out and the meanings are given below:

1. Seeing the problem

   It indicates the ability of the learner to perceive the problem in its totality.

2. Predicting Consequences

   This refers to the individual's ability to foresee situations and their related outcomes.

3. Divergent Thinking

   Ability to visualise varied solutions and trends.

4. Originality

   It is a measure of originality where originality is the ability to make an original, rare or uncommon response revealing cleverness or ingenuity.

5. Feasibility

   It indicates the possibility of doing.

6. Unconventionality

   This refers to the extent of deviation from the normal happening around us.

7. Cost effectiveness

   It refers to the extent to which there is benefit, profit, etc. Compared to the resources spent.

8. Science & Technological/Cultural Comprehension

   These refer to the abilities to perceive the changes taking place in the wake of Science and Technology advancements and cultural shifts.

9. Approach

   It is the way in which the task has been looked at and handled.

10. Analysis, synthesis and conclusion

    These refer to the abilities to draw inferences.

3. *Evaluation of Classroom Activities*

3.1. The teachers should realise that the brains of the students constitute a nation's greatest asset. From their minds will come the future scientific discoveries, future works of art and literature, further advances in technology and social organisation; in short, all future progress. Recognition and acknowledgment of potentialities is one of the most important teacher skills needed to nurture futuristic thinking. It can be developed in the classroom only in an atmosphere of psychological safety. The children should have the freedom to express whatever ideas that crop up in their minds without any fear or pressure from any quarter. They should have a permissive atmosphere to express their thoughts and ideas and sudden flashes of insight. There should not be any emphasis on uniformity and counteractive responses. All sorts of free-wheeling must be welcome. The classroom sessions should never be a time of "Cold War" or "Wet Blanket". The use of all "Killer Phrases" should be avoided. The soil of democratic organisation and administration is essential.

3.2. The evaluation of classroom activities shall be in the form of continuous assessment. However, while the students are engaged in a number of classroom activities, during the whole year in their 10th class, one activity per term may be evaluated for the purpose of rating. The assessment shall be done as given in the Proforma. The object of the Proforma is to evaluate an individual with reference to his/her futuristic thinking. Each component is assessed by assigning scores individually on a five point rating score and can be calculated by adding up the scores marked for all the components.

3.3. The rating of the performance of the individual may be done as per the table given below: The Maximum score being 30.

Score	*Rating*
Upto 12	Low
13-15	Satisfactory
16-18	Good
19-21	Very Good
22 and above	Outstanding

4. *Project Work*

4.1. The Project Work may be submitted in the form of a Project Report or in the form of a model. The choice shall be left to the students. The project should be challenging, demanding the maximal exertion of his mental resources. It should require application and augmentation of knowledge and skills acquired by the student.

4.2. As far as possible, every student should be encouraged to formulate his own proposal, discuss it with his teacher and execute it. In such cases where the student's interests and capacities are involved, sugge st such tasks which he can manage. On no account should the teacher impose a task/problem on a student even though it may be a really useful one.

4.3. The student shall discuss any changes he wishes to make in the topic/design of the project with the teacher and be guided by him. The student shall perform the work undertaken regularly and systematically (maintaining complete records of the works), appraise the teacher of the progress of the work every month and seek his guidance at all stages of the execution of the project.

4.5. The evaluation of the project work shall be summative in nature. The assessment shall be done as given in the Proforma. The object of the Proforma is to evaluate the quality of the project report/model submitted with reference to his/her futuristic thinking. Each component is assessed by assigning scores individually on a five point rating scale. For every individual, the performance score can be calculated by adding up the scores marked for all the components.

4.6. The rating of the performance of the individual may be done as per the following table. The maximum score being 30.

Score	*Rating*
Upto 12	Low
13-15	Satisfactory
16-18	Good
19-21	Very good
22 and above	Outstanding

5. *Overall Grading*

5.1. Rating for classroom activities and the project work may be shown separately.

5.2. For calculating the overali performance grade, the scores obtained in classroom activities and the project work may be put together and the present CBSE system of 9 point scale may be followed for the sake of uniformity with other subjects under elective area. The grading may easily be done as the raw scores are readily available for classroom activities and project work.

PROFORMA

Evaluation (Classroom Activities and Project Work)

Components	*Rating Score*				
	1	*2*	*3*	*4*	*5*
1. Seeing the Problem					
2. Predicting Consequences					
3. Divergent Thinking					
4. Originality					
5. Feasibility					
6. Approach					
7. Science and Technology/ Cultural Comprehension					
8. Unconventionality					
9. Analysis, Synthesis and Conclusions					
10. Cost-effectiveness					
Total Score:					

APPENDIX - C

Futurology: A Bibliographical Review

In this book a thesis has been advocated that only such Public Administration Experts can help in Bureaucratic Re-building exercise who also happen to be Futurologists. The titles contained in this Bibliographical Review do constitute a useful reading. This section also includes some exercises and futurology gaines.

A. Futurology
B. Methodologies
C. Technological Forecasting
D. Technology Assessment
E. Social Prognostics and Political Forecasting
F. Systems Science and Futurology
G. Educational Futures
H. Urban Futures
I. Management and Futurology
J. Futurology: General (Cases, Applications, Energy, Transportation, Food, Economics, Materials, etc.)

Note : 1. This classification is not mutually exclusive. Division has been done only for the sake of convenience.
2. 48 (1), 62, 1970 denotes Vol. 48, No.1, Page 62, Year 1970 for the journal references.
3. TF and SC= Technological Forecasting and Social Change
4. IFF = Institute for the Future
5. RFF = Resources for the Future
6. TA = Technology Assessment
7. TF = Technology Forecasting
8. LRP = Long Range Planning

PART - I

Bibliography

A. Futurology

1. Ackoff, R.L., *Redesigning the Future*, Wiby Interscience, New York, 1974.
2. Albertson, P. and M. Barnett; *Managing the Planet*, Prentice Hall, New Jersey, 1974.
3. Amara, R., Futures Field: Functions, Forms and Critical Issues, *Futures*. 6 (4), 289-301, 1974.
4. Anderson, G., Methods in futures studies, *Technological Forecasting and Social Change*. 5, 303-17, 1973.
5. Andover, J.J., Futurism: For Fun and Profit; *IEEE Spectrum*, 10 (17), 37, 1973.
6. Arthur, D.R., *Survival: Man and His Environment*, English Universities, London, 1969.
7. Baade, F., *The Race to the Year 2000*, Double-day, New York, 1962.
8. Balke, B., *Planning the Technical Future*, Universities, 10 (4), 297, 1968
9. Beckwith, B., The next 500 years, University Exposition, 1967.
10. Behrman, B., The Forecasters Forecast for the Year 2000, *UNESCO Features*, No. 644, p. 17, 1972.
11. I. Bestuzhev-Lada, Forecasting: An Approach to the Problems of the Future, *International Social Science Jl.* 21 (4), 526, 1969.
12. Blivin, B., *Preview of Tomorrow*, Knopf, New York, 1953.
13. Boylan, B., D.G. Brenan and H. Kahn, *Alternatives to Assured Destruction*, Hl-1603-RR, Hudson Institute, New York, 1972.
14. Braaten, C. and R.W. Jenson, *Futurist Options*, Panelist Newman, New Jersey, 1970.
15. Bright, J.R., Evaluating signals of technological change, *Harv. Busin Review* 48(1), 62, 1970.
16. Brown, H., *The Challenge of Man's Future*, Viking, New York, 1954.
17. Brown, H.J., Bonner and J. Weir, *The Next Ninety Years*, Calif Inst. of Tech. Pasadena, 1967.
18. Cadbury, G.A.H., *Our Technical Future*, chartered Mech. Engr, 1970.
19. Calder, R., *The World in 1984*, Penguin, Baltimore, 1965.

20. Chase, S., *The Most Probable World*, Penguin, Hardmondsworth, 1969.
21. Clarke, Arthur. C., *Profiles of Future: An Inquiry into the Limits of the Possible*, Pan Books, London, 1973.
22. Clarke, R., The Need for Alternative Technologies, *American Review*, 19 (4), 75-84, 1975.
23. Clarke, I.F., The First Forecast of the Future, *Futures* 1, 325-330, 1970.
24. Cooper, O., *Future is Before Us*, Broadman, Tennurse, 1973.
25. Craver, J.K., Effect of the Future on Today's Decisions, *Long Range Planning* 6 (2), 29-34, 1973.
26. Cross, N., D. Elliott and R. Roy, *Man Made Futures*, Hutchinson, London, 1974.
27. Daedalus, 96 (3), *Towards the Year 2000*, 639-990, 1967.
    The year 2000, Baselines for the future, Alternative futures.
    Centralization and decentralization, Need for models;
    The next 30 years, Can social predication be evaluated;
    Forecasting and technological forecasting;
    University Cities in the year 2000;
    Efforts to control human behaviour;
    Biological man in the year 2000;
    Problems of privacy in 2000;
    Psychological perspectives in 2000;
    On meritocracy;
    Future international society;
    World Order 2000;
    International System in the next century;
    Nature and limitations of forecasting;
    Four Futures.
28. Dalkey, N., *Predicting the Future*, P-3948, Rand Corp. Banta Monica, 1968.
29. De Jouvenel, B., *The Art of Confecture*, Basic Books, New York, 1967.
30. Nike, L. De, The Danger of Dire Predictions, *Futurist*, 6 (3), 118, 1972.
31. Dobrov, G.M., Forecasting as a means for Scientific and Technology policy control, *Tech. Forecast*, 4 (1), 5-18, 1972.
32. Dror, Y., A Third Look at Futures Studies, *TF & SC* 5, 109-112, 1973.

33. Drucker, P.F., *The Age of Discontinuity*, Harper and Row, New York, 1968.
34. Dunstan, M. and P.W. Garlan, *Worlds in the Making*, Prentice Hall, New Jersey, 1970.
35. Ebling and Heath, *The Future of Man*, Royal Geographical Society, London, 1972.
36. Encel, S.; Science, Technology and the Future, *Search*, 5 (8), 387, 1974.
37. *Engineering News Record* 192(18), 30 April, 1974. Probing the future, (1) To 2000 and Beyond, (2) Defusing the cities, (3) Tomorrows housing, (4) Water, (5) Energy in crisis and transition (6) Opening the transportation bottleneck (7) future of labour force, (8) Will solid wastes bury us, (9) Tomorrows tools and methods, (10) Future materials, (11) Design of environments, (12) Under the seas and in outer space, (13) Planning for change, (14) 100 years of constructions, (15) A Century of probing the future.
38. Enzer, S., A Case Study using Forecasting as a Decision Making Aid, WP-2, IFF, Menlopark, 1969.
39. Falk, R.A., *A Study of the Future Worlds*, Orient Longman, New Delhi, 1975.
40. Europe 2000, *Future is Tomorrow*, M. Nijhoff, Prague, 1974.
41. Flechtheim, O.K., *History and Futurology*, Verlag Anton Hain, Germany, 1966.
42. Flechtheim, O.K., *Futurology Today-Directions and Scope*, University, 11(1), 75, 1968.
43. Frejka, T., *Future of Population Growth: Alternate Paths to Equilibrium*, Wiley, New York, 1973.
44. Foreign Policy Association, Toward the Year 2018 Cowles, New York, 1963.
45. Furnas, C.C., *The Next Hundred Years*, Williams and Wilkins, Baltimore, 1936.
46. *Futures, Human Futures*, IPC Science and Technology Press, Sussex, 1974.
47. Gabor, D., *Inventing the Future*, Penguin, Harmondsworth, 1964.
48. ———, Inventing the Future, is now, Dell, New York, 1973.
49. Goeschel, H., Technology and Mankind's Future, *Universities* 12 (1), 21, 1969.

50. Gordon, J., *The Future*, St. Martins Press, New York, 1965.
51. Gordon, T.J., *Current Methods of Futures Research*, P-11, IFF, Menlopark, 1971.
52. Griffith, P.B., *Future is not What it used to be*, Simon and Schuster, New York, 1970.
53. Hall, P., *The Planner*, Special Futurology Edition, Vol. 60(4), 1974.
54. Handler, P., *Biology and the Future of Man*, Oxford University Press, New York, 1970.
55. Haydon, B., The Year 2000, p. 3571, Rand Corp., Santa Manica, 1967.
56. Heilbrones, R.L., An Inquiry into the Human Prospect, Norton, New York, 1974.
57. ———, Second Thoughts on the Human Prospect, Futures 7 (1), 31-40, 1975.
58. Heinlein, L.J., *The Past through Tomorrow*, Doubleday, New York, 1968.
59. Helmer, O., An Agenda for Futures Research, *Futures* 7(1), 3-14, 1975.
60. Henry, N., The Future as Information, *Futures*. 5, 392-400, 1973.
61. Hetman, F., Language of Forecasting, *Futuribles*, Paris, 1969.
62. Holst, J.H., *Peacekeeping: Some Policy Issues for the Future*, H1-1117/2-RR, Hudson Institute, New York, 1968.
63. Hoos, I.R., *Criteria for Good Futures Research*, TF and SC 6, 113-132, 1974.
64. Hughes, D., Towards a Recycling Society, *New Scientist*, 61, 113-132, 1974.
65. ———, Towards a Recycling Society, *New Scientist*, 61, (880), 58, Jan. 10, 1974.
66. Jackson, R.M., Politics and Futurology, *Futures* 6(5) 420, 1974.
67. Japan Society of Futurology, Proceedings of the International Futures Conference, Kodansha, Japan, 1970, Volume 1. The role of future and Future Research; The role of imagination and futures research, problems in social and cultural forecasting, Delphi and Cross impact techniques; Assumptions in futures research, Typological survey of futures research; Science Fiction as a forecasting methodology;

Information and epistemology in futuristics; Futurism: Pros and Cons.; Use of the future for Development policy; Critical Futurology; Futures Research and its role in the world; Scientific basis of Futurology; Forward looking for today and tomorrow; Forecasting methods in social sciences; Methodology of futurology; General system of prognostication; Systems analysis for policy planning; Forecasting analysis and Decision making; Social forecasting and prognostication; Prospective conflictology of futures research; Forecasting as an aid to planning; Human revolution; Spread of soft technology; Flexible system in Education; Value in leisure Political innovation.

68. Japan Society of Futurology; Proceedings of the International Futures Conference, Kodansha, Japan 1970; Vol. 2 Social change; Technological Innovations and Education for Future; Technology of the Future; Social Impact of Computerization; How to Introduce Change in Complex Systems; Delphi Technique, Futures Studies; Social and Cultural Consequences of Automation; How men can Shape their future; Policy and Future; Research Social indicators; SINIC — An Approach to the Futures; Forecasting interactions between technological and social changes, A policy view of futures studies; Futurology and Philosophy of techniques; Education for futurism; Educating man for the 21st Century. Aesthetical education in future; Towards a new technology of education; Futures Studies and Educational policy; Problems of education and the future; Handling of increasing leisure; Future town as an act of choice; Resources conserving urbanism; Future urbanisation patterns; Tomorrows transportation; Human living standards in the future.

69. Japan Society of Futurology Proceedings of the International Future Conference, Kodansha, Japan, 1970. Vol. 3 New Values; Social systems and world futures; Way to stimulate political innovations; Social and political innovations; Measuring social innovation; Alternative Domestic Political Futures; Innovation in Bureaucratic systems; Future planning in corporate environment; International Technology Assessment; Socio-Political Decision processes in social planning; Future

from the point of view of a critical theory; Law of nations and futurology; Future of Human society; Evolution or revolution; A valid dilemma, changing oceanic circulation; A model of technological development.

70. Jantsch, E., Forecasting the Future, *Science Jl* 3 (10) 40-48, 1967.
71. Jaspers, K., *Future of Mankind*, University of Chicago, Chicago, 1961.
72. Jungk, R. and J. Galtung, *Mankind 2000*, Allen and Unwin, London, 1969.
On the Future of International System; Looking Forward to 1999; Material Resources; Solution of World Food Problem; Communication in the year 2000; TV from space; Education and Future; Medicine and our future society; Future of Cybernetics; Professional futurist; Future research, Is Futurology the answer to the challenge of the future; Prognostication and Prognoseology; Social prognostics, Towards a goal of goals; Computer based system for the exploration of possible futures for 2000.
73. Jungk, R., The Future of Future Research, *Science Jl* 3(10), 3, 1967.
74. ———, Imagination and the Future, *International Soc. Sci. Jl.* 21 (4), 557, 1969.
75. Kahn, H., and A.J. Weiner, *The year 2000-A Framework for Speculating about the Next 33 Years*, Macmillan, New York, 1967.
76. ———, Some notes for a paper on Resources, power, pollution and other depletion and scarcity type issues, HI-1625-D, Hudson Institute: New York, 1972.
77. ———, *A Glimpse at the Seventies*, HI-1259-p, Hudson Institute, New York, 1969.
78. ———, The world of 1980, HI-122172-p, Hudson Institute, New York 1869.
79. ———, The World of 1990, HI-1570-P, Hudson Institute, New York, 1969.
80. ———, *World Futures*, Sci. Jl. 3(10), 120, 1967.
81. Kahn, H., and B. Bruce-Briggs, *Things to Come: Thinking about 70's and 80's*, Macmillan, New York, 1972.
82. Karlik, J., *Implementing the Year 2000 Ideology*, HI-970/2, Hudson Institute, New York, 1968.

83. Kaya, Y. and Y. Suzuki, Global Constraints and a New Vision for Development-Part-I, *TF and SC* 6, 277, 1974.
84. Kaya, Y. and Y. Suzuki, Global constraints and a new vision for development-Part-II. *TF and SC* 6, 371, 1974.
85. Kettle, J., *Footnotes on the Future*, Methuen, London, 1970.
86. Kiefer, D.M., The Futures Business, *Chem. and Engg. News*, pp. 62, August 11, 1969.
87. Kostelanetz, R., *Human Alternatives: Visions for us now*, William Morrow, New York, 1971.
88. Laithwaite, E.R., Rules of the Planet Earth, *Elect. Review* 194(4), 104, Feb. 8, 1974.
89. Linstone, H.A., A University for the Post-industrial Society. TF and SC 1,1970.
90. ———, Four American Futures: Reflections on the role of planning. *TF and SC* 4(1), 41, 1972.
91. ———, On discounting the Future. *TF and SC* 4, 335, 1972.
92. Livingston, D., Science Fiction and Futurology, *Futurist*, 2 (6), 47-68, 1968.
93. Lundborg, L.B., *Future without Shock*, Norton, New York, 1974.
94. Marien, M., Herman Kahn's things to come, *Futurist* 7 (1), 7, 1973.
95. Martin, A., *The last generation: The end of Survival*, Fontana, London, 1975.
96. Mc Hale, J., Towards the Future, *Teilhard Review*, Vol. 3(1), 1968.
97. ———, *The Future of the Future*, George Braziller, New York, 1969.
98. ———, *World Fact and Trends: Where man is Headed-A Multidimensional View*, Collier, New York, 1972.
99. ———, The Changing Pattern of Futures Research in the USA, *Futures*, pp. 257-271, 1973.
100. Miller, D.C., Is To-day Tomorrow, *Futurist*, 7(4), 175, 1973.
101. Mishan, E.J., To Grow or Not to Grow: What are the Issues, *Encounter*; 40(5), 9-29, May 1973.
102. Morgan, C.H., *Mans Long Term Future Prospects*, HI-1630-P, Hudson Institute, New York, 1972.

103. Muckehirm, M., *Future as Shared Hope*, Sheed, New York, 1968.
104. Nicol, H., *The Limits of Man*, Constable, London.
105. Peccei, A., Problems of World Future, *TF and SC* 1 (3), 229-233, 1970.
106. Pierre, A.J., *On the Future Environment of International Peacekeeping in the Third World*, HI-1067/3-RR, Hudson Institute, New York, 1968.
107. Piganiol, P., Futurology and Prospective Study, *Internat. Soc. Sci. Jl* 21(4), 515, 1969.
108. Platt, J.C., What we must do, *Science*, 166. 1115-1122, 1969.
109. ———, How Can Man Shape the Future, *Futures*, pp. 32-47, March 1971.
110. Pocock, B.M., Futurology and Planning, *Long Range Planning*. 8(1), 64-69, 1975.
111. Podhoretz, N., Does Literature have a Future, *Amer Review*. 19(3), 53-59, 1975.
112. Polak, F.L., Prognostics, Elsevier, Amsterdam, 1971.
113. ———, Image of the Future, Elsevier, Amsterdam, 1973.
114. Prehcda, R.W., *Designing the Future*, Chilton Books, Philadelphia, 1967.
115. Rescher, N., *Future as an Object of Research*, p. 3593, Rand Corp., Santa Monica, 1967.
116. Ridker, R.G., To Grow or Not to Grow, *Science*. 182 (4119), 1315, Dec. 1973.
117. Rochberg, R., *Some Comments on the Problem of Self-Affecting Predictions*, p. 3735, Rand Corp., Santa Monica, 1967.
118. Rolansky, J.D., Shaping the future, 1971 Nobel Conference, North-Holland, Amsterdam, 1972.
119. Rye, J., *Futurism*, Dutton, New York, 1972.
120. Schneider, J.H., The Population Explosion-Can it Shake the Climate? *AMBIO*, 3(3), 150-155, 1974.
121. Secretariat for Future Studies, To choose a Future, *SFFS*, Stockholm, 1974.
122. Secretariat for Future Studies, Man in the Communications System of the Future, *SFFS*, Stockholm, 1974.
123. Seth, S.C., (ed.) *The Base Document on Futurology*, NCST Publication (Cyclostyled).

124. ———, (ed.), *An outlook for India's Future: (2000 AD): A Summary of Methodology, Approach and Views.*
125. Seth, Z.C., Mankind 2000, *Indian Administrative and Management Review.* 5 (2), 10, 1973.
126. *Science Journal*, Vol. 3(10), 3-120, 1967, Futures Special, Science, Energy, automation, Communication Space, Transport, Food, Materials, Population.
127. Siebker, M. and Y. Kaya, The Club of Rome from Tokyo: Towards a global vision of human problems, *TF and SC.* 6, 231-260, 1974.
128. Simmonds, W.H.C., How to make sure you have a Future, Innovation. 12, 38-43, 1970.
129. Starr, C., Parameters of Technological Growth, *Science* 177, p. 518, August 1972.
130. Taviss, I., Futurology and the Problem of Values, *International Social Science Jl*, 21 (4), 574.
131. Teilhard de Chardin, *The Future of Man*, Collins, London, 1964.
132. Theobald, R. and J.M. Scott, *Teg's 1994: An Anticipation of the Near Future*, Swallow Press, Chicago, 1972
133. ———, *Futures Conditional*, Bobbs-Merrill, New York, 1972.
134. Thompson, G., *Forseeable Future*, Cambridge University Press, Cambridge, 1955.
135. Toffler, A., *Future Shock*, Ramdom House, New York, 1970.
136. ———, *Futurists*, Ramdom House, New york, 1972
137. Watson-Watt, R., Man's Means to his end, Heineman; London 1962.
138. Wilkinson, J., *Retrospective Futurology*, CSDI, Santa Barbara, 1974.
139. Wilson, A. and D. Wilson, The four faces of the future, *TF and SC* 7, 5-12, 1975.
140. Wolstenholme, G., *Man and His future*, Churchill, London, 1967.

Future of Man, Future of Mind; World Population; Future of Infections and Malignant Diseases; Longevity; World resources; Biological Future; Agricultural Productivity and population; Engenics and genetics; Sociological aspects of future; Growth and development of social groups.

B. Methodologies

1. Aiso, M., Forecasting techniques, *IBM Systems* Jl. 12(2), 187-209, 1973.
2. Alderson, R.C., Requirement Analysis, Forecasting and Technology Planning using Pattern, *TF and SC* 3 (2), 255, 1972.
3. Amara, R., Forecasting : From Conjectural Art Towards Science, *Futurist* 6(3), 112, 1972.
4. ———, Some views on the use of expert judgement. *TF and SC*. 3 (3), 279-289, 1972.
5. Amert, R.H., Comparison of Delphi Forecasting Studies in 1964 and 1969, *Futures* 2 (1), March 1970.
6. Augimeri, R.M., Forecasting the Future, Australian Chem. Engr. 13(5), 21, 1971.
7. Bar-Zakay, S.N., Technology Transfer Model, AD-731271, NTIS, Virginia, 1970.
8. Barch, J.L., and R.J. Twery, Forecasting techniques in R&D Planning, *Chem. Engg. Prog*. 66 (6), 15, 1970.
9. Bendes, A.D., A.E. Strack, G.W. Ebright and G. Von Haunalter, Delphi Study Examines Developments in Medicine, *Futures* 2, 289-303, 1969.
10. Bell, D., Twelve modes of prediction. In *Survey of Social Sciences*, Penguin, Baltimore, 1965.
11. Bereano, P.L., A Proposed Methodology for Assessing Alternative Technologies, *Tech. Assess*. 1 (3), 179, 1973.
12. Blackman, A.W., Normex Forecasting of Jet Engine Characteristics, *TF and SC*. 2, 61-76, 1970.
13. ———, The Use of Bayesian Techniques in Delphi forecasts. *TF and SC*. 2, 261-268, 1971.
14. ———, Forecasting through Dynamic Modeling, *TF and SC*. 6, 291-307, 1972.
15. ———, A Mathematical Model for Trend Forecasts, *TF and SC*. 3, 441-452, 1972.
16. ———, The Market Dynamics of Technological Substitutions, *TF and SC*. 6, 41-63, 1973.
17. ———, A Cross Impact Model Applicable to Forecasts for Long Range Planning, *TF & SC*. 5, 233, 1973.
18. ———, The use of Dynamic Modeling for Conditional Forecasts of Resource Allocation Policies, *TF and SC*. 6,191-208, 1974.

19. Bright, J.R., Can We Forecast Technology, *Management Thinking*, pp. 12-15, July 1968.
20. ———, A few kind words for trend extrapolation. *Futures* 5(4), 344-1973.
21. Brewer, G.D., *Gaming: Prospective for Forecasting*, p. 5178, Rand Crop., Santa Monica, 1974.
22. Brown, T.A., *An Experiment in Probabilistic Forecasting*, R-944-ARPA, Rand Corp., Santa Monica, 1973.
23. Brown, R.G., *Smoothing, Forecasting and Prediction of Discrete Time Series*, Prentice Hall, New Jersey, 1963.
24. Business Planning Group, *Delphi: The Bell Canada Experience*, Bell Canada, Montreal, 1972.
25. Bulter W.F., and R.D. Kayesh, *How Business Economists Forecast*, Prentice Hall, New Jersey, 1966.
26. Mc Burney, W.J., Financial Forecasts Emerge from the Shadows, *Futurist* 6 (5), 204, 1972.
27. Cazes, C., Applied Futures Research in France, *Futures* 5 (3), 277-280, 1973.
28. Cetron, M.J., and B. Bartocha, A Forecasting Model to Aid Research and Development Planning, *Futures* 1, 479-487, 1969.
29. Cetron, M.J., Forecasting Technology, *International Science and Technology*, p. 83, September, 1967.
30. Clarke, I.F., Ciecero Syndrome, *Futures* 6(2), 160, 1974.
31. Chambers, J.C., How to Choose the Right Forecasting Technique, *Harv Busi Rev.* 49(4), 45, 1971.
32. Chavchanidze, V., Induction of psychointellectual activity in long term forecasting and planning: Psychoheuristio programming, *TF and SC* 1 (2), 129-139, 1969.
33. Clark, G.H., *Brainstorming*, Double-day, New York, 1958.
34. Cottrell, A., Problems of Predicting Future World Trends, *Nature* 245, p. 280, 1973.
35. Dalkey, N., and O. Helmer, An Experimental Application of Delphi Method to the Use of Experts, *Mgmt. Sci.* 9, 458-467, 1963.
36. ———, *The Delphi Method and Experimental Study of Group Opinion*, RM-5888 DR, Rand Corp., Santa Monica, 1969.
37. ———, *An Elementary Cross Impact Model*, R. 677-ARPA Rand Corp., Santa Monica, 1971.

38. ———, Elementary Cross Impact Model, *TF and SC* 3 (3), 341-351, 1972.
39. Day, L.H., *Delphi Research in the Corporate Environment*. Bell Canada, Montreal, 1972.
40. Dewhurst, R.F.J., *Business Cost-benefit Analysis*, Business Books, London, 1972.
41. Doan, H.D., The Trouble with Forecasts, *Chem. Engg. Prog.* 69(12), 7,1973.
42. Dressler, F.R.S., Subjective Methodology in Forecasting. *TF and SC*. 3(4), 427-429, 1972.
43. Drox, Y., *Design for Policy Sciences*, Elsevier, Amsterdam, 1971.
44. ———, Ventures in Policy Sciences, American Elsevier, New York, 1971.
45. Duval, A., E. Fontela and A. Gabus, *Cross Impact: A Hand Book of Concepts and Applications*, Battelle, Geneva, 1974.
46. Eckenrode, R.T., Weighting Multiple Objectives, *Mgmt. Sci.* 12(3), 180-192, 1965.
47. Enzer, S., A Case Study using Forecasting as a Decision Making Aid, *Futures* 2(4), 314, 1970.
48. Fisher, G.H., *Some Comments on Conceptual Framework for Comparing Alternatives*, p-4506, Rand Corp., Santa Monica, 1970.
49. Fisher, J.C., and R.H. Pry, A Simple Substitution Model of Technological Change. *TF and SC*. 8, 75-88, 1971.
50. Foster, R., E. Leonard and R. Rea, A Scenario Generating Methodology, Art Associates, Cambridge, 1970.
51. Franco, G.R., Selecting Efficient Forecasts, *Futures* 5(4), 383-391, 1974.
52. Fusefeld, A.R. and R.N. Foster. The Delphi Technique: Survey and Comment, *Business Horizons* 14, 63, 1971.
53. Fusefeld, A.R., Technological Progress Function: A New Technique for Forecasting. *TF and SC*. 1, 301-312, 1970.
54. Geschka, H., G.R. Schaude and H. Schlicksupp, Modern Techniques for Solving Problems, *Chem. Engg*. Vol. 80.91 Aug. 6, 1973.
55. Gordon, T.F. and H. Hayward, Initial Experiments with the Cross Impact Method of Forecasting. *Futures* 1, 100, 1968.
56. Gordon, T.J., Cross-impact Matrices, *Futures* 1, 527-531, 1969.

57. ———, *The Current Methods of Futures Research*, p-11 IFF, Menlo Park, 1971.
58. Gordon, T.J., R. Cochberle and S. Enzer, *Research on Cross-Impact Technique with Applications to Selected Problems in Economics, Political Science and TA*, R-12, IFF, Menlo Park, 1970.
59. Gordon, T.J., and O. Helmer, *Report on a Long Range Forecasting Study*, p. 2082, Rand Corp., Santa Monica, 1964.
60. Hall, A.D., Three Dimensional Morphology of Systems Engineering, *IEEE Trans on Systems Science and Cybernetics*, RP 156-160, April 1969.
61. Helmer, O., and N. Rescher, On the Epistemology of the Inexact Sciences, *Mgmt. Sci.* 6, 25-52, 1959.
62. ———, *Long range Forecasting's Roles and Methods*, p-7, IFF, Menlo Park, 1970.
63. ———, Cross-impact Gaming, *Futures*, Feb. 1972.
64. Helmer, O., R. de Brigard and R. Buchele, *A Simulation Game of the Study of State Policies*, R-9, IFF, Menlo Park, 1970.
65. Herzog, H.W., An Environmental Assessment of Future Production Related Technological Change: 1970-2000, *TF and SC.* 75, 1973.
66. Hirschman, W.B., *Profit from the Learning Curve, Harward Business Review*, Jan, 1 Feb. 1964.
67. Hodges, S. and D. Kennett, Practical Problems of Gravity Modelling. *Long Range Planning* 6(4), 41, 1973.
68. Huckfeldt, V.E. and R.C. Judd, *Methods for Large-scale Delphi Studies.* WICHE, Colorado, 1975.
69. ———, *Issues in Large-scale Delphi Studies. TF and SC.* 6, 75-88, 1974.
70. Hudson, B.J.F., New Protein Foods-A Delphi, *Chem. and Industry*, No. 6. 251-254, 1972.
71. Jantsch, E., Toward a methodology for systemic forecasting, *TF and SC.* 1(4), 409-419, 1970.
72. Johnson, H.E., Some Computational Aspects of Cross Impact Matrix Forecasting, *Futures*, June 1970.
73. Kothari, R., *A Note on Theory and Methodology in the Study of the Future*, NCST Panel on Futurology, New Delhi, 1974.
74. Klee, A.J., *The Utilization of Expert Opinion in Decision Making*, AICHE, Jl. 18(6), 1107, 1972.

75. Lanford, H.W., A Penetration of the Technological Forecasting Jungle, *TF and SC* 4, 208-225, 1972.
76. Leclercz, R., The Use of Generalized Logic in Forecasting, *TF and SC* 2(2), 193-194, 1970.
77. Lee, O.B., Requiem for Large scale Models. *AIP Jl.* May 1973.
78. Leibson, I., and C.A. Trischman, Decision trees, *Chem. Engg.* 79, p. 99, 24 Jan. 1972.
79. Linstone, H.A. and M.A. Turoff, *The Delphi Method: Techniques and Applications*, Addison and Wesley, Reading 1975.
80. Lipinski, A.J., H.M. Lipinski L.R.H. Randolf, Computer Assisted Expert-Interrogation, *TF and SC*, 5, 3-18, 1973.
81. Livingston, D., Science Fiction as a Source of Forecast Material, *Futures*, 1 (3), 232-238, 1969.
82. Marien, M., *The Hot List Delphi: An Exploratory Survey of Essential Reading for the Future*, Syracuse University Res. Corp. Syracuse, 1972.
83. Martino, J.P., An Experiment with the Delphi Procedure for Long Range Forecasting, *IEEE Trans on Engg Mgmt*, EM-15 (3), 138, 1968.
84. ———, Correlation of Technological Trends, *TF and SC*. 1, 347-354, 1970.
85. ———, The lognormality of Delphi estimate, *TF and SC*. 1, 355, 1970.
86. ———, The Optimism-Pessimism Consistency of Delphi Panelists, *TF and SC*. 2, 221, 1970.
87. Maruyama, M., A New Logical Model for Futures Research, *Futures*, 5(5), 435-437, 1973.
88. Marley, B. Clark, Delphi Method and Urbanisation, *Long Range Planning*. 7 (6), 81-83, 1974.
89. Maruyama, M., Endogenous Research versus Experts from Outside, *Futures* 6, 389-394, 1974.
90. Massey, H.G., *Cost, Benefit and Risk-Keys to evaluation of Policy Alternatives*, p. 5197, Rand Corp., Santa Monica, 1974.
91. McHale, J., The Changing Pattern of Futures Research in the USA, *Futures*, 5(3), 257, 1973.
92. Meadone, A. and S.J. Parnes, Evaluation of Training in Creative Problem Solving-Brainstorming, *Jl of Appl. Psych.* 43(3), 189, 1959.

93. Merritt, T.P., Forecasting the Future, *Long Range Planning*, 7(3), 54, 1974.
94. Mesarovic, M. and E. Pestel, A Global Seeking and Regionalized Model for Analysis of Critical World Relationships. The Conceptual Foundation, *Kebernetics* 1, 79, 1973.
95. ———, An interactive decision stratum for the multi-level world model, *Futures*, 5(4), 357-366, 1973.
96. Mitroff, I.I. and M. Turoff, On Measuring the Conceptual Errors in Large Scale Social Experiments: The Future as Decision. *TF and SC* 6, 389, 1974.
97. Mohn, N.C., Application of Trend Concepts in Forecasting Typesetting Technology, *TF and SC*, 3(2), 1972.
98. North, H.Q. and D.L. Pyke, Probes of the technological futures. Harv Buri Review. 47(3), 68-82, 1969.
99. NCST Panel on Futurology Background Papers and Special Notes for Discussion: *Futurology*, NCST, New Delhi, 1974.
100. Pearce, S.F., Computerised Forecasting in Western Europe, *IMRA Jl.* pp. 11-27, 1973.
101. Prest, A.R. and R. Turvey' Cost Benefit Analysis: A Survey, *The Economic Jl.* pp. 683-735, Dec, 1965.
102. Pyke, D.L., Mapping - A System Concept for Displaying Alternatives, *TF and SC.* 2, 311-320, 1971.
103. ———, A practical approach to Delphi, Futures 3, 143, 1971.
104. Quade, E.S., *Systems Analysis: A Tool for Choice*, p. 4860, Rand Corp., Santa Monica, 1972.
105. Rabitsh, E.K., Input-output Analysis and Business Forecasting, *TF and SC.* 3(4), 453, 1972.
106. Reid, G.W., *A Multistructural Demand Model for Water Requirement Forecasting*, PB-190813, NTIS, Virginia, 1970.
107. Ribeill, G., Elements and Methods of Industrial Forecasting, *Futures.* 6(5), 395, 1974.
108. Roberts, P., Models of the Future, *Omega*; 1(5), Oct. 1973.
109. Rochberg, R., *Information Theory, Cross Impact Matrices and Pivotal Events*, P-8, IFF, Menlo Park, 1970.
110. Rochberg, R., T.J. Gordon and O. Helmer, *The Use of Cross-Impact Matrices for Forecasting and Planning*, R-10, IFF, Menlo Part, 1970.

111. Randsepp, E., *Synecties: Enhancing the Group Creativity*, Hydro Proce 50, p. 133, Jan. 1971.
112. Sackman, H., *Delphi Assessment: Expert Opinion Forecasting and Group Process*, R-183-FR, Rand Corp., Santo Monica, 1974.
113. Sahal, D., Generalized poisson and Related Models of Technological Innovation, *TF and SC*. 6(4), 403-436, 1974.
114. Salamoik, J.R., W. Wenger and E. Helfer, *Construction of Delphi Statements*, p. 13. IFF, Menlo Park, 1971.
115. Schoenermann, P.T., Forecasts and Model Building, *IMRA Jl*. 6, 130. 1970.
116. Sharif, M.N., and G.A. Uddin, *A Procedure for Adapting Technological Forecasting Models, TF and SC*. 7(1), 99, 1975.
117. Sheppard, W.J., Relevance Analysis in Research Planning, TF 1, 371, 1970.
118. Simmonds, W.H.C., An Analysis of Industrial Behaviour and its use in Forecasting, *TF and SC*, 3(2), 205, 1972.
119. Stefflre, V., Long Term Forecasting and the Problem of Wars, *Futures*, 6(4), 302, 1974.
120. Sule, O., Futures Research in Czechoslovakia, *Futures*, 5(6), 578, 1973
121. Swager, W.L., Technological Forecasting in Research and Development, *Chem. Engg. Prog*. 65(12), 39, 1969.
122. Swett, B.H., Fundamental theory and Problems Related to Long-range Forecasting, AD-854590, NTIS, Virginia, 1968.
123. Teeling Smith, G., Medicines in 1990: Experience with a Delphi Forecast, *Long Range Planning* 5. pp. 59, 1971.
124. Theobald, R., Alternative Methods of Predicting the Future, *Futurist*. 3(2), 43, 1969.
125. M. Turoff, The Design of a Policy Delphi, *TF and SC*. 2(2), 141, 1970.
126. ———, Delphi Conferencing: Computer based conferencing with anonymity, *TF and SC*. 3, 159, 1972.
127. ———, Delphi and its Potential Impact on Information Systems, AFIPS conference proceedings, Vol 39, pp. 317.
128. ———, An Alternative Approach to Cross Impact Analysis, *TF and SC*. 3, 309, 1972.
129. Wagle, B., Some Statistical Aids in Forecasting, *The Statistician*, 15(2), 1965.

130. Wagle, B., Some Recent Developments in Forecasting Techniques, *Jl. of Inst Petro*, 1966.
131. Weimberg, A.M., Criteria for Scientific Choice, *Minerva 1(2)*, 159, 1963.
132. Zernan, M., Remarks on Teratological Forecasting Models. *TF and SC*. 6, 209, 1974.
133. Zuricky, F., Discovery, Invention, Research, through the monophological Approach, Macmillan, New York, 1968.

C. Technological Forecasting

1. Armytage, W.H.G., Technological Forecasting, Proceedings of the Inst. of Mechanical Engrs. 184, 1970.
2. Arnfield, R.V., *Technological Forecasting*, Edinburgh Univ. Press, Edinburgh, 1969.
3. Ayres, R.U., *Technological Forecasting and Long Range Planning*, McGraw Hill, New York, 1969.
4. Blackman, A.W., The Role of Technological Forecasting in Analysis and Planning of New Ventures, 72-DE-26, ASME, New York, 1972.
5. ———, New Venture Planning; The Role of Technological Forecasting. *TF and SC*. 5, 25, 1973.
6. Blchm, H. and K. Steinbuch, *Technological Forecasting in Practice*, Saxin, Farnborough, 1973.
7. Bright, J.R., Technological Forecasting: New Tools for an Old Responsibility, *Res Mgmt*, DPSO-65, July 1972.
8. Bouladon, G., Technological Forecasting Applied to Transport, *Futures*. 2, 15, 1970.
9. Bright, J.R., Technological Forecasting for Industry and Government, Prentice Hall, New Jersey, 1968.
10. Bright, J.R. and M.E.P. Schoeman. *A Practical Guide to Technological Forecasting*, Prentice Hall, New Jersey, 1973.
11. Bright, J.R., A Brief introduction to Technology forecasting: Concepts and exercises, Pemaquid Press, Texas, 1972.
12. Bruno, A.V., J.D. Montgomery and E. Capener, Technological Forecasting in Small Companies, *Mgmt Review*. 15(1), 49-65, 1973.
13. Bruno, A.V., T.E. Bibbeds and J.J. Digiovanni, A reassessment of Technological Forecasting in a Small Company. *Slogan Mgmt Review*, 15(3), 89, 1974.

14. Carter, A.P., Technological Forecasting and Input Output Analysis, *TF and SC* 1(4), 331-345, 1970.
15. Cetron, M.J. and C.A. Ralph, *Industrial Applications of Technological Forecasting*, Wiley Interscience, 1971.
16. Cetron, M.J., Using Technological Forecasts. *Science and Technology*, p. 57, July 1968.
17. ———, *Technological Forecasting*, Gordon & Breach, New York, 1969.
18 ———, A Method for Integrating Goals and Technological Forecasts into Planning. *TF & SC* 2, 23, 1970.
19. Cetron, M.J. and D.N. Dick, TF: Practical Problems and Pitfalls, IEEE *Trans Engg Mgmt. EM*-16(4), 161-172, 1969.
20. Curril, D.L., Technological Forecasting in Six Major UK. Companies, *Long Range Planning* 5(i), 72-77, 1972.
21. Dror, Y., Technology Forecasting and Policy Making Reform, *TF & SC*. 1(2), 109, 1969.
22. Dory, J.P. and Lodd, R.J., Does TF Really Work, *Harvard Business Review*, 48(168), 16, Nov/Dec. 1970.
23. Fields, S.R., Technological Forecasting, BNWL-1466, NTIS, Virginia, 1970.
24. Gestenfeld, A., *TF J. of Business*, 44(i), 10, 1971.
25. Hrusha, A., Science Forecasting and its Limits, *Futures*. 6(2), 153, 1974.
26. Hayden, S., How Industry is Using TF, *Mgmt Review*, 59 (5), 4, 1970.
27. Isenson, R.S., Technological forecasting in perspective, *Mgmt. Sci*. 13 (2) P-B70, Oct. 1966.
28. Jantsch, E., *Technological Forecasting in Perspective*, OECD, Paris, 1967.
29. ———, Technological Forecasting: A Tool for a Dynamic Science Policy, *Chem. Age of India*. 19 (7), 499, 1968.
30. ———, Technological Forecasting in Corporate Planning, *Long Range Planning*. 1 (1), Sep. 1968.
31. Khol, R., What Good is Technological Forecasting, *Mach. Design*. pp. 114-120, 14 Dec. 1972.
32. Kiefer, D.M., Industry Maps Tomorrows Technology, *Chem. & Engg. News*, pp. 11-19, 28 Feb. 1972.
33. Lanford, H.W., *Technological Forecasting Methodologies*, American Mgmt. Association, New York, 1972.

34. Lanford, H.W., Approaches to Technological Forecasting as a Planning Tool, *Long Range Planning*. 7 (4), 49, 1974.
35. Lenz, R.C., *Technological Forecasting*, AD- 408085, U.S. Dept of Commerce, Virginia, June 1962.
36. Lien, A.P., P. Anton and J.W. Duncun, *Technological Forecasting Tools Techniques and Applications*, American Management Association, New York, 1968.
37. Linstone, H.A., Technology Forecasting: Planning Tool or Toy, *IEEE Spectrum*. 11(4), 42, 1974.
38. Lipinsky, E.S., Relevance Tree Techniques in Technological Forecasting, *Jl of Paint Tech* 41(453) 17A, 1969.
39. Martino, J.P., Seamans Competitive Model for Technological Growth, *TF & SC* 2, 107, 1970.
40. ———, Technology Forecasting: Tools for Looking Ahead, *IEEE Spectrum*, p. 32, Oct. 1972.
41. ———, *An Introduction to Technological Forecasting*. Gordon & Breach, New York, 1972.
42. ———, Technological Forecasting in Industry, *Futurist*, 6(4), 167, 1972.
43. ———, *Technological Forecasting for Decision Making*, American Elsevier, 1972.
44. ———, Correlation of Technological Trends, TF & SC 1, 347, 1970.
45. ———, Effect of Errors in Estimating the Upper Limit of a Growth Curve, *TF & SC* 4, 77, 1972.
46. Mencher, A G., *A Future for Technology Management Today*, Oct. 1970.
47. Mitroff, I.I. and M. Turoff, Technology forecasting and assessment: Science or Mythology, *TF & SC*. 5(2), 113, 1970.
48. North, H.Q. and D.L. Pyke, Technological Forecasting in Planning for Company Growth, *IEEE Spectrum*, p. 30, Jan. 1968.
49. ———, Technological Forecasting to Aid Research and Development Planning. *Res Mgmt* 12(4), 289, 1969.
50. Novik, O. and F.S. Pardee, Reducing Lead Time through Improved Technological Forecasting, *TF & SC*, 1(2), 141, 1969
51. Olenzak, A.T., Technological Forecasting: A Pragmatic Approach, *Chem Engg Prog*. 68(6), 27, 1972.

52. Olenzak, A.T., How Useful is Technological Forecasting. *Hydrocarbon Proc*, Vol. 53(5), 157, 1974.
53. Pananos, W.J., *An Introduction of Technological Forecasting*, AD-755 523, NTIS, Virginia, 1973.
54. Quinn, J.B., Technological Forecasting, *Harvard Business Review.* 45(2), p. 91, March/April, 1967
55. Richta, R. and O. Sule, Forecasting and the Scientific and Technological Revolution, *Intern Soc Sci. Jl.* 21(4), 563, 1969.
56. Rhyne, R., Technological Forecasting within Alternative Whole Futures Projections, *TF & SC* 6, 133, 1974.
57. Roberts, E.B., Exploratory and Normative Technological Forecasting. A Critical Appraisal, *TF & SC.* 1(2), Nov. 1969.
58. Rooney, J.W., *A Survey and Critique of Technological Forecasting: Methods*, D-736541, NTIS, Virginia, 1971.
59. Sahai, D., A Generalized Logistic Model for Technological Forecasting, *TF & SC.* 7(l), 81, 1975.
60. Swager, W.L., Technological Forecasting in Research and Development, *Chem Engg Prog.* 1965.
61. ———, Industrial Implications of Technological Forecasting, *Engg Economist*, pp. 19-34, 1966.
62. ———, Technological Forecasting for Practical Planning, *Petro Mgmt*, pp. 61-66, July 1966.
63. ———, Strategic Planning. The Roles of Technological Forecasting, *TF & SC.* 4, 85, 1972.
64. ———, Technological Forecasting in Planning, *Business Horizons*, Feb. 1973.
65. Tureff, M. and I.I. Mitreff, Technological Forecasting. The Whys behind the Hows, *IEEE Spectrum.* 10, (3), 62, 1973.
66. Vogel, P.H., A Basis for Technological Forecasting, *TF & SC* 1, 313, 1970.
67. Weber, E., G.K. Teal & A.G. Schillinger, *Technology Forecast for 1980*, Van Nostrand, New York, 1971.
68. Wills, G., R. Wilson, N. Manning and R. Hildebrandt, *Technological Forecasting: The Art and its Managerial Implications*, Penguin Books, Harmondsworth, 1972.
69. Wills, G., D. Ashton and B. Taylor, *Technological Forecasting and Corporate Strategy*, BUP-Cross by Lockwood, London, 1969.

70. Rohatgi, P K. and B. Bowonder, Potential use of technological forecasting in planning materials research, *NML Tech. Jl.* 14, 141, 1972.
71. ———, Technological forecasting for planning research and production in Chemical Industries; *Chem Age of India.* 24(9), 575, 1973.
72. ———, Technological forecasting: Relevance for India. *Economic Times.* 13 (315) 5, 30 Jan. 1974.
73. ———, Technological Forecasting for planning industries; *Economic Times.* 13 (314), 5, 29 Jan. 1974.
74. ———, Technology Forecast as applied to Indian environment, Proceedings of IEEE Annual Meeting, January 1974.
75. ———, Technological forecasting and research inputs in the area of birth control technology, *Jl. of Sci. Ind. Res.* 33 (12), 625, 1974.
76. ———, Technological Forecasting for Planning Research in the Area of Metals and Alloys. *Minerals & Metals Review.* 1(1) 7, 1975.
77. ———, *Technological Forecasting: Relevance, Applicability and Efforts in a Developing Country; TF & SC* 7 (3), 293-256, 1975.

D. Technology Assessment

1. Alpher, R.A., Technology Assessment: Its role in Corporate Planning, *Research Mgmt.* 16 (5), 18, 1973.
2. Anon, A., Blueprint for Survival, *Ecologist*, 13 Jan. 1972.
3. Altonpohl, D., Technology Assessment in Industry, GP-DA AP-650, Swiss Aluminium, Zurich, 1972.
4. Baram, M.S., Social Control of Science and Technology, *Science.* 172, 535, 1971.
5. ———, *Technology Assessment and Social Control Science.* 180 (4085), 465, 1973.
6. Barker, A.A. and J.A. Fowbr, *Technology Assessment*, Bioscience. 19 (10), 34, 1969.
7. Bedford, M.T., A Technology Assessment of Future Home Communications, *Business Planning Paper*-12, Bell Canada, Montreal, 1973.

8. Bedford, M.T., Technology Assessment and the Future of Educational Technology. *Business Planning* Paper-14, Bell Canada, Montreal, 1973.
9. Bell, D., The Impact of Automation, *American Review.* 19 (3), 46, 1975.
10. Bereano, P.L., A Proposed Methodology for Assessing Alternate Technology, *Technology Assessment.* 1 (3), 179, 1973.
11. Black, G., *Technology Assessment - What Should it Be,* PB-201 471, NTIS, Virginia, 1971.
12. Blum, W. and D. Altenpohol, Technology Assessment and Corporate Social Adult, Swiss Aluminiu, Zurich, 1973.
13. Bordman, S.L., Technology Assessment: Improving the Accuracy of Benefit-Cost Analysis, *IEEE Spectrum,* 10 (9), 72, 1973.
14. Brooks, H. and R. Bowers, The Assessment of Technology, *Scientific American*: 222 (2), 13, 1970.
15. Brown, B.A. and J.D. Goldhar, *High Energy Laser Technology Assessment.* Vol. 2, AD-A010101, Dept. of Army, Washington, 1975.
16. Brown, E.A. and M.V. Jones, *High Energy Laser Technology Assessment.* Vol. 1, AD-A010100, Dept. of Army, Washington, 1975.
17. Brubaker, S., *To Live on Earth: Man and His Environment in Perspective,* John Hopkin's Uni. Press, Maryland, 1972.
18. Cetron, M J. and B. Bartocha, *Technology Assessment in a Dynamic Environment.* Gordon and Breach New York, 1973.
19. Carpenter, R.A., Technology Assessment: Total Impact Analysis, Paper presented at the Symposium on Technology Assessment, Tokyo, 1973.
20. Coates, J.F., Technology Assessment: The Benefits the Costs, the Consequences; *Futurist*; pp. 225-230, Dec. 1971.
21. ———, Technology Assessment, McGraw Hill Year Book, *Science Technology,* 1974, McGraw Hill, New York, 1974.
22. ———, Technology Assessment: How Will it Work, *Standardisation News.* 2 (11) 30, 1974.
23. ———, Some Methods and Techniques for Comprehensive Impact Assessment, *TF & SC.* 6, 341, 1974.
24. ———, Bell Strikes again, Art International, *The Lugano Review,* 18 (10), 64, Dec. 1974.

25. ———, Technology Assessment and Public Wisdom, *Jl Wash Acad. Sci.* 65(1), 3, 1975.
26. Coates, V.T., *Technology and Public Policy: The Process of Technology Assessment in Government* (3 vols), George Washington University. Washington, 1972.
27. ———, Technology in Balance, *Futurist*, 7 (2), 66, 1973.
28. ———, Technology Assessment - Where it Stands Today, *Res. Mgmt.* 16 (5), 12, 1973.
29. ———, Technology Assessment: New Demands for Information, *Chem. Eng. Prog.* 70 (11), 41, 1974.
30. Commoner, B., Closing Circle, A Knopf, New York, 1971.
31. Daddario, E.Q., Needs for a National Policy, *Physics Today*, 22, 33, 1969.
32. ———, Priorities for the Future: Guidelines for Technology Assessment. 1971 *Britannica Year Book*, pp. 292-311, 1972.
33. Davis, R.C., Applying Technology Assessment in the Multiproduct Company, *Futures*. 6, 413, 1974.
34. Day, L.H., The Corporate Role in Technology Assessment. A Case Example, Business Planning Paper-13, Bell Canada, Montreal, 1973.
35. Dickey, J.W., D.M. Glancy and E.M. Jennelle, *Technology Assessment*. Lexington Books, Lexington, 1973.
36. Douglas, J.D., *Technological Treat*, Prentice Hall, New Jersey, 1971.
37. Edmunds, S. and J. Letey, *Environmental Administration*, McGraw Hill, New York, 1973.
38. Enzer, S., *Cross Impact Techniques in Technology Assessment*. p. 15, Institute for the Future, Menlo Park, 1971.
39. Enzer, E., Cross Impact Techniques in TA, *Futures*. 4 (1), 30, 1972.
40. EPA, *Alternative Futures and Environmental Quality*. Environmental Protection Agency, Washington, 1973.
41. Falkenmark, M. and G. Lunch, Impact of Water Resources on Population. Paper Presented at UN World Population Conference, Bucharest, 1974.
42. Feldman, P., Group Judgemental Data in Cross Impact Analysis and Technology Assessment. Business Planning Paper-19, Bell Canada, Montreal, 1973.

43. ———, Cross Impact Matrix Applications in Technology and Policy Assessment. Business Planning Paper-15, Bell Canada, Montreal, 1973.
44. ———, A Technology Assessment of Computer Assisted Instruction Use in Colleges. Report, Bell Canada, Montreal. 1973.
45. Fisher, A.C., J.V. Krutilla and C.J. Cicohetti, The Economics of Environmental Preservation: A Theoretical and Empurical Analysis, *American Economic Review*, Sep. 1972.
46. Flajser, S. and A.L. Porter, Toward a Science for Technology Assessment, *Trends in Engineering* 26 (4), 16, 1974.
47. Freeman, C., Technology Assessment and its Social Context, *Stadium Generale*. 24, 1038-1050, 1971.
48. Fuller, W., *Social Impact of Modern Biology*, Routledge and Kegan, London, 1971.
49. Goldman, D.T., Solid Wastes: A Technological Assessment *Chem. Engg. Prog*. 69 (9), 33, 1973.
50. Gordon, T.J. and H.S. Becker, The Cross Impact Matrix Approach to Technology Assessment, *Res. Mgmt*. pp. 73-81, July 1972.
51. Graverr, J K., A Practical Method for Technology Assessment, Paper Presented at the First International Congress on Technology Assessment, Hague, 1973.
52. Hall, C.C., Assessing Assessment, *Technology Review*, p. 58, January 1972.
53. Hamilton, M., The New Genetics and the Future of Man, William Erdsman, New York, 1972.
54. Headley, J.C. and J.N. Lewis, *The Pesticide Problem: An Economic Approach to Public Policy, Resources for the Future*, Washington, 1970.
55. Henderson, H., Technology Assessment and the Citizen, *The Trend in Engg*. 26 (2), 9, 1974.
56. Herfindahl, O.C. and A.V. Kneese, *Quality of the Environment: An Economic Approach to Some Problems in Using Land, Water and Air*, RFF, Washington, 1965.
57. Hertman, F., *Society and the Assessment of Technology*. OECD. Paris, 1974
58. Hilton, B., *Ethical Issues in Human Genetics*, Plenum, New York, 1972.

59. Holdren, J.P., Energy and Prosperity, *Bull Atomic Scientist*. 31 (1), 26, 1975.
60. Hollingsworth, R.E., Environmental Statement: LMFBR Demonstration Plant, WASH-1509, USAEC, Washington, 1972.
61. Iyengar, M.S., Technology Assessment and its relevance to the Developing Countries, Paper Presented at the First International Congress on Technology Assessment, Hague, 1973.
62. Jacobsen, W.E., A Technology Assessment Methodology, MTR-6009, Mitre Corp. McLean, 1971.
63. Jones, M.V., *Generating Social Impact Scenarios; A Key Step in Making Technology Assessment Studies*, N72-24978, NTIS, Virginia, 1972.
64. Kantrowiz, A., The Test: Meeting the Challenges of New Technology, *Bull Atomic Scientists*. 24(9), 21, 1969.
65. Kash, D.E. and I.L. White, Technology Assessment; Harnessing the genius, *Chem. and Engg. News* p. 36, 29 Nov., 1971.
66. ———, *Energy under the Oceans: A Technology Assessment*. Univ. of Oklahoma, Norman, 1973.
67. Kasper, R.G., *Technology Assessment*, Praeger, New York, 1972.
68. Kiefer, D.M., Technology: Talk about Assessment, *Chem. and Engg. News*. 47 (53), 11, 1969.
69. D.M. Kiefer, Technology Assessment: Approach with Caution, *Chem. and Engg. News*, 47, p. 26, 20 Oct. 1969.
70. ———, Technology: Its values, its Effects, *chem. and Engg. News*, 47 (49), p. 18, 24 Nov. 1969.
71. ———, Technology Assessment, *Chem. and Engg. News* 48. pp. 42-54, Oct. 5, 1970.
72. ———, A stance for Industry in Technology Assessment, *Chem. and Engg. News*, 48 (29), p. 20, 13 July 1970.
73. ———, Step Forward in Assessing Technology, *Chem. and Engg. News*, 50, p. 34, 20 March, 1972.
74. Knezo, G.T., Technology Assessment, *Tech. Assessment*. 1 (1), 62, 1972.
75. Lock, G.S., The Developing Responsibility of Technology Assessment. *Engineering Jl*. 56 (9), 18, 1973.

76. Martino, J.P., The Role of Forecasting in Technology Assessment, *Futurist*. 6 (5), 210, 1972.
77. Mayo, L.H., The Contextual Approach to TA: Implications for One-factor-fix Solutions to Complex Problems, N71-38781, NTIS, Virginia, 1971.
78. Medford, D., Environmental Harassmentor Technology Assessment, Elsevier, Amsterdam, 1973.
79. ———, Technology Assessment, *New Scientist*. 58 (847), 24 May, 1973.
80. Mitre Corporation, *A Technology Assessment Methodology and Volumes*, PB-202 778, NTIS, Virginia, 1971.
    Volume 1, *Basic Propositions*
    Volume 2, *Automotive Emissions*
    Volume 3, *Computer - Communication network*
    Volume 4, *Enzymes*
    Volume 5, *Mariculture - Sea Farming*
    Volume 6, *Water Pollution - Domestic Wastes*
81. Morgenthau, H., *Science: Servant or Master*, New American Library, New York, 1972.
82. National Academy of Sciences, Technology: Processes of Assessment and Choice. USGPO, Washington, 1969.
83. National Academy of Engineering, A Study of Technology Assessment, USGPO, Washington, 1969.
84. OECD, Methodological Guidelines for Social Assessment of Technology, OECD, Washington, 1975.
85. Parker, E.B. and D.A. Dunn, Information Technology: Its Social Potential, *Science*. 176, 1332-1399, June, 1972.
86. Poat, Marwick, Mitchell and So, *A Survey of Technology Assessment Today* NSF-C631, NSF, Washington, 1972.
87. Piel, E.J. and J.G. Truxal. *Man and His Technology: Problems and Issues*, McGraw Hill, New York, 1973.
88. Poleman, T.J. and D.K. Freebairn, *Food, Population and Employment: The Impact of Green Population*, Praeger, New York, 1973.
89. Porter, A.L. and J.J. Best, Technology Policy Assessment Research in the Social Management of Technology, *Trend in Engg*. 26 (2), 22, 1974.
90. Press, S.J. and A.J. Herman, *Methodology for Subjective Assessment of Technological Advancement*. R-1375, Rand Corp., Santa Monica, 1975.

91. Raymond, B. and J. Frey, Technology Assessment and Microwave Diodes, *Sci. Amer*. 226 (2), 13, 1972.
92. Roessner, J.D. and J. Frey, Methodology for Technology Assessment, *TF & SC*. 6, 163-169, 1974.
93. Russel, B., *Impact of Science on Society*, Union Books, London, 1968.
94. Sackman, H. and N. Nie, Information Utility and Social Choice, AFIPS, Montvale, 1970
95. Salaneik, G.R., Choosing Technology for a Better World, *Futurist*. 6(3), 208, 1972.
96. Schwortz, E.S., *Overskill: The Decline of Technology in Modern Civilization*, Quadrangle Books, New York, 1971.
97. Secretariat for Future Studies. Technology Assessment in Sweden : 9 Case Studies, SFFS, Stockholm, 1973.
98. Sinclair, T.C., Technology Assessment in U.K. *Technology Assessment*. 1(2), Oct. 1972.
99. Starr, C., Social Benefit versus Technological Risk, *Science* 165, 1232-1238, 1969.
100. ———, Technology Assessment, *Res. Mgmt*. 13 (6), 409, 1970
101. State Centre for Science Policy and Technology Assessment, Proceedings of Symposium on Manganese Module Deposits in the Pacific, SCFSPTA, Hawai, 1972.
102. Steneck, N.H., *Science and Society : Past, Present and Future*, Univ. of Michigan, Ann. Arbor, 1975.
103. Stober, G.J. and D. Schumacher. *Technology Assessment and Quality of Life*. Elsevier, Amsterdam, 1973.
104. Strasser, G., Technology Assessment: A Fad or a new way of life, Science Policy Reviews, 5 (1), 7, 1972.
105. ———, *Technology Assessment-What it Means to Civil Engineer*, ABCE Engineering issues, Pill, Jan. 1973.
106. ———, Technology Assessment: What it is, Where it is, *Research/Development*, pp. 48-51, Sept. 1973.
107. Toeffler, A., *Eco-spasm Report*, Bantam, New York, 1975.
108. Trimble, G., *Legal and Administrative Aspects of an Aquaculture Policy for Hawai: An Assessment*, WINCHE, Colorado, 1972.
109. Tanenbaum, M., Technology Assessment, *Res. Mgmt*. 13 (6), 427, 1970.
110. Teniene-Buchot, P.K., Technological Assessment of External Effects, *Research Policy* 2 (1), 1973.

111. Waller, R.A., Assessing the Impact of Technology on the environment, *Long Range Planning*. 8 (1), 43, 1975.
112. Walker, C.R., *Technology, Industry and Man: An Age of Acceleration*, McGraw Hill, New York, 1968.
113. Warner, A.W. and A.S. Eichner. *The Impact of Science and Technology*, Columbia Univ. Press, New York, 1966.
114. Weinberg, A.M., In Defence of Science. *Science*, 168 141-149, 1970.
115. Wenk, E., Managing Technology for a human society. *Trend in Engg*. 21 (2), 3, 1974.
116. Wolf, M., Potential Impacts of Solar Energy, *Energy Conversion*. 14 (9), 20, 1974.
117. A Collection of Authors, The Social Assessment of Technology, *International Social Sci. Jl.*, 25 (3), 1973.

E. Social Prognostics and Political Forecasting

1. Akzin, B., On Conjecture in Political Science. *Political Studies*. 14(1), 1, 1960.
2. Baier, K. and N. Rescher, *Values and the Future*, Free Press, New York, 1971.
3. Baran, P., *On the Impact of the New Communications Media upon Social Values*, P-3, IFF, Menlo Park, 1969.
4. Barbeau, C., *Future of the Family*, Bruce Publishing, New Jersey, 1971.
5. Beer, S., *Platform for Change*, Wiley-Interscience, New York, 1975.
6. Bell, D., *Twelve Modes of Prediction -A Preliminary Sorting of Approaches in the Social Sciences*, Daedalus, p. 865, 1964.
7. ———, *Coming of Post-industry Society-A Venture in Social Forecasting*, Heineman, London, 1974.
8. ———, A Just Equality, *American Review*, 20 (1), 85, 1975.
9. Bell, W. and J.A. Man, *The Sociology of the Future*, Russel Sage Foundation, New York, 1971.
10. Benn, A.W., Social and Political Implications of Automation, *Electronics and Power*, July 1968.
11. Bereano, P.L., The Scientific Community and the Crisis of Belief, *American Scientist*. 57 (4), 484, 1969.
12. Bernard, J., *Future of Marriage*, Bantam, New York, 1973.

13. Bernard, J., *Future of Motherhood*. Dial, New York, 1974.
14. Best, F., *Future of Work*, Prentice Hall, New Jersey, 1974.
15. Bestuzhev-Lada, I.B., *A Window Toward the Future and the Present Stage of Social Forecasting*, MIR, Moscow, 1970.
16. Bockle, F., *Future of Marriage as an Institution*, Seabury, New York, 1970.
17. Boguslaw, R., The New Utopians: A Study of Systems Design and Social Change. Prentice Hall, New Jersey, 1965.
18. Boulding, E., Futurology and the Imaging Capacity of the West, *Teilhard Review*; 7 (1), 1972.
19. ———, Family as an Agent of Social Change, *Futurist*, 6 (5), 186, 1972.
20. Bliss, K., *Future of Religion*, Int. Publn. Service, New York, 1970.
21. Bruce-Briggs, B., *Looking Forward: A Survey of Forecasts of Social Trends*, Hi-1494-D, Hudson Institute, New York, 1971.
22. ———, The Case for Optimism. *SPAN*. 16 (11), 7, 1975.
23. Brown, B.S., Mental Health in the Future, *Annals of American Academy of Poli & Soc Sci*, 408, 62-69, 1973.
24. Chratham, H., *Your Sexual Future*, Pinnacle Books, New York, 1972.
25. Christakis, A.N., A New Policy Science Paradigm, *Futures*. 5 (6), 543, 1973.
26. Conger, D.S., Social Inventions, *Futurist*. 7 (4), 149, 1973.
27. Conover, P.W., The Potential for an Alternate Society, *Futurist*, 7 (3), 111, 1973.
28. ———, The Alternate Society; its Sources and its Future, *TF & SC* 5,295, 1978.
29. Cornish, S., The Future of Marriage, *Futurist*. 6 (3), 103, 1972.
30. Cournand, A. and M. Meyer, Overcrowding: A Disease of Social Growth, *Futures*, 5 (3), 287, 1973.
31. De. Engard, P. and O. Helmer, *Some Potential Society Developments*: 1970-2000 R-7, IFF.
32. Dreikurs, R., Equality: The Lifestyle of Tomorrow, *Futurist*. 6 (4), 1972.
33. Dror, Y., *Futures in Government*, p. 3909, Rand Corp., Santa Monica, 1968.
34. ———, The Role of Futures in Government, *Futures* 1, 40-46, 1968.

35. Y. Dror, *Public Policy Making Reexamined*, Chandler, San Francisco, 1968.
36. ———, The Prediction of Political Feasibility. *Futures*. 1 (4), 282, 1969.
37. ———, *Policy Analysis: A Theoretical Framework and Some Basic Concepts*, p. 4156, Rand Corp., Santa Monica, 1969.
38. ———, *A Policy Sciences View of Future Studies: Alternative Futures and Present Action*, p. 4305, Rand Corp., Santa Monica, 1970.
39. ———, *Alternative Domestic Political Futures: Research Needs and Research Design*, p. 4306, Rand Corp., Santa Monica, 1970.
40. ———, *Crazy States, Health-Legington*, Legington, 1971.
41. Edwards, D.V., Political Forecasting. In J.R. Bright and M.E.F. Shoeman, (eds.) *A Guide to Practical Forecasting*, Prentice Hall, New Jersey, 1973.
42. Edwards, D.E., *International Political Analysis*, Holt, Rinehart and Winston, New York, 1969.
43. Eggers, O.R., An Answer of Monotonus Monogramy. *Futurist*. 7 (2), 61, 1973.
44. Encel, S., The Use of Socio-Technical Systems in Forecasting, Sixth World Congress on Sociology, Toronto, 1970.
45. Feinberg, G., *The Prometheus Project: Mankind's Search for Long Range Goals*, Doubleday Anchor, New York, 1969.
46. Friedman, Y., Arguments for a Poor World, *Futures*, F 6 (4), 334, 1974.
47. Gabor, D., The Mature Society, Praeger, New York, 1972.
48. Gappers, G., The Development of a Pattern Model for Social Forecasting, *Futures* 5(4), 367, 1973.
49. Gordon, T.J. and R.H. Ament, *Forecasts of Some Technological and Scientific Developments and Their Societal Consequences*, R-6, IFF. Menlo Park, 1969.
50. Gretler, A. and P. Mandl, *Values, Trends and Alternatives in Swiss Society*. Praeger, New York, 1973.
51. Gueron, S., Reflections on Social Forecasting, *Futures* 5(6), 526, 1973.
52. Harman, W.W., *Notes on the Coming Transformation*, SRI, Menlo Park, 1975.
53. Harris, J.K., Communal Livings as an Alternative Future, *Futurist*, 6(5), 192, 1972.

54. Hart, P.A., The Future of the Government Process. *Annals of American Acad Polit & Soc Sci*. 408, 94-103, 1973.
55. Heller, A., On the Future of Relations Between the Sexes, *Inter Soci Sci Jl*, 21(4), 535, 1969.
56. Helmer, O., *Social Technology*, Basic Books, New York, 1966.
57. ———, *Methodology of Societal Studies*, P-3611, Rand Corp., Menlo Park, 1967.
58. ———, *Political Analysis of Future*, P-1, IFF, Menlo Park, 1969.
59. Howe, L.K., *Future of the Family*, Simon and Schuster, New York, 1963.
60. Henshel, R.L., Sociology and Prediction, *American Sociologist*, 6, 213, 1971.
61. Hopkins, F.S., Futures Possible, Probable and Preferable, *Futurist*, 7(3), 128, 1973.
62. Hoos, I.R., *Systems Analysis in Public Policy: A Critique*, Univ. of Calif., Berkeley, 1972.
63. Horowitz, I.L., Engineering and Sociological Perspectives on Development: Interdisciplinary Constraints in Social Forecasting, *International Social Sci Jl*. 21 (4), 545, 1969.
64. Howell, J.A., An Alternative Approach to Relative Indices of Development and Potential for Change of the Nation State, *TF & SC*. 5, 253, 1973.
65. Ikle, F.C., Social Forecasting and Problem of Changing Values, p. 4550, Rand Corp., Santa Monica, 1971.
66. Institute Riceche applicate documentazione estudi, IRADES Edizioni Previsionali 1972. Social Forecasting Documentation, 1972.
67. Jantsch, E., *Technological Planning and Social Futures*. John Wiley, New York, 1972.
68. Jones, P.M.S., Preliminary Thoughts on Social Forecasting, PAU-M16, HMSO, London, 1970.
69. Keller, S. and S. Lindberg, When Parents can Choose, Which Sex it will be, *Futurist*, 6(5), 193, 1972.
70. Knesse, A.V. and B.T. Bower, *Environmental Quality Analysis: Theory and Method in Social Sciences*, John Hopkins Univ. Maryland, 1972.
71. Kahn, H., Some Preliminary Thoughts and Suggestions for Study in the Quality of Life in the 21st Century, Hl-1714-DF, Hudson Institute, New York, 1972.

72. Keller, S., Future Role of Women, *Annals of Amer. Acad. Poli. & Soc. Sci.* 408, 1-12, 1973.
73. Kent, S., *Future Sex*, Paperback Lib, New York, 1974.
74. Kohyama, R. and T. Yoshida, Techniques of Social Forecasting, Nihon Keiza Shimbun, Tokyo, 1969.
75. Kostelanetz, R., *Human Alternatives: Visions for Us Now*, Morrow, New York, 1971.
76. ———, *Social Speculations: Visions of Our Time*, Morrow, New York, 1971.
77. Kothari, R., *Footsteps into the Future*, Allied, New Delhi, 1974.
78. Little, D.L., Social Indicators and Public Policy, *Futures* 7 (1), 41-51, 1975.
79. Martin, J., and A.R.D. Norman, *Computerized Society*, Prentice Hall, New Jersey, 1970.
80. Maruyama, M., and J.A. Dator, *Human Futuristics*, Social Science Res. Institute, Honolulu, 1971.
81. McHale, J., *The Socio-Future*, Centre for Integrative Studies, New York, 1969.
82. ———, Changing Values in a Revolutionary Age, *Future Markets*. 1 (11 and 12), 11-16, 1969.
83. ———, Problems in Social and Cultural Forecasting, Proceedings Second International Future Research Conference, Kyoto, 1970.
84. ———, The Transnational World, *Ekistics*. 29 (175) June 1970.
85. Mendlovitz, S.H., *On the Creation of Just World Order: Preferred worlds for the 1990's*, Orient Longman, Madras, 1975.
86. Mesthene, E.G., *How Technology Will Shape the Future*, Science. 159, 135, 1968.
87. Michael, D.N., *The Unprepared Society: Planning for a Precarious Future*, Basic Books, New York, 1968.
88. ———, Technology and the Management of Change from the Perspective of a Culture Context, *TF & SC* 5, 219, 1973.
89. Miles, I.D., Social forecasting. From Impression to Investigation, *Futures*. 6 (3), 240, 1974.
90. Miles, I.D., C. Freeman and M. Jahoda, Progress and Problems in Social Forecasting, SSRC Seminar on Forecasting, Falmer, 1974.
91. Miller, S. and P. Roby, *The Future of Inequality*, Basic Books, New York, 1972.

92. Mitroff, I.I. and L.V. Blankeship, On the Methodology of the Holistic Experiment: An Approach to the Conceptualization of Large Scale Social Experiments, *TF & SC* 4, 339-353, 1973.
93. Moore, W.E., *Technology and Social Change*, Quadrangle Books, Chicago, 1972.
94. Morsell, J.A., Ethnic Relations of the Future, *Annals of American Acad. Polit. Soc. Sci.* 408, 83, 1973.
95. Newitt, J., Health Care and the Social System : Looking Ahead to the 1980's, HI-1545-D, Hudson Institute, New York, 1972.
96. Otto, H., Man-Woman Relationships in the Future, *Futurist.* 7 (2), 55, 1973.
97. Parkman, R., *Technological Society*, Pergammon, London, 1972.
98. Parker, S., *Future or Work and Leisure*, Praeger, New York, 1972.
99. Philips, B.S., *Worlds of the Future: Exercises in the Social Imagination*, C.E. Marrill, Columbus, 1972.
100. Platt, J., Social Traps, *Amer Psychologist*, 28 (8), 641, 1973.
101. Potter, V.R., *Bicethics: Bridge of the Future*. Prentice Hall, New Jersey, 1971.
102. Powelson, J.P., Why are the Poor so Poor in Less Developed Countries. *Human Organisation*. 34 (1), 101, 1975.
103. Quade, E.S., *Analysis for Public Policy Decisions*, p. 4863, Rand Corp., Santa Monica, 1972.
104. Schwortz, P., Counter-culture Views of the Future, *Futurist*, 7 (3), 119, 1973.
105. Shostack, A.Br., Social Policy: Tomorrows Reform Agenda, *Futurist*. 7 (3), 107, 1973.
106. Sontheimer, K., *Prediction as the Aim and Problem of Modern Social Science*, Universital. 14 (1), 1, 1971.
107. Sulc, O., Interactions between Technological and Social Changes, *Futures* 1, 402, 1961.
108. Taylor, G.R., *Rethink: A Paraprimitive Solution*, E.P. Dulton, New York, 1973.
109. Theobald, R. and J.M. Scott, *Tegs 1994: An Anticipation of the Near Future*, Swallow Press, Chicago, 1972.
110. Tiselins, A. and S. Nillsson, The Place of Value in a World of Facts-Nobel Symposium, Almquist Wiksell, Stockholm, 1970.

111. Toch, H.H., The perception of future events : Case studies in social prediction, *Public opinion quarterly*. 22, 57-66, 1958.
112. Unwin, J.O., *Future of Religion, Exposition*, New York, 1973.
113. Van Dam, A., Three Worlds. Two Futures, One Society, *Futurist*, 7(2), 84, 1973.
114. Wallia, C.S., *Toward Century 21*, Basic Books, New York, 1970. Science, Technology and Human Values; Thical issues in Future Medicine, Population and Environment; Some Futures for the Social Sciences, New Communication Media; Thinking Computer, Technology Forecasting; Future Transportation; International Political Futures Social impacts of Urbanisation; Future of Religion; Affection Education—the Future; Inner Human Experience and the Future.
115. Wiener, A.J., *Faust's Progress: The Changing Economic and Social Climate for Technological and Economic Growth*, HI-1493/2, -RR, Hudson Institute, New York, 1971.
116. ———, *The Future of the Family*, Family Service Association of America, USA, 1974.
117. William, C., Inventing a future civilization, *Futurist* 6(4), 137, 1972.
118. Winthrop, C.H., The Sociologist and the Study of the Future, *American Sociologist*, May 1958.
119. Wilcox, L.D., R.M. Brooks and G.E. Klongan, *Societal Indicators and Social Monitoring*, Elsevier, Amsterdam, 1974.
120. L.A. Zurcher, The Mutable Self, *Futurist* 6(5), 181, 1972.
121. A collection of authors, No growth society Daedulus, 102(4), 1-229, 1972.

F. Systems Science and Futurology

1. Ackoff, R.L., The systems, revolutions, *Long Range Planning*. 1(6), 2, 1974.
2. Arni, V.R.S., Concepts and Measurements in the Innovation Process, Chemical Age of India, Bombay, 1972.
3. Athinger, E.O., *Global Systems Dynamics*, Krager, New York, 1970.
4. Behrens, W., D.H. Meadows, D.L. Meadows and J. Randers, The limits of growth : Hard sell for a computer view of Doomsday, *Science*, p. 1088, March 1972.

5. Beer, S., *Designing Freedom*, CBC, Toronto, 1974.
6. Beherns, W.W., *Dynamics of Natural Resource Utilization*, Simulation. 19(3), 91,1972.
7. Boguslav, B., *The New Utopians: A Study of Design and Social Change*, Prentice Hall, New Jeresy 1965.
8. Boyian, E., *A Responsible Approach to the Limits of Growth*, HI-1678-D, Hudson Institute, New York, 1972.
9. ———, *A Critical Analysis of Forrester's World Dynamics*, HI-1632-DP, Hudson Institute, New York, 1972.
10. Clark, J., S. Cole, R. Curnow and M. Hopkins, Experimental Socio-Economic Models of Europe, *Futures* 6, 499, 1974.
11. Cole, H.S.D., C. Fraeman, M. Jahoda and K.L.R. Pavitt, *Thinking About the Future: A Critique of the Limits of Growth*, Chatto Windus, London, 1973.
12. Cole, H.S.D., Limitations of Large Scale Models in Forecasting, *The Planner*, 60(4), 646, 1974.
13. ———, The Structure of World Models, *Futures*, 5(1), 14, 1973.
14. Cole, H.S.D. and R.C. Curnow, Backcasting the World Dynamic Models, *Nature* 243(5402)), 63, 1973.
15. Cole, H.L.D., The Evaluation of the World Models, *Futures* 5(1), 108, 1974.
16. Cole, S., World Models, Their Progress and Applicability, *Futures* 6, 201, 1974.
17. Dator, J.D., The limits to the limits to growth, *Ind Adm Mgmt Review*. 6(1), 23, 1974.
18. Forrester, J.W., Industrial Dynamics: A Major Breakthrough for Decision Makers, *Harv Business Review*, 36(4), 37, July 1958.
19. ———, *Industrial Dynamics*, MIT, Cambridge, 1961.
20. ———, *Principles of Systems*, Wright-Allen, Cambridge, 1968.
21. ———, *Industrial Dynamics*, MIT, Cambridge, 1971.
22. ———, Counter-intuitive Behaviours of Social Systems, *Simulation* 16(2), 61-76, 1971.
23. ———, A National Model for Understanding Social and Economic Change, *Simulation Today* 24(32), 125, 1975.
24. lyengar, M.S., Are There any Limits to Growth? *Ind Adm & Mgmt Review*. 5(1), 52, 1973.
25. Jantsch, E., Forecasting and the Systems Approach: A Critical Survey, *Policy Sciences*. 3, 474, 1975.

26. Lee, K.N., How Should We Read the Limits to Growth, *Trend in Engg*. 26(2), 33, 1974.
27. Little, D.L. and R. Feller, *STAPOL-Simulation Game Series*; WP-12, WP-13, WP-14, IFF, Menlo Park, 1971.
28. Little, D.L., *Models and Simulation*, WP-6, IFF, Menlo Park, 1970.
29. Marstrand, P.K. and K.L.R. Pavitt, The Agricultural Subsystem, *Futures*, 5(1), 55, 1973.
30. Meadows, D.L., *Global Equilibrium*. Wright-Allen Cambridge, 1972.
31. ———, *The Limits to Growth*, Wright Allen, Cambridge. 1972.
32. Mearovic, M.D., D. Macko and Y. Takahara, *Theory of Hierarchical Multilevel Systems*, Academic Press, New York, 1970.
33. Mearovic, M.D. and J. Pestel, *Mankind at the Turning Point:* Second Report of the Club of Rome, Potomac Associates, London, 1974.
34. Mitroff, I.I. and F. Sagasti, Epistemology as General Systems Theory, *Philo Soci Sci* 3, 117, 1973.
35. Morgan, C.H., *World Dynamics under Scrutiny*, HI-1601-DP, Hudson Institute, New York, 1972.
36. McPherson, P.K., A Perspective on Systems Science and Systems Philosophy, *Futures*. 6(3), 219, 1974.
37. Nordhans, W.D., World Dynamics: Measurement Without data. *Economic Jl*. Dec. 1973.
38. Quade, E.S. and W.I. Boucher, *Systems Analysis and Policy Making*, Elsevier, New York, 1968.
39. Rothkopf, M., World Models Won't Work, *New Scientist*, 22 March 1973.
40. Sagasti, F.R., A Conceptual Systems Framework for the Study of Planning Theory, *TF & SC*. 5, 379, 1973.
41. Simmon, H., Systems Dynamic & Technocracy, *Futures*. 5 (2), 212, 1973.
42. Smernoff, B.J., *A Preliminary Critique of World Dynamics*, HI-1552-D, Hudson Institute, New York, 1971.
43. West C. Churchman, *Design of Inquiry Systems*, Basic Books, New York, 1972.
44. Maddox, J., Are the Limits to Growth Real? *Environment and Change*. 2 (1), 23, 1973.

G. Educational Futures

1. Anlyan, W.G., *Future of Medical Education*, Duke, North Carolina, 1973.
2. Christenson, G.A., *Future of the University*, University of Oklahoma, Norman, 1969.
3. Disch, R., *Future of Literacy*, Prentice Hall, New Jersey, 1973.
4. Eldrege, H.W., University Education in Future Studies, *Futures*. 7(1), 15-30, 1975.
5. *Europe 2000; Educating Man for the 21st Century: Perspectives in Primary Education*, Nijhoff, Hague, 1974.
6. *Europe 2000; Educating Man for the 21st Century: University of the Future*; Nijhoff, Hague, 1974.
7. *Europe 2000*; Project I; Volumes, Nijhoff, Hague, 1974, *Future of European Education, Access to Education and Division of Labour, Education in Industrialized Countries, Individual Orientation in Education.*
8. Faure, E., *Learning to Be: Education Today and Tomorrow*, UNESCO-Stirling, New Delhi, 1973,
9. Grayson, L.P., Education Beyond Horizon, *Science*, 170, 1376-1382, 1970.
10. Green, T., *Educational Planning in Perspective*, IPC Science and Technology Press, Survey, 1974.
11. Hencley, S.P. and J.R. Yates, *Futurism in Education*, McCutcham, Berkeley, 1973.
12. Harkins, A., Futurizing a University, *Futurist*, 7(4), 172, 1973.
13. Haskins, C.P., Education: Thoughts on an Unchartered Future, *Daedalus*, 104(1), 234, 1975.
14. Hipple, T.W., Future of Education, Good year, New Jersey, 1970
15. Illich, I.D., *Deschooling the Society*, Penguin, Harmondsworth, 1973.
16. Licklider, J.C.R., *Libraries of the Future*, MIT, Cambridge, 1965.
17. Marien, M., *Alternative Futures for Learning*, Syracuse University Research Corp. Syracuse, 1971.
18. Michael, D.N., *On Learning to Plan and Planning to Learn*, Jossy-Bass, London, 1974.
19. Molnar, T., *Future of Education*, Fleet, New York, 1970.
20. Mood, A., *Future of Higher Education*, McGraw Hill, New York, 1973.

21. Ozmon, H., *Utopias and Education*, Burgers Publishing Co., Minneapolis, 1969.
22. Peterson, A.D., *Future of Education*, Fernhill, New Jersey, 1968.
23. Shane, H.G., *Educational Significance of the Future*, Phi Delta Kappa Educational Foundation, Bloomington, 1973.
24. ———, Education for Tomorrows World, *Futurist* 7(3), 103, 1973.
25. Tibble, J.W., *Future of Teacher Education*, Routledge & Kegan Paul, Boston, 1971.
26. Vermilye, D., *Future in the Making: Current Issues in Higher Education*, Jossey Bass, San Franscisco, 1973.

H. Urban Futures

1. Armytage, W.H.G., *Yesterdays Tomorrows: A Historical Survey of Future Societies*, Univ. of Toronto Press, Toronto, 1968.
2. Bonladon, G., Man, the City and the Automobile in the Future, *Futures* 6(1), 59, 1974.
3. Bruce-Briggs, B., *Future of Housing and Urban Development Policy*, HI-1724-RR, Hudson, New York, 1972.
4. Chinoy, E., *The Urban Future Lieber*, Atherton, New York, 1974.
5. Dahinden, J., *Urban Structures for the Future*, Pall Mall, 1972.
6. Dantzig, G.B. and T.L. Saaty, *Compact City: A Plan for a Liveable Urban Environment*, Freeman, San Francisco, 1973.
7. Downs, A., Alternate Forms of Future Urban Growth, *Jl. of American Institute of Planners*, p. 4, Jan 1970.
8. Eldredge, H.W., *Taming Megalapolis*, Anchor Doubleday, New York, 1967.
9. ———, *World Capitals: Toward Guided Urbanization and Urbanism*, Doubleday, New York, 1974.
10. ———, Alternative Possible Urban Futures, *Future*, 6(1), 26, 1974.
11. Elwood, R., *Future City*, Trident, New York, 1973.
12. Forrester, J.W., *Urban Dynamics*, MIT, Cambridge, 1969.
13. Ginzberg, E., *Future of Metropolis: People, Jobs and Income*, Olympus Publishing Co., Salt Lake City, 1974.
14. Gore, M.S. and J.C. Sharma, City size and costs; *Indian International Centre Quarterly*, p. 29, April, 1975.
15. Hall, P., *Future Metropolis*, Weindened and Wiscolson, London, 1966.

16. Hellman, H., *The City in the World of Future*, M. Evans, New York, 1970.
17. Mayur, R., *Urbanisation in India in the year 2000*, NITIE, Bombay, 1974.
18. ———, An Alternative Model of Urban Life, *Young Indian*, pp. 20, 32, Oct. 1974.
19. McHale, J., *Future City: Notes on a Typology*, Ekistics' 28 (165), 2969.
20. Lapatra, J.W., *Applying Systems Approach to Urban Development*, Dowden & Budchipson-John Willey, New York, 1973.
21. McHale, J., Technology and the Future City, *Architectural Design*, *49*, November, 1970.
22. Desarovic, M.D. and A. Rcisman, *Systems Approach and the City*, Elsevier, Amsterdam, 1972.
23. Miller, B., N. Pinney and W. Saslow, *Innovation in New Communications*, MIT, Cambridge, 1972.
24. Mitscherlich, A., The Town of the Future and Society, *Universities*. 16(3), 193, 1974.
25. Nogellbarg, M. and D.L. Little, *Selected Urban Simulation and Games*, WP-4, IFF, Menlo Park, 1970.
26. Page, J.K., Integrating Town and Country to Conserve Resources, *Futures*, 5(4), 401, 1973.
27. Owen, W., *The accessible city* (Telecommunication and Life Style), Brocking Institution, Washington, 1972.
28. Rodwin, L., Future Metropolis, Braziller, New York, 1968.
29. Starr, R., *Urban choices: The City and its Critics*, Penguin, Baltimore, 1967.
30. Strong, A.L., *Planned Urban Environments*, John Hopkins, Baltimore, 1971.
31. Stulman, J., *Creative Systems in Housing*, World Institute Council, 4 (2), 1971.
32. Theobald, R., *Habit and Habitat*, Prentice Hall, New Jersey, 1973.
33. Wager, W.W., Building the City of Man, Freeman, San Francisco, 1971.
34. A Collection of Authors, *The Future Metropolis*, Daedulus. 90 (1), 3-193, 1961.
35. Gappert, G., Assessment and Acceptability of Urban Futures, *Futures*. 6(1), 43, 1974.

I. Management and Futurology

1. Ahamad, B., and M. Blaug, *Practice of Manpower Forecasting*, Elsevier, Amsterdam, 1972.
2. Ansoff, H.I. and J.M. Steward, Strategies for Technology Based Industries, *Harv Busi Review*, p. 71, Nov/Dec 1967.
3. Blackman, A.W., Ten New Product Successes for the 1970's, *Business Horizons*, June, 1972.
4. Boettinger, B.H., Technology and Managers Future, *Harv Busi Review*, 48 (6), 4, 1970.
5. Bogart, D.H., Changing Views of Organisation, *TF & SC*. 5, 163-177, 1973.
6. Brewer, G.D., Innovation, Social Change and Reality, *TF & SC*. 5, 19-24, 1973.
7. Byrnes, W.G. and B.K. Chesterton; *Decisions, Strategies and New Ventures*, Allen-Unwin, London, 1973.
8. Chambers, J.C., S.K. Mullick and D.D. Smith, *An Executives Guide to Forecasting*, Wiley Interscience, New York, 1974.
9. Connor, J.T., What is Ahead fc. Management in 2000, *Hydrocarbon Process*. 52(10), 151, 1974.
10. Cooper-Jones, D., *Business Planning and Forecasting*, Business, London, 1974.
11. Cowan, *Future of Planning*, Sage, California, 1973.
12. Doktor, R., On the Creation of Demand for Technological Innovation, *TF & SC*. 6(2), 219, 1974.
13. Cleveland, H., *The Future Executive*, Harper & Row, New York, 1972.
14. Dror, Y., Futures Studies and Management Development, *Futures*. 5(6), 636, 1973.
15. Fisher, L., Long Term Forecasting of Demand for Industrial Products, *IMRA Jl*, 5, PP3, 1969.
16. Gabor, D., *Innovations: Scientific, Technological and Social*, OUP, London, 1972.
17. Glenn, J., Forecasting Techniques as Teaching Methods, *TF & SC*. 5, 95, 1973.
18. Hendry, I.C., Three Parameter Approach to Long Range Forecasting. *Long Range Planning*, 5(1), 40, 1972.
19. Jantsch, E., *Design for Evolution: Self Organisation and Planning in the Life of Human Systems*. Braziller, New York, 1975.

20. Jones, P.M.S., *Technological Forecasting as a Managerial Tool*, PAU-MIO, HMSO, London, 1969.
21. ———, *Market Research in an R & D Environment*, IMRA, Lichfield, 1971.
22. Lindley, B.C., TF and Corporate Long Range Planning, *Electronics and Power*. 16, 363, 1970.
23. Love, P.L.,. Forecasting Advanced Technology, *Industrial Marketing Management*, pp. 91-105, Dec., 1973.
24. Madden, C.H., *Of Clash of Culture: Management in an Age of Changing Values*, National Planning Association, 1972.
25. Makridakis, S. and S. Wheel Wright, Integrating Forecasting and Planning. *Long Range Planning*, 6(3), 53, 1973.
26. Mapstone, E., Forecasting for Sales and Production, *Chem Engg* 80, 126, 14 May, 1973.
27. Maruyama, M., Paradigms and Communication, *TF & SC*. 5, 135, 1973.
28. ———, Hiearchists, Individualists Mutualists: Three Paradigms among Planners, *Futures*. 6, 103, 1974.
29. Morrell, J., *Management Decisions and the Role of Forecasting*, Penguin, Harmondsworth, 1972.
30. Nicholson, R.L.R., *Technological Forecasting as a Management Technique*, PAU-M7, HMSO, London 1969.
31. Ozbekhan, H., On some of the Fundamental Problems in Planning, *TF & SC*. 1(3), 235, 1970.
32. Povac, F.J. and M.F. Dague, Forecasting by Product Life Cycle Analysis, *Res Mgmt*. 15(4), 66, 1972.
33. Seth, S.C., Future Research in Management, *Indi Admn & Mgmt Review*. 6(1), 10, 1974.
34. ———, Management 2000: An Indian Scenario, *Indian Management*, pp. 1-4, May, 1975.
35. Smith, W.E., Resources and Long Range Forecasts, *Bull Atomic Scientists*. 29(5), 21, 1973.
36. Steiner, G.A., *Top Management Planning*, Macmillan, London, 1969.
37. Thompson, G.B., and E. Herbert, A Gentle Approach to Corporate Change. *TF & SC*. 5, 179, 1973.
38. Twiss, B.C., *Managing Technological Innovation*, Longman, London, 1975.

39. Van Dam, A., The Multinational Corporation vis-a-vis Societies in Transformation, *TF and SC*. 5, 281, 1973.
40. Venu, S., The Multinationals and Developing Societies. *Futures*, 6 (2), 133, 1974.
41. Wheelright, S.C. and S. Makridakis, *Forecasting Methods for Management*, Wiley-Interscience, New York, 1973.
42. Wilson, I.H., Futures Forecasting for Strategic Planning at General Electric, *Long Range Planning*. 6(2), 39, 1973.

J. Futurology : General

(Cases. Applications, Energy, Transportation, Food Materials)

1. Agarwal, S.N., K. Rohatgi, B. Bowonder and P.K. Rohtagi, *A Delhi Study of Future Foods in India Food Policy*, 1(1), 136, 1975.
2. Allen, C., Engineering Water Resources for 2070, *Mech Engg*. p. 7, July, 1971.
3. Allen, J.E., *Future of Aeronautics*, Intl. Publns Service. New York, 1970.
4. Anon, Medicine 2001, *New Scientists*, p. 758, 27 Sep. 1973.
5. ———, Can technology meet our future energy needs. *Chem. Engg. Prog*. 69(6), 21, 1973.
6. Anerson, J.E., PRT: Urban Transportation of the Future, *Futurist*, 7(1), 16, 1973.
7. Ash, J.C.K. and D.J. Smythe. *Forecasting the U.K. Economy*, Saxon. Farnborough. 1974.
8. Ayres, R.U., Food: The Future Science Jl, 3(10), 100, 1967.
9. Ayres, R.U. and R.P. Mckenna. Alternatives to Internal Combustion Engine, John Hopkins Univ., Maryland, 1972.
10. Baade, F., Food Reserves of a Starving World. *Universities*. 9(4), 343, 1967.
11. Baran, P., The future of newsprint 1970-2000. R-16, IFF, Menlo Park, 1971.
12. ———, *On the State of Art of the Computer Development by the Year 2000*, p. 10, IFF, Menlo Park, 1971.
13. Bergsten, C.F., *Future of the International Economic Order*, Lexington Books.
14. Bethke, F.J., The Future of Computing: Is the Sky the Limit, *Computers and People*. 24(9), 25, 1975.
15. Bezdek, R.H., Long Range Economic and Man-Power Forecasting. *Long Range Planning* 8(1), 31, 1975.

16. Bhagwati, J.N., *Economics and World Order: From the 1970's to the 1990's*. Orient Longman, New Delhi, 1972. *Haves and havenots around 2000, Future of Poor Countries, World Economics and World Future. International Monetary System in 2000, Indian Perspectives 1990-2000.*
17. Bjerrun, C.A., Forecast of Computer Development and Applications: 1968-2000. *Futures*. 1, 331, 1969.
18. Borgstrom, G., *World Food Resources*, Inter text Books, Bucks, 1973.
19. ———, *The Hungry Planet*, Macmilan, London 1965.
20. ———, The World Food Crises, *Futures* 1, 342, 1969.
21. ———, *The Food Population Dilemma*, AMBIO, 3(3-4), 109, 1974.
22. Bose, A., A. Mitra, P.B. Desai and J.N. Sharma, *Population in Indias Development: 1947-2000*, Vikas, Bombay, 1975.
23. Bosman, H.W. and F.A. Alting, *Future of International monetary System*, Lexington. Lexington, 1970.
24. Bouladon, G., The Introduction of Innovation in Urban Transport, *Transportation Planning and Tech*. 1, 3-9, 1972.
25. Bowonder, B. and P.K. Rohatgi, *Future, Energy Systems of India, To appear in Energy Policy,*
26. ———, Future of Steel Technology India, to appear in *Jl. of Sci. Ind. Res.*
27. Brennan, D.G., *Fashions in Military Technology: Fifty Years Hence*, HI-951-P, Hudson, New York, 1968.
28. Brookes, L.G., Energy Resources and World Economic Growth, *Long Range Planning*, 6(3), 39, 1973.
29. Brooks, G.W., Aircraft Structures for the Day after Tomorrow, *Astronautics and Aeronautics*, July 1973.
30. Brooks, D.B., J.V. Krutilla, *Peaceful Use of Nuclear Explosives: Economics*, RFF, Washington, 1969.
31. Brown, L.R., *World without Borders*, Random House, Westminster, 1972.
32. Burn, D., *Future of Steel*, Transatlantic, Levit Town, 1971.
33. Carter, A.P., Economics of Technological Change, *Scientific American*, April, 1966.
34. Chaturvedi, M.C., *Water in Second India*, Ford Foundation, New Delhi, 1975.
35. Chaplin, G. and D. Glenn, *Hawai 2000*, Univ. Press of Hawai, Honolulu, 1973.

36. Clawson, M., *Policy Directions for U.S. Agriculture: Long Range Choices in Farming and Rural Living*, John Hopkins Univ. Press, Maryland, 1968.
37. Clement, R.C., Conservation: A Positive Position, *TEEE Spectrum*, 10(8), 44, 1973.
38. Commoner, B., Improving Resource Productivity: A Way to Support the Growing World Population, *AMBIO* (3) (3-4), 136, 1974.
39. Convery, F.J., Forestry and LRP, *Long Range Planning* 6 (2), 27, 1973.
40. Cook, E., Energy Sources for the Future, *Futurist*. 6(4), 142 1972.
41. Crawford, W.D., Electric Power in the 21st Century, *Profe Engineering*. 41(2), 20, 1971.
42. Daly, H.E., *Toward a Steady State Economy*, Freeman, San Fincisco, 1973.
43. Darmstadter, J., Energy in the World Economy, *Development Digest*, July 1972.
44. ———, Limiting the Demand for Energy Possible, Probable? Reprint 116, RFF, Washington, 1974.
45. D.S. Davies, Raw materials for chemicals of the future. Chem, and Industry, pp 1132, 15 Dec. 1973.
46. Day, L.H., An Assessment of Travel/Communications Substitutabilities, *Futures*. 5 (6), 559, 1973.
47. Decker, R.L., *Economic Developments to the Year 2000*. Gordon and Breach, New York, 1974.
48. ———, Future Economic Developments: A Delphi Survey, *Futures* 6(2), 142, 1974.
49. Dent, E.J., *Future of Music*, Pergamon, London, 1966.
50. Doctor, R.D., *Energy Demand in the Future: Reducing the Growth Rate*, p. 4992, Rand Corp., Santa Monica, 1973.
51. Doerr, W., Future Prospects of Research into Diseases and the Position Today, *Universities*, 12 (3), 193, 1970.
52. Dunham, K., How Long Our Minerals Last? *New Scientists*. 61 (881), HP 129, 17 Jan 1974.
53. Ehrlich, G.E., Health Challenges of the Future, *Annals of American Academy of Polit and Sco. Sci*. 408, 70-82, 1973.
54. Enzer, S., *Some Prospects for Residential Housing by 1985*, R. 13, IFF, Menlo Park, 1971.

55. Enzer, S., *Some Developments in Plastics and Competing Materials by 1985*, R-17, IFF, Menlo Park, 1971.
56. Falkenmark, M., How can We Cope with the Water Resources Situation by the Year 2015, *AMBIO*, 3 (3-4), 114, 1974.
57. Fink, D.G., Electronics Next 25 Years, *IEEE Trans. Indu. Appli.* IA. 8 (2), 93, 1972.
58. Fisher, J.C., Energy crisis in perspective, Wiley-Interscience, New York, 1974.
59. Fisher, J.L., Water Resources in the Future: Directions and Prospects, *Proc. ASCE 98*, 3 July, 1972.
60. Fried lander, G.D., Technology Forecasting : Energy's Hazy Future, *IEEE Spectrum*. 12 (5), 32, 1975.
61. Gale, M., Towards Super Cereals, *New Sci.* 61 (883), 284, 1974.
62. Good, I.J., *Scientist Speculates* (p 233, Multipurpose Plants) : An Anthology of partly baked ideas, Heinemann, London, 1962.
63. George, F.H. and J.D. Humpheries, The Robots are Coming, Newton-Abbot, London, 1974.
64. Graham, W.B., *A Look to the Future* (Military Technology) p. 5251, Rand Corp., Sant Monica, 1974.
65. Greenberge, M., *Computers and the World of the Future*, MIT, Cambridge, 1968.
66. Hamil, R., The Future of Oceans, *Futurist*. 6(3), 109, 1972.
67. ———, Depletion of Fossil Fuels, *Futurist*, 6 (4), 152, 1972.
68. Hammond, A.L., Energy and the Future, Academic Press, New York, 1973.
69. Hansen, K., World Chemistry and its Task for the Future, *Universities*, 9(4), 351, 1967.
70. Harris, C.C., *Urban economies-1985, Health*, Farnborough, 1973.
71. Heginbotham, W.B., Industrial Robots: Present and Future, *Chart Mech Engr*, 20(9), 78, 1973.
72. Hellman, H., Transportation in the World of Future, M. Evans, New York, 1968.
73. Helmer, O., On the Future State of Union, R-27, IFF, Menlo Park, 1972.
74. Hempel, G., Sea as a Source of Good, *Universities*. 13(3). 239, 1971.

75. Hendrickson, R., *Future of Money*, Prentice Hall, New Jersey, 1970.
76. Hoffman, G.A., Future Electric Automobiles, *Futures*. 1, 173-183, 1969.
77. Hunt, H., *Forecasting and Need for Research and Development*, *Futures*. 1, 382, 1969.
78. Hupkes, G., Future of Motor Car: Alternative Scenarios, *Futures*. 5(5), 457-468, 1973.
79. Illich, I.D., *Energy and Equity*, Rupa. Bombay, 1974.
80. Jenkins, G.I., Energy Forecasting in UK. *Petroleum Review*. 26(310), 302, Oct. 1972.
81. Johnson, H., Why Worry about Future Energy Needs. *New Scientist*. 61(888), 620, 1974.
82. Johnson, N., Communications and the Year 2000. *Ind Admn & Mgmt Review* 6(1), 47, 1974.
83. Kahn, H., *Synoptic Context One-The prospects for mankind and a year 2000 ideology*, HI-1648/4-D, Hudson, New York, 1972.
84. ———, *What if the Rich Stop Aiding the Poor*, UNESCO, Geneva, 1973.
85. ———, *Future of the Corporation*, Mason-Lipscomb New York, 1974.
86. Kahn, H. and C. Morgan, *Some World Economic and Population Scenarios for the 21st Century*, Hudson, New York, 1972
87. Kahn, H., and B. Smernoff, *Can the Green Revolution be Sustained*, HI-1583/2-p, Hudson, New York, 1972.
88. Kaufmann, F., Hard and Soft Health Technology of the Future, *Tech Fore & Soc Change*. 5, 67, 1973.
89. Kiefer, D.M., Chemicals 1992, *Chem & Engg News*, p. 6, July 10, 1972.
90. Kniffler, A., Rail Transport of the Future as a Problem of Today, *Universities*, 15(1), 21, 1973.
91. Kolber, H. and J. Schulze, Chemical Products of the Future, *Universities*. 13(3), 217, 1971.
92. Kneese. A.V., R.U. Ayres and R.C. Darge, *Economics and the Environment: A Materials Balance Approach*, RFF, Washington, 1970.
93. Kovas, F.J., Technology Forecasting: Tires, *Chem Tech* 1, 18, 1971.

94. Kovatch, G., J.B. Barber, R.F. Casey and G. Zames, *Transportation Systems Technology-a 20 Year Outlook*; PB-204-400, NTIS, Virginia, 1971.
95. Lahiri, A., *Minerals and Metals: 2000 AD in India*, ORG, Baroda, 1975.
96. Landsberg, H.H., L.L. Fischman and J.F. Fisher, *Resources in American Future: Latterns of requirements and availabilities: 1960-2000*, John Hopkins Univ., Maryland, 1964.
97. Lawrence, S.A., *International Sea Transport - The Years Ahead*, Harnborough, Hants, 1972.
98. Leisester, C., *Britains 2001 AD: A Forecast of the UK Economy*, HMSO, London, 1972.
99. Malenbaum, W., World Resources for the Year 2000, *Annals of American Acad Poli & Soc Sci.* 408, 30, 1973.
100. ———, *Material Requirements in the United States and Abroad in the Year 2000*, Univ of Pennsylvania, USA, 1973.
101. Mandel, H., Nuclear Reactors and the Future, *Universities*, 13(1), 35, 1970.
102. Marsham, T.N., Nuclear Power-The Future, *Atom.* 196, 46, Feb. 1973.
103. Martin, A., *The Last Generation-The End of Survival*, Fontana, London, 1974.
104. Martin, J., *Future Developments in Telecommunications*, Prentice Hall, New Jersey, 1973.
105. Martino, J.P., Technological Forecasting for the Chemical Process Industries, *Chem Engg.* 78(29), 54, Dec. 1971.
106. Mitre Corporation, Proceedings of the Symposium of Energy, Resources and the Environment, MTR-72-190 (5 volumes), Mitre Corp, McLean, 1972.
107. McHale, J., World Energy Resources in the Future, *Futures*. 1(1), August, 1968.
108. ———, *Future of Mind*, University Review. 3(3), Autumn 1970.
109. McLean, M. and M. Hopkins, Problems of World Food and Agriculture: Projections, Models and Possible Approaches. *Futures*. 6(4), 157, 1972.
110. Miller, S.M. and P. Roby, Economic Inequality: Will It Increase? *Futurist*. 6(4), 157, 1972.

111. Nair, C.K.N., Natural Rubber Research upto 2000 AD, Rubber Planters conference, India, 1974.
112. National Materials Advisory Board, A Delphi Exploration of the U.S. Ferro Alloy and Steel Industries, NMAB-277, NAS-NAE, Washington, 1971.
113. Nelson, L., Future Nuclear Reactors, *Electrica Review*, 193,(13), 409, 1973.
114. Notess, C.B., Trads in Urban Transportation. *Transportation Engg Jl*, TE3, p. 655, 1973.
115. Office of Health Economics, Medicine in the 1990's OHE, London, 1969.
116. C/o. OF Iaherty' People, transport systems and the urban scene, *Int Jl Envi Studies*. 3, 265, 1972.
117. Othmer, D.F., Energy: Prospects for the Rest of the Century, *Mech Engg*. 96(8), 18, 1974.
118. Paddock, W. and P. Paddock, *Famine, 1975*, Weidenfeld and Nicolson, London, 1967.
119. Page, W., Population Forecasting, *Futures*, 5(2), 179, 1973.
120. Parikh, K.S., India in 2000-Fuels or Second India and Energy, Indian Statistical Institute, New Delhi, 1975.
121. Pavitt, K.L.R., Malthus and Other Economists, *Futures* 5(2), 157-178, 1973.
122. Picard, P., The Future of Automobile Paper 980A, SAE, New York, 1965.
123. Price, D.K., Purists and Politicians, *Science* 163 (3862), p. 25, 1969.
124. Rao, V.M., Second India's Prospects for Food, Ford Foundation, New Delhi, 1975.
125. Richardson, P.W., Automotive Engines for the 1980's, *Chem. Tech*, 4(11), 660, 1974.
126. Roberts, F., Next Fity Years in Engineering Materials, *Chem Engr* No. 260, 144, 1972.
127. ——, Future Resources for Engineering Materials Chart, *Mech Engr*. p. 69, April, 1973.
128. Rose, D.J., Rational Development of Options: Energy as an Example, Special Lecture, MIT, Cambridge, 1971.
129. Rothkopf, M.H., *An Economic Model of World Energy 1900-2020 Long Range Planning*.

130. Ruttan, V.W., *The Economic demand for Irrigated Acreage: Preliminary Projections*, John Hopkins Univ Press, Maryland, 1965.
131. Sardana, P.K., V. Kumar & K.R. Parameswar, Technological Forecasting through Scenario Construction. (Energy Systems in India), Lok Udyog 8(4), 49, 1974.
132. Schell, F.L., People Movers: Yesterday, Today and Tomorrow, *Traffic Quarterly* 28(1), 5, 1974.
133. Schmilt, W.H., Planetary Food Potential. *Annals of New York Academy of Sciences*. 118, 645, 1965.
134. Schneider, J.J., A Future for Airships, *Automotive Engg*. 83(7), 40, 1975.
135. ———, *Future Lighter than Air Concepts*, SAE-750618, SAE, Warrendale, 1975.
136. Schneider, S.H., The Population Explosion: Can it Shake the Climate, *AMBIO* 3(3-4), 150, 1974.
137. Schriever, B.A. and W. Seifert, Air Transportation 1975 and Beyond, MIT, Cambridge, 1968.
138. Schurr, S.H., *Energy, Economic Growth and the Environment*, John Hopkins Univ Press, Maryland, 1972.
139. Schwartz, A.M., *Detergents of the Future, Soap, Cosmetics and Chemical Specialities*, p. 31, Sep, 1973.
140. Second Indian Series of Studies. *The Indian Economy in 2000 AD*, TECS, Bombay, 1975.
141. Second Indian Series of Studies. *The Transportation in the Second India*, TECS, Bombay, 1975.
142. Second Indian Series of Studies, *Industry in the Second Indian TECS*, Bombay, 1975.
143. Singer, S.F., Is there an Optimum Level of Population, McGraw Hill, New York, 1971.
144. Smernoff, B.J., *Military Technology in the 1980's*, HI-1559/D, Hudson, New York, 1972.
145. Smil, V., Forecast of Energy Trends and the Impact of Environment, *Electrical Review*, 192(8), 286, Feb., 1973.
146. Smith, M., When Psychology Grows Up-A Delphi, *New Scientist*. 64(918), 90, 1974.
147. Stolte, D., Tomorrows Television-Analyses and Prognoses, *Universities*. 15(3), 209, 1973.

148. Sullivan, E.A., *Future: Human Ecology & Education*, Etc Publ. Illinois, 1975.
149. Surrey, A.J., Can we Improve the Quality of Energy Forecasts and their Interpretation, *Elec Review*, 191(20), 664, 17 Nov. 1972.
150. ———, The Future Growth of Nuclear Power: Demand & Supply, Energy Policy, p. 107, Sep., 1973.
151. ———, The Future Growth of Nuclear Power: Choices and Obstacles, Energy Policy, p. 208, Dec., 1973.
152. Swaminathan, M.S., Our Agricultural Future, Sardar Patel Memorial Lecture 1973, All India Radio, New Delhi, 1973.
153. ———, Agriculturalon Spaceship Earth, Coromandel Lecture, Coromandel Fertilizers, New Delhi, 1973.
154. Swiss, M., Energy and the Future, *Chart Mech. Engr*, 21(8), 99, 1974.
155. Tape, N.W., Future Trends in Food Processing and Marketing, *Cand Jl Pub Health*. 59(12), 467, 1968.
156. Taylor, J.G., The Shape of Minds to Come, Weybright and Talley, New York, 1971.
157. Timm, B., Chemistry and Nutrition in 2000 AD, *Universities*, 13(2), 119, 1971.
158. Turn, R., *Computer in the 1980's: Trends in Hardware Technology*, p. 5189, Rand Corp., Santa Monica, 1974.
159. ———, *Computers in the 1980's*, columbia Univ. Press, New York, 1974.
160. U.S. Bureau of Mines, Mineral Facts and Problems (Bureau of Mines Bulletin. No. 650) USGPO, Washington, 1970.
161. Varon, B., Enough of Everything for Everyone, Forever? *Finance and Develop* 12(3), 17, 1975.
162. VITA, *Village Technology Handbook*, PB-207491, NTIS, Virginia, 1970.
163. Vyas, B.J., B. Bowonder and P.K. Rohatgi, Technological Forecasting for Foundry Industries in India. IISc, Bangalore, 1975.
164. Weinberg, A.M., Long Range Approaches for Resolving the Energy Crisis, *Mech. Engg*. 95(6), 14, 1973.
165. Wheat Croft, S., Aeroplanes for the Eighties, *Astronautics Aeronautics*. 12(3), 34, 1974.

166. Weizsacker, C.F.V., Nuclear Energy as the Most Important Energy Source during the Last Decades of the 20th Century, *Universities*. 12(2), 97, 1970.
167. Wiener, A.J., The Future of Economic Activity, *Annals of American Academy of Political and Soci. Sci*, 408, 47, 1973.
168. Wilkins, L.T., Crime and Criminal Justice at the Turn of the Century, *Annals of American Academy of Poli. and Soc. Sci*. 408, 13, 1973.
169. Winsche, W.E., Hydrogen: Its Future Role in the Nations Energy Economy, *Science*. 180 (4093), 1325, 1973.
170. World Future Society, *Energy: Todays Choices, Tomorrows Opportunities*, World Future Society, Washington, 1974.
171. Wollman, N. and G.W. Bonem, *The Outlook for Water*, John Hopkins Univ. Press, Maryland, 1971.
172. Wright, F.L., Future of Architecture, *Horizon*, New York, 1973.
173. Young, B.P., *A New World in the Morning-The Biopsychological Revolution*. Westminister, Philadelphia, 1972.
174. Zraket, C.A., Energy Resources for the year 2000 and Beyond, MTP-401, Mitre Corp. McLean, 1975.
175. A Collection of Authors. Technology Forecasting. *IEEE Spectrum*. 22(4). 41,-76. 1975. (Electronics, Communications, Computers, Instrumentation, Components).
176. A Collection of Authors, Materials towards the Year 2000, *Materials Engg*. pp. 34-63, Nov. 1969.

PART II

Bibliography

Abrol, Sunil : 'The Profile of a Personnel Man in 2000 AD". In the *Management Review*, Vol. 13, No. 2, 1986.

Adieseshiah, M.S. :"Education and Future of India", in *Education or Catastrophe*, (eds.), P.S. Sundaram and A.B. Shah, Vikas Publishing House, Delhi, 1976.

Agwani, M.S. : "Prospects for Indo-West Asian Relations". In *India: A Study in Futurism*, (ed.) S.R. Gupta, Abhinav Publications, New Delhi, 1976.

Ahmad, Aqueil : "Scientific and Technical Human Resources Development in India". In *Short Studies in Futures Research*, NCST, Government of India, 1980.

Ambannavar, Jaipal, P. : *Second Indian Studies Population*, The Macmillan & Co., Delhi, 1975.

Apte, P.M. : "Planning for Human Settlement : Housing". In *Short Studies in Futures Research*, NCST, Government of India, 1980.

Arora, Satish, K. : "India in 1997 : Social Future". In *India: A Study in Futurism*, (ed.) S.R. Gupta, Abhinav Publication, New Delhi, 1976.

Arora Satish : 'India's Next Quarter Century: Experience and Prospects'. In *India and Foreign Review*, Vol. 12, No. 6, 1975.

Atal, Yogesh : "Communication". In *India Since Independence*, (ed.) S.C. Dube, Vikas Publishing House, Delhi, 1977.

——— : "Sociology and the Future". In *International Social Science Journal*. No. 108, 1968.

Bagchi, P.P. : "Availability, and Cost of Transport Fuels over the Next Fifteen years in India and Other Countries of SAARC" In *Journal of Transport Management*, Vol. 9, No. 9, 1985.

Bajpai, U.S. : "The South Asian Situation". In *World Focus*, Vol. 7, No. 11-12, 1986.

Balan, K. : *A Better India By 2000 AD*. Intellectual Publishing House, New Delhi, 1987.

Banerjee, B.N : *India on Threshold of the 21st Century*, Paribus Publications, New Delhi, 1986.

Banerjee, Subrata : "Co-operation with Developing World". In *World Focus*, Vol. 7 No. 11-12, 1986.

Banerjee, Utpal K. : "Technology Management for the Future of India". In *Short Studies in Futures Research*, NCST, Government of India, 1980.

———: "Social Communication and Social Indicators: A Futuristic Analysis". In *Short Studies in Futures Research*, NCST, 1980.

Basu, D.N. : "Consumption Pattern and Life Style". In *India in Perspective*, Vol. I, Operations Research Group, Arnold-Heinemann, New Delhi, 1978.

Bhagwati, Jagdish N. (ed.) : *Economics and World Order from 1970's to the 1990's*, Orient Longman Ltd., New Delhi, 1972.

Bhaskara Rao, B.: "Housing". In *India in Perspective*, Vol. 3, Operations Research Group, Arnold-Heinemann, New Delhi, 1978.

———.: "Housing 2000 A.D. : A Long Range Perspective for India". In *Urban Perspectives-2001*, (eds.), C.S. Chandrasekhara and Deva Raj, National Institute of Urban Affairs, New Delhi, 1978.

Bhatt, V.V. : *Two Decades of Development, The Indian Experiment*, Vora and Co. Publishers, Bombay, 1973.

——— : *Development Perspectives : Problems Strategy and Policies*, Pergamon Press, London, 1980.

Bhende, Asha A: "Social Welfare Services". In *Second Maharashtra by 2005*. Tata Economic consultancy Services, Popular Prakashan, Bombay, 1977.

——— : "Health and Sanitation". In *Second Maharashtra by 2005*. Tata Economic Consultancy Services, Popular Prakashan, Bombay, 1977.

——— : "Family Planning". In *Second Maharashtra by 2005*. Tata Economic Consultancy Services, Popular Prakashan, Bombay, 1977.

Birla Institute of Scientific Research : *India 2001*, Arnold-Heinemann, New Delhi, 1976.

Bhatia, S.K. : "Personnel Function in 21st Century". In *The Management Review*, Vol. 13, No. 2, 1986.

Bose, A.N. : "Meeting the Food Requirement in 2000 A.D." In *Science and Culture*, Vol. 46, No. 5, 1980.

Bose, Ashish, Ashok Mitra, P.B. Desai and J.N. Sharma (eds.). *Population in India's Development 1947-2000*. Vikas Publishing House, Delhi, 1974.

Bose, Ashish: "The Urban Context". In *India Since Independence*, (ed.) S.C. Dube, Vikas Publishing House, Delhi, 1977.

——— : *India's Urbanization 1901-2001*, Tata Mcgraw Hill Co., Delhi, 1978.

——— : "Some thoughts on India's Urban Future". In *Urban Perspectives-2001*, (eds.), C.S. Chandrasekhara and Deva Raj. National Institute of Urban Affairs, New Delhi, 1978.

Bowonder, B. : "Future of Transportation". In *Short Studies* in *Futures Research*, NCST, Government of India, 1980.

Centre for Applied Systems in Development: *Technological Forecasting in Pulses in India in 2001 AD*, Pune, 1987 (Mimeographed).

Chandrasekhara, C.S. and Deva Raj (eds.) : *Urban Perspectives-2001*. National Institute of Urban Affairs, New Delhi, 1978.

Chandrasekharan, Raj Kumari and Asha Sukumaran : "Profiles of Education for Women in 2000 AD." In *Experiment in Education*, Vol. XV, No. 2, February, 1987.

Chatterjee, Ateryi: "Some Implications of the Future Trend of Urbanization". In *Population in India's Development 1947-2000*, (ed.) Ashish Bose et al., Vikas Publishing House, Delhi, 1974.

Chaturvedi, M.C. : *Second India Studies: Water*, The Macmillan Co., New Delhi, 1976.

Chavan, B.W.: "State Domestic Product". In *Second Maharashtra By 2005*, Tata Economic Consultancy Services, Popular Prakashan, Bombay, 1977.

Chhabra, Hari Sharan : "All-round cooperation with Africa". In *World Focus*. Volume. 7, No. 11-12, 1986.

Damle, Y.B. : "Youth". In *India Since Independence*, (ed.) S.C. Dube, Vikas Publishing House, Delhi, 1977.

Dandekar, Kumudini : "Population Growth and Composition". In *Second Maharashtra by 2005. A Study in Futurology*, Tata Economic Consultancy Services, Popular Prakashan, Bombay, 1977.

Das, S.R. : "Energy Scene in India". In *Yojana*, Vol. 27, No.19, 1983.

Das Gupta, Chidananda : "Indian Cinema : Dynamics of Old and New". In *India 2000: The Next Fifteen Years*, (ed.) James R. Roach, Allied Publishers, Delhi, 1986.

Dave, J.M. : "Some Considerations of Environmental Issues of Urban Growth". In *Urban Perspectives-2001*, (eds.) C.S. Chandrasekhara and Deva Raj, National Institute of Urban Affairs, New Delhi, 1978.

Dayal, Ishwar : "Public Administration Major Tasks Ahead". In *Indian Management*, Vol. 23, No. 1, 1984.

De, Sankar Lal and Bhuvana Krishnamurthy : "Transportation". In *Second Maharashtra by 2005*, Tata Economic Consultancy Services, Popular Prakashan, Bombay, 1977.

Deoras, P.J. : "Population". In *Second Maharashtra by 2005*, Tata Economic Consultancy Services, Popular Prakashan, Bombay, 1977.

Deshpande, S.H. : "Rural Development". In *Second Maharashtra by 2005*, Tata Economic Consultancy Services, popular Prakashan, Bombay, 1977.

——— : "Special Backward Areas". In *Second Maharashtra by 2005*, Tata Economic Consultancy Services, Popular Prakashan, Bombay, 1977.

Deva Raj : "Introduction". In *Urban Perspectives-2001* (eds.), C.S. Chandrasekhara and Deva Raj, National Institute of Urban Affairs. New Delhi, 1978.

Dube, S.C.(ed.) : *India Since Independence*, Vikas Publishing House, New Delhi, 1977.

——— : *Man, Society and Education: Some Questions Concerning a Preferred Future*, National Council of Educational Research and Training, New Delhi, 1977.

——— : "Unfinished Tasks". In *India Since Independence*, (ed.) S.C. Dube, Vikas Publishing House, Delhi, 1977.

Dutt, V.P. : "China in 2000: Outlook is not Unpromising". In *Patriot*, Feb. 2, 1987.

Ezekiel, H. : *Second India Studies: Industry*, The Macmillan Co., Delhi, 1975.

Ezekiel, H. : Second India Studies: Overview, The Macmillan Co., Delhi, 1978.

Ezekiel, Hannon and Madhoo Pavaskar : *Second India Studies Services,* The Macmillan Co., Delhi, 1976.

Frejka, Tomas : *The Future of Population Growth— Alternative Paths to Equilibrium,* John Wiley & Sons, 1972.

Gangal, S.C. and Anurag Gangal: "Gandhi and Global Problems-A vision for the Twenty-first Century". In *Foreign Affairs Reports,* Vol. XXXIII, No. 11-12, 1984.

Gangal, S.C. : "Gandhi and the Major World Problems: A Contemporary and Futuristic Perspective". In *Gandhi Marg,* Vol. 9, No.1, 1987.

Ghosh, Santosh : "Regiopolis 2000 : A study in Intermediate Urbanization with new growth centres". In *Short Studies in Futures Research,* NCST, Government of India, 1980.

Goon, A.M. and N.K. Chandra : "Projecting India's Population to 2001 AD". In *Manpower Journal,* Vol. XVIII, No. 2, 1982.

Gopalakrishnan, T.R. : "Transportation". In *India in Perspective,* Vol. 3. Operations Research Group, Arnold-Heinemann, New Delhi, 1978.

Government of India : *The Seventh Five Year Plan 1985-90,* Vol. I, Planning Commission, New Delhi, 1985.

Gupta, P.C. : "Telecommunication Beyond 2000 AD". In *Science and Culture,* Vol. 50, No. 10, 1984.

Gupta, Shyam Ratna (ed.) : *India: A Study in Futurism,* Abhinav Publications, New Delhi, 1976.

———: "Buckminister Fuller World of 2001 AD-An Interview". In *India: A Study in Futurism,* (ed.) S.R. Gupta, Abhinav Publications, New Delhi, 1976.

Gupta, S.P. : "Long Range Planning-1990, Strategies and Progress". In *India Towards 1990s.* (ed.) R.K. Mishra, Patriot Publishers, New Delhi, 1976.

Guru, D.D. : "The Future of India's International Economic Policy". In *Southern Economist,* Vol. 26, No. 5, 1986.

Hadden, Susan G. : "Environmental Protection and Economic Development in India". In *India 2000: The Next Fifteen Years,* (ed.) James R. Roach, Allied Publishers, New Delhi, 1986.

Haque, T. : "A Perspective of Agrarian Change for and Towards 2000 AD". In *Indian Review of Management and Future,* No. 2, 1986.

Harish Chandra : "Winds of Change in Indian Tourism in 1980-85 and Beyond". In *Quarterly-Economic Report of the Indian Institute of Public Opinion,* Vol. 29, No. 2, 1985.

Hasan, Ibnul, : "Indo-Pakistan Relations, 2085 AD". In *Pakistan and Gulf Economist,* Vol. IV, No. 19, 1985.

Hazari, R.K. : "India as a Major Power in the 21st Century". In *Mainstream,* Vol. 24, No. 2, 1986.

Hebber, V.G. : "Mineral Resources". In *Second Maharashtra By 2005,* Tata Economic Consultancy Services, Popular Prakashan, Bombay, 1977.

Hussain, Abid : "Technology : Key to Renaissance". In *World Focus,* Vol. 7, No.11-12, 1986.

Hussain, Ashique : "Urban Development". In *Second Maharashtra by 2005,* Tata Economic Consultancy Services, Popular Prakashan, Bombay, 1977.

ICSSR and ICMR : *Health for All: An Alternative Strategy,* Indian Institute of Education, Pune, 1981.

Institute for Social and Economic Change : *Population Projections for Karnataka 1981-2001,* Bangalore, 1985.

Iyengar, M.S. : "Pattern of Education in the year 2000 Education or Catastrophe". In *Indian Administrative and Management Review,* Vol. 2, No. 4, 1970.

Iyengar, R. Narayan : "Prediction of Food Production including Rainfall Uncertainties". In *Short Studies in Future Research,* NCST, Government of India, 1980.

Iyengar, Sultana an M.S. Iyengar: "The Technology of the Future and its Relevance of Developing Countries". In *International Symposium on Science, Technology & Development,* March 20-25, 1987.

Jayaraman, Kunthala: "System of Education in 2000 AD". In *Short Studies in Futures Research,* NCST, Government of India, 1980.

Jha, J.S. : "Prospectives for Development of Steel Industry upto 2000 AD in India". In *Lok Udyog,* Vol. 17, No. 6. 1983.

——— : "Higher Technical Education in India—Problems and Prospects". In *Shaping the Technology Era,* (eds.), O.N. Wakhlu and G.L. Labru, B.R. Publishing Corporation, Delhi, 1985.

Joshi, B.I.C. Krishnayya and S.K. Sharma, "Technological Assessment and Impact Analysis of Creating a National Market Place". In *Short Studies in Futures Research,* NCST, 1980.

Joshi, P.C. : "Peasants and Politics—Two faces of Peasantism". In *India Towards 1990s*. (ed.) R.K. Mishra, Patriot Publishers, New Delhi, 1986.

Joshi, P.C. : "Agriculture". In *India's Economic Development Strategies 1951-2000 AD*, (ed.), J.N. Mongia, Allied Publishers, New Delhi, 1986.

Kalhan, Promilla : "Women". In *India Since Independence*, (ed.), S.C. Dube, Vikas Publishing House, Delhi, 1977.

Kalkundrikar, Anil B. : "The Future of Prices in India". In *Acarsh*, Vol. 1, No. 4, 1985.

Kapur, J.C. : *India in the Year 2000.* India International Centre, New Delhi, 1975.

Kapur, J.C. : "Energy Perspectives for Urban Future". In *Urban Perspectives-2001*, (eds.) C.S. Chandrasekhara and Deva Raj, National Institute of Urban Affairs, New Delhi, 1978.

Khan, Rasheeduddin, : "Polity and Politics in India—The Contexts and Parameters". In *India Towards 1990s*, (ed.), R.K. Mishra, Patriot Publishers, New Delhi, 1986.

Khusro, A.M. : *The Future of Developing Economies*, Indian Council of Cultural Relations, New Delhi, 1980.

Kidwai, Jamal : "Do this, this, this and also this". In *Yojana*, Vol. 30, Nos. 14 & 15, 1986.

King, Robert D. : The Language Issue Revisited". In *India 2000: The Next Fifteen Years*, (ed.), James R. Roach. Allied Publishers, Delhi, 1986.

Kirpal, Prem: "Education Needs Qualitative Change". In *Yojana*, Vol. 30, No. 1 & 2, 1986.

Kothari, Rajni : *Footsteps into the Future*, Orient Longman, New Delhi, 1974.

——— : "World Order Perspective on the Future". In *India: A Study in Futurism*, (ed.), S.R. Gupta, Abhinav Publications, New Delhi, 1976.

——— : *Nation Building and Political Development in India Since Independence*, (ed.), S.C. Dubey, Vikas Publishing House, Delhi, 1977.

Koti, Raghunath, K. : "Forest Resources". In *Second Maharashtra by 2005*, Tata Economic Consultancy Services, Popular Prakashan, Bombay, 1977.

Koti, Raghunath, K. : "Secondary Sector". In *Second Maharashtra By 2005,* Tata Economic Consultancy Services, Popular Prakashan, Bombay, 1977.

——— : "Summary and Conclusion". In *Second Maharashtra By 2005: A Study in Futurology,* Tata Economic Consultancy Services, Popular Prakashan, Bombay, 1977.

Koti, Raghunath. K.: and K.V. Santhanam: "Growth of Economy". In *Second Maharashtra by 2005,* Tata Economic Consultancy Services, Popular Prakashan, Bombay, 1977.

Koti Raghunath, K. and D.V. Alate : "Primary Sector". In *Second Maharashtra by 2005,* Tata Economic Consultancy Services, Popular Prakashan, Bombay, 1977.

Krishna Iyer, V.R. : "What do we need to mould Kismet of India 2001". In *Yojana,* 1986, Vol. 30, No. 14 and 15.

Kulkarni, R.R. : "Recreation". In *Second Maharashtra by 2005,* Tata Economic Consultancy Services, Popular Prakashan, Bombay, 1977.

Kulkarni, R.R. and K.C. Sharma : "Communication". In *Second Maharashtra by 2005,* Tata Economic Consultancy Services, Popular Prakashan, Bombay, 1977.

Kumar, Satish : "Pakistan : Reconciliation Possible". In *World Focus,* Vol. 7, No. 11-12, 1986.

Kurien, C.T. : "Paradoxes of Planned Development: The Indian Experience". In *India 2000: The Next Fifteen Years,* (ed.), James R. Roach, Allied Publishers, 1986.

Lahiri, A.: "Water Resources". In *India in Perspective,* Vol. 2, Operations Research Group, Arnold Heinemann, New Delhi, 1977.

Lahiri, A. : "Minerals and Medals". In *India in Perspective,* Vol. 2, Operations Research Group, Arnold Heinemann, New Delhi, 1977.

Lal, Sham: "Entering the 21st Century". In *India International Centre Quarterly,* Spring, 1987.

Luthra Pran Nath : "The Crisis of Urbanization: 1985-2000 AD", *Monthly Commentary on Indian Economic Conditions,* Vol. 27, No. 5, Annual Number, 1985.

Madan, T.N. : "Indian Society : The Rural Context". In *India Since Independence,* (ed.), S.C. Dube, Vikas Publishing House, Delhi, 1977.

Mahesh Chand : "Future Growth of Households in India 1976-2001". In *The Journal of Family Welfare*, Vol. XXXIV, No. 2, 1977.

Majumdar (Chatterjee) Atreyi : "Problems of Urbanization in India by 2001 AD : A Demographic View". In *Urban Perspectives-2001*, (eds.) C.S. Chandrasekhara and Deva Raj, National Institute of Urban Affairs, New Delhi, 1968.

Malgavkar, P.D. and V.A. Pai Panandiker : *Population and Development*, Samaiya Publications, Bombay, 1982.

Malik, Amita : "Culture and the Arts". In *India Since Independence*, (ed.), S.C. Dube, Vikas Publishing House, Delhi, 1977.

Martino, J. : *Technological Forecasting for Decision Making*, American Elsevier, New York, 1972.

Mathur, Girish : "NAM and South-South Cooperation", In *World Focus*, Vol. 2, No. 11-12, 1986.

Mayur, Rashmi : "Dimensions of Urban Pollution". In *Urban Perspectives 2001*. (eds.) C.S. Chandrasekhara and Deva Raj. National Institute of Urban Affairs, New Delhi, 1978.

——— : "Decentralized Metropolitan Developments in India in the year 2000 AD". In *Short Studies in Futures Research*, NCST, Government of India, 1980.

——— : "Urbanization in India in the year 2000 AD". In *Urban Problems and Policy Perspectives*, (Ed.) Gopal Bhargav, Abhinav Publications, New Delhi, 1981.

Mehta, J. : *Second India Studies: Economy*, The Macmillan Co. Ltd., Delhi, 1976.

Mehta. J. : "Urbanization in 2001 AD : A Sociological Perspective". In *Urban Problems and Policy Perspectives*, (ed.) Gopal Bhargava, Abhinav Publications, New Delhi, 1981.

Menezes, Francis, A.: "Power in Organizations : Can this change in 2000 AD". In *Short Studies in Futures Research*, NCST, Government of India, New Delhi, 1980.

Menon, V.K. Narayana : "Traditional Culture, New Mediums, Interaction and Diffusion". In *India 2000: The Next Fifteen Years*, (ed.) James R. Roach, Allied Publishers, New Delhi, 1986.

Menon, V.K.S. : "Productivity Techniques in the Future". In *Integrated Management*, No. 128, 1976.

Minault, Gail : "Women in Contemporary India: The Quest for Equal Participation and Justice". In *India 2000 : The Next Fifteen Years*, (ed.) James R. Roach, Allied Publishers, New Delhi, 1986.

Ministry of Shipping and Transport : *Road Development Plan for India (1981-2001)*, Indian Road Congress, New Delhi, 1984.

Misra, K.P. (ed.) : *The World Towards, 1990s*, Patriot Publishers, New Delhi, 1986.

Mishra, Ashok : "The Future of Urbanization in relation to Metropolitan and Industrial Centres in the Eastern Region". In *Urban Perspectives-2001*, (eds.) C.S. Chandrasekhara and Deva Raj, National Institute of Urban Affairs, New Delhi, 1978.

Mohmood, Arshad : "Post-Harvest Foodgrain Losses in India in 2000 AD". In *Southern Economist*, Vol. 25 (24), 1987.

Mongia, J.N. (ed.) : *India's Economic Development Strategies 1951-2000 AD*, Allied Publishers Pvt. Ltd., New Delhi, 1986.

Mongia, J.N. : "Housing and Urban Renewal". In *India's Economic Development Strategies, 1951-2000 AD*, (ed.) J.N. Mongia, Allied Publishers, New Delhi, 1986.

Moolgaokar, S. : "Moving to the Twenty-First Century". In *Man and Development*, Vol. VII, No. 1, 1986.

Mukarji, Nirmal: "We may remain the same in 2001 Unless". In *Yojana*. Vol. 20, Nos. 14 and 15, 1986.

Mulkh Raj : "Housing Strategy Till 2001". In *Urban perspectives-2001*, (eds.) C.S. Chandrasekhara and Deva Raj, National Institute of Urban Affairs, New Delhi, 1978.

Murthy, S.G.N. : "Manufacturing Activity". In *India in Perspective*, Vol. 3, Operations Research Group, Arnold-Heinemann, New Delhi, 1978.

Muthuswamy, M. : "Co-operatives in 2000 AD". In *The Co-operator*, Vol. 19, No. 4, 1981.

Nagarajan, R. : "Energy". In *India in Perspective*, Vol. 2, Operations Research Group, Arnold-Heinemann, New Delhi, 1977.

Naik J.P.: "Education". In *India Since Independence*, (ed.) S.C. Dube, Vikas Publishing House, Delhi, 1977.

Nair, V.S.M. : "Housing". In *Second Maharashtra by 2005*. Tata Economic Consultancy Services, Popular Prakashan, Bombay, 1977.

Nair, V.S.M.: "Tertiary Sector". In *Second Maharashtra by 2005*, Tata Economic Consultancy Services, Popular Prakashan, Bombay, 1977.

Nanda, Biren: "India in 2000 AD: A Few Perspectives". In *The Administrator*, Vol. 25, No. 2, 1980.

Narain, Virendra: "International Politics and Indian Polity". In *India Towards 1990s*. (ed.), R.K. Mishra, Patriot Publishers, New Delhi, 1986.

Narang, A.S. and Subhendu R. Raj : *Indian Society at the Turn of the Century: An Overview*, Working paper of the XII Indian Social Science Congress, Mysore, 1987 (Mimeo).

Nath, D.C. : "Police in 2001 AD". In *The Indian Police Journal*, Vol. XXV, No. 1, 1978.

Nath, V. : "Urbanization in India, Review and Prospects". In *Economic and Political Weekly*, Vol. XXI, No. 8, 1986.

——— : "Urbanization". In *India's Economic Development Strategies 1951-2000 AD*. (ed.) J.N. Mongia, Allied Publishers, New Delhi, 1986.

National Committee on Science and Technology: *Short Studies in Futures Research*, Government of India, New Delhi, 1980

National Productivity Council : *Study on Technology Forecasting Assessment based on Long range quantitative Modelling for Indian Paper Industry*. In 3 Volumes, Bangalore, 1986 (Mimeo).

Operations Research Group : *India in Perspective*, Vol. 2, Arnold-Heinemann, New Delhi, 1977.

——— : *India in Perspective, Development Issues*. Vol. I, Arnold-Heinemann, New Delhi, 1978.

——— : India in Perspective, Vol. 3, Arnold-Heinemann, New Delhi, 1978

——— : "Population Projections". In *India in Perspective*, Vol. I, ORG, Arnold Heinemann, New Delhi, 1978.

Palaniswamy, S.P. and S. Gangopadhyay : *Technological Forecasting in Transportation* (A Delphi Study), Department of Science and Technology, Government of India, 1979 (Mimeo.).

Panchmukhi, V.R.: "Foreign Trade and Balance of Payment". In *India's Economic Development Strategies, 1951-2000 AD*. (ed.) J.N. Mongia, Allied Publishers, New Delhi, 1986.

Pande, C.S. : *Economic Development and Futures Report 2000 and Beyond*, Economic and Scientific Association, Calcutta, 1985.

Pant, Pitamber: "International Developmental Strategy and Indian Perspectives; 1990-2000". In *Economics and World Order from the 1970s to the 1990s,* (ed.) Jagdish, N. Bhagwati, Orient-Longman Ltd., New Delhi, 1972.

Parikh, G.D. and V.K. Sinha: "Education". In *Second Maharashtra by 2005,* Tata Economic Consultancy Services, Popular Prakashan, Bombay, 1977.

Parikh, Kirit: *Second India Studies: Energy,* The Macmillan & Co., New Delhi, 1976.

Patankar, P.G.: "Energy Demand Management in the Transport Sector". In *Journal of Transport Management,* Vol. 11, No. 2, 1987.

Patel, Shirish, B.: "The Future of Bombay—An Alternative Approach in Urban Planning". In *Population in India's Development—1947-2000.* (ed.) Ashish Bose, et. al. Vikas Publishing House, New Delhi, 1974.

Patel, Surendra J: *The India We Want: Its Economic Transition,* Manaktala & Sons, Bombay, 1966.

———: "Seventh Plan and Beyond (1985-2000)". In *Mainstream,* Vol. 25, No. 19, 1987.

Patra, Saral : "Bangladesh: Needed Mutual Trust". In *World Focus,* Vol. 7, No. 11-12, 1986.

Paul, A.P. : "Management Education: Future Trends in 1976-2000 AD". In *Short Studies in Futures Research,* NCST, Government of India, 1990.

Pavaskar, M.G. : "Water Resources". In *Second Maharashtra by 2005,* Tata Economic Consultancy Services, Popular Prakashan, Bombay, 1977.

——— : "Manpower and Employment". In *Second Maharashtra by 2005,* Tata Economic Consultancy Services, Popular Prakashan, Bombay, 1977.

——— : "Energy Resources". In *Maharashtra by 2005,* Tata Economic Consultancy Services, Popular Prakashan, Bombay, 1977.

Pavaskar, Madhoo : *Second India studies: Transport,* Popular Prakashan, Bombay, 1978.

Pavaskar, Madhoo and R.R. Kulkarni : *Second India Studies: Communication,* Popular Prakashan, Bombay, 1978.

Premi, Mahendra K. : "Demographic Aspects of Educational Planning in a Long Term Perspective". In *Educational Planning: A Long Term Perspective,* (ed.) Moonis Raza, Concept Publishing Co., New Delhi, 1986.

Raghavachari, M. : "India's Freight Transport Problem, Problems and Prospects". In *Short Studies in Futures Research,* NCST, Government of India, 1980.

Raghavachari, S.: "Population Projections, 1976-2001". In *Population in India's Development 1947-2000,* (ed.), Ashish Bose et al., Vikas Publishing House, New Delhi, 1974.

Raghavan, J. Veera: "Directions of Educational Change Towards 2001", Paper Presented in a Seminar on *Education in 2001,* State Planning Commission, Madras, 1983 (Mimeo).

Rahman, A.: "Science and Technology". In *India Since Independence,* (ed.) S.C. Dube, Vikas Publishing House, Delhi, 1977.

Rajan, M.S. : "The Indian Subcontinent : Role of External Powers". In *India: A study in Futurism,* (ed.), S.R. Gupta, Abhinav Publishers, New Delhi, 1976.

Rajeshwari V.V. : "Food and Population Planning in India". In *Gramodyog,* Vol. XXXIII No. 4, 1987.

Raj Krishna : "The Economic Outlook for India". In *India 2000: The Next Fifteen Years,* (ed.) James R. Roach, Allied Publishers, Delhi, 1986.

Ram, Vinay Bharat : "Prospects of Urban Employment in 2000 AD". In *Indian Journal of Industrial Relations,* Vol. 13, No. 1, 1977.

Raman, M.V. : "A Demographic Profile of Calcutta". In *Population in India's Development 1947,* (ed.), Ashish Bose et al., Vikas Publishing House, Delhi, 1974.

Ramesh, Jairam and J.N. Maggo, : *Towards a Perspective on Energy Demand and Supply in India in 2004/05,* Government of India, Delhi, 1985.

Rammurti, Acharya: "Our Revolution Towards 2000 AD". In *Gandhi Vigvau,* Vol. 5, No. 2, 1982.

Rangnekar, D.K. : "Food Scenario: 2000 AD". In *Short Studies in Futures Research,* NCST, Government of India, New Delhi, 1980.

Rao, R.K. : *Disease Patterns and Drug Demand in India by the year 2000 AD*, Administrative Staff College of India, Hyderabad, 1986 (Mimeo).

Rao, K. Vinayak : "Planning for Our Energy Needs in 2000 AD". In *Yojana*, Vol. 27, No. 22, 1983.

Rao, M.S.V. and Sanjay Gupta : "Delhi Master Plan 2001-A Critical Review of Transportation Sector". In *Indian Highways*, Vol. 15, No. 2, 1987.

Rao, V.K.R.V. : *India's National Income 1950-1980*, Sage Publications, New Delhi, 1983.

Rao, V.M. : *Second India Studies: Food*, The Macmillan Co., New Delhi, 1983.

Raza Moonis : "Education and the Future". In *Educational Planning-A Long Term Perspective*, (ed.) Moonis Raza, Concept Publishing Co., New Delhi, 1986.

Reddy, V. Eshwara: "A Model of Education for the Future". In *Journal of Indian Education*, Vol. II, No. 1, 1977.

Roach, James R. (ed.) : *India 2000 : The Next Fifteen Years*, Allied Publishers, New Delhi, 1986.

Rohatgi, P.K. and Kalpana Rohatgi: "Methodologies of Technological Forecasting and their application to Long-Term Educational Planning". In *Educational Planning-A Long Term Perspective*, (ed.) Moonis Raza, Concept Publishing Co., New Delhi, 1986.

Roy, Bunker : "Action is Called Right Now to Avoid a Rude Shock". In *Yojana*, Vol. 30, Nos. 14 and 15, 1986.

Sackman, H. : *Delphi Assessment: Expert Opinion, Forecasting and Group Process.*

Saggar, R.K. and J.N. Mongia : "Transport". In *India's Economic Development Strategies 1951-2000 AD*, (ed.) J.N. Mongia, Allied Publishers, New Delhi, 1986.

Sahay, Raghuvir : "Literature". In *India since Independence*, (ed.), S.C. Dube, Vikas Publishing House, Delhi, 1977.

Sankar, T.L. : "Energy". In *Population in India's Development 1947-2000*, (ed.) Ashish Bose et al. Vikas Publishing House, Delhi, 1974.

Sastry, S.M.Y. : "Urban Management Perspective 2001". In *Urban Perspectives-2001*, (eds.) C.S. Chandrasekhara and Deva Raj, National Institute of Urban Affairs, New Delhi, 1978.

Sathyamurthy, T.V. ; "India and the Global Power Configuration The Next Twenty Five Years". In *Journal of Social Studies*, No. 36, 1984.

Schwarz, Brita, Uno Svedin and Bjorn Wittrock : *Methods in Future Studies*, West-view Press, Colorado, 1982.

Sen, Biman : "Education and India in 21st Century". In *University News*, Vol. XXIV, No. 15, 1986.

——— : "Education for one world: A Long-Term Perspective". In *University News.*

Sen, Lalit K. and G.R. Dawar : "Perspective for Development till 2000 AD". In *Commerce,* Vol. 135, No. 3475, 1977.

Sen, Mohit: "The Third World-Theoretical Sketch". In *The World Towards 1990's,* (ed.) K.P. Misra, Patriot Publishers, New Delhi, 1985.

——— : "Transformations and Alternatives-India's Polity in the 1990s. In *India Towards 1990s,* (ed.) R.K. Mishra, Patriot Publishers, New Delhi, 1986

——— : "Doing the Business in a Business like Way". In *Yojana,* Vol. 33, Nos. 14 and 15, 1986.

Sengupta, Bhabani : *Ethnopolitical Inter-state Tensions and Conflicts in South Asia, Prognosis for the Next 15 Years*, Centre for Policy Research, New Delhi, 1986 (Mimeo).

Seth, S.C. : "Management 2000 AD: An Outline Scenario". In *Indian Management,* Vol. 15, No. 9, 1976.

——— : *India The Next 7000 Days,* Wiley Eastern Limited, New Delhi, 1985.

——— : "Rural Futures: A Conceptual Developmental Framework". In *Co-operative Perspective.* Vol. 21, No. 3, 1986.

——— : "Training Bureaucrats for the Twenty-first Century-Some Reflections". In *Management and Labour Studies,* Vol. 12, No. 2, 1987.

Singh, Balwant : "Perspective on Police Crime, Law and Order-2000 AD". In *Police Research and Development,* July-Sept., 1985.

Sethi J.D. : "The Asian Balance of Power". In *India: A Study in Futurism,* (ed.) S.R. Gupta, Abhinav Publications, New Delhi, 1976.

Shah, C.H. : "Agricultural Production". In *India in Perspective,* Vol. 3, Operations Research Group, Arnold-Heinemann, New Delhi, 1978.

Shrivastava, O.S. : *A Text Book of Demography*, Vikas Publishing House, New Delhi, 1983.

Singh, B.B. And Ajab Singh : "Perspectives of Urbanization in the National Capital Region of India by 2001 AD". In *National Geographer*, Vol. XX, No. 2, 1985.

Singh, Jasjit : "Towards Deterrence Conventional Air Power in the 1990s". In *Indian Deterrence Review*, Vol. 2, No. 2, 1986.

Singh, S.P. et al: "An Economic Analysis of Interstate Disparities in Milk Production and Institutional Facilities in India". In *Agricultural Situation in India*, Vol. 40, No. 10, 1986.

Sinha, Durganand : "Bring Radical Changes in Education". In *Yojana*, Vol. 30, No.1 and 2, 1986.

Sinha, J.N. : "Some Aspects of Employment-A Long View". In *Population in India's Development 1947-2000*, (ed.), Ashish Bose et al., Vikas Publishing House, 1974.

Sinha, K.A. : "Coal Prospect and Perspective for the Year 2000". In *Energy Management*, Vol. 11, No. 1, 1987.

Sivaramakrishnan, K.C. : "Calcutta 2001-Triumph by Survival". In *Population in India's Development 1947-2000*, (ed.) Ashish Bose et al. Vikas Publishing House, New Delhi, 1974.

Sivaraman, B. : "Growth Pattern for Rural Sector by 2000 AD". In *Indian and Foreign Review*, Vol. 13, No. 7, 1976.

Srinivasan, A.N. : "Executive Development in India-A Delphi Study". In *Short Studies in Futures Research*, NCST, Government of India, New Delhi, 1980.

Srinivasan, N.S. : "Challenging Urban Transportation Problems". In *Urban Perspectives 2001*, (eds.) C.S. Chandrasekhara and Deva Raj, National Institute of Urban Affairs, New Delhi, 1978.

Srinivas, M.N. : "On Living in a Revolution". In *Indian 2000 : The Next Fifteen Years*, (Ed.) James R. Roach, Allied Publishers, New Delhi, 1986.

Srinivasan, N.S. : "Future Scenario of Road Transport in India". In *Indian Highways*, Vol. 15, No. 2, 1987.

Srivastava, Anand P. : *Teaching and Learning in XXI Century*, The Learning Laboratory, New Delhi, 1987.

Subramanian, V. : "Public Administration". In *Second Maharashtra by 2005*, Tata Economic Consultancy Services, Popular Prakashan, Bombay, 1977.

Subrahmanyam, K. : "India's Security Needs in 1975-2000 AD". In *India: A Study in Futurism,* (ed.) S.R. Gupta, Abhinav Publications, New Delhi, 1976.

Sundaram K. : "Registrar General's Population Projections, 1981-2001-An Appraisal and an Alternative Scenario". In *Economic & Political Weekly,* Vol. 19, No. 34, 1986.

Swaminathan, M.S. : "Higher Education into the 21st Century". In *Journal of Higher Education,* Vol. 7, Nos. 1-2, 1981.

Tamil Nadu Board of Continuing Education: *Education in Twenty-First Century,* State Resource Centre for Non-formal Education, Madras, 1987.

Taimni, K.K. : "Co-operative Management Process". In *Indian Management,* Vol. 19, No. 10, 1988.

Tata Economic Consultancy Services : *Second Maharashtra by 2005-A Study in Futurology,* Popular Prakashan, Bombay, 1977.

Thapar, Romesh : "Living in 2001-A Crowded Tangled Future". In *Yojana,* Vol. 30, Nos. 14 and 15, 1986.

Trivedi, H.N. : "Future of Indian Shipping: A 20 year Scenario". In *Foreign Trade Review,* Vol. XVII, No. 1, 1982.

Unni, K.R. "Community Housing". In *Short Studies in Futures Research,* NCST, Government of India, 1980.

UNO : Population Growth and Policies in Mega Cities, Calcutta, New York, 1986.

UNO : Population Growth and Policies in Mega Cities, Bombay, New York, 1986.

UNO : Population Growth and Policies in Mega Cities, Delhi, New York, 1986.

Vasudeva, Aruna : Communication with the Masses—A Delphi Study in Multi-Media Chices, Department of Science and Technology, 1981 (Mimeographed).

Venkatraman, B. and D. Vanugopal : "Public Order". In *India Since Independence,* (ed.) S.C. Dube, Vikas Publishing House, New Delhi, 1977.

Verma, J.R. : "Emerging Trends in Pictorial and Plastic Arts". In *India: A Study in Futurism,* (ed.) S.R. Gupta, Abhinav Publications, New Delhi, 1976.

Viswam, S. : "Lots of Hope in SAARC". In *World Focus,* Vol. 7, Nos. 11-12, 1986.

Wakhlu, O. N. and G.L. Labru (eds.) : *Shaping the Technology Era*, B.R. Publishing Corporation, Delhi, 1986.

Wallace, Paul: "Centre State Relations in India". In *The Federal Dilemma, in India: 2000: The Next Fifteen Years* (ed.) James R. Roach, Allied Publishers, New Delhi, 1986.

Weiner, Myron: "India's Minorities—Who are They? What do They Want". In *India: 2000: The Next Fifteen Years*, (ed.) James R. Roach, Allied Publishers, New Delhi, 1986.

Zadoo, V.D. : "Man Made Hazards in Environment". In *Shaping the Technology Era*, (eds.) O. N. Wakhlu and G.L. Labru, B.R. Publishing Corporation, Delhi, 1985.

APPENDIX D

How ICMF Can Help Indian Industry and Public System

By Our Staff Futurist

This report is about the ICMF's In-House Training/Workshop Programmes

The Indian Council of Management and Future (ICMF), is a registered professional society. It is an independent, non-political, non-ideological and non-profit making body.

This Council, through its programmes, is creating awareness of future and the importance of its study. It is engaged in training professional managers, both in the Government and in the public and the private sectors, acquainting them how to use the tools and techniques of Technology Forecasting and long-range planning to learn how to draw up corporate strategic plan. This Council's special programmes also include exposition to the new concept (introduced by India's leading Futurologist, Dr. S.C. Seth) of Anticipatory Management.

Aims and Objects of In-House Training/Workshops

Futurology / Futures Research is now acknowledged world-wide as an important input to management education and practice. In the Soviet Union they use the term 'prognostics'. There exists a body of knowledge and administrative and managerial opinion which strongly suggests that future should be handled independently through several meaningful conclusions for a given long-range time-frame. Scholars who belong to such a school of thought believe that if we can exercise any control whatsoever, it should only be in trying to share and hopefully influence things that lie ahead in the future. We should, in today's investment, also accommodate the future needs of our people with prior preparation. The emphasis of such anticipatory management is not so much with prediction. It is concerned more with using the tools and techniques of future scanning in order to take more judicious current day decisions and plans. The futuristic approach, thus, helps us to develop the building blocks for "Management for and towards Future". Most mature societies are now using Futurology as a major training input both in the public administrative system as well as in the industrial management education, through long-range planning and allied corporate strategies. The inter-disciplinary body of knowledge available on the subject provides to the top policy makers and planners, several alternatives and blue-prints. Today futuristic data is being sought by more than 50 Governments through the help of their own future analysis and future scanning groups or through the work of more than 1000 professional institutions which are engaged in this work world-over. In fact, global modelling is now integral to the policy and programme commitments of most of the organizations in the UN systems.

Relevance to Top-Management in the Corporate Sector

The key task of an alert management is to identify the nature of uncertainty towards which a corporate entity moves into the future. Nobody intends to make claims for accurate forecasting. An alert management is one which can make timely use of all the tools and techniques of future research whereby it can identify the challenge of the coming decades to industry and in its operations accommodate the long-range perspective as identified in terms of change factors—be they demographic, educational, economic, organizational, technological, or political

The scenario building for searching policy-options is common in many advanced countries in the Governmental sector. However, futuristic techniques are now commonly used by important companies world-over. Most of these applications are to be practical problems. Monsanto, for example, has successfully applied cross impact analysis to a variety of future-oriented problems including new product development and training of professionals. General Electric has incorporated trend impact analysis in its "Futurescan" monitoring and forecasting system and Pilikington Brothers Ltd., the British Glass Company, has used cross impact simulation to help it gain a better understanding of a pension fund issue. In fact, Delphi technique is commonly used even for assessing future marketing potential.

Need for Forecasting, Monitoring and Future Scanning

Such an input in the Indian Corporate Management requires an intensive exposure and training of top executives in the field of Futures Research and Technology Forecasting. Monitoring and Forecasting is an attempt to make explicit the assumptions held about the future, to identify developments and, ultimately, to try to shape and guide the organization as far as practical, based on the analysis of long-range trends.

The focus of the monitoring activity in the identification of specific trends and events which individually, or by their interaction, suggest possible hazards or opportunities for the organisation and which, should therefore be considered in developing corporate strategy and plans.

Advantages

Each company ought to put itself some of the following questions. These are only illustrative in nature. As training input specific company-oriented hypothetical questions should be raised by top management from time to time. This can help them stretch their mind beyond day to day obligations and generate an Anticipatory-Management-Culture in the company. These illustrative questions are as follows:

1. How can you minimize resistance to change and innovation?
2. How can you improve the communication of important/future technological changes to top management and to your colleagues? Do you know what your company/organization will be doing after

20 years and how and where? What could be your undertakings plans for future diversification?

3. What causes success or disaster in marketing efforts?
4. How to use forecasting techniques to reach alternative technical planning strategies and options? How can they be fed into your corporate planning?
5. How can you better evaluate R&D Proposals and establish appropriate R&D Programmes?
6. How to catalogue and fulfil the future needs of your organization?
7. How to take decisions in uncertainty?
8. How to improve your internal and external markets over a time?
9. How to maintain uninterrupted supply of scarce resources?
10. How to develop a sound technological superstructure to ensure steady profits?

The Main Features of the In-House Training/Workshop Programme

This Council organizes a 5-day programme of In-House Training/Workshop which will cover the following aspects of Anticipatory Management :

(i) Concepts and relevance of futures studies to socio-economic development;

(ii) Tools, techniques, methodologies of future scanning and analysis giving a brief introduction to technology forecasting, social forecasting and technology assessment;

(iii) The scenarios in a few selected basic need areas as seen by some of the experts in Futures Research;

(iv) Relating anticipatory management to (a) decision making process and new organizational forms; (b) perspective planning, and (c) new training obligations;

(v) Developing alternative scenarios for organizations future growth.

These workshops are run on highly participative lines and do offer sufficient scope for discussion. They are provided some special and relevant issues of Council's outstanding quarterly journal *Indian Review of Management and Future*. Additional material is also provided which includes conceptual and thematic reading material, including futurology exercises. Time permitting, brain-storming session, are also conducted. The Faculty for this programme includes India's leading futurologist and systems analyst.

For further details write to:

Office Secretary,
Indian Council of Management and Future,
E B-166, Maya Enclave,
New Delhi-110064.
(Tele : 5402903)

Index